Irene Checa-García and Laura Marqués-Pascual (Eds.)
Current Perspectives in Spanish Lexical Development

Studies on Language Acquisition

Series Editors
Luke Plonsky
Martha Young-Scholten

Volume 68

Current Perspectives in Spanish Lexical Development

Edited by
Irene Checa-García and Laura Marqués-Pascual

DE GRUYTER
MOUTON

ISBN 978-3-11-221379-7
e-ISBN (PDF) 978-3-11-073041-8
e-ISBN (EPUB) 978-3-11-073050-0
ISSN 1861-4248

Library of Congress Control Number: 2023939559

Bibliographic information published by the Deutsche Nationalbibliothek
The Deutsche Nationalbibliothek lists this publication in the Deutsche Nationalbibliografie;
detailed bibliographic data are available on the internet at http://dnb.dnb.de.

© 2025 Walter de Gruyter GmbH, Berlin/Boston
This volume is text- and page-identical with the hardback published in 2023.
Typesetting: Integra Software Services Pvt. Ltd.
Printing and binding: CPI books GmbH, Leck

www.degruyter.com

Preface

The present collection reflects increasing scholarly focus on lexical development in Spanish. Although there has been a volume dedicated to teaching vocabulary from a meaning-oriented perspective (Bracroft and Muñoz-Basols 2022) and a special issue at the Journal of Spanish Language Teaching dedicated to vocabulary teaching (Sánchez Rufat and Jiménez Calderón 2015), there has been no other work in Spanish that includes other areas of vocabulary studies besides teaching. In the respect, vocabulary studies in Spanish were still lagging behind those in English.

This volume, then, grows out of a public call for papers on diverse aspects of vocabulary acquisition, with an emphasis on quantitative and data-driven approaches. Each chapter was reviewed first by one of the two editors, then by two to three anonymous reviewers, then by the other of the two editors, and finally anonymous reviewers gave a final round of feedback for the entire volume. In a few cases the referees were the authors of other chapters, but more commonly they were outside referees chosen for their specific expertise. All chapters went through several rounds of reviews and revisions. Authors of chapters with a similar topic had the opportunity of reading a revised version of those other chapters and were able to connect results and reference other studies in the volume, in order to create a solid, cohesive and interconnected collection of studies.

We would like to thank all the anonymous reviewers for generously offering their time to this endeavor and significantly improving its quality and rigor, and we thank the authors for their patience through this process. We would also like to thank Michaela Göbels at De Gruyter Mouton, and Luke Plonsky, Series Editor for Studies on Language Acquisition for their support.

For both of us, language teachers, the possibility of contributing to the further development of vocabulary studies in Spanish was a long overdue task that we hope will help other educators and inspire future researchers.

Irene Checa-García
Fort Collins, Colorado

Laura Marqués-Pascual
Santa Barbara, California

Contents

Preface —— V

List of contributors —— XI

Section I: **Lexicon at the crossroads: The interplay of lexicon with other areas of language**

Laura Marqués-Pascual and Irene Checa-García
Chapter 1
The trajectory of Spanish vocabulary studies and challenges ahead —— 3

Milagros Fernández-Pérez and Miguel González-Pereira
Chapter 2
The role of the lexicon in language acquisition: An issue in need of study —— 25

Danielle Daidone
Chapter 3
The relationship between self-rated vocabulary knowledge and accuracy of phonological forms —— 49

Section II: **Measures of lexical competence and development in Spanish**

Juan-Andrés Villena-Ponsoda, Antonio-Manuel Ávila-Muñoz, José-María Sánchez-Sáez
Chapter 4
Individual lexical breadth and its associated measures. A contribution to the calculation of individual lexical richness —— 75

Irene Checa-García, Austin Schafer
Chapter 5
L1 to L2 lexical development transfer? A within subjects study on lexical richness measures —— 109

Judith Borràs, Àngels Llanes, Goretti Prieto Botana
Chapter 6
Development of lexical deployment as a result of a short-term study abroad experience in Costa Rica —— 137

Marco Berton and Laura Sánchez
Chapter 7
Effects of passive vocabulary knowledge and task type on lexical sophistication in L2 Spanish writing —— 161

Section III: Attitudes and emotions in the lexicon

Elisabet Llopart-Saumell
Chapter 8
"Learn the rules like a pro, so you can break them like an artist": On the emotional effects of breaking word-formation rules —— 189

Stefan DuBois
Chapter 9
Do L2 Speakers sound strange when using slang? L1 attitudes toward L2 Use of peninsular Spanish colloquial lexical items —— 215

Section IV: Approaches to teaching L2 lexicon

Claudia Helena Sánchez-Gutiérrez, Pablo Robles-García, César Hoyos Álvarez
Chapter 10
Vocabulary in the L2 Spanish classroom: What students know and what their instructors believe they know —— 245

Nausica Marcos Miguel, Mari Félix Cubas Mora
Chapter 11
Interpreting the designated curriculum: Teachers' understanding of vocabulary instruction and adherence to the textbook —— 269

Eve C. Zyzik, Laura Marqués-Pascual
Chapter 12
Do you really know this word? Dimensions of vocabulary knowledge in Spanish textbooks —— 303

Index —— 329

List of contributors

Antonio-Manuel Ávila-Muñoz
Associate Professor in General Linguistics
Departamento de Filología Griega, Estudios Árabes, Lingüística General, Documentación y Filología Latina
Universidad de Málaga
amavila@uma.es

Marco Berton
Senior Lecturer of Spanish
Department of Language, Literature and Intercultural Studies
Karlstad University
marco.berton@kau.se

Judith Borràs
Adjunct Professor in English Philology
Department of English
University of Design and Technology
judith.borras@esne.es

Irene Checa García
Associate Professor of Spanish Linguistics
Department of Modern and Classical Languages
University of Wyoming
irene.checa@uwyo.edu

Mari Félix Cubas Mora
Visiting Professor
Department of Hispanic Languages and Literatures
University of Pittsburgh
mfc24@pitt.edu

Danielle Daidone
Assistant Professor of Spanish
University of North Carolina, Wilmington
daidoned@uncw.edu

Stefan DuBois
Assistant Professor of Spanish and First Year Coordinator
Center for World Languages and Cultures
University of Denver
stefan.dubois@du.edu

Milagros Fernández-Pérez
Full Professor of General Linguistics
Deparment of Spanish Language and Literature, Literary Theory and General Linguistics
Universidade de Santiago
magos.fernandez.perez@usc.es

Miguel González-Pereira
Associate Professor in General Linguistics
Deparment of Spanish Language and Literature, Literary Theory and General Linguistics
Universidade de Santiago
miguel.gonzalez.pereira@usc.es

César Hoyos Álvarez
PhD candidate in Spanish linguistics
Department of Spanish and Portuguese
University of California, Davis
cehoyosalvarez@ucdavis.edu

Àngels Llanes
Associate Professor of English
Department of English and Linguistics
University of Lleida
angels.llanes@udl.cat

Elisabet Llopart-Saumell
Assistant Professor at the Department of Translation and Language Sciences
Member of the Institute for Applied Linguistics
Universitat Pompeu Fabra
elisabet.llopart@upf.edu

List of contributors

Nausica Marcos Miguel
Assistant Professor
Department of Translation, Interpreting and Communication
Ghent University
nausica.marcosmiguel@ugent.be

Laura Marqués-Pascual
Teaching Professor and Language Program Director
Department of Spanish and Portuguese
University of California, Santa Barbara
lampas@ucsb.edu

Goretti Prieto-Botana
Teaching Professor of Spanish
Latin-American and Iberian Cultures Department
University of Southern California
botana@usc.edu

Pablo Robles-García
Assistant Professor of Spanish Linguistics
Department of Language Studies
University of Toronto, Mississauga
p.roblesgarcia@utoronto.ca

Laura Sánchez
Senior Lecturer of Spanish
Department of Teaching and Learning
University of Stockholm
laura.sanchez@su.se

Claudia Sánchez-Gutiérrez
Associate Professor of Spanish
Graduate Program Chair
Director of the First-Year Spanish Program
Department of Spanish and Portuguese
University of California, Davis
chsanchez@ucdavis.edu

José-María Sánchez-Sáez
Assistant Professor
Department of Pedagogy of Mathematics and Social and Experimental Sciences
Universidad de Málaga
jmss@uma.es

Austin Schafer
MS Candidate
Department of Computer Science
University of Wisconsin, Eau-Claire
austin.schafer3@gmail.com

Juan-Andrés Villena-Ponsoda
Emeritus Professor
Departamento de Filología Griega, Estudios Árabes, Lingüística General, Documentación y Filología Latina
Universidad de Málaga
vum@uma.es

Eve Zyzik
Full Professor of Spanish
Department of Languages and Applied Linguistics
University of California, Santa Cruz
ezyzik@ucsc.edu

Section I: **Lexicon at the crossroads: The interplay of lexicon with other areas of language**

Laura Marqués-Pascual and Irene Checa-García
Chapter 1
The trajectory of Spanish vocabulary studies and challenges ahead

1 Introduction: Aspects in vocabulary studies

Vocabulary is commonly recognized as an essential building block in acquiring a language, whether L1, L2, or additional languages, not only by researchers (Qian and Lin 2019), but also by learners themselves (Meara 1980, Webb and Nation 2017), who consider it a difficult aspect of language learning, and one that hinders their success the most. This impression that learners have is corroborated by research. For instance, Schmitt (2010) shows how vocabulary is possibly the most easily lost linguistic aspect after having been acquired and explains this loss by the fact that vocabulary has fewer rules and possibilities for generalization. Research on vocabulary is, however, quite complex, since it is a multifaceted construct that includes 1) its description, 2) ways to assess its knowledge and acquisition development, and 3) its pedagogy (Sánchez-Rufat and Jiménez-Calderón 2015, Webb 2020). These multiple aspects of vocabulary explain research trends in those three areas.

As in other linguistic fields, vocabulary research presents the initial challenge of determining what it means to know a lexical item, what a lexical item is, and in what form it is stored and accessed (Pellicer Sánchez 2015, Barcroft and Muñoz-Basols 2021). Although meaning is a central part of vocabulary, research has shown that vocabulary learning involves many additional layers of knowledge (see Fernández Pérez and González Pereira, this volume). For example, Nation (2001, 2013) identified nine dimensions of vocabulary knowledge related to form, meaning, and use involved in what it means to know a word, and these dimensions both entail receptive and productive knowledge (see Zyzik and Marqués-Pascual, this volume, for an overview of Nation's framework).

Lexicon knowledge has also been studied by distinguishing between its size (lexical breadth) and its quality (lexical depth). Lexical breadth refers to how many words are known, that is, the size of a mental lexicon. Lexical depth is a more complex term, which refers to how well a word is known (see Schmitt 2014, for more details about the concept of vocabulary depth and its relationship to vocabulary size). According to Webb (2022: 42), lexical depth refers to "different

---
Laura Marqués-Pascual, University of California, Santa Barbara
Irene Checa-García, University of Wyoming, Laramie

https://doi.org/10.1515/9783110730418-001

types of word knowledge that need to be learned in order to fully know a word", that is, how well the properties of lexical items are known, including compositionality, combinatorial properties, appropriate contexts and registers, connotations, etc. Thus, while vocabulary breadth refers to the inventory and hence many items, lexical depth focuses on how well each item is known, and in this sense, it can be related to Nation's (2000, 2013) theory of what it takes to know a word.

Past this initial hurdle, there is still the question of how to measure development and sequences in its acquisition. Numerous ways of measuring vocabulary size and knowledge have been devised for English as an L2. Most of these tests assess receptive vocabulary and aim to gauge learning based on the link between form and meaning; that is, learners are presented with words of different frequency levels and asked if they know the most basic meaning of the word, or asked to match each word with its correct meaning among those provided, such as the most widely known Vocabulary Size Test (Nation 2013), the Vocabulary Levels Test (Schmitt et al. 2001), the Swansea Levels Test (Meara and Miralpeix 2016), or lexical availability tests that make use of associative tasks (Read 2000). Productive vocabulary is believed to be more difficult to estimate, and reliable tools to assess it are very scarce. The Lexical Frequency Profile (Laufer and Nation 1995) can give the percentage of words in a text belonging to different frequency bands, although it cannot provide an estimate of vocabulary size.

The development of such tests for Spanish has lagged behind, and the plethora of different tests for English (see Read 2020 for an overview of these tests) has not inspired the creation of similar vocabulary tests for Spanish until recently (further discussion of some vocabulary tests developed for Spanish as an L2 will be presented in Section 4). In addition to these controlled tests which mainly measure receptive and productive vocabulary knowledge, there are many measurements of lexical performance in spontaneous writing and speech. These measures usually assess three aspects of performance: complexity, accuracy, and fluency (CAF). The treatment of each of these aspects has been rather unbalanced, with measures of complexity being utilized much more frequently than those of accuracy and fluency. As a case in point, the measure used most frequently, lexical diversity (Castañeda and Jarvis 2014), is only one of the three measures of complexity/richness (see Section 3.1 for further discussion of these measures and their terminology), but often is equated to lexical richness.

Finally, besides description and assessment, vocabulary research has intensely looked at pedagogical methods, in particular in relation to the four strands proposed by Nation (2007): meaning-focused input, meaning-focused output, language-focused learning, and fluency development (Webb 2020). Pedagogically oriented vocabulary studies have also looked at the materials and the curriculum (see Marcos Miguel and Cubas and Sánchez-Gutiérrez et al., in this volume).

Vocabulary studies, however, have not been an island, and their strong emergence in the last two decades has been due in part to the connection between the lexicon and other aspects of a language, such as grammatical processes (grammaticalization, lexicalization) and a different view on combination of words as less free and more grammar ruled (constructions, collocations, colloconstructions). In response, many studies have been devoted to the study of multiword items, especially -their description and acquisition process. There are also studies examining the mutual influence of lexical and other kinds of linguistic knowledge, mainly grammatical and phonetic (see Daidone, this volume, for an example of phonetic knowledge influence, and Fernández-Pérez and González-Pereira, this volume, for other examples of such studies).

Similarly, the increased number of tools for analysis – corpora, concordance tools, and eye-tracking, among others – has made it possible to study vocabulary knowledge and development in a more precise, representative, and quantitative manner, with the emergence of a new line of research on vocabulary processing (Camblin et al. 2007; Blumefeld and Marian 2007, and an overview of using eye tracking to research L2 processing, including lexical processing, in Roberts and Syanova-Chanturia 2013, as examples).

In the next sections, we will discuss the general evolution of vocabulary studies (Section 2) with special attention to the acquisition of Spanish vocabulary (Section 2.1), for which we will present current resources (Section 3). We then discuss some challenges and areas that need further development (Section 4). We conclude this introduction with an overview of the organization of this volume and its chapters (Section 5).

2 Overview of research on vocabulary development

In part because of its complexity and in part because of its vastness, the study of vocabulary has lagged somewhat behind when compared to the study of the acquisition and development of other linguistic areas such as grammar or even phonetics (Meara 1980). In a recent introduction to a collective volume in honor of Norbert Schmitt, McCarthy (2020) reviews the beginnings of vocabulary research in the 80s. Previously, a more formal approach to language that viewed grammar as independent of the lexicon, be that in the form of structuralism or generativism, had prevented the development of this line of research. Moreover, the emergence of the communicative approach in the 70s and 80s meant that vocabulary and other areas of linguistic knowledge were not thought of explicitly (Mc-

Carthy 2022, Mitchell 1994: 36). However, in the 80s, McCarthy himself and some of his colleagues started changing this view. McCarthy (1984) and Carter and McCarthy (1988) proposed the need for a focus on vocabulary research with a specific focus on teaching and learning. Meanwhile, Meara (1980) and Meara and Ingle (1986) focused on researching the acquisition of vocabulary. In 1982, Paul Nation put forward his influential proposal with a seminal paper making the case for researching vocabulary acquisition in different modes (oral vs. written), through both indirect and direct instruction. His work underlines the need to look at how much input is needed for vocabulary acquisition (measured in the number of repetitions or encounters with an item). Nation is also responsible for emphasizing the effect of word difficulty and many other implicated factors, such as word frequency, its relationship to L1 translation or cognates, the complexity of the linguistic form, etc.

The next decade saw the prolific application of these new research trends into pedagogical approaches to L2s, dominated by a lexical angle, as shown by works such as *The Lexical Syllabus* (Willis 1990) or *Lexical Approach* (Lewis 1993, and the more practical volume Lewis 1997), as well as the learning strategies inventories published by Schmitt (1997). Then, in the year 2000, an explosion of works in corpus linguistics, propitiated by numerous online and free tools and resources, and the appearance and resurgence of several linguistic theories of a marked lexicalist tendency, such as Construction Grammar (Goldberg 2003), Pattern Grammar (Hunston and Francis 2000), Emergence Grammar (Hopper and Bybee 2001), and Linear Unit Grammar (Sinclair and Mauranen 2006), led to a growth of works focused on the lexicon (see Fernández-Perez and González Pereira, this volume). Likewise, the acquisition of multiword units increasingly started to get more attention and entered the sphere of L2 teaching methods (Lewis 2000, Wray 2002, Schmitt 2004, Boers and Lindstromberg 2009, and for a recent summary of empirical results in the area see Pellicer Sánchez and Boers 2018). As a result of all these studies, the amount of research focused on vocabulary knowledge and vocabulary teaching has increased exponentially in the last 15 years or so, at least for the English language. While before 2010, there were only two volumes dedicated to vocabulary (Schmitt and McCarthy 1997, and Bogaards and Laufer 2004), the last decade has seen a good number of not only collective volumes (Webb 2020, Szudarski and Barclay 2022) but also research manuals and books dedicated to explaining how to get vocabulary data and develop resources (word lists, Nation 2006; eye-tracking, Conklin et al. 2018 and Godfroid 2019; general research guidance, Nation and Webb 2011; Schmitt 2010). In addition, several journal issues have been dedicated to vocabulary in recent years, such as *Foreign Language* (2010, edited by Averil Coxhead), *RELC Journal* (2012, edited by Paul Nation), *Language Teaching Research* (January 2017, edited by Batia Laufer; and May 2017, edited by Anna Siyanova-Chanturia) and finally *Language Teaching* (2018, edited by Stuart Webb).

2.1 The research landscape of Spanish vocabulary learning and teaching

The research landscape for vocabulary acquisition and its teaching and learning in Spanish has developed more slowly, emerging more strongly in the 2000s, with the exception of lexical availability studies, which do have ample tradition in this language (López Morales 1995). While the English tradition has looked more into frequency lists and different measurements, Spanish researchers have preferred to focus on theme-oriented lexicons available to the learners (Jiménez Catalán 2014, and Villena-Ponsoda et al., this volume). Still, in the last two decades at least, there has been an effort to import the interests most frequently visited in the English tradition into research focused on Spanish vocabulary acquisition. Comprehension studies, especially in the L1, have developed tests and word lists parallel to those for English, incorporating more aspects of vocabulary knowledge in recent years (see Fernández-Pérez and Gómez-Pereira, this volume). Production studies have centered often on lexical deficits in L2 and its causes (Lozano and Medikoetxea 2013), with a focus on transfer and the effect that types of lexical items can have on such transfer (Sánchez Rufat 2015). Although the most frequent route of transfer has been from L1 to L2 (see Checa-García and Schafer, this volume), there have been some studies also focusing on the reverse route (Hohenstein et al. 2006, Botezatu et al. 2020).

Another area of recent expansion is that of lexical development in Spanish as an L2 during or after a study abroad experience (Llanes, Tragant and Serrano 2012, Serrano, Tragant and Llanes 2012, Tracy-Ventura 2017, Tracy Ventura, Huensch and Mitchell 2021, and Zaytseva, Miralpeix and Pérez-Vidal 2019), although much less has been done with respect to L2 maintenance (but see Graham 2012 and Pearce 2018 who looked at missionaries' vocabulary attrition after being back from their missionary/immersion experience, and Tracy-Ventura, Huensch and Mitchell 2021, who looked into lexical diversity among Spanish L2 learners up to three years after study abroad).

While research on Spanish as a heritage language has increased significantly in the last two decades, studies focused on the vocabulary knowledge, development, and use by Spanish heritage language speakers are scarce in comparison to that of other areas. Some studies have suggested that heritage learners have a strong command of vocabulary if we compare them with L2 learners (e.g., Montrul and Foote 2014), and the limited range of contexts and registers heritage learners are initially exposed to (mainly at home and family environments only) have been found to have an effect on their vocabulary size (Belpoliti and Bermejo 2019: 98). For instance, heritage learners tend to have a higher command of grammatical words than L2 learners, and, since they have learned their native language at home, they are typically much more familiar with daily life vocabulary. In contrast, L2 learners tend to have a higher command of vocabulary for classroom management and certain academic topics. A few recent studies have used lexical availability and decision tasks (Fairclough 2011, Montrul and Foote 2014, Zyzik 2014, Zyzik and Sánchez 2019) in order to investigate the vocabulary knowledge of Spanish bilinguals, sometimes comparing it to that of native English speakers and Spanish L2 learners (Checa-García and Marqués-Pascual 2021), or with the purpose of placing Spanish heritage speakers in the appropriate course of study. Fairclough and Belpoliti (2016) used a lexical decision task in combination with measures of lexical diversity and lexical sophistication and concluded that the lexical richness of Spanish heritage learners is characterized by a reduced vocabulary that consists of the repetition of the same high-frequency words. A few studies have used lexical measures in spontaneous writing in order to investigate heritage learners' lexical development over time. Both Marqués-Pascual (2021) and Marqués-Pascual and Checa-García (2023) studied the lexical development of Spanish heritage learners in a study abroad context, whereas Bowles and Bello-Uriarte (2019) did so in an instructional context at home.

Measuring lexical development is necessary to study, improve and assess the effectiveness of different teaching approaches, activities, and techniques employed in the classroom (see in this volume Marcos-Miguel and Cubas-Mora, Sánchez-Gutiérrez et al., Zyzik and Marqués-Pascual). Two volumes with a pedagogical focus on Spanish L2 vocabulary have recently been published. First, a special issue for the *Journal of Spanish Language Teaching*, (edited by Sánchez Rufat and Jiménez Calderón in 2015) mentions how the emergence of new tools and resources, mainly in the form of L2 corpora, has been a propeller of new empirically based studies centered around vocabulary acquisition and teaching of Spanish L2 vocabulary, albeit sometimes with methodological problems (p. 101). Also focused on vocabulary learning and teaching, and specifically on Meaning-Oriented instruction, is the volume edited by Barcroft and Muñoz-Basols (2021). This volume presents studies of incidental and intentional vocabulary learning, and include applications and teaching suggestions for cognates, testing, and many of the topics we saw regularly present in vocabulary research, with the exception of CAF measurement.

Two major approaches to vocabulary teaching in Spanish are discussed in these two volumes: the *Lexical Approach* or *enfoque léxico* (as proposed by Jiménez Calderón and Sánchez Rufat 2016, and Sánchez Rufat and Jiménez Calderón

2019) and *Data-Driven Learning* (as discussed in Ascensión-Delaney et al. 2015, and Fernández-Pérez and Gómez-Pereira, this volume).

The *enfoque léxico* by Jiménez Calderón and Sánchez Rufat (2016) revolves around the application of a set of methodological principles which assume a central role for the lexicon in the process of learning a second language. Although their approach shares some commonalities with the Lexical Approach by Lewis (1993, 1997, 2000), their proposal is based on eight (psycho)linguistic principles, each with its pedagogical implications, all of them compatible with communicative language teaching. This approach particularly emphasizes the inclusion of various aspects of word knowledge (see Zyzik and Marqués-Pascual in this volume for a description of such aspects), the network nature of lexical knowledge, and attention to different types of lexical items (multiword items, chunks, and collocations, etc.), among other aspects. In order to implement their approach to vocabulary teaching, Jiménez Calderón and Sánchez Rufat (2016) recommend that the selection of target vocabulary should take into account both a learners' needs assessment and results from corpora and lexical availability studies (p. 21). Secondly, and most importantly, the resulting pedagogical recommendations work well within the tenets of a task-based and communicative language teaching approach centered around vocabulary teaching.

The work of Asención-Delaney et al. (2015) provides some ideas on how to incorporate the results of data-driven studies of vocabulary into teaching. Specifically, they present guidelines on how to use concordance searches from native corpora. Within this approach, it is the learners who generate concordances from a reference corpus and use them to explore lexical regularities and frequent combinations, and complete activities based on the results of their search. The use of concordances in the classroom can contribute to the incidental and autonomous learning of the student but can also be used in explicit teaching activities in the classroom.

Finally, studies in Spanish vocabulary acquisition, as it happened with studies on English vocabulary acquisition, have expanded to include multiword items (collocations, phraseology, chunking, etc.), in part as a consequence of seeing the lexicon as an intricate part of language structure (see Fernández-Pérez and González-Pereira in this volume). In the last decade, a number of works have centered around teaching multiunits (Baralo et al. 2012, Castells et al. 2016, Salazar and Molero 2013) as well as L2 production (Yuldashev et al. 2013), applications of phraseology to L2 learning (Bertrán et al. 2011), and multiword presence in textbooks, yet are still in need of improvement (López-Jiménez 2013).

3 Current resources for Spanish vocabulary research

As mentioned in Section 2.2, since the early 2000s there has been a sharp increase in the publication of several key resources for the study of the lexicon in Spanish. In what follows, we briefly discuss available reference and learner's corpora, teaching standards, vocabulary lists, tests, lemmatizers, and other lexical analysis tools.

There are now many corpora available in Spanish for native language and L2 production. Reference corpora of a language provide access to millions of authentic productions by native speakers, which enables a descriptive approach to variation and use. These corpora offer at least three main uses: 1) statistics on the frequency of occurrence of lexical units, 2) concordances in which lexical elements appear in a contextualized form, and 3) the identification of collocations and other multiword or formulaic units. The Royal Spanish Academy of Language (*Real Academia Española* or RAE), has compiled two corpora of native Spanish: *CREA* (https://www.rae.es/banco-de-datos/crea) and *CORPES XXI* (https://apps2.rae.es/CORPES/view/inicioExterno.view), both with oral and written registers represented. The *Corpus del Español Actual*, compiled by Davies (2006) offers a corpus of similar scope and several search capabilities as well. In addition, there have been projects to capture production in multiple areas of the Spanish speaking word, such as the *Macrocorpus de la norma lingüística culta de las principales ciudades de España y América* (MC-NC), the *Corpus del Proyecto para el estudio sociolingüístico del Español de España y de América* (PRESEEA), the *Corpus Oral de Referencia de la Lengua Española Contemporánea* (CORLEC), only for Peninsular oral Spanish, and the *Corpus del Proyecto Estudio gramatical del español hablado en América* (EGREHA). All of them, with the exception of the CORLEC, are based on oral interviews, and some of them are socially stratified. These corpora offer multiple possibilities of exploration in any of the directions shown in Cruz Piñol (2012) and Rufat (2018).

Spanish learner corpora are slowly emerging and being shared. Currently, the two main ones are the CAES (*Corpus de Aprendices de Español* by Rojo and Palacios 2016, https://galvan.usc.es/caes/) and the CEDEL2 (*Corpus Escrito del Español como L2;* Lozano 2009, http://cedel2.learnercorpora.com/search) They feature a great diversity of tasks, genres, and topics that are included in the prompts to which learners have to respond. They can be searched according to the learner's level, L1 and task, and sometimes other features. The collection methods vary, from classroom exercises to specifically produced for the corpus and a mix of both, as in CEDEL2, and *The New England Corpus of Heritage and Second Language Speakers*, although it is very limited in the number of speakers interviewed. Finally, the *Corpus of Written Spanish of L2 and Heritage Speakers* (COWS-L2H; Davidson et al. 2020 and Yamada et al. 2020) is a Spanish learner corpus composed of written samples by students enrolled in the Spanish language courses offered at the University of California, Davis.[1] Other corpora may allow for some searches but are not published nor available to download at the moment.

These corpora resources combined with some analytical tools can be very powerful. Thus, the use of lexical competence measures (see Section 4.1 for types and terminology on those measures) applied to texts in learner corpora can provide an estimation of students' productive vocabulary size (Kyle 2020; Laufer and Nation 1995). For example, lexical diversity measures can yield a valuable estimation of such vocabulary size, which can then be compared across levels of proficiency and offer an approximation of learners' lexical proficiency (Crossley, Salsbury, McNamara and Jarvis 2010). However, a careful selection of the materials is necessary to ensure that the productions are sufficiently similar in task type and topic, as they have been shown to affect lexical richness measures (Fernández Mira et al. 2021; Crossley et al. 2019).

In terms of reference for creating a target vocabulary, both standards by different institutions and frequency and availability lists have been used. Frequency lists constitute a great resource for vocabulary research and teaching. The *Corpus del español* (https://www.corpusdelespanol.org) by Davies (2006), identifies the 5,000 most frequent word families in Spanish from the data extracted from its Spanish corpus and includes a frequency list of lemmas with word type information as well as register, making it possible to do searches online, and also available for purchase. *A Frequency Dictionary of Spanish. Core Vocabulary for Learners*, by Davies and Davies (2018) and based on the Davies corpus, is one of the most widely used resources nowadays when selecting target vocabulary for teaching materials and presents a list of the 20,000 lemmas, also available for purchase in electronic form[2]. The *Open Subtitles* set of corpora (Lison and Tiedemann 2016) also offers a word frequency list (not lemmas) in a number of languages, based on movie subtitles. Because these lists are based on the same movies subtitled to dif-

---

[1] COWS-L2H is freely available in plain text format to all researchers under a Creative Commons license, via a GitHub repository from which the data can be downloaded: https://github.com/ucdaviscl/cowsl2h.

[2] The electronic list allows to find frequency in some registers only (academic, oral, etc.) but not by country. There are also discrepancies between the electronic list available for purchase and the list published in the book.

ferent languages, it is also a parallel corpus of several languages that have been used to compare them, mainly at the grammatical level, and for translation studies.

As mentioned previously, lexical availability has been researched extensively in Hispanic studies. Most efforts are grouped around the Dispolex project (http://www.dispolex.com/info/el-proyecto-panhispanico), directed by Humberto López Morales. Different teams in different areas of the Spanish-speaking world are collecting availability lists on basic semantic fields ("centros de interés"), all at the end of the general education period, around 18 years of age. Different teams are at different stages of the process, but there are several publications already available with their results so far, and the lists can be searched and downloaded after registering on the site. In addition to "centro de interés" and the location of the project, the researcher can select sex and sociocultural level.

In terms of reference guidelines for language teaching, there are vocabulary standards to varying degrees of generality, such as the proficiency guidelines for vocabulary described in the *Common European Framework of Reference for Languages* (2001) and its *Companion Volume* (2020). In these two documents vocabulary and grammar are considered as a whole; lexical and grammatical competence are considered to go hand in hand. Specifically for Spanish, the reference levels described by the Instituto Cervantes in its *Plan Curricular* (2006) include a special mention of multiword lexical units such as collocations and idiomatic expressions and of recognizing the combinatorial properties of these units. The *Performance Descriptors for Language Learners* (2012) put forward by the American Council on the Teaching of Foreign Languages also emphasize the importance of formulaic language and idiomatic expressions for increased proficiency.

As briefly discussed in Section 1, while there are a number of tests for assessing lexical proficiency in L2 English, there are not so many tests available for the assessment of lexical proficiency vocabulary knowledge in L2 Spanish. Examples of such test are the Spanish Vocabulary Levels Test, developed by Chandler (2021), and the 3K-LEx (Robles-García 2020)[3] measures the written recognition (Nation 2013) of nouns, verbs, and adjectives. These tests are receptive vocabulary size tests, which usually assume that if a high percentage of the words in a sample from a specific frequency band is known, all the words in that frequency band will also be known. While knowing the size of the lexicon is important, current vocabulary tests usually measure only word recognition or word association ap-

---

3 The 3K-Lex (https://github.com/problg00/3K-LEx) is a *yes/no* lexical decision test. The complete test contains 108 real words (36 words pertaining to each of the three first 1,000-frequency bands) which were randomly selected from Davies and Davies (2018) Spanish lemmatized frequency dictionary, as well as 54 pseudowords.

propriate to its meaning, thus focusing only on lexical breadth. However, in order to acquire a more accurate picture of vocabulary development, measures of breadth and richness need to be complemented with measures of vocabulary depth (Yanigisawa and Webb 2019). The chapter by Fernández-Pérez and González-Pereira in this volume reviews in more detail some of these tests and those for the first language and explains how the incorporation of more meaning-form aspects and multiword testing is increasingly being included in these tests, but still needs to be developed further.

In order to make use of some of the resources mentioned earlier, and in particular word lists and corpora, several analysis tools are needed. The first of these tools, especially important for a flexive language like Spanish, is a lemmatizer. Good lemmatizers are hard to come by, and there is no exception here for Spanish. The program CLAN has a module for tagging parts of speech (POS), and a lemmatizer extractor for Spanish, but it requires that the data be transcribed in the CHAT format. A python package (SpaCy) also lemmatizes but does not rely on POS tagging and presents frequent problems. In the R environment, there is a tree tagger for Spanish, however, its accuracy is rated lower than its English counterpart. All in all, the accuracy of Spanish lemmatizers and POS taggers is unreliable compared to English, for native production, so their accuracy when confronting L2 production's mistakes is likely to be even lower.

Other resources that allow lexical analyses without the need for coding (concordance programs, frequency results programs, programs that calculate more accurate measures of diversity, etc.) are available for English but not for Spanish. For instance, the "Logonostics" (https://www.lognostics.co.uk/) website, as well as the website "Textinspector" (https://textinspector.com/), offer interesting measures for lexical production, but their tools are currently designed for English and there is explicit advice on their sites not to use them with other languages, such as Spanish. A quick test of its accuracy for Spanish vs. a manual calculation by the authors of this chapter revealed very large differences in types counts, for instance. A work around this issue is the use of the lemmatizers seen above, accompanied by a manual review of problematic items, and the use of the R package koRpus (https://cran.r-project.org/web/packages/koRpus/index.html) to calculate diversity indexes and other measures.

4 Some challenges researching vocabulary development

The study of vocabulary development has been hindered by a number of obstacles. First, the vastness of an ever-growing and relatively fast-changing aspect of language, with words appearing and disappearing and changing meaning even within generations of speakers, has made it difficult to systematize its study. Second, the abundance of terminology has complicated delimiting with precision what needs to be studied, to understand the concepts behind the numerous measurements, and even to compare results among studies sometimes using the same measures for different properties and vice versa (for instance, diversity has been measured in many different ways and the number of words per T-unit has been used as a measure of fluency as well as a measure of complexity; additionally, diversity has also frequently been equated to lexical richness, which includes more aspects than just diversity). Third, many indexes have been proposed for measuring different concepts, making older ones obsolete, but still being used by many researchers (the clearest example is the use of TTR or Giraud's indexes instead of the less text-length-dependent ones MTLD and MATTR, see a comparison of diversity indexes in Catalonian by Torruella and Capsada 2013). Fourth, for many of the measures proposed, different units could be used, and there is not much research on which units to use and why (a notable exception is the study by Jarvis and Hashimoto 2021). Finally, as we saw in the last section, for some indexes, the calculation gets fairly sophisticated and though there are online tools for English, such tools are lacking in Spanish. In the following section, we clarify some frequent terminological confusions and set the terminology practices adopted in this volume.

4.1 Terminological clarifications

As we mentioned above, the lack of consistent terminology makes it difficult to interpret different studies and compare their results, particularly with respect to measures of production and the different terms used to name them. In his study of these inconsistencies in terminology, Jarvis (2013) proposed the term "lexical deployment" for the overall ability to effectively use vocabulary. This term would cover accuracy, including contextual adequacy, fluency, as well as what we will term here "lexical richness" rather than "lexical complexity".

The term "lexical complexity" has been used (Johnson 2017) to refer to a number of qualities of the vocabulary that is known and produced by speakers. However, besides the overarching nature of the term "lexical complexity", with a similar meaning if not identical to that of the proposed term "lexical deployment", the term can also be interpreted as referring to the morphological and phonological complexity of a particular lexical item, rather than overall knowledge. For this reason, it makes better sense to reserve the term "lexical complexity" for the morphological complexity of lexical items, and perhaps even morphosyntactic complexity. Thus, following Castañeda and Jarvis (2014), in this volume, we prefer to use the term "lexical deployment" as the hypernym that refers to overall proficiency in vocabulary, while we will reserve the term "lexical complexity" for a particular measure of lexical deployment among other possible measures. This overall proficiency in vocabulary would include accuracy (in terms of presence and absence of different kinds of errors), fluency (as a measure of the production of lexical units by a certain amount of time), and what traditionally has been called in other areas "complexity" which, in the case of vocabulary studies, has also been frequently termed "lexical richness". The lack of terminological consistency has gone hand in hand with the variety of ways for measuring the different aspects of lexical deployment.

The term "lexical richness" was introduced a long time ago by Yule (1944). With this term, Yule referred to the number of words an author displayed in their publications, and it was akin to the size of their lexicon inventory (not vocabulary known but used). Later on, different authors interpreted the concept in different ways. For instance, Halliday (1985) interpreted "lexical richness" as informational density, Malvern et al. (2004) thought of it as the diversity of the vocabulary used, and Laufer and Nation (1995) used it to refer to the difficulty of the words used. Recent studies, however, have used it to refer to a construct that includes all of these ideas, as a general measure of vocabulary development (Castañeda and Jarvis 2014, Jarvis 2013, Kyle 2020), and it is in this sense that it will be used in the volume, as the compound of lexical diversity, lexical density, and lexical sophistication.

Each of these concepts contributing to lexical richness has been measured in different ways, in particular lexical diversity. Lexical diversity is understood as the variety of vocabulary used (McCarthy and Jarvis 2007). A high degree of lexical diversity is indicative of less repetition of the same words within a sample. Many measurements have been proposed. The initial ones were shown to be correlated with the extension of the production in words, so newer measures that are less affected by this correlation have been proposed (McCarthy and Jarvis 2010). Despite the empirical testing of best lexical diversity indexes, many relatively recent studies still employ older indexes such as Guiraud's or TTR (Serrano et al. 2012, Llanes et al. 2012, Waldvogel 2014, among others). In addition to the variety of different calculations for the same measurement of lexical richness, the lexical units for the calculation can vary, from orthographic words, to lemmas, to word families. Lexical density, the amount of content items per total (grammatical and lexical) items, can also be computed using different units, in this case types or tokens, although less research has been done in this respect.

Finally, lexical sophistication, or one's command of less frequent words, measures the degree to which a text includes words that are less frequent in the language at large. It has been calculated so far by looking at the overall frequency or ranking of those words in a frequency list of the language in question. However, using other types of frequency rankings as a baseline may be preferable depending on the goals of the study, such as the frequency of the word in the input, or the frequency of the word in certain registers/modes vs. native speaker overall frequency, depending on the goals of the study. Moreover, the calculation of sophistication can be done on the basis of count-frequency or band-frequency. Band-frequency divides the lexical items considered into groups of more or less frequency, such as 1000 more frequent words, etc. Thus, it turns a quantitative variable (frequency of tokens) into a categorical one, losing information. In an empirical study comparing both methods (Crossley et al. 2013), a count-based way of computing sophistication was shown to be more sensitive to detect group differences. However, a majority of studies, at least for Spanish (Belpoliti and Bermejo 2019, Bertón and Sánchez, this volume, Borrás et al., this volume, Fairclough and Belpoliti 2016, Tracy-Ventura 2017, Waldvogel 2014) have used a band method, which makes easy to measure progress in acquiring vocabulary beyond a certain threshold of frequency (typically beyond 2000 most frequent words) and make more sense when not comparing groups such as in Belpoliti and Bermejo (2019) and Fairclough and Belpoliti (2016). For a use of a count-based comparison, see Marqués-Pascual and Checa-García (in press), Checa-García and Marqués-Pascual (2021) and Checa-García and Schafer, this volume.

Lastly, as discussed in Sections 2.1 and 3, vocabulary studies in Spanish have often focused on investigating "lexical availability". This term refers to the degree to which a term is accessible to a speaker, and it is studied by asking speakers to produce vocabulary related to a certain meaning (typically a semantic field, such as "body parts" or "emotions," etc.), called "centros de interés" (Jiménez Catalán 2014). The idea is that not all words are known the same in terms of processing and accessing, so what words are accessed first and faster provides valuable information about the language lexicon, as valuable if not more as frequency lists (see Villena-Ponsoda et al, this volume, for a revision and a new proposed way of calculating lexical availability).

With the aim of clarifying the concepts and measures presented above, Figure 1 presents a summary table including most of the terms reviewed in this section.

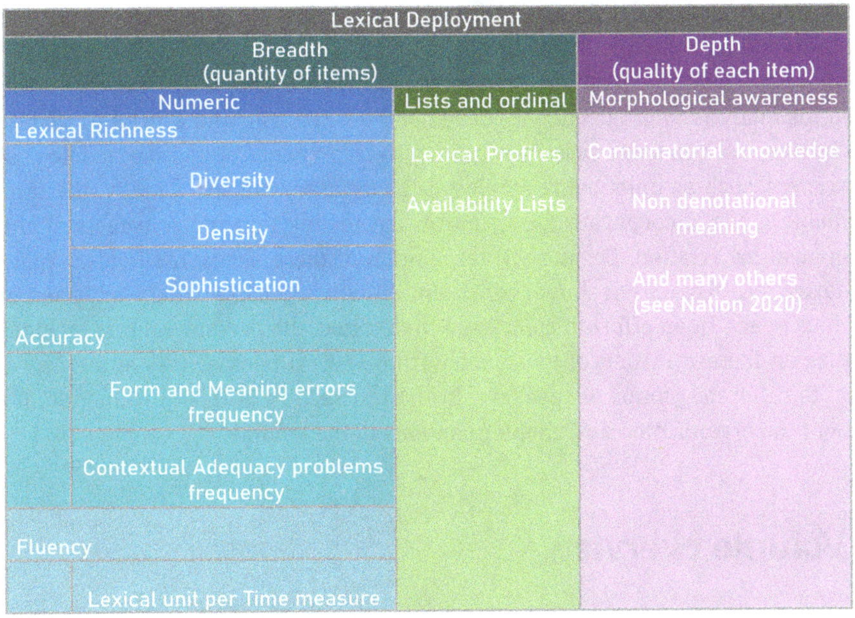

Lexical Deployment		
Breadth (quantity of items)		**Depth** (quality of each item)
Numeric	Lists and ordinal	Morphological awareness
Lexical Richness	Lexical Profiles	Combinatorial knowledge
Diversity	Availability Lists	Non denotational meaning
Density		
Sophistication		And many others (see Nation 2020)
Accuracy		
Form and Meaning errors frequency		
Contextual Adequacy problems frequency		
Fluency		
Lexical unit per Time measure		

Figure 1: Lexical deployment conceptual organization.

5 What still needs to be done. Suggestions for future research

Section 3 presented some of the tools currently available for the study of Spanish vocabulary. As mentioned, despite the availability of reference corpora for Spanish, the availability of corpora for L2 Spanish learners is still limited. In their review of Spanish corpora, Parodi and Burdiles (2019) discuss that most learner corpora are designed with research in mind. Thus, there is still a need for corpora with a language teaching focus that are designed for learners, as well as more adequate and exhaustive frequency lists for Spanish. Regarding vocabulary testing, current vocabulary tests usually measure only lexical breadth. However, to acquire a more accurate picture of development, measures of vocabulary size and tests of lexical availability need to be complemented with measures of vocabulary depth.

    Given the possibility of L1 transfer into the L2 when creating the interlanguage, another line of research should look into whether vocabulary transfer happens and whether this transfer is only negative or if positive transfer can favor vocabulary development in an L2. A further related question is if the transfer is only of items, or if there are lexical abilities that could be transferred (see Checa-García and Schafer, this volume).

Together with the need for some corpus data, there is perhaps a more urgent need for analysis tools specifically developed for Spanish, and a need to update the indexes used in some cases, in addition to terminological and methodological awareness, such as units being employed for different indexes. Finally, the tests available could incorporate more multiword testing and more aspects of the form-meaning relation. Despite the recognition of these needs, the field of Spanish lexical acquisition has shown consistent growth and more is to be expected in the next years. In an effort to contribute to this goal, the present volume includes studies on the acquisition of vocabulary from several perspectives and with respect to different groups of speakers. In the last section of this introduction, we present the organization and chapter contents in the volume.

6 Volume overview

The aim of the volume is to be of interest to readers looking for studies that present theory, research, and practice or a combination of these elements, centered around the lexical acquisition of Spanish. Consequently, the volume is organized into four sections corresponding to those areas.

Section I, *Lexicon at the crossroads: the interplay of lexicon with other areas of language* is composed of chapters that provide an overview of vocabulary studies, look into the history, and needs of research in this area (Chapter 1 and Chapter 2) and examine the relationship of vocabulary knowledge and other forms of linguistic knowledge, such as phonetic awareness, offering an example of what new theories claim (Chapter 3).

Section II, *Measures of lexical competence and development in Spanish* looks into measures used in the study of lexical competence and presents studies that have made use of one or more of these measures (Chapters 4, 5, 6, and 7). A goal of this section is to include an explanation of different approaches to measuring vocabulary knowledge, explain different indexes developed, and exemplify different applications in the four studies reported. This area has been frequently studied in other languages, particularly English, but as we saw, is in need of new tools, updating of indexes, more terminological rigor, and more explicit detail in the methods and their reasoning. We hope that the studies in this section will offer some ideas in this respect, as well as represent the possibilities for group comparison, time effect studies, and transfer research that these indexes offer.

Section III, *Attitudes and emotions in the lexicon* discusses attitudes and emotions towards vocabulary, both in terms of one's lexical use (Chapter 8) and of perceptions towards someone else's vocabulary use (Chapter 9). This section helps represent studies with a more sociolinguistic approach, often a less visited area in lexical acquisition studies.

Finally, Section IV, the most pedagogical and applied section, *Approaches to teaching L2 vocabulary*, is devoted to issues related to teaching Spanish vocabulary in the L2 classroom, all of them in the U.S. higher education setting. It begins with a focus on both instructors and learners and what both groups think they know (Chapter 10), then discusses the instructor's adherence to the proposed curriculum (Chapter 11) and ends with a narrower focus on the treatment of vocabulary and activity types in current Spanish textbooks (Chapter 12). These three chapters are based on both pedagogical practices and research, since both should be considered when developing a program of vocabulary learning with the goal of closing the gap between theory, research, and practice. A common complaint in articles with a pedagogical focus is the lack of correspondence between didactic materials and research advancements in the field of vocabulary knowledge and acquisition. This last section attempts to bridge this gap by following the precedence of the two other volumes in the field (Barcroft and Basols 2022 and Sánchez Rufat and Jiménez Calderón 2015). The present volume follows that line of work in hopes of expanding the research landscape of lexical competence in Spanish.

References

Asención-Delaney, Yuli, Joseph Collentine, Karina Collentine, Jersus Colmenares & Luke Plonsky. 2015. El potencial de la enseñanza del vocabulario basada en corpus: Optimismo con precaución. *Journal of Spanish Language Teaching* 2(2). 140–151.

Baralo, Marta, Marta Genís & María Eugenia Santana. 2012. *Vocabulario. B2*. Madrid: Anaya.

Barcroft, Joe & Javier Muñoz-Basols. 2021. *Spanish Vocabulary Learning in Meaning-oriented Instruction*. London/N.Y.: Routledge.

Belpoliti, Flavia & Encarna Bermejo. 2019. *Spanish heritage learners' emerging literacy: Empirical research and classroom practice*. Routledge.

Bertrán, Antonio Pamies, Lucía Luque Nadal & José Manuel Pazos Bretaña (eds.) 2011. *Multi-lingual Phraseography, Second Language Learning and Translation Applications*. Hohengehren: Schneider Verlag.

Blumenfeld, Henrike K. & Viorica Marian. 2007. Constraints on parallel activation in bilingual spoken language processing: Examining proficiency and lexical status using eye-tracking. *Language and cognitive processes* 22(5). 633–660.

Boers, Frank & Seth Lindstromberg. 2009. *Optimizing a lexical approach to instructed second language acquisition*. N.Y: Springer.

Bogaards, Paul & Batia Laufer. 2004. *Vocabulary in a second language: Selection, acquisition, and testing*. Vol. 10. Amsterdam/N.Y: John Benjamins.

Botezatu, Mona Roxana, Judith F. Kroll, Morgan I. Trachsel, & Taomei Guo. 2020. Second language immersion impacts native language lexical production and comprehension. *Linguistic Approaches to bilingualism* 12(3). 47–376.

Bowles, Melissa & Adrián Bello-Uriarte. 2019. What Impact Does Heritage Language Instruction Have on Spanish Heritage Learners' Writing? In Masatoshi Sato & Shawn Loewen (eds.), *Evidence-Based Second Language Pedagogy*, 219–240. New York, NY: Routledge.

Camblin, C. Christine, Peter C. Gordon, & Tamara Y. Swaab. 2007. The interplay of discourse congruence and lexical association during sentence processing: Evidence from ERPs and eye tracking. *Journal of Memory and Language* 56(1). 103–128.

Castells, Sergi Torner & Elisenda Bernal Gallen. 2016. *Collocations and other lexical combinations in Spanish: Theoretical, Lexicographical and Applied Perspectives*. N.Y. & Philadelphia: Taylor & Francis.

Carter, Ronald & Michael McCarthy. 1988. *Vocabulary and Language Teaching*. N.Y.: Longman.

Castañeda-Jiménez, Gabriela & Scott Jarvis. 2014. Exploring Lexical Diversity in Second Language Spanish. In Kimberly L. Geeslin (ed.), *The Handbook of Spanish Second Language Acquisition*, 498–513. Wiley Blackwell.

Chandler, Paul. 2021. New vocabulary levels tests for L2 Spanish. In Joe Barcroft and Javier Muñoz-Basols (eds.), *Spanish Vocabulary Learning in Meaning-Oriented Instruction*,1st edn. N.Y: Routledge. https://doi.org/10.4324/9781315100364

Checa-García, Irene & Laura Marqués-Pascual. 2021. Lexical Richness Measures in Spanish Heritage, Native and L2 Learners. Paper presented at the *8th National Symposium of Spanish as a Heritage Language*. Virtual Conference, May 2021.

Conklin, Kathy, Ana Pellicer-Sánchez & Gareth Carrol. 2018. *Eye-tracking. A guide for Applied Linguistics Research*. Cambridge: Cambridge University Press.

Crossley, Scott A., Tom Cobb & Danielle S. McNamara. 2013. Comparing count-based and band-based indices of word frequency: Implications for active vocabulary research and pedagogical applications. *System* 41(4). 965–981.

Crossley, Scott A., Kyle Kristopher & Ute Römer. 2019. Examining lexical and cohesion differences in discipline-specific writing using multi-dimensional analysis. *Multi-Dimensional Analysis: Research Methods and Current Issues* 6. 189–216.

Crossley, Scott, Tom Salsbury, Danielle S. McNamara & Scott Jarvis. 2010. Predicting lexical proficiency in language learner texts using computational indices. *Language Testing*, 28(4). 561–580.

Cruz Piñol, Mar. 2012. *Lingüística de corpus y enseñanza del español como 2/L*. Madrid: Arco Libros.

Davidson, Sam, Aaron Yamada, Paloma Fernández Mira, Agustina Carando, Claudia H. Sánchez Gutierrez & Kenji Sagae. 2020. Developing NLP Tools with a New Corpus of Learner Spanish. In *Proceedings of the 12th Language Resources and Evaluation Conference*, pages 7238–7243, Marseille, France. European Language Resources Association.

Davies, Mark. 2006. *A Frequency Dictionary of Spanish*. London and New York: Routledge.

Davies, Mark & Kathy Hayward Davies. 2018. *A frequency dictionary of Spanish: Core vocabulary for learners*. N.Y: Routledge.

Fairclough, Marta. 2011. Testing the lexical recognition task with Spanish/English bilinguals in the United States. *Language Testing*, 28. 273–297.

Fairclough, Marta & Flavia Belpoliti. 2016. Emerging literacy in Spanish among Hispanic heritage language university students in the USA: a pilot study. *International Journal of Bilingual Education and Bilingualism*, 19(2). 185–201.

Fernández-Mira, Paloma, Emily Morgan, Sam Davidson, Aaron Yamada, Agustina Carando, Kenji Sagae, & Claudia H. Sánchez-Gutiérrez, C. H. 2021. Lexical diversity in an L2 Spanish learner corpus: The effect of topic-related variables. *International Journal of Learner Corpus Research* 7(2). 230–258.

Godfroid, Aline. 2019. *Eye tracking in second language acquisition and bilingualism: A research synthesis and methodological guide.* N.Y: Routledge.

Goldberg, Adele. E. 2003. Constructions: A new theoretical approach to language. *Trends in cognitive sciences* 7(5). 219–224.

Graham, C. Ray. 2012.Vocabulary attrition in adult speakers of Spanish as a second language. In Lynne Hansen (ed.), *Second Language Acquisition Abroad: The LDS Missionary Experience*, 135–184. Amsterdam/N.Y.: John Benjamins.

Halliday, Michael K. 1985. *An Introduction to Functional Grammar.* 1st edn. London: Edward Arnold.

Hohenstein, Jill, Ann Eisenberg & Letitia Naigles. 2006. Is he floating across or crossing afloat? Cross-influence of L1 and L2 in Spanish–English bilingual adults. *Bilingualism: Language and cognition* 9(3). 249–261.

Hopper, Paul & Joan Bybee (ed.). 2001. *Frequency and the Emergence of Linguistic Structure.* Amsterdam/N.Y.: John Benjamins.

Hunston, Susan & Gill Francis. 2000. *Pattern grammar: A corpus-driven approach to the lexical grammar of English.* Amsterdam/N.Y.: John Benjamins.

Jarvis, Scott. 2013. Capturing the diversity in lexical diversity. *Language Learning* 63. 87–106

Jarvis, Scott & Brett James Hashimoto. 2021. How operationalizations of word types affect measures of lexical diversity. *International Journal of Learner Corpus Research* 7(1). 163–194.

Jiménez Catalán, Rosa María (ed.). 2014. *Lexical availability in English and Spanish as a second language.* Vol. 17. N.Y.: Springer Science & Business Media.

Jiménez Calderón, Francisco & Sánchez-Rufat. 2016. Posibilidades de aplicación de un enfoque léxico a la enseñanza comunicativa del español. In Gerardo Nieto Caballero (ed.), Nuevas aportaciones al estudio de la enseñanza y aprendizaje de lenguas, 11–23. Cáceres, Universidad de Extremadura.

Johnson, Mark D. 2017. Cognitive task complexity and L2 written syntactic complexity, accuracy, lexical complexity, and fluency: A research synthesis and meta-analysis. *Journal of Second Language Writing* 37. 13–38.

Kyle, Kristopher. 2020. Measuring lexical richness. In Stuart Webb (ed.), *The Routledge handbook of vocabulary studies*, 454–476. N.Y.: Routledge.

Laufer, Batia & Paul Nation. 1995. Vocabulary size and use: lexical richness in L2 written production. *applied Linguistics*, 16. 307–322.

Llanes, Àngels, Elsa Tragant & Raquel Serrano. 2012. The roles of individual differences in a study abroad experience: The case of Erasmus students. *International Journal of Multilingualism* 9(3). 318–342. https://doi.org/10.1080/14790718.2011.620614

Lewis, Michael. 1993. *The lexical approach.* Hove, UK: Language Teaching Publications.

Lewis, Michael. 1997. *Implementing the lexical approach.* Hove, UK: Language Teaching Publications.

Lewis, Michael (ed.). 2000. *Teaching collocation: Further developments in the lexical approach.* Hove, UK: Language Teaching Publications.

Lison, Pierre & Jörg Tiedemann. 2016. OpenSubtitles2016: Extracting large parallel corpora from movie and TV subtitles. In *Proceedings of the 10th International Conference on Language Resources and Evaluation* (LREC 2016), 923–929. European Language Resources Association (ELRA).

López-Jiménez, María Dolores. 2013. Multi-word lexical units in 12 textbooks. *Revista española de lingüística aplicada* 26. 333–348.

López Morales, Humberto. 1995. Los estudios de disponibilidad léxica: pasado y presente. *Boletín De Filología* 35(1). 245–259. Accessed at https://ultimadecada.uchile.cl/index.php/BDF/article/view/19231

Lozano, Cristobal. 2009. CEDEL2: Corpus Escrito del Español como L2. In Carmen. M. Bretones Callejas, José Francisco Fernández Sánchez, José Ramón Ibáñez Ibáñez, María Elena García Sánchez, M. Enriqueta Cortés de los Ríos, Sagrario Salaberri Ramiro, M. Soledad Cruz Martínez,

Nobel Perdü Honeyman, and Blasina Cantizano Märquez (eds.), *Applied linguistics now: Understanding language and mind/La lingüística aplicada actual: Comprendiendo el lenguaje y la mente*, 197–212. Almería: Universidad de Almería.

Lozano, Cristóbal & Amaya Mendikoetxea. 2013. Learner corpora and second language acquisition. *Automatic treatment and analysis of learner corpus data* 59. 65–100.

Malvern, David, Brian Richards, Ngoni Chipere, & Pilar Durán. 2004. *Lexical Diversity and Language Development: Quantification and Assessment*. New York: Palgrave MacMillan.

Marqués-Pascual, Laura. 2021. The impact of study abroad on Spanish heritage learners' writing development (Chapter 10). In Rebecca Pozzi, Tracy Quan and Chelsea Escalante (eds.), *Heritage Speakers of Spanish and Study Abroad*. N.Y.: Routledge.

Marqués-Pascual, Laura & Irene Checa-García. 2023. Lexical development in Study Abroad: Heritage Speakers and L2 learners. *Study Abroad Research in Second Language Acquisition and International Education* 8(1). 115–141. https://doi.org/10.1075/sar.21012.mar

McCarthy, Michael J. 1984. A new look at vocabulary in EFL. *Applied linguistics* 5(1). 12–22.

McCarthy, Michael. 2020. Fifty-five years and counting: A half-century of getting it half right? *Language Teaching*, 54(3). 343–354. doi:10.1017/S0261444820000075

McCarthy, Michael J. 2022. Foreword. In Paweł Szudarski, and Samuel Barclay (eds.), *Vocabulary theory, patterning and teaching*. Vol. 152. Jackson, TN: Multilingual Matters.

McCarthy, Philip M. & Scott Jarvis. 2007. Vocd: A Theoretical and Empirical Evaluation. *Language Testing*, 24(4). 459–488.

McCarthy, Philip M. & Scott Jarvis. 2010. MTLD, vocd-D, and HD-D: A validation study of sophisticated approaches to lexical diversity assessment. *Behavior research methods* 42(2). 381–392.

Meara, Paul & Stephen Ingle. 1986. The formal representation of words in an L2 speaker's lexicon. *Interlanguage studies bulletin* 2(2). 160–171.

Meara, Paul & Imma Miralpeix. 2016. *Tools for Researching Vocabulary*. Bristol, Blue Ridge Summit: Multilingual Matters.

Meara, Paul. 1980. Vocabulary acquisition: A neglected aspect of language learning. *Language Teaching* 13(3–4). 221–246.

Mitchell, Rosamond. 1994. The communicative approach to language teaching: An introduction. In A. Swarbrick (ed.), *Teaching Modern Languages*, 33–42. London: Routledge.

Molero, Clara María & Dánica Salazar. 2013. Análisis contrastivo, criterios de selección y didáctica de las colocaciones léxicas en el aula de español. In Ana Kuzmanović Jovanović, Jelena Filipović, Jasna Stojanović & Jelena Rajić (eds.) *Estudios Hispánicos del siglo XXI*, 359–365. Belgrado: University of Belgrado.

Montrul, Silvina & Rebecca Foote. 2014. Age of acquisition interactions in bilingual lexical access: A study of the weaker language of L2 learners and heritage speakers. *International Journal of bilingualism* 18(3). 274–303.

Nation, Ian Paul. 1982. Beginning to learn foreign vocabulary: A review of the research. *RELC journal* 13(1). 14–36.

Nation, Ian Paul. 2006. How large a vocabulary is needed for reading and listening? *Canadian modern language review* 63(1). 59–82.

Nation, Ian Paul. 2007. The four strands. *International Journal of Innovation in Language Learning and Teaching* 1(1). 2–13.

Nation, Ian Paul. 2013. *Learning vocabulary in another language*. 2nd edn. Cambridge: Cambridge University Press.

Nation, Ian Paul. 2020. The different aspects of vocabulary knowledge. In Stuart Webb (ed.), *The Routledge handbook of vocabulary studies*, 15–29. N.Y: Routledge.

Nation, Ian Paul & Stuart Alexander Webb. 2011. *Researching and analyzing vocabulary*. Boston, MA: Heinle, Cengage Learning.

Parodi, Giovanni & Gina Burdiles. 2019. Corpus y bases de datos. In Javier Muñoz-Basols, Elisa Gironzetti & Manuel Lacorte (eds.), *The Routledge Handbook of Spanish Language Teaching: metodologías, contextos y recursos para la enseñanza del español L2*, 596–612. Abingdon: Routledge.

Pearce, Nancy. 2018. *What Makes it Stick: Factors in Lexical Maintenance of LDS Spanish Speaking Return Missionaries*. M.A. University of Wyoming.

Pellicer Sánchez, Ana. 2015. Developing automaticity and speed of lexical access: The effects of incidental and explicit teaching approaches. *Journal of Spanish Language Teaching*, 2. 126–139.

Pellicer Sánchez, Ana & Frank Boers. 2018. Pedagogical approaches to the teaching and learning of formulaic language. In Anna Siyanova-Chanturia & Ana Pellicer-Sánchez (eds.), *Understanding formulaic language*. 153–173. New York, NY: Routledge.

Read, John. 2020. Key issues in assessing vocabulary knowledge. In Stuart Webb (ed.), The Routledge Handbook in Vocabulary studies, 545–560. London, UK: Routledge.

Robles-García, Pablo. 2020. 3K-LEx: Desarrollo y validación de una prueba de amplitud léxica en español. *Journal of Spanish Language Teaching*, 7(1). 64–76.

Rojo, Guillermo & Ignacio Palacios. 2016. Learner Spanish on computer: The CAES Corpus de Aprendices de Español project. In Margarita Alonso-Ramos (ed.) *Spanish learner corpus research: Current trends and future perspectives*, 55–87. Amsterdam: John Benjamins. https://doi.org/10.1075/scl.78.03roj

Qian, David D. & Linda H. F. Lin. 2019. The relationship between vocabulary knowledge and language proficiency. In Stuart Webb (ed.), *The Routledge handbook of vocabulary studies*, 66–80. London: Routledge.

Roberts, Leah & Anna Siyanova-Chanturia. 2013. Using eye-tracking to investigate topics in L2 acquisition and L2 processing. *Studies in Second Language Acquisition* 35(2). 213–235. doi:10.1017/S0272263112000861

Sánchez Rufat, Anna. 2015. *El verbo dar en el español escrito de aprendientes de L1 inglés: estudio comparativo entre hablantes no nativos y hablantes nativos basado en corpus*. Ph.D. Dissertation, Universidad de Extremadura.

Sánchez Rufat, Anna. 2018. Enseñanza-aprendizaje del componente léxico – semántico. In María Martínez-Atienza de Dios and Alfonso Zamorano (eds.), *Teoría y metodología para la enseñanza de ELE. II. Enseñanza – aprendizaje de los componentes lingüísticos*, 73–108. Madrid: EnClaveELE.

Sánchez Rufat, Anna & Francisco Jiménez Calderón. 2015. New perspectives on the acquisition and teaching of Spanish vocabulary/Nuevas perspectivas sobre la adquisición y la enseñanza del vocabulario del español. *Journal of Spanish Language Teaching* 2(2). 99–111.

Sánchez Rufat, Anna & Francisco Jiménez Calderón. 2019. Vocabulario. In Javier Muñoz- Basols, Elisa Gironzetti & Manel Lacorte (eds.), *The Routledge Handbook of Spanish Language Teaching: metodologías, contextos y recursos para la enseñanza del español L2*, 229–242. Abingdon/Nueva York: Routledge.

Schmitt, Norbert. 1997. Vocabulary learning strategies. *Vocabulary: Description, acquisition and pedagogy*. Cambridge: Cambridge University Press.

Schmitt, Norbert (ed.). 2004. *Formulaic sequences: Acquisition, processing, and use*. Vol. 9. Amsterdam/N.Y.: John Benjamins Publishing.

Schmitt, Norbert. 2010. *Researching vocabulary: A vocabulary research manual*. N.Y: Springer.

Schmitt, Norbert. 2014. Size and depth of vocabulary knowledge: What the research shows. *Language learning*, 64(4). 913–951.

Schmitt, Norbert & Michael McCarthy (eds.). 1997. *Vocabulary: description, acquisition and pedagogy*. Cambridge: Cambridge University Press.

Schmitt, Norbert, Diane Schmitt & Caroline Clapham. 2001. Developing and exploring the behaviour of two new versions of the Vocabulary Levels Test. *Language Testing*, 18(1). 55–88.
Serrano, Raquel, Elsa Tragant & Àngel Llanes. 2012. A longitudinal analysis of the effects of one year abroad. *The Canadian Modern Language Review* 68(2). 138–163.
Sinclair, John McHardy & Anna Mauranen. 2006. *Linear unit grammar: Integrating speech and writing*, vol. 25. Amsterdam/N.Y.: John Benjamins Publishing.
Szudarski, Paweł & Samuel Barclay (eds.). 2022. *Vocabulary theory, patterning and teaching*, vol. 152. Jackson, TN: Multilingual Matters.
Torruella, Joan & Ramon Capsada. 2013. Lexical Statistics and Typological Structures: A Measure of Lexical Richness, *Procedia – Social and Behavioral Sciences* 95. 447–454. https://doi.org/10.1016/j.sbspro.2013.10.668.
Tracy-Ventura, Nicole. 2017. Combining corpora and experimental data to investigate language learning during residence abroad: A study of lexical sophistication. *System* 71. 35–45.
Tracy-Ventura, Nicole, Amanda Huensch & Rosamond Mitchell. 2021. Understanding the Long-Term Evolution of L2 Lexical Diversity: The Contribution of a Longitudinal Learner Corpus. In B. Le Bruyn & M. Paquot (eds.), *Learner Corpus Research Meets Second Language Acquisition*, 148–171. Cambridge: Cambridge University Press. doi:10.1017/9781108674577.008
Waldvogel, Dieter. 2014. An analysis of Spanish L2 lexical richness. *Academic Exchange Quarterly* 18(2). 8.
Webb, Stuart (ed.). 2020. *The Routledge handbook of vocabulary studies*, vol. 2. London: Routledge.
Webb, Stuart. 2022. Innovations in Measures of Breadth and Depth of Vocabulary Knowledge. In Paweł Szudarski & Samuel Barclay (eds.), Vocabulary Theory, Patterning and Teaching, 41–58. Jackson, TN: Multilingual Matters.
Webb, Stuart & Paul Nation. 2017. *How Vocabulary is Learned*. Oxford: Oxford University Press.
Williams, Joy, Norman Segalowitz & Tatsiana Leclair. 2014. Estimating second language productive vocabulary size: A Capture-Recapture approach. *The Mental Lexicon* 9(1). 23–47. doi.org/10.1075/ml.9.1.02wil
Willis, Dave. 1990. *The lexical syllabus*, vol. 30. London: Collins. 17. *How vocabulary is learned*. Oxford: Oxford University Press.
Wray, Alison. 2002. *Formulaic language and the lexicon*. Cambridge/N.Y.: Cambridge University Press.
Yamada, Aaron, Sam Davidson, Paloma Fernández-Mira, Agustina Carando, Kenji Sagae & Claudia H. Sánchez-Gutiérrez. 2020. COWS-L2H: A corpus of Spanish learner writing. *Research in Corpus Linguistics* 8(1). 17–32. https://doi.org/10.32714/ricl.08.01.02
Yanagisawa, Akifumi & Stuart Webb. 2019. Measuring Depth of Vocabulary. In Stuart Webb (ed.), *The Routledge handbook of vocabulary studies*, 371–386. New York, NY: Routledge.
Yuldashev, Aziz, Julieta Fernandez & Steven L. Thorne. 2013. Second language learners' contiguous and discontiguous multi-word unit use over time. *The Modern Language Journal* 97(1). 31–45.
Yule, George Udny. 1944. *The Statistical Study of Literary Vocabulary*. Cambridge, UK: Cambridge University Press.
Zaytseva, Victoria, Inma Miralpeix & Carmen Pérez-Vidal. 2019. ESL Written development at home and abroad: taking a closer look at vocabulary. *International Journal of Bilingual Education and Bilingualism*. https://doi.org/10.1080/13670050.2019.1664392
Zyzik, Eve. 2014. Causative verbs in the grammar of Spanish heritage speakers. *Linguistic Approaches to Bilingualism* 4(1). 1–33.
Zyzik, Eve & Ruben Sánchez. 2019. Beyond accuracy: Heritage speakers' performance on two kinds of acceptability judgment tasks. *Applied Psycholinguistics* 40. 645–671. https://doi:10.1017/S0142716418000760

Milagros Fernández-Pérez and Miguel González-Pereira

Chapter 2
The role of the lexicon in language acquisition: An issue in need of study

1 Introduction. The value of the lexicon in language acquisition

The conception of language from an atomized perspective as a rule-governed *product* has led to the prioritization of grammar over other components. It is the aim of this chapter to underline the significance of the lexicon in the dynamics of L1 acquisition and in the processes of learning and teaching L2. If language is seen as an *activity* that is learned and used, there are at least two reasons why lexical development is crucial. First, because words are the only possible basis for phonic progress (Golinkoff and Hirsh-Pasek 1999), and second, because the flow of words itself channels the emergence of grammar (Bates and Goodman 1999). These two reasons effectively motivate all specialists in L1 and L2 acquisition research; without progress in the acquisition of a speaker's lexical repertory there can be no progress in verbal competence.

Our contribution aims to highlight and contextualize how research into the value of lexical development has refocused the role of the other components in L1 and L2 learning (Section 2), in particular how the number of different words is decisive for the natural flow of phonetics (Section 2.1., 2.2.) and, above all, for the gradual building of grammar (Section 2.3, 2.4.). It also explains how the implementation of skills in relation to meaning goes hand in hand with the building up of grammatical and usage-based content. Thus, the holistic view of lexical-grammatical approaches and of corpus orientations which emphasize the importance of praxis are of prime concern in this chapter, as communicative mastery of the lexicon in a language requires combinatorial skills in structures and selection tactics in interchange frames.

Note: This study forms part of the research project "Adquisición fónica y Corpus. Tratamiento en PHON del corpus Koiné de habla infantil" (Phonetic acquisition and Corpus. The treatment in PHON of the Koiné corpus of child speech) (FFFI2017-82752-P), funded by FEDER/Ministerio de Ciencia, Innovación y Universidades –Agencia Estatal de Investigación (2017).

Milagros Fernández-Pérez, Miguel González-Pereira, Universidade de Santiago de Compostela, Spain

https://doi.org/10.1515/9783110730418-002

More specifically, two guiding principles will inform our methodology and approach here, with the aim of confirming the central role of the lexicon in an active vision of verbal usage and language acquisition. On the one hand, and in light of an observational approach based on corpus data, we include descriptive studies that are based on registers of evolving production in different communicative frameworks and which facilitate the learning of lexical patterns appropriate for diverse situational and interactional contexts (Section 3). On the other hand, we take into account research with a more traditional evaluative format which includes data from sheets and questionnaires reflecting the *language-product* taken as one model (Section 3.1.). Possible convergent evidence derived from both approaches will thus confirm the central role of lexical development for language acquisition in a holistic sense (Section 4).

2 Lexical acquisition and language components

The relevance of lexical development in the dynamics of language acquisition is crucial for two main reasons: (a) without uttered words (*chunks*, Brown 1973, Peters 1983) there is no basis on which sounds can emerge; (b) without words that combine (*constructions*, Tomasello 2003, Goldberg 2005) there are no structures leading to grammar. These two reasons motivate the research for all specialists in L1 and L2 acquisition. That is, without progress in the development of the lexical stock, there can be no progress in verbal competence. In this section we will highlight and contextualize how levels of lexical development have been shown to influence the progress of other components in L1 and L2; and we will discuss how the number of different words acquired is decisive in the natural progression of phonetics and, above all, for the gradual building up of grammar (Bates and Goodman 1999).

2.1 The lexicon and phonetic progress in L1 acquisition

The predominance in linguistics of formal and static views of language has led to the prime role of grammar at the expense of the other components.[1] However, in

---

[1] As early as 1997 D. Slobin had emphasized the need to consider the *process* prior to the *product*: "the important term is development, rather acquisition. Much attention has been paid to the initial state and the endstate, while the processes of change over time have been too often slighted, ignored and explained away" (Slobin 1997:16).

acquisition, lexis and sounds go hand in hand: in order to estimate the degree of solidity of acquired sounds, key criteria are the presence of these sounds in *type* data (not just *tokens*) and above all their functional weight in the lexicon as a whole (how many oppositional pairs they support, Hoff-Ginsberg 1997).

As Lleó notes (1997: 20), among the tests for measuring and comparing phonetic acquisition data, "En primer lugar, es importante saber el *número de palabras* o *número de tipos léxicos* que una criatura tiene en su lexicón a lo largo de una secuencia de puntos temporales" ["First of all, it is important to know the *number of words* or *number of lexical types* that a child has in its lexicon over a sequence of time points"], because one cannot approach phonetic development without considering its role in the pronunciation of the lexical items available for communication.

In studies on the phonetic development of L1, the approach to estimating both the sequence of the emergence of sounds and the degree of the rootedness of sounds emphasizes the functional influence of sounds in the system: the oppositional pairs supported, plus their frequency, determine the appearance (more or less early) of phonetic units, as well as the margins for their establishment in verbal competence. It thus depends on the lexical *types* in oppositional pairs in each linguistic system and is not a consequence of the degree of articulatory "difficulty". The study by Ingram (1989) marked a turning point here, in that it emphasized the functional profitability of phonetic units: they must appear in multiple lexical units rather than in a small number of widely used words. As Hoff-Ginsberg (1997: 169) notes,

> It is important to understand that the relevant factor according to Ingram's functional hypothesis is not the frequency with which children hear the sound but rather the frequency with which the sound is used in different words. For example, in English, the initial sound in *the* and *this* is very frequently heard because it is used in a few very high-frequency words. However, because the sound is not involved in many different words, its functional significance is low. And it is interesting to note that the *th* sound [ð] is a late-acquired sound in children acquiring English.

At the same time, the procedures for assessing the evolution of phonetic development in L1 acquisition include elicitation materials with words not only appropriate to the cognitive-referential flow of the initial verbal stages, but, even more importantly, which are selected to include oppositional pairs that guarantee the solidity of the sounds emitted. Thus, the tests designed for English by Grunwell (1985) incorporate elements that prompt the production of different words and aim to outline the functional implications of *phonetic patterns*: only in this way can the symbolic stock of sounds be ensured.

In a similar way, Bosch (2004) developed an elicitation system to estimate phonetic progress in Spanish, by means of images that induce the production of

32 words containing the 62 phonetic elements in question. The expected lexical items are based on two conditions: that they accommodate children's cognitive levels, and that they include a certain functional weight of the sounds. As Bosch (2004: 27) says,

> No hay que olvidar que los segmentos vocálicos y consonánticos se adquieren como partes de palabras y no de forma aislada. Por tanto, toda consideración sobre la realización de determinados sonidos en el habla no debería llevarse a cabo sin tener en cuenta las unidades léxicas de las cuales forman parte, su posición dentro de la sílaba y el contexto fonético en que se producen.

> [It should not be forgotten that vowel and consonant segments are acquired as parts of words and not in isolation. Therefore, any consideration of the realization of particular sounds in speech should not be carried out without taking into account the lexical units of which they form part, their position within the syllable, and the phonetic context in which they are produced]

The importance of the lexicon in approaches to the phonetic component of acquisition has been acknowledged in recent linguistic thought. It was Vihman who introduced the term *Whole-word Approaches* in this area, based on the distinctions between *selected* and *adapted* words, essential for dealing with the development of idiosyncratic phonetic *templates* (Vihman and Keren-Portnoy 2013; Vihman 2019). Vihman's proposal allows for both approaches to acquisition: in terms of the model-pattern (*selected words*) and in terms of particular gradual development (*adapted words*) and makes it possible to accommodate idiosyncratic progress in the particular dynamics of each learner.

2.2 The role of lexicon in teaching/learning of the phonetic component

This interweaving of lexical and phonetic progress is also assumed in most current approaches to the teaching/learning of the phonetic component. The characterization of phonetic competence in the *Common European Framework of Reference for Languages* (*CEFR* 2001) thus focuses (section 5.2.1.4.) on knowledge and skills in the production and reception of segmental and suprasegmental elements conducive to the intelligibility of messages. Such promotion of the teaching of phonetic competence as part of communicative competence is further reinforced in the recent *CEFR* companion volume, which renews and updates the descriptors of phonological control "to focus on intelligibility as the primary construct in phonological control, in line with current research" (Council of Europe 2020: 243). In addition, a specific "Phonology" column was added to the table of qualitative aspects of spoken language use (Council of Europe 2020: Appendix 3). At the same time, the descriptors in its phonologic evaluation focus on progress in the control of phonetic elements with functional value ranging from pronunciation "of a very limited repertoire of learnt words and phrases" that can be understood with some effort (A1) to the ability to use "the full range of phonological features in the target language with a high level of control" at level C2.[2]

On these lines, the communicative approach to language teaching has led to major reformulations in the teaching of pronunciation and a change in dominant methods. For years, the "phono-articulatory method" was predominant, focusing on teaching pronunciation through conscious articulations of L2 sounds based on articulatory descriptions. This method mainly uses two types of activities: exercises for the mechanical repetition of those sounds that cause the most problems for learners, and "minimal pairs" for the contrast of those phonetic features that are relevant because they frequently distinguish lexical items (cf. Padilla García 2015: 72–74). A sample of this type of exercise focused on articulatory practice of words and on the reinforcement of distinctive contrasts in minimal pairs can be seen, for example, in didactic materials developed by Siles Artés (1994) and his multiple proposals such as "Lea estas palabras y distinga los elementos de cada par: *fila/pila, fino/pino*" ["Read these words and distinguish the elements of each pair: *fila/pila, fino/pino*"] (Siles Artés 1994: 53). These techniques for teaching pronunciation expressly centered on articulation and word contrasts have been criticized from the perspective of the communicative approach. The main criteria for criticisms here are: their repetitive and mechanical character; their focus on units of the phonological system characterized by articulatory features within a structural approach oriented towards the correction of errors; and a decontextualized practice of the pronunciation of lexical units, far removed from communicative use. This has led to a kind of teaching of pronunciation closer to the "verbo-tonal method" (Padilla García 2015: 75–79), which prioritizes perception and suprasegmental features, reducing the weight of articulatory phonetics and the role of error correction to avoid foreign accent.

Privileging of fluency over phonetic correction in accordance with the principles of communicative teaching should not, however, imply that the teaching of phonetic skills is detached from lexical development and the pronunciation of words. As Iruela (2007) argues, the teaching of pronunciation should be aimed at ensuring that learners achieve effective use of phonetic competence in real communicative situations, for which three teaching domains should be distinguished:

---

2 *CFER* introduces six common reference levels that can be grouped into three wide categories: basic user (A1 and A2), independent user (B1 and B2) and proficient user (C1 and C2).

"pronunciation-centered teaching", "meaning-centered teaching", and "learning-centered teaching" (Iruela 2007: 7). Pronunciation-focused teaching, which aims to provide knowledge of the phonological system of the L2, would revolve around "enabling activities" which "no son comunicativas ni pretenden serlo [. . .] como por ejemplo las de contraste de pares mínimos" ["are not communicative and are not intended to be [. . .] such as minimal pair contrast activities"] (Iruela 2007: 9). Although these types of exercises do not involve communicative practice by learners, they enable them to engage in communicative activities, since intelligibility and fluency cannot be achieved without the identification and production of the phonetic elements with which meaningful expressions of L2 lexical items are constructed.

In the most recent proposals for the teaching of Spanish pronunciation we therefore no longer find designs centered exclusively on exercises with isolated words and phrases to practice segmental and suprasegmental units with distinctive value, but minimal pairs of words are indeed still found, together with other more playful and communicative activities. This can be seen, for example, in Goméz Sacristán (2008: 33): "*toro/doro, tos/dos*", or in Bueno Hudson (2013), whose proposed activities for teaching pronunciation to teachers of Spanish as a foreign language (ELE) begin with listening to word pairs: [péro] / [péro], [kóro] / [kóðo], [péya] / [péra] (19).

Over and above the necessary updating of approaches and methods, the teaching of the phonetic component must not lose sight of the fact that it is a matter of providing the student with the knowledge and skills necessary for the control of those elements with which the expression of words and meaningful constructions is configured. Along the same lines, an interesting suggestion can be found in Padilla García (2015: section VII), whose phono-cognitive approach to teaching pronunciation proposes a model that integrates and places the traditional exercises of listening and repetition, contrast and correction within three phono-cognitive processes: perception, reflection and production, developed in six sequential phases, which "permitirán la identificación, la producción y la consolidación de las nuevas categorías fonológicas o la reorganización de las existentes" ["will allow the identification, production and consolidation of new phonological categories or the reorganization of existing ones"] (Padilla García 2015: 107). We continue to see, then, a necessary interweaving of phonetic and lexical progress, which is evidenced by the fact that the most significant pronunciation errors, and those which require correction to the greatest extent, are those which impede communication because the appropriate phonological label is not used to differentiate the corresponding words or constructions which carry meaning (Padilla García 2015: 84–85).

2.3 The lexicon and grammatical progress in L1 acquisition

The almost exclusively central nature of the grammatical component in much linguistic theory has overridden and obscured the relevance of the lexicon and has even promoted the idea of its dependence on grammar. However, regardless of the obvious and incontestable fact that "without words, there are no grammatical structures", in dynamic approaches such as those demanded by processes of acquisition, there is room for neither the autonomy nor the primacy of any single component. A holistic approach to how language is built up is required. On the other hand, the common cliché that identifies "speaking a language" with "knowing its grammar" has for some time now been replaced by "speaking a language means having the communicative skills for effective interaction". This entails a global view of linguistic tactics and skills rather than atomized perspectives within a modular approach. Slobin's irony here (2001: 442–443) is emphatic:

> The modules that are postulated often have names that evoke suspicion: they are the names of our own academic fields (linguistics, mathematics, physics, biology) or subfields (closed-class morphemes, grammaticizable notions). Could God or Evolution have anticipated the academic and intellectual organization of late twentieth-century America?

The work of Bates and Goodman (1999) marked a turning point for modular theory by attributing a crucial role in the grammatical acquisition process to the lexical stock. On the basis of concrete data derived from longitudinal and cross-sectional studies using McArthur inventories and other estimation procedures, it was concluded that the minimum threshold of words for the gradual emergence of word combinations in constructions is 300. According to Bates and Goodman (1999: 38),

> The evidence shows that the emergence and elaboration of grammar are highly dependent on vocabulary size throughout this period (between 8 and 30 months of age), as children make the passage from first words to sentences and go on to gain productive control over the basic morphosyntactic structures of their native language.

The findings, which show this interdependence in habitual situations, illustrate the same trend in atypical situations, which was also reported in Bates and Goodman (1999). In late-developing children, children with Williams syndrome, children with Down's syndrome, and even Specific Language Impairment children and those with brain damage, grammar is but a function of vocabulary, and constructional complexity depends on the size of the lexicon (Bates and Goodman 1997).

Alongside the empirical evidence, the authors adduce five cognitive-theoretical reasons for the integrated lexical-grammatical nature of grammar. Thus, it is not possible to maintain the modular conception for reasons of: (1) *perceptual boot-*

strapping (understood through nuclear content, only a sufficient lexical stock allows top-down processing of grammatical forms); (2) *logical bootstrapping* (the sequential order of word dominance places grammatical units at the end: "Children cannot understand relational terms until they understand the things that these words relate" Bates and Goodman 1999: 55; what Tomasello and Merriman 1995 call *grammatical glue*); (3) *syntactic bootstrapping* (sentence-level information is exploited only when words are learned to be used in different combinations, the *cut and paste* stage (Tomasello 2003), and requires novelties in vocabulary to extend syntagmatic possibilities); (4) *nonlinear dynamics of learning in a neural network* (lexical-grammatical acquisition does not always reflect identical variables); and (5) *lexically based grammar* (suitable for examining in a natural way the process of the emergence of verbal strategies in processes of acquisition).

In short, whether tacitly, or in an explicit way, as in the case in Bates and Goodman (1999), it has been common to consider the lexicon as an essential source for building grammar. Cognitive theories along the lines of Langacker (2008), and more specifically in the wake of *construction grammar* (Goldberg 2005), accommodate the holistic view which is essential in order to approach the acquisition of grammar from a lexical orientation. Not for nothing is the concept of *emergence grammar* (Hopper 1998) introduced as a representation of the gradual sprouting of grammatical knowledge from lexical sources used in discourse. Plans and systems in language learning for estimating the level of competence go hand in hand with lexical stock and the rules for combining words. And the learning of formal grammar is only introduced/valued once a sufficient lexical background is available. The *collostructions* approach (how *lexemes* and the *constructions* in which they occur have an impact on each other), as defined by Stephanowitsch and Gries 2003, strongly supports the lexico-grammar.

2.4 The lexicon and its relationship with grammar in teaching/learning L2

This same perspective is increasingly present in language teaching and has radically modified the way in which the teaching of the lexicon is conceived. Having overcome those traditional methods that tended to approach the learning of an L2 as the memorization of isolated words, the rise and predominance of the communicative approach has led to a focus on the *incidental learning* processes of vocabulary and grammar. This maximalist and reductionist formulation of communicative proposals held that the mere exposure of students to multiple significant contexts conducive to constant interaction in the classroom would make possible the gradual acquisition of vocabulary and grammar. This, in turn, led to the suspension for a time of a reflective approach to the role of lexicon and its relationship to grammar in L2 learning processes.

Without abandoning the development of communicative competence as the axis of language teaching, since the 1990s, *focus on form* proposals have arisen that once again pay attention to linguistic components and that assume and demonstrate the need for approaches that integrate *incidental learning* and *intentional learning* through *explicit teaching* (Barcroft 2015: 25–26; Schmitt and Schmitt 2020: 161–164). However, this reincorporation into the classroom of lexical and grammatical elements cannot lead to a return to modular approaches. Pedagogical grammar must be oriented towards its use in discourse, assuming that grammatical elements are explained and processed in a way that is based on their meaningful contribution to communication (Bustos Gisbert 2018: 48–54), which requires a view that embraces lexical-grammatical integration. The relevance of explicit teaching, which favors the learner being able to process the constructional patterns of the language consciously, demands that we do not lose sight of the symbolic character of the language and the priority of the dimension of meaning in any linguistic description, as once again cognitive linguistics has shown. In line with the contributions of cognitive models that take *constructions* as the basic descriptive units, the L2 teacher should always bear in mind what Castañeda Castro (2019: 266) states:

> La fluidez de un hablante nativo se funda no tanto en la aplicación analítico-deductiva de reglas de gran alcance determinadas por principios formales generales, sino en la disponibilidad inmediata de cientos de miles de rutinas construccionales específicas de carácter léxico, en gran parte ya pre-ensambladas.
>
> [The fluency of a native speaker is based not so much on the analytical-deductive application of powerful rules determined by general formal principles, but on the immediate availability of hundreds of thousands of specific constructional routines of a lexical-grammatical nature, these to a great extent already pre-assembled]

It seems unnecessary to highlight here the central role of lexical competence in language teaching oriented towards the objective of achieving fluency in meaningful discourse, as Baralo argues (2007: 384). The "lexical approach" in the teaching of languages must be seen within this vindication of the central role of the lexicon in approaches that, while maintaining the importance of communicative competence, seek to recover the need for complementary explicit teaching of incidental learning. This method, which perhaps has its most significant expression in the work of Lewis (1993), implies a radical break from any consideration of the dependence of the lexicon on grammar. In accordance with the lines of research already outlined on the acquisition of L1, the lexical approach is configured around clear "key principles" such as "Language consists of grammaticalized lexis, not lexicalized grammar. The grammar/vocabulary dichotomy is invalid; much language consists of multi-word 'chunks'" (Lewis 1993: vi).

As Racine (2018) points out, the theoretical background of the lexical approach derives from findings in corpus linguistics and the development of the distinction between an open-choice principle and an idiom principle. In contrast to the notion of languages as grammatical structures with gaps in which elements of the vocabulary are inserted to make sentences, the idea is that as speakers we identify and produce numerous lexical chunks that constitute the basis of our meaningful constructions: "This kind of reconceptualization – from "slot-and-filler" grammar-vocabulary to chunks of prefabricated language – is central to the lexical approach" (Racine 2018: 3). The lexical approach thus extends to the field of language teaching those crucial contributions in L1 acquisition by authors such as Peters (1983), who argue for the role of *speech formulas* and for the conceptualization of the units of linguistic acquisition not as isolated words or any other structurally characterized element, but rather as *chunks*, that is, lexical, mono-verbal or multi-verbal units which are extracted and processed from discourse through the recognition of the global semantic function that they have. However, these lexical chunks not only configure the repertoire of constructions with which production can advance in terms of fluency, but they are the basis from which the grammar emerges. Indeed, such lexical units, these "extracted units", initially stored as assembled pieces, will be the object of gradual segmentation and analysis that, through a process of discovering the underlying patterns of regularity – the grammar –, will make possible the production and variation of new constructions (cfr. Peters 1983). Lewis's lexical approach thus presupposes a common basis in L1 acquisition and L2 learning processes, supported by the central role of chunks, of segmented lexical units, as a source from which grammar flows. These units are mostly multi-verbal, extracted and processed by a *joint meaning-related* function in the most frequent communicative situations.

> It now seems plausible that an important part of language acquisition is the ability to produce lexical phrases as unanalyzed wholes or 'chunks', and that these chunks become the raw data by which the learner begins to perceive patterns, morphology, and those other features of language traditionally thought of as 'grammar'. Within such a model, phrases acquired as wholes are the primary resource by which the syntactic system is mastered (Lewis 1993: 95).

Whether or not the theoretical posits and the specific methodological proposals of the lexical approach are assumed, the truth is that its influence is perceived in most current approaches to the explicit teaching of the lexicon, in which the study of vocabulary in its combinations predominates and special attention is paid to conscious work with collocations and other types of formulaic sequences, these variable in terms of the degree of idiomatic fixation or compositionality of their meaning. Starting from the idea that the mental lexicon does not store and process isolated elements but is organized in multiple association networks (phonetic, semantic, etc.), work with combinatorial networks – collocations in a broad sense – is especially useful in L2 classrooms and has an increasing presence in the design of activities for working with the lexicon.

If we focus on Spanish as an L2, there are many studies that pursue this idea of promoting the use of combinatorial dictionaries, such as *Redes* and *Práctico*, developed by Bosque (2004, 2006), as extremely useful tools for students of L2 Spanish to carry out tasks that allow them to discover the most frequent selectional restrictions with which lexical units are built in Spanish and to develop their own hypotheses of lexical classes drawn from various elements of vocabulary (cf., for example, Rufat 2018: 97–98). Teaching proposals in L2 Spanish focusing on working with formulaic constructions and collocations are even more common given the growing influence of phraseology as a separate field in language teaching. We might consider, for example, Higueras García (2006) or Sánchez Rufat and Jiménez Calderón (2013); the latter, after a critical review of the lexical approach, proposes an activity in which students use input from corpora to develop collocations by discovering the elements with which those lexical units are usually combined.

In all cases, these are approaches to teaching the lexicon that assume the transversal and central nature of lexical competence, which implies knowledge and skills relevant to phonetic/orthographic, morphological, syntactic, semantic, sociolinguistic and pragmatic development (cfr. Baralo 2007: 385–386; Ivanova 2020: 47).

3 Observational and evaluative proposals to the development of the lexicon, with special attention to studies on Spanish

An approach to the development of the lexicon implies not overlooking the fact that it is an interplay of perceptual processing combined with word tasks, as well as with a gradual symbolic repository of the lexical stock itself. Thus, it is not enough to cumulatively register words, but rather it is essential to contemplate their contexts of use and validate their representational load. As Hernández Sacristán (2006: 202) explains:

un término común como «perro» puede contener inicialmente un esquema de uso que permite referir a cualquier tipo de animal. Este esquema reduce drásticamente su ámbito referencial a medida que se incrementa el volumen léxico con otros términos que designan animal (. . .) Esta condición abierta del significado es la esperable de la naturaleza simbólica del lenguaje humano y es lo que hace que su localización como entidad definida y aislable resulte una empresa mal fundamentada.

[a common term such as "dog" may initially contain a usage scheme that allows it to refer to any type of animal. This scheme drastically reduces its referential scope as the volume of the lexicon increases with other terms that denote animal (. . .) Such an open condition of meaning is to be expected, given the symbolic nature of human language, and is what makes a term's location as a defined and isolatable entity a poorly founded undertaking]

In acquisition processes, a conception that only addresses the lexicon as a previously structured system is not the most advisable path. More appropriate are those conceptions that consider vocabulary in its contexts of use (*concordances*, *collocations* and *collostructions*), where meanings and their symbolic roots are confirmed and verified. Pragmatic and word combinatorial filters must also be present. A syntagmatic approach, versus a single-unit one, is also of great value in the study of the lexicon. "Associationist-cognitivist" approaches allow these variables (pragmatics and syntagmatic) to support lexical organization in gradient models based on *series, hierarchies*, and *associative lexical fields*; and, to a greater or lesser extent, these are the procedures that underlie today's lexical tests and assessments of acquisition.

Has this syntagmatic approach with inclusion of pragmatic and combinatorial information been used in empirical research? We argue that there are basically two methodological paths being taken in current studies on the acquisition of the lexicon, be it in L1 or L2: the observational perspective, with greater validity at the present time and which go hand in hand with cognitive, based-in-usage theoretical approaches using corpora (*concordances, collocations* and *collostructions*); and approaches of an evaluative nature, with the tests and development assessments that normally go together with more traditional theoretical approaches based on a pre-established and formally configured lexical system. Along each of these paths, conceptions about meaning are found, which, to whatever degree convergent or complementary, are in fact different.

3.1 Resources for observational and evaluative approaches to L1 lexicon development

In studies that address the development of the lexicon through the observational route and by resorting to documentary records found in corpora, we typically find parameters that go beyond the regulated vision of the language, such as attention, perception and motivation, and these are of crucial importance in the dynamics of acquisition and learning. Some experts in cognitive substrates have explained acquisition dynamics at early ages. Tomasello (2003), for example, has highlighted the requirements of *joint attention* and *intention-reading* to address not only the processes of the emergence of the lexicon, but also its symbolic sediment and solidity in the learner's word stock (O'Madagain and Tomasello 2021). There is, therefore, a firm link between development – cognitive and verbal – and the course of socialization and culturalization in life. Basic cognitive abilities become useful and advantageous according to the contextual circumstances that favor them. Not all children have the same vocabulary, and not all L2 learners enjoy identical conditions for the consolidation of word stock. Whatever the methodological path, we must consider cognitive parameters and contextual variables in dealing with the acquisition of the lexicon. Furthermore, in the design of a significant number of L1 acquisition corpora, cognitive and social variables are incorporated, either through labelling in the recorded conversations, or through profile characteristics in each of the children. An example is our own *Corpus Koiné de habla infantil* (https://sla.talkbank.org/TBB/phon/Spanish/Koine).

By contrast, it is not so common for evaluative tests of L1 acquisition to consider such dimensions. Thus, a consolidated vocabulary comprehension test with versions for different languages, such as the *PEABODY* (Dunn et al. 2006), uses a static and limited view of the lexicon (abstract words are absent), although the 125 items organized into 18 categories are applied by means of age strata and the results of progress in the accumulation of words at different phases. There are more general tests of verbal development, such as the *Prueba de lenguaje oral de Navarra Revisada, PLON-R* (Revised Navarre Oral Language Test, Aguinaga et al. 2001) and the *Exploración del Lenguaje Comprensivo y Expresivo, ELCE* (Exploration of Comprehensive and Expressive Language, López Ginés et al. 2002), which show a less constrained conception of lexical ability.

In the *PLON-R* various tasks are designed to (a) prompt word choice, and (b) test the ability to group words (by similarity) or exclude words (by differences). These tasks are aimed at obtaining non-categorical, closed-response answers, but above all to yield results that are symptomatic of cognitive skills and the symbolic storage of words. It does not matter so much that "spoon" and "fork" are not differentiated as it is that they are grouped together for "eat," or that they are contrasted with "glass." In a similar vein, the *ELCE* includes two levels of application (and estimation): a *sensory-perceptual level* and a *pure verbal level*, with the aim of reflecting the gradual configuration of lexical skills:

El sujeto, al reconocer las palabras, está realizando a nivel neurofisiológico una actividad analítico-sintética, en la que los rasgos distintivos van siendo aislados y jerarquizados hasta que se completa la identificación. Es decir, implica la diferenciación de significados y su reconocimiento (López Ginés et al. 2002: 15). [The subject, when recognizing words, is carrying out an analytic-synthetic activity at the neurophysiological level, in which the distinctive features are isolated and hierarchized until the identification is completed. That is, it implies the differentiation of meanings and their recognition].

Progression in acquisition from comprehension of meanings to the verbal ability to express them is covered in this assessment battery (*ELCE*). From tasks for the recognition and initial generic comprehension of words, for example, "dog", "milk", "apple", to tests of the verbalization of differences between "dog" and "wolf", the identification of differences between "milk" and "white", the recognition of differences between "apple" and "pear", or of the association and combinations between "pear" and "it has the body of a pear".

In line with observational approaches, some methodological focuses address the acquisition of the lexicon in the L1 by combining the use of samples of usage in communicative frameworks and the assessment of the lexicon based on these samples. Such an approach incorporates a cognitive hint (of attention, perception, intentions) and the vision of meaning-in-context. The MacArthur inventories (Fenson et al. 1993) in the "words and gestures" and "words and sentences" booklets are an example of this formula. In *The Clinical Assessment of Language Comprehension* (Miller and Paul 1995) the understanding of meanings is considered to be regulated by cognitive factors and to be inextricably linked to the contexts in which the words appear.

3.2 Data-driven-learning: The use of native and learner corpora

Within studies on the acquisition and teaching of L2, the predominance of empirical methodologies based on the observation of samples of real use is also increasing. Advances in corpus linguistics have provided a solid basis for methodological proposals that fall within the area of *data-driven-learning* (DDL). This approach to language teaching allows faithful access to real usage for both native speakers and L2 learners, which enables the development of teaching materials based on the analysis of contextualized production and not on the mere intuition of the teacher. In this section, we present some of the resources available, as well as some of their applications, in particular to studying and teaching the lexicon.

Fortunately, in the field of Spanish as an L2 there are more and more databases available, thus favoring the growing presence of proposals for teaching supported by corpus samples. In Parodi and Burdiles (2019) we can see an especially useful updated review of Spanish corpora available online, in which they correctly distinguish between native Spanish (L1) and L2 Spanish (learner) corpora, and between written and oral corpora. Their analysis and evaluation lead to the conclusion that the availability of corpora for L2 Spanish learners is still limited, and more so for those with a language teaching focus; that is, corpora designed with research in mind predominate over those aimed at learners, and their use leads to more decisions about what to teach than about how to teach (Parodi and Burdiles 2019: 600–601, 606).

Focusing our attention, briefly, on the use of some of the corpus available for the teaching/learning of the lexicon, it is useful, when pointing out the main uses for which these corpora can be exploited, to distinguish between corpora of native use and those of learners. Reference corpora of a language provide access to millions of authentic productions by native speakers, which in itself enables a more descriptive than normative approach to variation in usage. In the area of lexicon, they offer at least three major avenues of use: statistics on frequency of occurrence of lexical units, concordances in which lexical elements appear in a contextualized form, and the identification of collocations and other multi-verbal lexical units of a formulaic nature. The two main corpora of native Spanish, *CREA* and *CORPES XXI*, offer multiple possibilities of exploitation in any of these directions, as can be seen, for example, in Cruz Piñol (2012) and Rufat (2018: 98–100).

The frequency of occurrence of lexical units registered in corpora offers information of great interest for the teaching of vocabulary, since it provides criteria based on real data when selecting the lexical elements that are given to learners at various levels of the development of their lexical competence. The *Corpus del español* (https://www.corpusdelespanol.org/) by Davies (2006), identifies the 5,000 most frequent word families in Spanish from the data extracted from its Spanish corpus. High frequency not only allows the identification of the most profitable lexical elements for effective communication, but also guarantees the repetition of their cognitive processing, essential for consolidated acquisition over time. However, frequency lists must be handled with caution, avoiding mechanical and unguided use, not only because, as Sánchez Rufat and Jiménez Calderón (2015: 102) note, they usually include words with many different contextual meanings without filtering the frequency of those different senses, but also because high frequency does not necessarily imply the relevance and usefulness of items for students, since their cognitive profiles and communicative interests might be different. Assuming diversity in individual cognitive development paths and the importance of motivating the learner in the incorporation of new lexical units that respond to their communication needs, we must embrace the observations of Schmitt and Schmitt (2020: 84): "Frequency lists can be particularly useful in designing syllabus, aiding the principled selection of words. In general, higher-frequency words should be taught before lower-frequency words, although this should not be seen as a straitjacket. Context of use should always be considered too".

Another way in which native corpora can be useful for L2 research and teaching is concordance searches. These are indeed among the best currently established ways of using corpora. Their usefulness in language teaching is, in fact, at the core of DDL methods and their application for lexical learning is at the base of the lexical approach. Concordances provide samples of lexical units in their contexts, which allows one to obtain information about their combinational behavior and to identify the grammatical constructions in which they are most common. As we have already noted, lexical learning should be understood as the axis on which grammatical development pivots, and concordances are an excellent resource to infer the lexical and categorical selection criteria that shape the constructions that are actually used in verbal communication. The use of concordances in the classroom, occupying part of the time previously devoted to word lists, can contribute to the incidental and autonomous learning of the student – who can infer the meaning of a word from its contexts and combinations –, but they should also be used in explicit teaching activities, and this requires teachers to plan the search for concordances with which to work (Asención-Delaney et al. 2015: 147–149). The analysis of concordances also stimulates an awareness of the high frequency of more or less fixed lexical combinations, which favors the identification and study of collocations and other idiomatic expressions, whose knowledge contributes to learners improving their expressive fluency early on.

In contrast to the methodologies that use native corpora described above, the development and exploitation of learner corpora is a more recent path, but one that is attracting more and more interest. In these databases, samples of oral/written production of people with different levels of competence are collected within the process of acquiring an L2. These learner corpora can also be used in the ways that native corpora are used, but their main usefulness is that they provide natural samples of the interlanguage of learners. A central theme in research on the processes of L2 acquisition is to describe and analyze the particular cognitive and communicative routes, that is, interlanguages, that emerge in the development of communicative competence (Lozano 2015: 181). Learner corpora are a basic tool for this purpose. To the extent that they collect productions of students with different L1, they are also an excellent source for the analysis of the influence of L1 and transfer processes, as well as for the analysis of errors and the detection of learning difficulties from real samples. In the field of the lexicon, these corpora can provide evidence of the socio-cultural dimension of vocabulary, and of differences between languages in terms of how representations of symbolic perceptions of the world are seen in terms of different frequencies of errors in the lexical domain of specific semantic fields according to L1. Some of these corpora allow for searches involving individual learner data, such as age and sex, as well as textual typology, and this allows us to analyze errors in the processing of certain lexical units, giving due weight to two factors of special relevance in understanding lexical development: the diversity of the different stages of cognitive development, and the influence of the learner's involvement according to the attention and interest aroused by the communicative situation.

Learner corpora for English are already abundant, while, as mentioned above, in the case of Spanish their appearance is much more recent. Among existing corpora of the written production of L2 Spanish learners, two stand out in that they offer rich materials and resources for research into the acquisition of the lexicon. The first is *CAES*, from the Cervantes Institute, prepared by a University of Santiago de Compostela research team led by Rojo and Palacios (https://galvan.usc.es/caes/). The size of the samples and the powerful search tools make it very useful for analyzing the written production of Spanish learners and for evaluating the differences in the ways in which the lexicon is acquired that we have pointed out. The second is *CEDEL2* (http://cedel2.learnercorpora.com/search), developed under the direction of Lozano. A specific characteristic of CEDEL2 is that it also includes subcorpora of native Spanish use and of five other L1 to facilitate the kind of contrasts needed when analyzing the peculiarities of interlanguages.

As we have already indicated, the teaching of vocabulary supported by corpora, typical of DDL, undoubtedly has great advantages by offering the learner rich and extensive input, which will favor the incidental learning of new words in contextualized and authentic uses. But it must be accompanied by explicit teaching activities that take into account those cognitive factors that influence the success of learning processes (Asención-Delaney et al. 2015: 141–144). Thus, mechanical practices that are limited to substituting input from teaching materials with that provided by corpus samples should be avoided. The changes that have emerged from cognitive and communicative approaches – with the idea of language teaching as a learner-centered activity and not a subject-centered one – should not be overshadowed by the current ease of access to numerous sources of real input. Each learner has a previous lexical range from which to process new lexical units so that learning can be consolidated. In addition to considering socio-cultural particularities, learning an L2 requires the planning of explicit teaching activities that favor engagement and cognitive development on the part of the learner. Indeed, Schmitt (2010) sees engagement as one of the "ten key issues" for vocabulary learning, considering it a decisive factor because "the more attention given to an item, and the more manipulation involved with the item, the greater the chances it will be remembered" (Schmitt 2010: 26).

With the same purpose of focusing on the importance of cognitive processing to promote consolidated learning of lexical units, Barcroft (2004) relates the level of *elaboration* in mental processing required by didactic activities to the probabilities of long-term learning. Consequently, among the five principles for effective instruction in the teaching of the vocabulary of an L2, Barcroft argues that activities requiring a significant processing effort aimed at semantic elaboration should be avoided in the initial phases of learning new lexical units, because this cognitive expenditure could inhibit the necessary prior acquisition of the formal characteristics of the new L2 lexical element (Barcroft 2004: 205). According to Barcroft (2015), in lexical-input-processing (lex-IP) there are at least three sub-processes: Form Processing, Semantic Processing, and Processing for Mapping. Vocabulary learning requires different types of tasks to consolidate each of these cognitive sub-processes and, according to the predictions of Barcroft's (2015) *type of processing-resource allocation (TOPRA) model*, when teaching L2 vocabulary we must assume that "each type of processing necessarily exhausts processing resources that now become unavailable for other types of processing" (Barcroft 2015: 64). Lexical teaching activities based on DDL should, therefore, seek to be appropriate to the type of lexical-input-processing (lex-IP) to be developed through contact with real-use input.

Language teaching methods supported by corpus-derived data are, therefore, the main path to follow in the teaching of the lexicon, because they facilitate access to authentic productions in which lexical units appear in their combinations, but, as in the theories on early-stage L1 acquisition of authors such as Tomasello (2003), it is also essential to focus on those factors that impact the effectiveness of cognitive processing of received verbal stimuli in L2 lexical learning. In this sense, DDL must be channeled within the path outlined in the communicative approach and must take advantage of corpus samples as an invaluable tool for the student to incorporate the lexical units learned in communicative activities that capture their attention and are attractive and motivating. In this way, the language teacher will be able to exploit corpora by means of explicit teaching that modulates the level of cognitive development required and that favors engagement, essential for learners to make the cognitive effort needed to acquire the kind of new L2 lexical units that are useful for their progress in communicative praxis.

4 Relevance of the lexicon to estimate progress in acquisition and to advance verbal competence

The process of language acquisition, whether in L1 or L2, involves stages of progression linked to the dimensions of skills. Comprehension skills have to be developed first, and only later can production skills be made effective. Finally, it will be possible to become proficient in the composition of texts as a result of the acquisition of literacy skills. In all these dynamics, the leading role of the lexicon is indisputable.

The prior need to understand requires a stock of referential units on which to configure and build meanings. Words/lexical elements are learned to represent that which has already been conceptualized. Hence there is an urgent need to have a sufficient lexical repertoire to activate comprehension. Words are the trigger for this. Children understand lexical blocks, *chunks*, in communicative contexts. The same process occurs for L2 learners: communicative words/constructions are understood in terms of their situational coordinates. Techniques to promote progress in listening skills are based, precisely, on the principle of understanding by lexical recognition, especially in the initial stages, because, as Field (2008: 330) notes, "identifying words with some degree of confidence provides the listener with 'islands of reliability' upon which hypotheses can be built". The phase of word learning, which has been considered a crucial element in the development of L2, is oriented fundamentally to the progressive development of passive skills.

Progress towards oral expression in L2 is channeled through the development of skills in word combinations. The selection of lexical elements to create grammatical structures in conversational frames requires learning not only morphosyntactic rules, but also the mastery of the meanings produced by syntagmatic distribution. Undoubtedly, tasks involved in conversation go beyond having access to lexical units and syntactic rules and require that the automated fluency of meanings in context increases. Production skills underline the integral nature of lexicon learning, and progress in these skills is necessary to project the symbolic network that accompanies every lexical unit: meanings-in-context and perceptual fluency to accommodate and refine the use of the lexicon.

Another area that requires the development of the lexicon is that of textual composition skills (and also, although not to the same degree, reading for comprehension), as these involve high levels of development in verbal competence, in both L1 and L2. The rhetorical rules used to create texts are very specific, but communication through written texts also demands linguistic skills that guarantee immediate effectiveness, not only regarding word choice, but most importantly their function and their impact from the recipient's perspective. Pragmatic aspects and formally established social practices condition the functional weight of lexical meaning and syntagmatic content. Oral fluency alone is not enough for communicative competence. Development of competence in social interaction that facilitates the rules for organizing and selecting the lexicon in different types of text is also necessary. Learning composition often emphasizes the social value of words/constructions.

The appropriateness of the learning method depends on the skills to be developed. Learning word lists perhaps establishes an initial, basic lexicon in the early stages of approaching the L2. Learning words also goes hand in hand with learning the phonetic system. It is probably in these early stages when the use of lexical development tests to calibrate the rate of acquisition and assess whether it is sufficient to undertake a comprehensive training in the language in question has some value and meaning.

The leading role of the lexicon in the development of communicative skills is evidenced by the fact that lexical competence is no longer conceived of simply as an adequate inventory of lexical items, something already recognized in language evaluation models, such as the *CEFR*. In fact, the characterization of lexical competence in *CEFR* (section 5.2.1.1.) includes multi-verbal lexical units and combinatorial selection factors, and the illustrative scales for the grading of lexical development present descriptors focused fundamentally on the range and control of the vocabulary suitable for different communicative situations. The core characteristic of level A1 is "a basic vocabulary repertoire of isolated words and phrases related to particular concrete situations", and progress through the levels goes hand in hand with the gradual mastery of the appropriate vocabulary in different everyday situations, until reaching a wide lexical repertoire that allows effective communication in all kinds of contexts at levels C1 and C2. In the characterization of the reference levels of lexical competence in *CEFR*, however, the domain of multi-verbal lexical units and idiomatic constructions only appears explicitly in the descriptors of the most advanced proficiency levels (C1 and C2). Teaching with the goal of advanced competence in an L2 requires a consideration of lexical meaning not only in isolated words, but above all in their syntagmatic combinations and in their real use, this from the most basic levels of development of communicative competence (Webb and Nation 2017). On these lines, an online diagnostic language testing system such as *Dialang* (https://dialangweb.lancaster.ac.uk/) is especially valuable, because all the lexical competence tests present contextualized vocabulary and include explicit language-oriented questions to evaluate mastery of word combinations, along with other elements related to semantic relations, word formation, and meaning.

An area of acquisition in which the development of the lexicon stands as a crucial element is *the teaching of the language for specific purposes*. The dynamics of this field include the goal of learning a specific terminological lexicon. There are even terminological reference works, such as *HSWL, A Hard Science Spoken Word List* (Dang 2018) for English in scientific fields. This area of learning words with a precise conceptual charge and with particular constructions and contexts of use might well be considered as a mirror image of the role that the lexicon plays in assessing the command of the language in general.

5 Conclusions: The critical weight of vocabulary in general linguistic development

In this chapter we have argued in favor of the critical weight of lexical development in the progress of the other linguistic components and skills. The importance of lexical acquisition has been shown in those studies that have compared and analyzed the results of *Dialang* tests in the different skills (listening, writing, reading, structures, vocabulary). According to Schmitt (2010: 4–5), comparison of the results in vocabulary sections of tests with those of other sections reveals very significant correlations, which would indicate that the level of lexical mastery can explain between 37% and 62% of the variation in learner proficiency in the different languages addressed.

We have also argued for the use of teaching materials and methods that consider this transverse nature of lexical competence and the need to approach it within its authentic and contextualized use. Such sources/repositories (electronic, audiovisual, textual) involve productions of the language that can be learned on the basis of how we outline progress in terms of lexicon-in-practice, and how we can build models of verbal proficiency in stages. At present, we can find corpora used in many teaching systems, with inventories taken as direct learning resources, or used as support materials in teaching and training manuals. One example here is *Cumbre* materials for students of L2 Spanish, which are supported by data provided by the contemporary Spanish *Cumbre* corpus developed by Sánchez Pérez et al. (1995).

This chapter has sought to emphasize the central role of lexical development in the processes of language acquisition and learning. Taking a holistic approach, it highlights how lexical stock serves as the basis for the emergence of the phonic component and of grammar. An appropriate means of addressing this central nature of the lexicon is through corpus linguistics, involving examples of real language use, which incorporate the kind of cognitive parameters and contextual variables that are essential for language acquisition and learning. Such a view has repercussions for pedagogy, which we have also highlighted. Implications for teaching include: the idea that language should be taught in its communicative use; that vocabulary must appear in its syntagmatic context; and that a learner's progress should not only be assessed in relation to the model of the language-as-product.

References

Aguinaga, Gloria, M. Luisa Armentia, Ana Fraile, Nicolás Uriz & Pedro Olangua. 2001. *PLON_R. Prueba Lenguaje Oral Navarra Revisada*. Madrid: TEA.

Asención-Delaney, Yuly, Joseph G. Collentine, Karina Collentine, Jersus Colmenares & Luke Plonsky. 2015. El potencial de la enseñanza del vocabulario basada en corpus: optimismo con precaución. *Journal of Spanish Language Teaching* 2(2). 140–151.

Baralo, Marta. 2007. Adquisición de palabras: redes semánticas y léxicas. In *Actas del Foro de español internacional: Aprender y enseñar léxico*, 384–399. https://cvc.cervantes.es/ensenanza/biblioteca_ele/publicaciones_centros/PDF/munich_2006-2007/04_baralo.pdf (accessed 10 March 2021).

Barcroft, Joe. 2004. Second language vocabulary acquisition: A lexical input processing approach. *Foreign language Annals* 37(2). 200–208.

Barcroft, Joe. 2015. *Lexical Input Processing and Vocabulary Learning*. Amsterdam: John Benjamins

Bates, Elisabeth & Judith Goodman. 1997. On the inseparability on grammar and the lexicon: Evidence from acquisition, aphasia and real-time processing. *Language and Cognitive Processes* 12(5–6). 507–586.

Bates, Elisabeth & Judith Goodman. 1999. On the Emergence of Grammar of the Lexicon. In Brian MacWhinney (ed.), *The Emergence of Language*, 29–80. London: Lawrence Erlbaum.

Bosch, Laura. 2004. *Evaluación fonológica del habla infantil*. Barcelona: Masson.

Bosque, Ignacio (ed.). 2004. *Redes. Diccionario combinatorio del español contemporáneo*. Madrid: Ediciones SM.

Bosque, Ignacio (ed.). 2006. *Práctico. Diccionario combinatorio práctico del español contemporáneo*. Madrid: Ediciones SM.

Brown, Roger. 1973. *A First Language: The Early Stages*. Cambridge, Mass: Harvard University Press.

Bueno Hudson, Richard. 2013. Propuestas para la enseñanza de la pronunciación y corrección fonética en español como lengua extranjera. *Actas del I Congreso Internacional de Didáctica de Español como Lengua Extranjera*, 15–35. Budapest: Instituto Cervantes. https://cvc.cervantes.es/ensenanza/biblioteca_ele/publicaciones_centros/PDF/budapest_2013/04_bueno.pdf (accessed 10 March 2021).

Bustos Gisbert, José Manuel. 2018. Enseñanza-aprendizaje del componente gramatical. In María Martínez-Atienza & Alfonso Zamorano Aguilar (eds.), *Teoría y metodología para la enseñanza de ELE. Vol II. Enseñanza-aprendizaje de los componentes lingüísticos*, 43–71. Madrid: enCLAVE ELE.

Castañeda Castro, Alejandro. 2019. Lingüística cognitiva. In Javier Muñoz-Basols, Elisa Gironzetti & Manuel Lacorte (eds.), *The Routledge Handbook of Spanish Language Teaching: metodologías, contextos y recursos para la enseñanza del español L2*, 261–278. Abingdon: Routledge.

CEFR: Council of Europe. 2001. *Common European framework of reference for languages: learning, teaching, assessment*. Cambridge, U.K.: Press Syndicate of the University of Cambridge.

Council of Europe. 2020. *Common European Framework of Reference for Languages: Learning, teaching, assessment – Companion volume*. Council of Europe Publishing: Strasbourg.

Cruz Piñol, M. 2012. *Lingüística de corpus y enseñanza del español como 2/L*. Madrid: Arco Libros.
Cumbre: Sánchez, Aquilino, Mª Teresa Espinet & Pascual Santos. 1996. *Cumbre. Curso de español para extranjeros. Nivel superior*. Madrid: SGEL.
Dang, Thi Ngoc. 2018. A Hard Science Spoken Word List. In Stuart Well (ed.), *Approaches to learning, testing, and researching L2 Vocabulary* (Special issue of the *International Journal of Applied Linguistics* 169), 44–71. Amsterdam: John Benjamins.
Davies, Mark. 2006. *A Frequency Dictionary of Spanish: Core Vocabulary for Learners*. London: Routledge.
Dunn, Lloyd, Leota Dunn & David Arribas. 2006. *PPVT-III Peabody. Test de Vocabulario en Imágenes*. Madrid: TEA.
Fenson, Larry, Philip Dale, J. Steven Reznick, Donna Thal, Elisabeth Bates, Jeffrey Hartung, Steve Pethick & Judith Reilly. 1993. *MacArthur Communicative Development Inventoires (CDI)*. San Diego: Singular Pub. Company.
Field, John. 2008. *Listening in the language classroom*. Cambridge: University Press.
Goldberg, Adele. 2005. *Constructions at Work: The Nature of Generalization in Language*. Oxford: Oxford University Press.
Golinkoff, Roberta & Kathy Hirsh-Pasek. 1999. *How Babies Talk. The Magic and Mystery of Language in the First Three Years of Life*. Harmondsworth: Penguin Books.
Gómez Sacristán, Mª Luisa. 2008. *Practica tu español. Ejercicios de pronunciación*. Madrid: SGEL.
Grunwell, Pamela. 1985. *Phonological Assessment of Child Speech (PACS)*. Windsor: NFER- Nelson.
Hernández Sacristán, Carlos. 2006. La unidad palabra y su significado: una perspectiva logopédica sobre la capacidad léxica. In Elena Garayzábal (ed.), *Lingüística Clínica y Logopedia*, 197–278. Madrid: Antonio Machado.
Higueras García, Marta. 2006. *Las colocaciones y su enseñanza en la clase de ELE*. Madrid: Arco Libros.
Hoff Ginsberg, Erika. 1997. *Language Development*. Pacific Grove, CA: Brooks/ Cole.
Hopper, Paul. 1998. Emergent Grammar. In Michael Tomasello (ed.), *The New Psychology of Language. Cognitive and Functional Approaches to Language Structure*, 155–175. New Jersey: Erlbaum.
Ingram. David. 1989. *First Language Acquisition. Method, Description, and Explanation*. Cambridge: Cambridge University Press.
Iruela, Agustín. 2007. Principios didácticos para la enseñanza de la pronunciación en lenguas extranjeras. *marcoELE. Revista de Didáctica Español Lengua Extranjera* 4. https://marcoele.com/descargas/4/iruela-pronunciacion.pdf (accessed 10 March 2021).
Ivanova, Olga. 2020. Why L2 vocabulary acquisition may be so difficult: Cognitive rationale and its pedagogical implications. In Nuray Alagözlü & Vedat Kiymazrslan (eds.), *Current Perspectives on Vocabulary Learning and Teaching*, 27–54. Newcastle upon Tyne: Cambridge Scholars.
Langacker, Ronald. 2008. *Cognitive Grammar. A Basic Introduction*. Oxford: Oxford University Press.
Lewis, Michael. 1993. *The Lexical Approach: The State of ELT and a Way Forward*. Hove: Language Teaching Publications.
López Ginés, Mª José, Ángeles Redón, Mª Dolores Zurita, Isabel García Martínez, Mercedes Santamaría & Julia Iniesta. 2002. *Exploración del lenguaje Comprensivo y Expresivo (ELCE)*. Madrid: CEPE.
Lozano, Cristóbal. 2015. Learner corpora as a research tool for the investigation of lexical competence in L2 Spanish, *Journal of Spanish Language Teaching* 2(2). 180–193.
Lleó, Conxita. 1997. *La adquisición de la fonología de la primera lengua y de las lenguas extranjeras*. Madrid: Visor.
Miller, Jon & Rea Paul. 1995. *The Clinical Assessment of Language Comprehension*. Baltimore: P. Brookes.

O'Madagain, Cathal & Michael Tomasello. 2021. Joint attention to mental content and the social origin of reasoning. *Synthese* 198, 4057–4078. https://doi.org/10.1007/s11229-019-02327-1 (accessed 20 March 2022).

Padilla García, Xose A. 2015. *La pronunciación del español. Fonética y enseñanza de lenguas*. Alacant: Publicacions Universitat d'Alacant.

Parodi, Giovanni & Gina Burdiles. 2019. Corpus y bases de datos. In Javier Muñoz-Basols, Elisa Gironzetti and Manuel Lacorte (eds.), *The Routledge Handbook of Spanish Language Teaching: metodologías, contextos y recursos para la enseñanza del español L2*, 596–612. Abingdon: Routledge.

Peters, Anne. 1983. *The Units of Language Acquisition*. Cambridge: Cambridge University Press.

Racine, John P. 2018. Lexical approach. In John I. Liontas (ed.), *The TESOL encyclopedia of English language teaching. Vol II. Approaches and methods in English for speakers of other languages*, 1–7. Hoboken: Wiley Online Library.

Rufat, Anna. 2018. Enseñanza-aprendizaje del componente léxico-semántico. In María Martínez-Atienza & Alfonso Zamorano Aguilar (eds.), *Teoría y metodología para la enseñanza de ELE. Vol II. Enseñanza-aprendizaje de los componentes lingüísticos*, 73–108. Madrid: enCLAVE ELE.

Sánchez Pérez, Aquilino, Ramón Sarmiento, Pascual Cantos and José Simón. 1995. *CUMBRE. Corpus lingüístico del español contemporáneo. Fundamentos, metodología y análisis*. Madrid: SGEL.

Sánchez Rufat, Anna & Francisco Jiménez Calderón. 2013. Combinatoria léxica y corpus como input. *Language Design* 14. 61–81.

Sánchez Rufat, Anna & Francisco Jiménez Calderón. 2015. New perspectives on the acquisition and teaching of Spanish vocabulary/Nuevas perspectivas sobre la adquisición y la enseñanza del vocabulario del español. *Journal of Spanish Language Teaching* 2(2). 99–111.

Schmitt, Norbert & Diane Schmitt. 2020 [2000]. *Vocabulary in language teaching*, 2nd edn. Cambridge: University Press.

Schmitt, Norbert. 2010. *Researching Vocabulary: A Vocabulary Research Manual*. Basingstoke: Palgrave Mcmillan.

Siles Artés, José. 1994. *Ejercicios prácticos de pronunciación del español*. Madrid: SGEL.

Slobin, Dan. 1997. The Universal, the Typological, and the Particular in Acquisition. In Dan Slobin (ed.), *The Crosslinguistic Study of Language Acquisition*, vol 5 (*Expanding the Contexts*), 1–39. Hillsdale: Erlbaum.

Slobin, Dan. 2001. Form-function relations: how do children find out what they are? In Bowerman, Melissa & Stephen Levinson (eds.), *Language acquisition and conceptual development*, 406–449. Cambridge: Cambridge University Press.

Stephanowitsch, Anatole & Stefan T. Gries. 2003. Collostructions: Investigating the interaction of words and constructions. *International Journal of Corpus Linguistics* 8(2). 209–243.

Tomasello, Michael. 2003. *Constructing a Language. A Usage-Based Theory of Language Acquisition*. Harvard: Harvard University Press.

Tomasello, Michael & William Merriman. 1995. *Beyond Names for Things. Young Children's Acquisition of Verbs*. New Jersey: Erlbaum.

Vihman, Marilyn. 2019. *Phonological Templates in Development*. Oxford: Oxford University Press.

Vihman, Marilyn & Tamar Keren-Portnoy. 2013. *The Emergency of Phonology. Whole-word Approaches and Cross-linguistic Evidence*. Cambridge: Cambridge University Press.

Webb, Stuart & Paul Nation. 2017. *How Vocabulary is Learned*. Oxford: Oxford University Press.

Danielle Daidone
Chapter 3
The relationship between self-rated vocabulary knowledge and accuracy of phonological forms

1 Introduction

For literate learners of a language, an entry in their second language (L2) mental lexicon for a word includes three core aspects: an orthographic representation, a semantic representation, and a phonological representation (see Ramus et al. 2010). Thus, an important component of lexical knowledge is knowing the phonological form of words, but research on L2 vocabulary acquisition has typically neglected to examine phonological forms in favor of focusing on orthographic and semantic representations. This is reflected in Beglar and Nation's (2014) review of vocabulary assessment, which includes almost entirely written tests of vocabulary. Well-known tests of English vocabulary knowledge include Nation's Vocabulary Levels Test and its updated versions (Schmitt, Schmitt and Clapham 2001), as well as the Vocabulary Size Test (Nation and Beglar 2007). For these types of vocabulary tests, the test taker matches written words with their definitions. While the Vocabulary Knowledge Scale (Wesche and Paribakht 1996) mixes both receptive and productive knowledge, it also only focuses on the written form, testing learners on a scale to assess the depth of their knowledge, from "I don't remember having seen this word before" to "I can write this word in a sentence: ____ (Write a sentence.)". Finally, typical "Yes/No" tests present participants with written words and nonwords, asking them to indicate which words they know. As Beglar and Nation (2014) state, "despite the importance of developing measures of aural vocabulary size, very little empirical work on tests designed to measure this construct exists" (p. 4).

Milton (2009) argues that this bias toward concentrating on orthographic forms is likely due to the ease of written tests and the unstated assumption in the field that knowledge of a written form implies knowledge of its phonological form (p. 93). However, research in L2 phonology has shown that L2 learners' phonological representations are often inaccurate or less detailed than those of native speakers (e.g., Cook et al. 2016; Cutler, Weber and Otake 2006; Daidone and Darcy 2014;

Danielle Daidone, University of North Carolina Wilmington

Darcy, Daidone and Kojima 2013; Darcy and Thomas 2019; Llompart 2021; Melnik and Peperkamp 2019). While some researchers have taken for granted that learners know the frequent words used in their study (Cutler, Weber and Otake 2006; Llompart 2021; Melnik and Peperkamp 2019) and others have manipulated frequency as a variable (Cook et al. 2016), the presence of inaccurate representations appears to be true even when an effort is made to ensure that learners know the words that were tested.

Darcy, Daidone, and Kojima (2013) tested intermediate and advanced English-speaking learners of German and Japanese on their perception and phonological lexical representations of difficult contrasts in these languages, specifically front rounded vowels for German and consonant length in Japanese. They found that the learners of German were able to discriminate front and back rounded vowels, and the learners of Japanese were able to discriminate singleton and geminate consonants. However, a lexical decision task revealed that both intermediate and advanced learners of Japanese had difficulty rejecting nonwords with a singleton consonant if the real word contained a geminate consonant; for example, they accepted *kipu [kipɯ] as a word when the real word is kippu /kippɯ/ 'ticket.' Similarly, the intermediate German learners had difficulty rejecting nonwords with a back rounded vowel if the real word contained a front rounded vowel. This is despite the fact that the words for the Japanese experiment were common words chosen from the first-year and second-year textbooks used by the students, and the participants in the German experiment were tested on their familiarity with the stimuli, and any participant with low written familiarity with the words was excluded. Darcy and Thomas (2019) also assessed familiarity for the words used in their experiment that examined the encoding of consonant clusters in L2 lexical representations by Korean learners of English. They found that participants rated all of the words as "very familiar" when given three options for familiarity, but nevertheless they tended to falsely accept test nonwords with an epenthetic vowel such as b[ʊ]lue for blue.

Similar findings on inaccurate lexical representations have also been reported for Spanish. Daidone and Darcy (2014) tested intermediate and advanced English-speaking learners on their lexical representations containing Spanish /r/, /ɾ/, and /d/ and their perception of these phonemes. They found that despite high accuracy in a discrimination task, in which the advanced learners' results did not differ from those of native speakers, in a lexical decision task both intermediate and advanced learners had difficulty rejecting nonwords with the incorrect rhotic, such as *quierro [ki̯ero] for the real word quiero /ki̯eɾo/ 'I want.' Learners had difficulty with these experimental words even though the researchers mainly used stimuli from the *Beginning Spanish Lexicon*, which provides data about words that are included in beginner Spanish textbooks (Vitevitch, Stamer and Kieweg 2012), and they checked that no participants had generally low familiarity with the words used.

Given these findings on learners' inaccurate phonological representations, it is not clear that knowledge of the meaning of a written form necessarily entails an accurate phonological form. Moreover, studies specifically examining the effect of orthography on lexical encoding accuracy have found mixed results. Some researchers have shown that orthography can help learners establish a difference between new non-native phonological contrasts (Escudero, Hayes-Harb and Mitterer 2008; Escudero, Simon and Mulak 2014; Showalter and Hayes-Harb 2013). For example, Escudero, Hayes-Harb, and Mitterer (2008) found that those Dutch-speaking learners of English exposed to orthographic forms of new words were able to establish a contrast between words differing in the difficult contrast /æ-ɛ/, whereas those participants only exposed to auditory input were less accurate. On the other hand, researchers have also found a negative effect of exposing learners to orthography when building new lexical representations, especially when the orthography does not match the sound-spelling correspondences of their first language (Escudero, Simon and Mulak 2014; Hayes-Harb, Brown and Smith 2018; Hayes-Harb and Cheng 2016; Hayes-Harb, Nicol and Barker 2010; Mathieu 2016; Rafat 2016). Escudero, Simon, and Mulak (2014) revealed that Spanish learners of Dutch were aided by the presence of orthographic forms only if the sound-spelling correspondences were similar to those in Spanish; new sound-spelling correspondences in Dutch hindered their performance. Similarly, Rafat (2016) showed that English-speaking learners of Spanish were negatively influenced by seeing Spanish orthographic forms that differed from English sound-spelling correspondences; for instance, the presence of <z> (/s/ or /θ/ in Spanish, depending on the dialect) often resulted in the pronunciation [z] as would be found in English. Other studies have observed no effect of exposing learners to orthography when acquiring words (Durham et al. 2016; Hayes-Harb and Hacking 2015; Showalter and Hayes-Harb 2015; Simon, Chambless and Kickhöfel Alves 2010). For example, Simon and colleagues taught English-speaking participants French novel words containing /u/ and /y/, either with orthography or without. They reported no difference in the accuracy of these vowels in word learning or perception between the group that was given orthography and the group that was exposed only to auditory forms. In sum, these studies show that orthography may help, but just as often may have no influence or even hinder learners' phonological acquisition of words. At the very least, this research reveals that learning the orthographic form of a word does not guarantee its phonological form will be remembered correctly.

This gap between knowledge of orthographic and phonological forms can have real-world consequences for learners, who may know a word in its written form but be unable to recognize it in speech, as evidenced in English by Carney (2021).

He found that Japanese-speaking learners of English had difficulty with listening comprehension even for texts that consisted of high-frequency vocabulary and orthographically known words. Therefore, it is unsurprising that written vocabulary knowledge is not a strong predictor of listening comprehension in English, while aural vocabulary knowledge very strongly predicts listening comprehension (Masrai 2020).

Given this disconnect between orthographic knowledge and phonological knowledge, researchers in English language teaching have begun to see the value of creating tests for learners' knowledge of the phonological form of words, as seen by the development of the Listening Vocabulary Levels Test (McLean, Kramer and Beglar 2015). For measures of aural vocabulary size, researchers have also used dictations, in which participants write down aurally presented sentences, and the number of corrected written keywords is tallied, or an aural "Yes/No" test such as AuraLex (Milton and Hopkins 2006), in which learners hear words and nonwords and indicate whether they know them or not. Some existing tests of productive knowledge do assess oral production, such as the Boston Naming Test (Kaplan, Goodglass and Weintraub 2001) and the Peabody Picture Vocabulary Test (PPVT) (Dunn and Dunn 1997). However, these tests were created for use with children or adult native speaker populations and have haphazardly been adapted for use with adult L2 learners.

For Spanish, few standardized tests of vocabulary knowledge exist for adult L2 learners, and they are exclusively written. The Lextale-Esp (Izura, Cuetos and Brysbaert 2014) asks learners to indicate which words they know from a list, and X_Lex (Meara 2005) asks learners to indicate whether each individually presented written form is a real word. Standardized aural tests of vocabulary have yet to be developed for Spanish, but given the transparent orthography of Spanish, it could be argued that written tests of vocabulary knowledge may in fact be sufficient for L2 learners. In the absence of such aural tests of L2 Spanish vocabulary, especially ones that test phonological form together with meaning, it is not clear whether previous results that have pointed to inaccurate phonological representations for Spanish words are truly due to a disconnect between learners' knowledge of the orthographic form of a word and its phonological accuracy, or are related more to experimental design decisions made in previous studies.

In Darcy and Daidone (2014), as well as other studies, the researchers did not take vocabulary knowledge into account on a trial-by-trial basis, and thus unknown words may have depressed accuracy levels in their results. They also did not look at differences in vocabulary knowledge as anything more than an exclusion criterion, when in fact gradation in vocabulary knowledge could help explain differences in performance between participants. Furthermore, that study, along with the majority of other studies examining L2 lexical representations, used an auditory lexical decision task in which participants heard stimuli and had to decide if they were real words or not. It may be that L2 learners know the correct pronunciation of a word, but they are willing to consciously accept slight deviations of the type tested in the experimental conditions because they are less confident in their answers or are used to hearing other non-native speakers, and thus have a lower threshold for acceptance. Therefore, a more in-depth analysis of participants' knowledge of the words used in an experiment may reveal that learners of Spanish do in fact display accurate phonological representations in accordance with their knowledge of the semantic and orthographic representations of those words, particularly when assessed with a task that requires them to choose the correct form of a word rather than indicate whether a form is a real word. The current study examines whether this is indeed the case.

2 Method

2.1 Research question

Does self-reported knowledge of the meaning of Spanish written words correspond with accuracy in their phonological form as evidenced by a forced choice task? Does this differ by proficiency level?

In order to address this question, the current study compares intermediate and advanced L2 learners' abilities to choose the correct phonological form of a word in a forced choice task with their self-rated familiarity with words as measured with a vocabulary rating task. Participants also completed a language background questionnaire to collect demographic information and to determine whether the learners understood sound-spelling correspondences in Spanish. These tasks are described in detail in the following sections.

2.2 Forced choice task

The forced choice task tested the Spanish /ɾ-d/ ("tap-d"), /ɾ-r/ ("tap-trill"), /r-d/ ("trill-d"), and /f-p/ contrasts. The first three contrasts served as test contrasts, and the last served as a control. Whereas the /f-p/ contrast exists in English, the /tap-d/, /tap-trill/ and /trill-d/ contrasts represent new sounds for English-speaking learners in various ways.

Although English has a single rhotic while Spanish has two – the tap and trill – the /tap-trill/ contrast has been shown to be discriminable for learners at all levels and even naïve English listeners (Daidone and Darcy 2014, 2021; Herd 2011; Rose 2010). Nevertheless, English-speaking learners perceptually assimilate both the tap and the trill chiefly to English /ɹ/ (Rose 2012), which may explain why this contrast is difficult for learners to accurately encode in words (Daidone and Darcy 2014, 2021).

While [ɾ] exists in English, at least for North American speakers, it is an allophone of /t/ and /d/ rather than a separate phoneme (Ladefoged and Johnston 2011: 74). Thus, English-speaking learners must acquire the Spanish tap as a separate phoneme rather than as an allophone of /d/. The different representational status of these sounds in English and Spanish may help explain why the /tap-d/ contrast has been found to be more difficult than /tap-trill/ in perception (Daidone and Darcy 2014, 2021; Herd 2011; Rose 2010), since sounds which are allophones in a speakers' first language are perceived to be perceptually similar (Boomershine et al. 2008). However, /tap-d/ has also been found to be more accurate in lexical encoding than /tap-trill/ (Daidone and Darcy 2014, 2021).

Despite the trill being a new rhotic for English-speaking learners, the /trill-d/ contrast has been shown to be relatively easy for learners, perhaps because the trill and /d/ are mainly perceptually assimilated to different English sounds (Rose 2012). Studies have found the /trill-d/ contrast to be more accurate than /tap-trill/ or /tap-d/ in perception and lexical encoding (Daidone and Darcy 2014, 2021; Herd 2011; Rose 2010).

Finally, the phonemes /f/ and /p/ exist in both English and Spanish, although /p/ has different phonetic properties across the two languages (Hualde 2005: 150). The contrast /f-p/ has served as a control contrast in previous research and has been shown to be more accurate in perception and lexical encoding than /tap-d/, /tap-trill/ and /trill-d/ (Daidone and Darcy 2014, 2021).

In sum, these contrasts were chosen because much is known about their L2 discriminability and lexical encoding accuracy from previous investigations (Daidone and Darcy 2014, 2021; Herd 2011; Herd, Sereno and Jongman 2015; Rose 2010). Nevertheless, the relationship between lexical encoding accuracy and gradations in vocabulary knowledge for words with these sounds has not been examined. Furthermore, while the orthographic representations of these sounds are transparent in intervocalic position, the Spanish orthographic contrast between the tap and trill, <r> vs. <rr> (e.g. *pero* /ˈpe.ɾo/ 'but' vs. *perro* /ˈpe.ro/ 'dog'), is new for English-speaking learners, for whom both a single and a double <r> represent /ɹ/ in their first language (e.g. *carrot* and *carat* /ˈkæ.ɹət/). Therefore, orthographic knowledge can also be examined as a factor in learners' lexical encoding accuracy.

In the forced choice task, participants heard two auditory stimuli containing the sounds of one of the aforementioned contrasts and decided which was the real Spanish word, such as *quiero* [ki̯ero] 'I want' vs. the nonword **quierro* [ki̯ero] (see Table 1 for examples).¹

Table 1: Example stimuli for the forced choice task.

		Word		Nonword	
		Orthography	IPA	Orthography	IPA
/tap-trill/ (test)	/r-*r/	aburrido	/a.bu.'ri.do/	aburido	/a.bu.'ri.do/
		tierra	/'ti̯e.ra/	tiera	/'ti̯e.ra/
	/r-*r/	dinero	/di.'ne.ro/	dinerro	/di.'ne.ro/
		parece	/pa.'re.se/	parrece	/pa.'re.se/
/tap-d/ (test)	/r-*d/	cultura	/kul.'tu.ra/	cultuda	/kul.'tu.da/
		fuera	/'fu̯e.ra/	fueda	/'fu̯e.da/
	/d-*r/	miedo	/'mi̯e.do/	miero	/'mi̯e.ro/
		médico	/'me.di.ko/	mérico	/'me.ri.ko/
/trill-d/ (test)	/r-*d/	ocurre	/o.'ku.re/	ocude	/o.'ku.de/
		arregla	/a.'re.gla/	adegla	/a.'de.gla/
	/d-*r/	estado	/es.'ta.do/	estarro	/es.'ta.ro/
		todavía	/to.da.'bi.a/	torravía	/to.ra.'bi.a/
/f-p/ (control)	/f-*p/	jefe	/'xe.fe/	jepe	/'xe.pe/
		oficina	/o.fi.'si.na/	opicina	/o.pi.'si.na/
	/p-*f/	grupo	/'gru.po/	grufo	/'gru.fo/
		zapato	/sa.'pa.to/	zafato	/sa.'fa.to/

Words ranged between 2 and 4 syllables, with the target phoneme appearing in intervocalic position as the onset of the 2nd, 3rd, or 4th syllable. The stimuli were recorded in a sound booth by two native Spanish speakers: 1) a male speaker from Costa Rica and 2) a female speaker from Puerto Rico. The speakers produced the stimuli with a standard Spanish pronunciation. Therefore, all /ɾ/ tokens were

---

1 Full stimuli list, data, and analyses are available at https://osf.io/4venh/

realized with one occlusion, all /r/ tokens were realized with at least two occlusions, and /d/ was realized as an approximant [ð̞].

There were 20 words for each of the contrasts, for example, 10 real words containing tap and 10 real words containing trill for the /tap-trill/ contrast. Each word-nonword pair was presented twice, once with the male speaker producing the real word and once with the female speaker producing the real word, theoretically resulting in a total of 40 trials per contrast. However, due to a recording error, the nonword *genedal* (cf. *general* /xeneɾal/ 'general') was not available for the female speaker, resulting in one less trial for the /tap-d/ contrast, for a total of 39 trials. Conversely, a coding error resulted in the duplication of the *corecto-correcto* (nonword-word) trial, bringing the total number of trials for the /tap-trill/ contrast to 41. Thus, there were 160 trials in the task, but with one less trial for /tap-d/ and one additional trial for /tap-trill/. During each trial in the task, a fixation cross appeared on the screen while participants listened to a stimulus spoken by the male speaker, followed by a 500 ms pause, and then a stimulus spoken by the female speaker, always in that order. Participants had 5000 ms from the beginning of the trial to respond, and the time between trials was 1000 ms. Participants also had to complete 10 practice trials at the beginning of the task. These trials, spoken by one female native Spanish speaker from Colombia, contained 5 words and 5 corresponding nonwords that differed in sounds other than the contrasts used in the test and control trials (e.g., *nada* 'nothing' vs. *bada*; *duda* 'doubt' vs. *dida*). The 5 word-nonword pairs occurred twice, once with the word first and once with the nonword first. For each practice trial, participants received feedback on whether their answer was correct, incorrect, or too slow. To proceed to the rest of the task, participants needed to score at least 8 out of 10, or the practice phase was repeated. Participants completed the forced choice task through a web browser with jsPsych (de Leeuw 2015) in about 10 minutes, with one break in the middle of the task. Trials were divided so that each block contained roughly an equal number per contrast, and trials were randomized within each block.

2.3 Vocabulary task

In order to examine a range of self-reported vocabulary knowledge rather than simply known/unknown, the vocabulary task for the current study was adapted from the Vocabulary Knowledge Scale (Wesche and Paribakht 1996). Given that the majority of studies on L2 vocabulary size as well as word familiarity checks for other types of L2 studies use Yes/No tests of receptive vocabulary knowledge

only, the scale of self-reported knowledge used in the current study did not require production, in contrast to the original Vocabulary Knowledge Scale. To clarify, while this self-assessment asked about productive knowledge, it did not require learners to write translations for the words or write them in a sentence. The 6-point scale given to learners was as follows, with only the text of each point on the scale visible rather than the numbers:
1) I didn't know this was a word
2) I recognize this word but I don't know what it means
3) I recognize this word and have a vague idea of what it means
4) I recognize this word and know more or less what it means
5) I know this word and can provide a translation in English
6) I know this word well, can provide a translation in English, and can use this word while speaking Spanish

2.4 Language background questionnaire

Each participant completed a language background questionnaire to elicit demographic information such as their age, gender, level of education, and history of residence, as well as their language learning history. In order to check the L2 learners' knowledge of Spanish sound-spelling correspondences, this questionnaire also asked them to "describe the difference in pronunciation of 'r' as in *pero* and 'rr' as in *perro*. If you don't know, please indicate that."

2.5 Participants

Participants in this study were intermediate and advanced English-speaking learners of Spanish, who constituted the experimental groups, and Spanish-speaking learners of English, who served as a control group. The intermediate learners were undergraduate Spanish majors and minors enrolled in a Spanish course at the fifth-semester level or higher. The advanced learners were graduate students who had taken graduate courses in Spanish. A postdoc in Hispanic linguistics also served as an advanced participant. Most of the advanced learners were teaching Spanish and studying Hispanic linguistics or Hispanic literatures and cultures, as were most of the native Spanish speakers. The English-speaking learners all grew up in monolingual households in which only English was spoken. In total, 42 L2 learners of Spanish and 11 native speakers were tested. However, 6 participants were excluded from the analyses for various reasons, such as failing the hearing screening (described below) or having too many timeouts on the forced choice task. This left data from 26 intermediate learners, 12 advanced learners, and 8 native Spanish speakers for the analyses. Demographic information about the participants is presented in Table 2.

Table 2: Demographic information for the participants.

	Intermediate L2 Learners N=26	Advanced L2 Learners N=12	Native Spanish Speakers N=8
Age at testing (years)	20.7 (2.5)	26.3 (3.3)	29.5 (2.5)
Age of onset for L2 learning[a]	12.7 (2.7)	13.8 (2.0)	10.6 (8.2)
Residence in a Spanish-speaking country (months)	1.0 (2.3)	13.1 (11.8)	
Age of arrival in the US			24.9 (4.0)
Self-rated L2 speaking ability (0–6)	3.1 (1.4)	5.6 (0.7)	5.1 (1.2)
Self-rated L2 listening ability (0–6)	3.5 (1.4)	5.4 (0.7)	5.6 (0.5)
Self-rated L2 reading ability (0–6)	4.0 (1.1)	5.7 (0.9)	5.4 (1.1)
Self-rated L2 writing ability (0–6)	3.9 (1.5)	5.5 (0.9)	5.1 (1.1)
Gender	20 female	6 female	3 female, 1 non-binary

Note: "L2" in the variables refers to Spanish for the English-speaking learners and English for the Spanish speakers. Means are given for rows 1–8, with standard deviations in parentheses.
[a]One Spanish-speaking participant listed their age of onset for L2 learning as "Middle school but formal instruction at the age of 18." This was not included in the summary statistics in the table.

2.6 Procedure

Participants completed the forced choice task, vocabulary knowledge task, and language background questionnaire as part of a larger study. After consenting to do the study, participants completed a bilateral hearing screening with 1000 Hz, 2000 Hz, and 4000 Hz pure tones at 20 dB HL, following the recommendations of Reilly, Troiani, Grossman, and Wingfield (2007). Pulsed tones were presented randomly, one time for each ear, and participants needed to indicate that they heard the tone by pressing the space bar. If an individual missed a tone, all of the tones were repeated once more before the test indicated a failure to pass. All participants needed to pass the hearing screening with 100% accuracy in order to proceed with the study. They were given a maximum of three attempts to pass the hearing screening, if necessary, after attempting to reduce any external noise that could be interfering. This task was administered through jsPsych and took approximately two minutes. Participants next completed a lexical decision task and oddity task that are not discussed in the current study, followed by the forced choice task. They then did a series of cognitive tasks and a vocabulary size task that are not analyzed here. Lastly, they completed the language background questionnaire and the vocabulary knowledge task. All testing took place one-on-one with the researcher in person. Participants wore Sennheiser HD 515 over-ear headphones for the tasks that presented auditory stimuli. The entire experiment lasted approximately 65–75 minutes and each person was paid $15 for their participation.

3 Results

In order to analyze the vocabulary knowledge task, learners' vocabulary ratings were converted to numerical values, with "1" representing no knowledge of the word and "6" representing high familiarity. Because equal difference could not be assumed between each value, vocabulary rating was treated as an ordinal variable. For example, the difference between "I didn't know this was a word" and "I recognize this word but I don't know what it means" is presumably conceptually larger than between "I know this word and can provide a translation in English" and "I know this word well, can provide a translation in English, and can use this word while speaking Spanish". Table 3 displays the median rating and range of ratings in parentheses for each group for each of the experimental contrasts.

Table 3: L2 learners' median vocabulary knowledge rating by contrast.

	/tap-trill/	/tap-d/	/trill-d/	/f-p/
Intermediate	6 (1–6)	6 (1–6)	6 (1–6)	6 (1–6)
Advanced	6 (3–6)	6 (all 6)	6 (5–6)	6 (5–6)

3.1 Relationship between vocabulary rating and forced choice accuracy

If self-rated vocabulary knowledge corresponds to the phonological accuracy of a word, we would expect a correlation between the rating given to a word and its accuracy in the forced choice task. In order to test this, Kendall tau-b correlations were run in R for intermediate and advanced learners individually, following the advice of Khamis (2008) for analyzing ordinal variables with a small number of levels. In these correlations, the variables were accuracy in a trial (0 or 1) and vocabulary rating for the word in that trial (1, 2, 3, 4, 5, 6). For the intermediate learners, there was a weak, positive correlation between accuracy in a trial and the vocabulary rating given to that word, $\tau_b = .12$, $p < .001$, with a 95% confidence interval of .08 to .15 for τ_b. For the advanced learners, although the initial analysis found a very weak but significant correlation, $\tau_b = .09$, $p < .001$, the 95% confidence interval went through 0 ([−.02, .20]), suggesting that there is no relationship between these variables. These findings of a weak to no correlation between vocabulary rating and accuracy in the forced choice task may be because the words were generally well known to the participants, especially the advanced learners, as seen in Table 3.

Additional analyses were conducted in order to determine if vocabulary rating could predict accuracy in the forced choice task for each contrast. Because the vocabulary ratings did not display much variation for the advanced group, both L2 groups were combined for these analyses. Figure 1 displays the average accuracy for each contrast in the forced choice task for each point along the vocabulary scale, with both L2 groups included. Diamonds represent mean values and the lines at 50% indicate chance level performance.

For each contrast (/tap-trill/, /tap-d/, /trill-d/, and /f-p/), a logistic regression was run with accuracy in each trial as the dependent variable (0 or 1) and orthogonal polynomials of the numeric vocabulary rating for that trial's word as the independent variables (vocab score, vocab score squared, vocab score cubed, vocab score to the fourth, and vocab score to the fifth). By analyzing vocab score in this way, it was possible to retain the ordered nature of the scale, that is, treat vocabulary rating as an ordinal variable, while at the same time assessing whether the relationship between vocabulary score and accuracy in the forced choice task was linearly increasing, or whether adding a curve to the regression line was needed in order to best model the data. For example, if only vocab score were significant, then the best fit for the data would be a straight line (i.e., a linear equation), whereas if vocab score squared were also significant, this would mean that adding a U-shaped curve (i.e., a quadratic equation) to the regression line would better model the data. As displayed in Table 4, only the linear trend was significant for the /tap-trill/ contrast, and the model was significant compared to the empty model with the intercept only, $\chi^2(5) =$

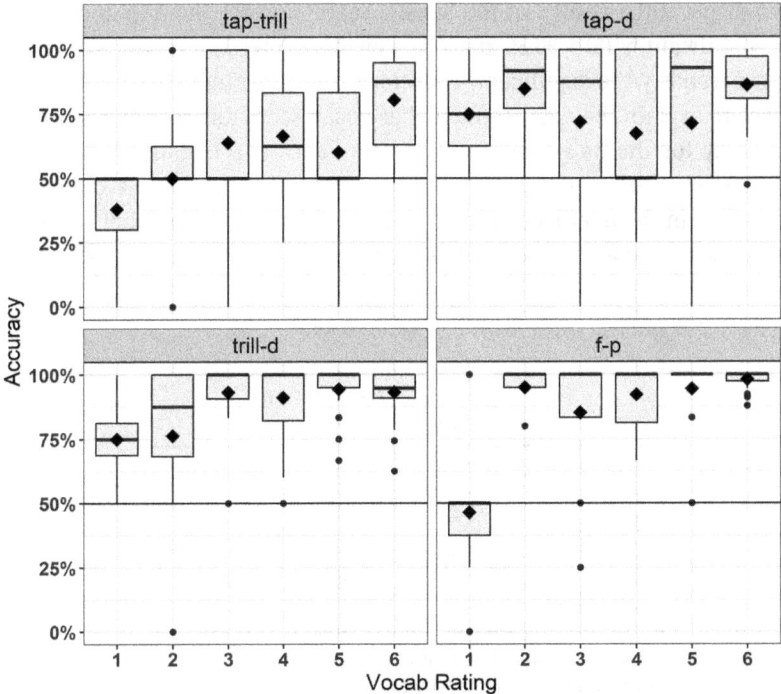

Figure 1: Accuracy in the forced choice task by vocabulary rating and contrast.

Table 4: Summary of logistic regression analysis for /tap-trill/ contrast.

Predictor	B	B 95% CI	Std Error B	z-value	p	
(Intercept)	1.22	[1.10, 1.33]	0.059	20.477	<.001	***
Vocab	15.40	[11.31, 19.56]	2.099	7.339	<.001	***
Vocab^2	1.82	[−2.37, 5.88]	2.098	0.865	0.387	
Vocab^3	2.87	[−1.15, 6.88]	2.044	1.403	0.160	
Vocab^4	2.25	[−1.79, 6.30]	2.061	1.091	0.275	
Vocab^5	2.13	[−1.88, 6.14]	2.038	1.044	0.296	

Note: $\chi^2(5)$ = 57.27, p < .001. B = unstandardized regression coefficient. Numbers in brackets indicate the lower and upper limits of a 95% confidence interval.
*p < .05, **p < .01, ***p < .001

57.27, p < .001. Thus, there was a linear relationship between vocab score and accuracy for the /tap-trill/ contrast in the forced choice task, such than a higher vocab score predicted higher accuracy.

Table 5 displays the results of the logistic regression for the /tap-d/ contrast, which was significant, $\chi^2(5) = 26.55$, $p < .001$. For this contrast, both the linear and the quadratic trends were significant. Therefore, a linearly increasing model was not sufficient to explain the data, and a higher vocab score did not always predict higher accuracy for the /tap-d/ contrast. Instead, adding a U-shaped curve (the quadratic equation) to the regression resulted in a better fit for the data. This trend is reflected in the averages in Figure 1 as well, where we see that the average accuracy by vocabulary rating for this contrast dips for ratings 3 through 5.

Table 5: Summary of logistic regression analysis for /tap-d/ contrast.

Predictor	B	B 95% CI	Std Error B	z-value	p	
(Intercept)	1.59	[1.46, 1.72]	0.068	23.460	<.001	***
Vocab	9.77	[5.02, 14.23]	2.330	4.194	<.001	***
Vocab^2	7.00	[2.53, 12.05]	2.353	2.973	0.003	**
Vocab^3	1.18	[−4.20, 5.63]	2.396	0.494	0.621	
Vocab^4	0.90	[−3.57, 5.61]	2.299	0.391	0.696	
Vocab^5	−0.03	[−4.45, 4.20]	2.190	−0.012	0.990	

Note: $\chi^2(5) = 26.55$, $p < .001$. B = unstandardized regression coefficient. Numbers in brackets indicate the lower and upper limits of a 95% confidence interval.
*$p < .05$, **$p < .01$, ***$p < .001$

The results of the logistic regression for the /trill-d/ contrast are shown in Table 6. This model was significant, χ2(5) = 26.55, $p < .001$. For this contrast, only the linear relationship was significant, showing that an increase in vocabulary rating predicted an increase in accuracy in the forced choice task.

Table 7 displays the results of the logistic regression for the /f-p/ contrast, which was significant, χ2(5) = 63.14, $p < .001$. Similar to the /tap-trill/ and /trill-d/ models, only the linear trend was significant, such that a higher vocabulary rating predicted higher forced choice accuracy for the /f-p/ contrast.

3.2 Analysis of forced choice accuracy for only well-known words

In order to further investigate the effect of proficiency, the data were divided by group and restricted to only the highest possible vocabulary rating. For a trial to be included for the L2 learners, that participant had to have chosen "I know this word well, can provide a translation in English, and can use this word while

Table 6: Summary of logistic regression analysis for /trill-d/ contrast.

Predictor	B	B 95% CI	Std Error B	z-value	p	
(Intercept)	2.29	[2.12, 2.46]	0.087	26.455	<.001	***
Vocab	9.04	[3.08, 14.65]	2.938	3.078	0.002	**
Vocab^2	−2.04	[−7.86, 3.53]	2.887	−0.707	0.479	
Vocab^3	2.88	[−2.77, 8.47]	2.836	1.017	0.309	
Vocab^4	3.92	[−1.79, 9.53]	2.870	1.367	0.172	
Vocab^5	−2.84	[−10.06, 3.45]	3.374	−0.842	0.400	

Note: $\chi^2(5) = 15.07$, $p = .010$. B = unstandardized regression coefficient. Numbers in brackets indicate the lower and upper limits of a 95% confidence interval.
$^*p < .05$, $^{**}p < .01$, $^{***}p < .001$

Table 7: Summary of logistic regression analysis for /f-p/ contrast.

Predictor	B	B 95% CI	Std Error B	z-value	p	
(Intercept)	2.90	[2.68, 3.14]	0.115	25.186	<.001	***
Vocab	18.69	[12.60, 24.52]	3.025	6.177	<.001	***
Vocab^2	−6.43	[−14.09, −0.01]	3.525	−1.824	0.068	
Vocab^3	−0.59	[−9.89, 6.55]	4.005	−0.146	0.884	
Vocab^4	−6.09	[−15.52, 1.38]	4.143	−1.469	0.142	
Vocab^5	1.44	[−5.30, 7.96]	3.325	0.432	0.666	

Note: $\chi^2(5) = 63.14$, $p < .001$. B = unstandardized regression coefficient. Numbers in brackets indicate the lower and upper limits of a 95% confidence interval.
$^*p < .05$, $^{**}p < .01$, $^{***}p < .001$

Table 8: Accuracy in the forced choice task for words with highest vocabulary rating only.

	/tap-trill/		/tap-d/		/trill-d/		/f-p/	
	Mean	SD	Mean	SD	Mean	SD	Mean	SD
Intermediate	74.1	15.4	81.5	10.9	90.9	8.7	97.6	3.5
	(48.3–94.3)		(47.3–97.3)		(62.5–100)		(87.9–100)	
Advanced	94.3	11.5	96.3	5.6	98.1	3.2	99.4	1.1
	(59.0–100)		(82.1–100)		(90.0–100)		(97.5–100)	
Spanish NS	97.9	2.4	98.4	2.4	98.7	1.4	99.1	1.3
	(95.1–100)		(94.7–100)		(97.3–100)		(97.5–100)	

Note: *All numbers are percentages. Numbers in parentheses show range of scores for each contrast.*

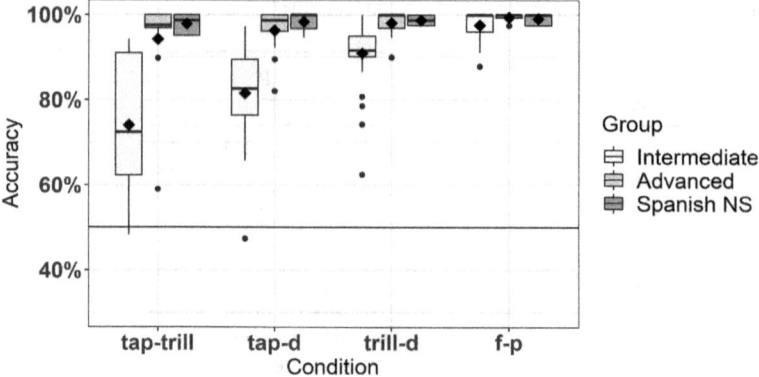

Figure 2: Accuracy in the forced choice task for words with highest vocabulary rating only.

speaking Spanish" for the word tested in that trial. These data are represented in Table 8 and Figure 2.

A two-way mixed ANOVA was run with *accuracy score* as the dependent variable, *group* (Intermediate, Advanced, or Spanish NS) as the between-subjects independent variable, and *contrast* (/tap-trill/, /tap-d/, /trill-d/, /f-p/) as the within-subjects independent variable. The Bonferroni correction method was used to adjust for multiple comparisons in post-hoc tests. Results showed that there was a significant interaction between group and contrast, $F(4.36, 93.67) = 8.56$, $p < .001$.[2] Post-hoc tests revealed that while there was no effect of group for the /f-p/ control contrast (adjusted $p = .52$), there were significant differences by group for the other three contrasts (all adjusted $p < .01$). For each of the contrasts /tap-d/, /tap-trill/, and /trill-d/, there was no difference between the advanced learners and the native speakers (all adjusted $p = 1$); however, there were significant differences between the intermediate learners and the other two groups for these contrasts (all adjusted $p < .05$). Contrast was only significant for the intermediate group, for whom all contrasts significantly differed from each other (all adjusted $p < .05$).

---

[2] Because the data violated the assumption of sphericity as shown by Mauchly's Test of Sphericity ($p < .001$), the Greenhouse-Geisser sphericity correction was applied to the degrees of freedom. The data were judged to be approximately normally distributed through an examination of the QQ plot; however, according to the results of Levene's tests, the FCLD data violated the assumption of homogeneity of variance in the /tap-trill/ ($p < .001$), /tap-d/ ($p = .034$), and /trill-d/ ($p = .044$) conditions. Box's M-test revealed that the homogeneity of covariance assumption was additionally violated ($p < .001$), and the data contained two extreme outliers. Therefore, a two-way mixed ANOVA with Robust Estimation was run with the R package WRS2 v.1.0–0 (Mair 2019) following Wilcox (2012). Results mirrored those of the traditional two-way mixed ANOVA, with a significant interaction between group and condition and significant main effects of group and condition.

In sum, while the advanced learners were as accurate as the native speakers across all contrasts, the intermediate learners were significantly less accurate than both the advanced and native speakers for the three test contrasts /tap-d/, /tap-trill/, and /trill-d/. The intermediate learners were least accurate for the /tap-trill/ contrast, followed by the /tap-d/ and /trill-d/ contrasts, respectively. For the /f-p/ control contrast, they were as highly accurate as the advanced learners and the native speakers.

3.3 Qualitative analysis of sound-spelling correspondence knowledge

Given that learners' understanding of sound-spelling correspondences could affect how they have phonologically encoded these words, an examination was also carried out on learners' responses to the question in the background questionnaire about the difference in pronunciation between intervocalic <r> and <rr>. Only 2 out of the 12 advanced learners did not give a reasonable explanation of the difference between tap and trill, along with 3 of the 26 intermediate learners. The majority of the advanced learners gave a linguistically-informed explanation of the difference. This was true for a small number of the intermediate learners, although most of them wrote about <rr> being "rolled". Three examples per group that were judged to be accurate are provided below verbatim:

Advanced Learners

(1a) The 'r' as in 'pero' is a tap sound similar to the 'tt' in the North American English word 'better', whereas the 'rr' is a trilled 'r' so the tip of your tongue has to tap your alveolar ridge multiple times

(1b) 'r' is a tap meaning the tongue hits the alveolar ridge only once, 'rr' is a trill meaning it rapidly hits the alveolar ridge around three times

(1c) The "rr" involves multiple tongue vibrations while the "r" has only one tongue tap.

Intermediate Learners

(2a) The difference in pronunciation between the two words is there is an emphasis when using a double "rr". One will roll the "rr" to make a trill sound but with the word "pero" you don't trill the "r".

(2b) The single "r" is pronounced with a "tap" of the tongue, whereas the double "rr" is pronounced in a "rolling" manner.

(2c) r is a short sound but rr is more of a rolling sound

The explanations that were judged to be at least partially inaccurate for each group are provided below verbatim:

Advanced Learners

(3a) rr is trilled, r is aveolar

(3b) longer trill in the second

Intermediate Learners

(4a) The rolled "r" sound

(4b) pero you do roll the 'r' but in perro, you do roll the 'r'

(4c) the trill r is sonora while the r is sordo.

For the advanced learners, the participant who stated that the <rr> represents a "longer trill" (implying that both sounds are trills) was in fact the participant with the lowest accuracy in the forced choice task, at 59%. Nevertheless, the learner who gave the second explanation that <r> is "aveolar" (implying that <rr> is not alveolar, when in reality both sounds have an alveolar place of articulation) did not have a lower score than the rest of the group; their accuracy was 97.5%. For the intermediate learners, the participant who gave the first explanation which does not clarify which spelling corresponds to the "rolled 'r' sound" had the 4th lowest score among this group, at 56.5%. The participant who gave the second explanation, which may not reflect inaccurate knowledge but instead a typo, scored a 91.4% in the forced choice. Finally, the participant who gave the third explanation, which is wholly inaccurate since both the tap and the trill are voiced, or *sonora*, rather than voiceless, or *sorda*, scored a 75.7% in this task, which was above average.

4 Discussion

This study sought to examine whether self-reported knowledge of the meaning of Spanish written words corresponded with accuracy in their phonological form and whether this differed by proficiency level. Although higher vocabulary rating was correlated with higher accuracy in the forced choice task, this association was weak for the intermediate learners and non-existent for the advanced learners. This may be due in part to the lack of substantial variation in vocabulary ratings, which were generally high for most of the words, especially for the advanced learners. Future studies using stimuli for which learners have more varied vocabulary ratings could provide better insight into this relationship.

Despite this limitation, when both groups were combined the regression analyses showed that better knowledge of the meaning of a word does predict a more accurate phonological representation. This is revealed by the linear relationship for the /tap-trill/, /trill-d/, and /f-p/ contrasts between vocabulary rating and accuracy in the forced choice task. Thus, in general, learners were more accurate at choosing the correct pronunciation of a word the higher they rated their knowledge of that word, although for /f-p/ this trend appears to be driven by differences between unknown words and all other levels of knowledge, rather than a more gradual increase in performance as knowledge increased, as shown by /tap-trill/ and /trill-d/. A linear increase in accuracy was not found for the /tap-d/ contrast, for which the quadratic function, or U-shaped curve, was also significant, signifying that learners' accuracy actually decreased for some of the higher ratings before increasing again. This could be due to several different possibilities. It may be that the gradations in knowledge that the scale was attempting to capture were not meaningful or well understood by the participants, and thus the scale would need to be reworded. It may also be that differences in how well a learner knows the meaning of a word do not appreciably impact the accuracy of its phonological form, and it is the ends of the scale, that is, simply knowing a word exists and being able to use it when speaking, that are the most useful metrics. However, these possibilities would not explain why only the /tap-d/ contrast showed this non-linear trend while the other contrasts did not. A more likely explanation may stem from the perceptual difficulty of this contrast. Studies have shown that the /tap-d/ contrast is the most difficult of the contrasts tested here (Daidone and Darcy 2014, 2021; Rose 2010; Herd 2011). For example, Herd (2011) found that intermediate learners of Spanish had 66% accuracy in identifying tap versus /d/ words after training, compared to 89% for /tap-trill/ and 97% for /trill-d/. Additionally, the nature of [ɾ] as an allophone of /d/ in English makes the Spanish tap and /d/ seem more similar in perception for learners, regardless of their actual acoustic characteristics (Boomershine et al. 2008). Because of the difficulty of /tap-d/, learners may struggle with hearing the difference between these options regardless of their familiarity with the word. Perhaps those learners who were not very familiar with a word containing one of these sounds listened more carefully for the correct form, while learners who were somewhat more secure in their knowledge of a word paid less attention to this difference, and those learners who chose that they can use this word while speaking Spanish were in fact better at recognizing this subtle difference.

When only words that were rated as "I know this word well, can provide a translation in English, and can use this word while speaking Spanish" were included for each participant, accuracy on the forced choice task still ranged greatly by individual for the intermediate group, who scored lower than both the advanced learners and native speakers for all of the test contrasts. They were capable of accurately completing the task when only phonemes that exist in their native language were tested, that is, /f-p/, but struggled to choose the correct pronunciation when tested on new L2 phonemes in the /tap-trill/, /tap-d/, and /trill-d/ contrasts. This is despite the accurate explicit knowledge of the sound-spelling correspondence for intervocalic tap and trill that the vast majority of learners displayed, and for those who did not, they were not uniformly less accurate. Even when knowing how a word should be pronounced based on its spelling and indicating that they could use this word when speaking Spanish, most intermediate learners could not select the correct pronunciation when given a clear choice between two options. Thus, knowledge of the meaning and spelling of a word does not appear to be sufficient for an accurate phonological representation. Moreover, accuracy appears to be driven more by proficiency level than the knowledge of individual words, as the advanced speakers were as accurate as the native speakers. These findings corroborate previous research that reported L2 phonological representations to be inaccurate or less detailed (e.g. Barrios and Hayes-Harb 2021; Cutler, Weber and Otake 2006; Daidone and Darcy 2014; Gor et al. 2021), and additionally this study shows that the difficulties learners have with storing accurate phonological representations cannot be explained away by the type of task used or participants' insufficient self-reported knowledge of the items tested.

5 Conclusions

These results have implications for both vocabulary teaching and testing. In the classroom, instructors cannot assume that knowing how a word is supposed to sound based on its spelling will lead to accurate representations of the sounds within that word. Spanish majors and minors, the intermediate learners in this study, need more training on perception and pronunciation when learning vocabulary, and they also could benefit from instruction on what is not an acceptable pronunciation of a word. This is true even for a language with a transparent orthography like Spanish. Moreover, if learners are only assessed on the written form of new vocabulary words, these tests may be missing critical information about the phonological accuracy of learners' vocabulary knowledge. The results of the intermediate learners for words well-known in writing indicate that if researchers are interested in learners' aural vocabulary abilities, the development of aural vocabulary tests for L2 learners or adaptation of such existing tests already in place for children is warranted, including for a language like Spanish. Furthermore, researchers should use caution if extrapolating phonological properties of L2 learners' lexicons such as phonological neighborhood density based solely on written tests. For example, if learners do not have a clear distinction between the Spanish tap and trill, their phonological forms for words such as *pero* 'but' and *perro* 'dog' may be merged, meaning that these words are not phonological neighbors of each other in their mental lexicons but rather homophones, or these representations may be separate but fuzzy to the extent that they are activated by similar words and each other.

Overall, these results reveal a disconnect between self-rated vocabulary knowledge and the accuracy of phonological forms. While having greater knowledge of a word predicts that it is more likely to have an accurate phonological representation, an accurate form is not guaranteed even when a word is well known. This is particularly true for intermediate learners, who often struggled to identify the real word when given a binary choice. Despite the relatively transparent orthography of Spanish, it is clear that phonological forms cannot be taken for granted based on knowledge of written forms. Additionally, it does not appear that learners' difficulty can be attributed to their lack of knowledge of sound-spelling correspondences. Thus, more time needs to be devoted to training the phonological forms of words in the classroom, and both instructors and researchers should use caution when using solely written instruments to assess learners' vocabulary knowledge, as they are likely to overestimate the accuracy of learners' phonological knowledge of these words.

References

Barrios, Shannon & Rachel Hayes-Harb. 2021. L2 processing of words containing English /æ/-/ɛ/ and /l/-/ɹ/ contrasts, and the uses and limits of the auditory lexical decision task for understanding the locus of difficulty. *Frontiers in Communication* 6(689470). doi:10.3389/fcomm.2021.689470.

Beglar, David & Paul Nation. 2014. Assessing vocabulary. In Antony John Kunnan (ed.), *The companion to language assessment*, 172–184. Hoboken, NJ: John Wiley & Sons. doi:10.1002/9781118411360.wbcla053.

Boomershine, Amanda, Kathleen Currie Hall, Elizabeth Hume & Keith Johnson. 2008. The influence of allophony vs. contrast on perception: The case of Spanish and English. In Peter Avery, B. Elan Dresher & Keren Rice (eds.), *Contrast in phonology: Perception and acquisition*, 145–171. Berlin: Mouton.

Carney, Nathaniel. 2021. Diagnosing L2 listeners' difficulty comprehending known lexis. *TESOL Quarterly* 55(2). 536–567. doi:10.1002/tesq.3000.

Cook, Svetlana V., Nick B. Pandža, Alia K. Lancaster & Kira Gor. 2016. Fuzzy nonnative phonolexical representations lead to fuzzy form-to-meaning mappings. *Frontiers in Psychology* 7(1345). doi:10.3389/fpsyg.2016.01345.

Cutler, Anne, Andrea Weber & Takashi Otake. 2006. Asymmetric mapping from phonetic to lexical representations in second-language listening. *Journal of Phonetics* 34(2). 269–284.

Daidone, Danielle & Isabelle Darcy. 2014. Quierro comprar una guitara: Lexical encoding of the tap and trill by L2 learners of Spanish. In Ryan T. Miller, Katherine I. Martin, Chelsea M. Eddington, Ashlie Henery, Nausica Marcos Miguel, Alison M. Tseng, Alba Tuninetti & Daniel Walter (eds.), *Selected Proceedings of the 2012 Second Language Research Forum: Building Bridges between Disciplines*, 39–50. Somerville, MA: Cascadilla Proceedings Project.

Daidone, Danielle & Isabelle Darcy. 2021. Vocabulary size is a key factor in predicting second language lexical encoding accuracy. *Frontiers in Psychology* 12(688356). doi:10.3389/fpsyg.2021.688356.

Darcy, Isabelle, Danielle Daidone & Chisato Kojima. 2013. Asymmetric lexical access and fuzzy lexical representations in second language learners. *The Mental Lexicon* 8(3). 372–420. doi:10.1075/ml.8.3.06dar.

Darcy, Isabelle & Trisha Thomas. 2019. When blue is a disyllabic word: Perceptual epenthesis in the mental lexicon of second language learners. *Bilingualism: Language and Cognition* 22(5). 1141–1159. doi:10.1017/S1366728918001050.

Dunn, Lloyd M. & Leota M. Dunn. 1997. *Peabody Picture Vocabulary Test*. 3rd edn. Circle Pines, MN: American Guidance Service.

Durham, Kristie, Rachel Hayes-Harb, Shannon Barrios & Catherine E. Showalter. 2016. The influence of various visual input types on L2 learners' memory for phonological forms of newly-learned words. In John M. Levis, Huong Le, Ivana Lucic, Evan Simpson & Sonca Vo (eds.), *Proceedings of the 7th Pronunciation in Second Language Learning and Teaching Conference*, 98–107. Ames, IA.

Escudero, Paola, Rachel Hayes-Harb & Holger Mitterer. 2008. Novel second-language words and asymmetric lexical access. *Journal of Phonetics* 36(2). 345–360.

Escudero, Paola, Ellen Simon & Karen E. Mulak. 2014. Learning words in a new language: Orthography doesn't always help. *Bilingualism* 17(2). 384–395. doi:10.1017/S1366728913000436.

Gor, Kira, Svetlana Cook, Denisa Bordag, Anna Chrabaszcz & Andreas Opitz. 2021. Fuzzy lexical representations in adult second language speakers. *Frontiers in Psychology* 12(732030). doi:10.3389/fpsyg.2021.732030.

Hayes-Harb, Rachel, Kelsey Brown & Bruce L. Smith. 2018. Orthographic input and the acquisition of German final devoicing by native speakers of English. *Language and Speech* 61(4). 547–564. doi:10.1177/0023830917710048.

Hayes-Harb, Rachel & Hui Wen Cheng. 2016. The influence of the Pinyin and Zhuyin writing systems on the acquisition of Mandarin word forms by native English speakers. *Frontiers in Psychology* 7(785). doi:10.3389/fpsyg.2016.00785.

Hayes-Harb, Rachel & Jane Hacking. 2015. The influence of written stress marks on native English speakers' acquisition of Russian lexical stress contrasts. *The Slavic and East European Journal* 59(1). 91–109.

Hayes-Harb, Rachel, Janet Nicol & Jason Barker. 2010. Learning the phonological forms of new words: Effects of orthographic and auditory input. *Language and Speech* 53(3). 367–381.

Herd, Wendy. 2011. *The perceptual and production training of /d,r,r/ in L2 Spanish: Behavioral, psycholinguistic, and neurolinguistic evidence*. Lawrence, KS: University of Kansas dissertation.

Herd, Wendy, Joan Sereno & Allard Jongman. 2015. Cross-modal priming differences between native and nonnative Spanish speakers. *Studies in Hispanic and Lusophone Linguistics* 8(1). 135–155. doi:10.1515/shll-2015-0005.

Hualde, José Ignacio. 2005. *The sounds of Spanish*. New York, NY: Cambridge University Press.

Izura, Cristina, Fernando Cuetos & Marc Brysbaert. 2014. Lextale-Esp: A test to rapidly and efficiently assess the spanish vocabulary size. *Psicológica* 35(1). 49–66.

Kaplan, Edith F., Harold Goodglass & Sandra Weintraub. 2001. *The Boston Naming Test*. 2nd edn. Philadelphia, PA: Lippincott Williams & Wilkins.

Khamis, Harry. 2008. Measures of association: How to choose? *Journal of Diagnostic Medical Sonography* 24(3). 155–162. doi:10.1177/8756479308317006.

Ladefoged, Peter & Keith Johnston. 2011. *A Course in Phonetics*. 6th edn. Boston, MA: Wadsworth.

Leeuw, Joshua R. de. 2015. jsPsych: A JavaScript library for creating behavioral experiments in a Web browser. *Behavior Research Methods* 47(1). 1–12. doi:10.3758/s13428-014-0458-y.

Llompart, Miquel. 2021. Phonetic categorization ability and vocabulary size contribute to the encoding of difficult second-language phonological contrasts into the lexicon. *Bilingualism: Language and Cognition* 24(3). 481–496. doi:10.1017/S1366728920000656.

Mair, Patrick. 2019. *WRS2: A collection of robust statistical methods*. R package version 1.0-0.

Masrai, Ahmed. 2020. Exploring the impact of individual differences in aural vocabulary knowledge, written vocabulary knowledge and working memory capacity on explaining L2 learners' listening comprehension. *Applied Linguistics Review* 11(3). 423–447. doi:10.1515/applirev-2018-0106.

Mathieu, Lionel. 2016. The influence of foreign scripts on the acquisition of a second language phonological contrast. *Second Language Research* 32(2). 145–170. doi:10.1177/0267658315601882.

McLean, Stuart, Brandon Kramer & David Beglar. 2015. The creation and validation of a listening vocabulary levels test. *Language Teaching Research* 19(6). 741–760. doi:10.1177/1362168814567889.

Meara, Paul M. 2005. X_Lex: The Swansea Vocabulary Levels Test. Swansea, UK: Lognostics.

Melnik, Gerda Ana & Sharon Peperkamp. 2019. Perceptual deletion and asymmetric lexical access in second language learners. *The Journal of the Acoustical Society of America* 145(1). EL13–EL18. doi:10.1121/1.5085648.

Milton, James. 2009. *Measuring second language vocabulary acquisition*. Bristol, UK: Multilingual Matters.

Milton, James & Nicola Hopkins. 2006. Comparing phonological and orthographic vocabulary size: Do vocabulary tests underestimate the knowledge of some learners? *Canadian Modern Language Review* 63(1). 127–147. doi:10.3138/cmlr.63.1.127.

Nation, Paul & David Beglar. 2007. A vocabulary size test. *The Language Teacher* 31(7). 9–13.

Rafat, Yasaman. 2016. Orthography-induced transfer in the production of English-speaking learners of Spanish. *The Language Learning Journal* 44(2). 197–213. doi:10.1080/09571736.2013.784346.

Ramus, Franck, Sharon Peperkamp, Anne Christophe, Charlotte Jacquemot, Sid Kouider & Emmanuel Dupoux. 2010. A psycholinguistic perspective on the acquisition of phonology. In Cécile Fougeron, Barbara Kuehnert, Mariapaola Imperio & Nathalie Vallee (eds.), *Laboratory Phonology 10: Variation, Phonetic Detail and Phonological Representation*, 311–340. Berlin: De Gruyter Mouton. doi:https://doi.org/10.1515/9783110224917.

Reilly, Jamie, Vanessa Troiani, Murray Grossman & Arthur Wingfield. 2007. An introduction to hearing loss and screening procedures for behavioral research. *Behavior Research Methods* 39(3). 667–672.

Rose, Marda. 2010. Differences in discriminating L2 consonants: A comparison of Spanish taps and trills. In Matthew T. Prior, Yukiko Watanabe & Sang-Ki Lee (eds.), *Selected proceedings of the 2008 Second Language Research Forum*, 181–196. Somerville, MA: Cascadilla Proceedings Project.

Rose, Marda. 2012. Cross-language identification of Spanish consonants in English. *Foreign Language Annals* 45(3). 415–429. doi:10.111/j.1944-9720.2012.01197.x.

Schmitt, Norbert, Diane Schmitt & Caroline Clapham. 2001. Developing and exploring the behaviour of two new versions of the Vocabulary Levels Test. *Language Testing* 18(1). 55–88. doi:10.1177/026553220101800103.

Showalter, Catherine E. & Rachel Hayes-Harb. 2013. Unfamiliar orthographic information and second language word learning: A novel lexicon study. *Second Language Research* 29(2). 185–200. doi:10.1177/0267658313480154.

Showalter, Catherine E. & Rachel Hayes-Harb. 2015. Native English speakers learning Arabic: The influence of novel orthographic information on second language phonological acquisition. *Applied Psycholinguistics* 36(1). 23–42. doi:10.1017/S0142716414000411.

Simon, Ellen, Della Chambless & Ubiratã Kickhöfel Alves. 2010. Understanding the role of orthography in the acquisition of a non-native vowel contrast. *Language Sciences* 32(3). 380–394. doi:10.1016/j.langsci.2009.07.001.

Vitevitch, Michael S., Melissa K. Stamer & Douglas Kieweg. 2012. Short research note: The beginning Spanish lexicon: A web-based interface to calculate phonological similarity among Spanish words in adults learning Spanish as a foreign language. *Second Language Research* 28(1). 103–112. doi:10.1177/0267658311432199.

Wesche, Marjorie & T. Sima Paribakht. 1996. Assessing second language vocabulary knowledge: Depth versus breadth. *Canadian Modern Language Review* 53(1). doi:10.3138/cmlr.53.1.13.

Wilcox, Rand. 2012. *Modern statistics for the social and behavioral sciences: A practical introduction*. New York, NY: Taylor & Francis.

Section II: **Measures of lexical competence and development in Spanish**

Juan-Andrés Villena-Ponsoda, Antonio-Manuel Ávila-Muñoz, José-María Sánchez-Sáez

Chapter 4
Individual lexical breadth and its associated measures. A contribution to the calculation of individual lexical richness

1 Introduction

The majority of studies on lexical richness conducted to date focus on written production, as such productions are relatively easy to access (Jarvis 2002; Malvern and Richards 2000; Malvern et al. 2004; Vermeer 2004). The use of spoken productions in research tends to involve a more complex data collection process, due to the highly individual nature of speech. Many studies have concentrated on analyzing the lexical production of either children and adolescents (see Ávila 1988; Verhoeven, van Leeuwe, and Vermeer 2011), adults (see Levelt 1989, 1993, 2001; Dell and O'Seaghdha 1992), native speakers (Goldfield and Reznick 1990; Díez-Villoria, Zubiauz de Pedro and Mayor Daller 2005; Milton and Treffers-Daller 2007; Cutillas et al. 2014; Jarvis and Daller 2013; Kaizumi and In'nami 2013), L2 language learners (Ellis 1994; Laufer and Nation 1995; Silva-Corvalan and Treffers-Daller 2016), or bilingual speakers (Bowles 2011; Bowles, Adams and Torh 2014; Montrul 2016; Checa-García and Marqués-Pascual 2020; Fairclough and Garza 2018). Certain research has even succeeded in developing theoretical indexes based on mathematical algorithms to predict the lexical richness of an entire city (Ávila-Muñoz 2016). Currently, several parameters are being used to determine "lexical richness", including content density, lexical sophistication, lexical accuracy and lexical diversity (Jarvis 2013: 13–44; Castañeda Jiménez and Jarvis 2013: 498–513).

Note: This work has been made possible thanks to the support of the Spanish State Research Agency project "Agenda 2050. The Spanish of Malaga: Processes of Spatial and Social Variation and Change" (PID2019-104982GB-C5-2). A preliminary Spanish version of certain parts of this chapter was published in Ávila-Muñoz and Villena-Ponsoda (2010), 37–81 and 177–286.

Juan-Andrés Villena-Ponsoda, Antonio-Manuel Ávila-Muñoz, José-María Sánchez-Sáez,
Universidad de Málaga, Spain

In this chapter, we present an original model for the measurement of "individual lexical breadth". With this construct, we try to represent lexical richness based on a solid and non-intuitive foundation, leading to the understanding that a speaker's lexical breadth is the quantitative reflection of his or her degree of lexical richness. Thus, lexical breadth is a statistically proven quantitative measure of lexical richness. The model presented here is based on both the size and specificity of the vocabulary produced by a speaker during a lexical test, i.e., on their available lexicon. A principal difference between our measure of individual lexical breadth and others relating to lexical richness is that our measure reflects a characteristic of the speakers and not of the written production they produce. We propose a number of indexes based on our model, notably, the Index of Lexical Decentralization (ILD) and the Index of Lexical Amplitude (ILA). Our intention is for these indexes to be used in addition to the four above-mentioned parameters (i.e., content density, lexical sophistication, lexical accuracy and lexical diversity) in the calculation of lexical richness.

Our model involves a revised interpretation of the traditional concept of "lexical availability", while still using association tests as source of data. It is based on previous work in the fields of socio- and psycholinguistic research (see Ávila-Muñoz 2016) in which association tests proved useful, despite the simplicity with which they allowed linguistic information to be obtained (López-Morales 1999; Hernández, Izura, and Ellis 2006; Ávila-Muñoz and Villena-Posoda 2010: 177–279).

2 Contextualization, methodology and study objectives

Research on lexical availability began in 1951, when the French Ministry of National Education appointed a committee to draw up a basic lexicon for teaching purposes (Gougenheim et al. 1954). The primary objective was the creation of a list of basic words for use in the curriculum of French as a foreign language. However, these pioneering researchers soon found that previous work was merely based on lexical frequency. In order to obtain the lexical frequency in a particular language, researchers use methods that facilitate access to the lexicon that has the highest degree of statistical stability. In other words, lists of lexical frequency obtained through such research include the words that speakers use to build a message, regardless of topic. It is well known that speakers tend towards using a reduced number of lexical and structural units – usually the most frequent. In fact, the variable "frequency of use" has proved one of the most important factors in language processing, both in production and decoding. Various frequency lists, or dictionaries, are available for the main western languages, and they are widely used. Two established examples are the frequency list by Davies (2006) for Spanish and the list by Lonsdale and Le Bras (2009) for French, both used in native as well as foreign language teaching (see Sánchez-García et al., this volume, and Zyzik and Marqués-Pascual, this volume). Nevertheless, frequency lists always include almost exclusively grammatical words, i.e. words without true lexical meaning, whereas non-grammatical words, those with proper lexical content, hardly ever feature and when they do, are quantitatively insignificant. This provides a false image of lexical frequency, since the latter are also frequently used by speakers, though only when the required communicative conditions for their use are fulfilled. These non-grammatical words are related to specific topics or refer to entities and objects and are, in most cases, nouns. They frequently co-occur and are almost always used when certain topics arise in conversation (de Kock 1983: 59–60).

Lists, or dictionaries, of lexical availability may therefore complement frequency lists in a way that provides a more realistic image – whereas the latter are excessively biased towards non-thematic lexicon, the former reflect the lexical production of speakers in specific communicative situations. Lists of lexical availability are based on the concept of "frequent situations", which is quite different from that of "frequent words" underlying frequency lists. Thus, the concept of the available lexicon is founded on the idea that certain frequently used words only occur in connection with specific topics.

In order to obtain a speaker's available vocabulary – and *not* their most frequent –, "association tests," a type of receptive vocabulary test, are usually carried out (see Samper-Padilla 1998, and Ávila-Muñoz and Villena-Ponsoda 2010). Association tests are based on a certain number of centers of interest (CI) presented via stimuli; around these, specific, related vocabulary emerge. This vocabulary is assumed to be the potential lexicon belonging to the active vocabulary of the speakers and that will be used whenever the topic represented by the stimulus of reference arises in conversation. The total number of words within an individual's list of available vocabulary for a specific CI is constrained by his or her reaction time, with speakers allowed to spend a maximum of two minutes on a single stimulus in both current and traditional research on lexical availability. Such research has shown that shorter reaction times correspond to the most available lexical items, hence, the ones occupying the first positions in the lists. In sum, available lexicon is part of a speaker's mental lexicon, but it does not occur in everyday linguistic interactions unless a specific topic arises.

In order to obtain the available lexicon for a CI, the so-called Lexical Availability Index (LAI) is used. The LAI is a numeric parameter that relates word frequency and rank order. The mathematical calculation on which the LAI is based weights the overall frequency of a certain word provided for a CI (i.e., the total number of speakers in a sample who provided the word) with its mean position in the lists (i.e., how high up it appears on average on the speakers' lists, reflecting how early it was produced). Thus, the most available words for a CI – those attaining LAI scores close to 1 within an interval between 0 and 1 – are the ones that occur the *most times* (a word's frequency) among the *first positions* (a word's rank position) in the lists obtained for the CI. Though this formula has undergone changes over time, its mathematical foundations are available in the work of Strassburger and López-Chávez (2000) (see also Strassburger and López-Chávez 1987; López-Morales 1989). The final version of the formula is:

$$d(p) = \sum_{i=1}^{n} \exp\left(C - \frac{i-1}{n1}\right) \frac{f_{pi}}{N_i}$$

where n is the highest position attained by a word, f_{pi} is its overall frequency in this position i, and N_i is the total number of speakers in the sample.

To return to the above-mentioned association tests, these consist of tasks that require participants to produce. When an individual is asked to write down a list of vocabulary relating to a particular stimulus, this task triggers a cognitive process, unique to the individual, that involves the interaction of several mechanisms of information processing. In such tests, participants are asked to spend a predefined amount of time – usually two minutes – writing down any vocabulary that comes to mind in relation to a stimulus, such as the human body, clothing, parts of a house, etc. (López-Morales 1999). No other instructions are given, although it is made clear that this is not an academic or intelligence test, meaning there can be no wrong answers.

For the association tests that provided the data for the present study, we used a uniformly allocated sample of speakers (N = 72), shown in Table 1, from the city of Malaga, Spain, stratified by age (Group 1: 20–34 years; Group 2: 35–54 years; Group 3: 55 years and over), gender (women, N = 36; men, N = 36) and educational level (Group 0: no education or uncompleted primary education; Group 1: uncompleted secondary education; Group 2: completed secondary education), to represent a population of 557,770, giving a sample/population ratio of 1/7746.

The informants were chosen based on the criteria established within the framework of the pan-hispanic PRESEEA project, for which the theoretical and methodological foundations can be accessed via the following link: http://www.linguas.net/portalpreseea/Metodolog%C3%ADa/tabid/474/Default.aspx [last accessed on June 16, 2022]. Many variables of post-stratification were considered as well, since it was assumed that some of these would be able to explain the lexical variation in the lists obtained. Sociolinguistic data were collected by means of a ques-

Table 1: Description of the speaker sample.

Education	Male				Female			
Age	0	1	2	Total	0	1	2	Total
20–34	4	4	4	12	4	4	4	12
35–54	4	4	4	12	4	4	4	12
> 55	4	4	4	12	4	4	4	12
	12	12	12	36	12	12	12	36

Note: Education:
0 = no education or uncompleted primary education
1 = uncompleted secondary education
2 = completed secondary education

tionnaire that subjects were required to fill in after completing the test. Via this questionnaire, participants provided extensive information in relation to social, psychosocial and social network variables.

The linguistic data were collected according to the usual process used in the field of lexical availability research, described above. For these tests, we used the following 20 centers of interest as stimuli: the human body; clothing; parts of a house (not including furniture); furniture in the home; food; objects laid on the table for a meal; the kitchen and kitchenware; the school: furniture and materials; heating, lighting, and means of ventilating a space; the city; the countryside; means of transport; agricultural and garden tasks; animals; games and entertainment; trades and professions; money and economy; internet and computers; colors; and the sea.

The linguistic information obtained from these stimuli has proved rich and comprehensive: the lexical data obtained so far in previous research have provided an invaluable source of information for studies on sociolinguistics, psycholinguistics, orthography, pedagogy, ethnolinguistics and dialectology as well as in general, for research in any other field interested in the study of lists of available lexicon.

Each test was conducted during a face-to-face interview between researcher and speaker, during the period 2005–2010.

The theoretical framework of prototype semantics seems to adequately represent the cognitive process that is initiated when an individual is asked write down a list of vocabulary relating to a particular stimulus. The same framework also provides a fundamental key to building more solid foundations for lexical availability and, thus, for a better understanding of lexical breadth (Ávila-Muñoz and Sánchez-Sáez 2016). Prototype theory was first proposed in the 1970s by Eleanor Rosch, within the field of psycholinguistics (Rosch 1973, 1975, 1977, 1978, 1988; Rosch and Mervis 1975; Rosch et al. 1976; Mervis and Rosch 1981). Since then, it has developed in two main directions. Firstly, the findings and proposals made by Rosch have been used in the field of information processing which aims to formally access human conceptual understanding and forms the base of artificial intelligence in order to produce models that explain the psychological disposition of lexicon and how this relates to the functioning of memory (Smith and Medin 1981; Medin and Smith 1984; Neisser 1987). Secondly, the cognitive implications of prototype theory on linguistics have undergone increasing development since the 1980s (Wierzbicka 1985; Lakoff 1987; Langacker 1987; Craig 1986; Holland and Quinn 1987; Rudzka–Ostyn 1988; Lehmann 1988; Hüllen and Schulze 1988; Tsohatzidis 1989; Taylor 1989). By combining principles from prototype theory and its cognitive extensions as well as advances from fuzzy set theory (Zadeh 1965; Zimmermann 2001), a satisfactory model for quantifying lexical richness can be developed (Ávila-Muñoz and Sánchez-Sáez 2014; Šifrar-Kalan 2017).

As described in Section 2 below, when building on the concept of "availability" as it is used in this model, each center of interest (CI) is assumed to link to a prototype that is itself created by the concept, or cognitive category, referenced. Speakers use this prototype as a gateway to their personal lexical network. "Accessibility" therefore refers to the act of entering the lexical network referenced. From this gateway, or access point, each speaker will move through his or her personal lexical network (Ávila-Muñoz and Sánchez-Sáez 2011). Once all the data provided by the informants during association tests are gathered, quantification of accessibility determines each word's degree of "centrality" for its category, described through the Index of Centrality (IC). The ensuing association between words and their respective degree of centrality reveals the lexical structure, or prototype, of a given center of interest (CI). Within this structure, the closer a word is to the prototype's center, the higher its IC. Hence, the words with the highest IC form the collective conceptual categorization, or collective cognitive prototype.

Accordingly, different zones of conceptual categorization can be established. The first will include the words with the highest IC, i.e., those most central to the category. As the IC decreases, the words will start to approach what can be called the line of "uncertainty". This is the limit beyond which, during an association test, an individual may question the relevancy to the stimulus of the word they are providing. In order to decide when a word belongs to the prototype's nucleus and, thus, when it can be classed as belonging to the collective prototype, we use the mathematical concept of "fuzzy set" (Zadeh 1965; Zimmermann 2001). This is a generalization of set theory in which an element's compatibility with its group is the focus rather than its belonging. Thus, different levels of compatibility can be established between elements and their set. This notion of compatibility corresponds to our concept of centrality, described above.

One of the tools from fuzzy set theory that can be used to establish these levels of compatibility is the determination of a word's "compatibility score", or "Fuzzy Expected Value", FEV – or even this tool's alternative, a word's "Weighted Fuzzy Expected Value", WFEV. Using these tools, we can establish limits for the degree of belonging and, thus, parameters for differentiating between elements that are "very characteristic" and "hardly characteristic" of a sample.

Our concept of centrality thus entails the perception of lexicon as a component constructed by speakers themselves (Aitchinson 2003). Since speakers belong to the same speech community, they share a large part of the lexicon of their language. The lexical core of any category (i.e., the collective prototype) will therefore be available to any speaker in the speech community, and an estimation of this core can be obtained through the lexico-statistical analysis of a set of word lists provided by informants during association tests such as those described above.

Given the foregoing, the objectives of our work are as follows:
1. To provide an easily understandable theoretical framework that offers a solid foundation for the concept of "lexical breadth".
2. To develop efficient mathematical parameters for the generation of measurements that determine individual lexical breadth and, thus, lexical richness.
3. To avoid restrictions observed in previous attempts to measure individual lexical availability – since the same type of data is used here as well. Existing models for the calculation of lexical availability exhibit the disadvantages of the additivity principle of probability and its effects if uncontrolled. In this model, the monotonicity principle is substituted for the additivity principle through the incorporation of fuzzy set theory, meaning that the higher the number of repetitions of a word within its set, the higher the probability that it will be provided.
4. To develop a flexible evaluation process that will allow for the continuous incorporation of new data and for the same process to be replicated by other researchers using different data.

3 Fundamentals. From availability to accessibility: A necessary transformation

As described above, for this model of language representation, lexicon is perceived as a component constructed by speakers themselves. It can therefore be assumed that all informants, as well as any other individual within the same speech community, will be capable of accessing vocabulary belonging to a prototype's nucleus. It follows that individual lexical breadth will be primarily determined by the more specific vocabulary provided by a speaker that is not as available to the rest of the community. Thus, the lists of available vocabulary for a given CI can be considered complementary, which results in new opportunities for quantitative analysis that have yet to be explored. The resulting hypothesis for this study is that an individual's lexical breadth will be higher if they provide words with a lower degree of centrality. This is logical, since, by definition, such individuals should be able to access the general vocabulary shared by the speech community easily, in addition to other less general words.

Our approach here to lexical availability builds on the simple assumption that members of the same speech community have certain vocabulary in common associated with frequently observed cognitive prototypes (Ávila-Muñoz and Villena-Ponsoda 2010). As discussed above, association tests are used to access this available vocabulary. For these tests, no restrictions are set regarding a provided word's morphology, proximity in terms of meaning to the CI's nucleus, further associations, etc. A sample of lists obtained during such tests can then be used to calculate the degree of availability for each word by relating word frequency and rank order (Strassburger and López Chávez 2000). The LAI – traditionally used for this purpose, described above in Section 1 – is a characteristic of the words provided and is useful for constructing both overall and category-specific vocabularies. However, to form part of this model, the LAI must undergo a profound transformation, so that it may characterize not the words but the informants. This transformation occurs via the following premises:

1. The stimulus that activates the association process is an access point to a network of lexical elements perceived by the individual as interrelated as well as related to the concept, or cognitive category, referenced in the stimulus.
2. The structure of this network is subjective and inherent to the individual, meaning it cannot be strictly extrapolated to others.
3. For various reasons, including both social and cultural factors, individuals within the same speech community develop similar lexical structures. We consider this shared sociocultural metastructure to constitute the vocabulary associated with a collective cognitive prototype; hence, the prototype does not exist in itself but is rather constructed by the members of the community. Most likely, a change in the group of speakers would therefore produce a change in the prototype.
4. When an individual is asked to provide a list of available vocabulary based on a stimulus, or prototype label, he or she first accesses words most closely related to the concept referenced. He or she then moves through his or her personal lexical network, searching for elements less closely related to the original access point and giving way to a list of words in a decreasing degree

of accessibility. There is the possibility that, should the individual feel he or she has moved too far from the stimulus, he or she will reenter his or her network via a new access point (Ávila-Muñoz and Sánchez-Sáez 2011), i.e., the individual will restart the wordassociation- process via a new access point by returning to the concept referenced.
5. Both the amount of vocabulary provided and the speed at which it is accessed – i.e., the time required to access all the words on a list – are relevant. It seems apparent why the number of words provided is not the sole determinant of lexical breadth, given each word's individual degree of compatibility with the prototype's nucleus (see Section 1). However, association tests currently in use only make it possible to consider a words' frequency rank order, meaning reaction time cannot be taken into account.
6. The rank order of the terms on a single list is relevant to determine their degree of accessibility, although its importance may be limited by the individual reentering his or her lexical network via a new access point.
7. The structure of a prototype is considered to consist of a nucleus and a periphery. The former is accessible to the entire community, whereas the latter is accessible to individuals depending on their degree of lexical breadth. The transition from nucleus to periphery is not abrupt but gradual.

The model underlying this study results from this last premise. Due to the format of the association tests, there are limitations regarding the extent to which the structure of a prototype may be represented. Although we assume that lexicon is structured as a multiconnected network, determining its layout would go beyond the scope of our work. Nevertheless, such a network is inherent in every informant and changes over time, as the speakers themselves change. We therefore resort to a simplified representation, in which the structure of a prototype consists of a network of terms organized by degree of accessibility. In this way, the need for the provision of information about the nature of the connections is removed and the focus is guided towards determining the ease with which terms provided during a test can be accessed.

Based on the premises above, we have developed a new model that is capable of measuring individual lexical breadth and can be linked to a specific area of mathematics due to the incorporation of fuzzy set theory (Zadeh 1965; Zimmermann 2001). As described, the latter is a generalization of set theory in which the compatibility of elements with their set is considered, instead of their belonging. In this way, different levels of compatibility can be established between elements and their set.

4 A Proposal for the calculation of individual lexical breadth

The measure of lexical breadth we propose (Index of Lexical Decentralization, ILD, see below, this section and Section 3.1) accounts for the quantity and specificity of the vocabulary provided by an individual and considers their degree of participation in the overall results of the studied sample. Our hypothesis is simple: the higher the number of specific words provided by a speaker – i.e., words with a lower degree of centrality –, the higher the speaker's lexical breadth. This is the result of considering that such individuals should be able to access the general vocabulary shared by the speech community easily, in addition to other less general words. Precise rank order should be inessential for the calculation of individual lexical breadth, due to the above-mentioned possibility of re-entry.

Our measure establishes an index for each speaker that represents his or her lexical breadth. The notion of lexical breadth underlies the speaker's lexical capacity or competence and, hence, the speaker's lexical richness, since it is based on the availability of each of the words he or she provided during the association test. For the creation of the index, we have employed approaches based on the probabilistic sum of values of non-availability of the vocabulary supplied by each speaker – i.e., a specific kind of operator that should not be confused with the sum of probabilities. It has been essential to develop an index capable of considering both the number of elements provided and their relevance to the cognitive category they represent, since the general vocabulary accessible to most of the community's members should not be given the same relevance as more specific vocabulary.

Words belonging to the nucleus of a prototype, also called nuclear vocabulary, should be of little relevance to the calculation of an individual's lexical breadth. However, terms that do not belong to the nucleus, also called non-prototypical vocabulary, should have greater weight in the calculation, the reason being that these terms indicate a higher degree of lexical breadth when provided, as they are not as widely used and are thus considered less accessible to the entire group of speakers. Consequently, a framework must be established according to which non-prototypical vocabulary is given greater weight than nuclear vocabulary (see Section 3.1 below).

Based on this logic, a viable proposal for measuring individual lexical breadth should account for two aspects: (a) the total number of words provided on a list (Index of Lexical Amplitude, ILA), and (b) the specificity of the terms provided (Index of Lexical Decentralization, ILD). These are not mutually exclusive; individuals that provide more specific vocabulary are generally capable of accessing general, shared vocabulary faster, thus resulting in a higher number of words provided, which corroborates the above-mentioned hypothesis, since speakers who provide more specific vocabulary are indeed also capable of accessing the words belonging to the shared nucleus.

4.1 Mathematical modeling of compatibility and decentralization

The model proposed above is capable of determining the collective lexical spectrum associated with each category represented in the association test for the population under study. As a result, we are in a position to establish the degree of "compatibility," between 0 and 1 of each word (e.g., *olmo* 'elm') with those included in the lists (e.g., *abedul* 'birch', *roble* 'oak', *arce* 'maple', etc.) for a given concept (*arbol* 'tree'). When the "compatibility score" of each word provided by the sample of speakers is observed in relation to that of the words provided by an individual, we gain insight into the degree of "centralization" or "decentralization" of their lexical spectrum, both for the lexical spectrum of an individual category and for that corresponding to all the categories.

Decentralization is the opposite of compatibility. If a word is related to the nucleus but shows a low degree of compatibility (i.e., it is non-prototypical) it should be assumed that it is not frequently used by the general population, meaning it will have a high degree of decentralization, or specificity. In this manner, a word's specificity is complementary to its compatibility, and a standardized operation within fuzzy set theory can be employed to calculate its degree of specificity: the complement operator. Within the fuzzy set framework, the score assigned to each element corresponds to the degree to which each element belongs to its set and the complement represents the degree to which it does not.

In the calculation of the Lexical Availability Index (LAI), the rank order of words is considered relevant. When subjects produce a list of available vocabulary, they presumably provide words that are more relevant to the stimulus, and therefore more central to the prototype, prior to words that are less relevant, and therefore more distant from the prototype's nucleus. Subjects may, however, re-enter their lexical network via a new access point whenever they consider they have moved too far from the nucleus. Nevertheless, when the data provided by all informants in a sample are combined to construct the lexical spectrum of a prototype, this re-entry is blurred in the result. It is for this reason that we believe the precise rank order should be disregarded when measuring individual lexical breadth, with emphasis only on the vocabulary provided by an individual and the lexical spectrum of the collective prototype. In a sense, this means that using the ILD instead of the LAI represents a step, as the ILD focuses only on the compatibility of a single word with its set.

If a word's (x) compatibility with the collective lexical spectrum (c) is expressed by $m_c(x)$, since its degree of compatibility must be in the interval [0,1], its degree of decentralization could be determined as $1 - m_c(x)$. The result expresses the word's distance from the nucleus. Irrespective of its position on a list, the degree of decentralization is calculated for every word provided by a subject. A single indicator must therefore be developed that aggregates each word's degree of decentralization. This is the way in which we use the Index of Lexical Decentralization (ILD) – which similarly takes values in the interval [0,1] –, since it is the expression of a term's distance to the nucleus.

The concept underlying the model that we have developed to determine a speaker's degree of lexical decentralization is the aggregated degree of decentralization of the vocabulary they provide. Two methods may be used to calculate this:

1. The first method would involve obtaining the aggregated degree of decentralization, by summing the degree of decentralization of each word. This approximation corresponds to the concept of cardinality as defined in fuzzy set theory.
2. The second method would involve establishing the degree of compatibility of a speaker's production with the concept of "wide lexical capacity", by constructing a fuzzy set over the set of speakers.

The first method can be interpreted directly and requires only a simple calculation, as indicated. The second method establishes an index with an upper and lower limit value that can be interpreted as the compatibility of the speaker's lexical production with the notion of "wide lexical capacity". Both approaches show advantages and disadvantages. In this work, we opt for the second method in order to stay within the same lines as the model of language representation, which also uses fuzzy sets.

Thus, in order to calculate each subject's degree of lexical decentralization, or their ability to access nonprototypical vocabulary, the Index of Lexical Decentralization (ILD) of each provided term is aggregated via the addition rule of probability:

$$a + b - a * b = 1 - (1-b)(1-a)$$

By generalizing to the set all the words provided by the speaker for a particular category, this results in the following formula:

$$d = 1 - \Pi_x(1 - (1 - m_c(x))) = 1 - \Pi_x\, m_c(x)$$

where x is every word provided on the speaker's list (c), and $m_c(x)$ is the degree of decentralization of a word with respect to the collective lexical spectrum of the category.

However, this process is not trouble-free: given that the probability additive aggregation operator value shows a consistent tendency to increase, never to decrease, should the degree of decentralization of a single word be valued as 1, the entire calculation will adjust to 0–1 range. As this situation would be uninformative, a control procedure is added by scaling the obtained decentralization measures through a parameter k, which must be determined in order to both control the above-mentioned increment and obtain an informative range. In this way, the calculation of individual lexical decentralization – the measure most closely related to the concept of lexical breadth – is given the following definite formula:

$$d = 1 - \Pi_x(1 - k \cdot (1 - m_c(x)))$$

4.2 Validation of the methodological instrument

In order to demonstrate the validity of our proposed measure, we analyzed – as described above in Section 1 – lists of available vocabulary provided by a sample of individuals from the city of Malaga in southern Spain, pre-stratified by age, gender and educational level (N = 72, Table 1), since the goal of the investigation was to produce a list, or dictionary, of lexical availability for the whole city (Ávila-Muñoz and Villena-Ponsoda 2010).

Each speaker produced a vocabulary list, which resulted in 72 lists containing 24,047 words, or tokens, for a total amount of 5,860 types (i.e. distinct words). Table 2 presents information on the cognitive stimuli used in the association tests. The selection of stimuli was based on previous work on available lexicon conducted in Spain and several other Spanish-speaking countries (see López-Morales 1989; Ávila-Muñoz and Villena-Ponsoda 2010).

We have created two separate measures – the development of which is described above in Section 2 – to determine individual lexical breadth: (a) quantity (Index of Lexical Amplitude, ILA), and (b) degree of decentralization (Index of Lexical Decentralization, ILD). The first index is a measure of the *total number* of words (types) provided by a subject in the test – this may be calculated to represent either all the included stimuli (ILA) or only a single stimulus (Stimulus Index of Lexical Amplitude, SILA). The second index is a measure of the *accumulated relative decentralization* of a speaker's vocabulary, i.e., the number of words provided that are *not common* to the community – this may also be calculated to represent either all the included stimuli (ILD) or only a single stimulus (Stimulus

Table 2: Number of tokens and types by cognitive stimulus.

Stimulus	Tokens	Types
01. The human body	1659	272
02. Clothing	1434	255
03. Parts of a house (not including furniture)	1217	128
04. Furniture in the home	1226	194
05. Food	1729	313
06. Objects laid on the table for a meal	1190	190
07. The kitchen and kitchenware	1297	281
08. The school: furniture and materials	1422	284
09. Heating, lighting, and means of ventilating a space	850	184
10. The city	1461	376
11. The countryside	1377	467
12. Means of transport	1278	177
13. Agricultural and garden tasks	919	254
14. Animals	1752	300
15. Games and entertainment	1306	350
16. Trades and professions	1519	354
17. Money and economy	1250	403
18. Internet and computers	1238	439
19. Colors	1430	187
20. The sea	1493	452
TOTAL	2707	5860

Index of Lexical Decentralization, SILD). The adapted hypothesis is that the more words a subject provides, the higher the probability that their lexical production will become decentralized, meaning they will provide less frequent words that are more technical, specialized or sophisticated (e.g., terms more typical of the literary or academic spheres). A strong and positive correlation is thus expected between lexical amplitude and lexical decentralization.

In order to prove this correlation, we used the two lexical variables ILA and ILD to analyze the data. In this study, we have considered lexical amplitude (LA) as the overall number of words provided for the 20 stimuli, and lexical decentralization (LD) as a quality of the vocabulary provided by an informant for a single stimulus, describing its degree of compatibility with the vocabulary proposed by other subjects for the same stimulus (SILD, described above). The SILD, also taking values in the interval [0,1], allows the vocabulary produced by an individual to be described through the synthesis of the degrees of non-prototypicality of all the words they provided for a stimulus. This index was calculated using the computer-based program *DispoCen*, created for this purpose by Ávila-Muñoz, Sánchez-Sáez and Odishelidze (2021). This program is used to obtain the ILD of a given set. The SILD will be closer to 1 if a speaker provides a high number of words for a stimulus that does not coincide with those provided by the rest of the speakers in the sample. In the case of the opposite, meaning if a speaker provides a lower number of such words, the SILD will be closer to 0.

As expected, the ILA and the ILD correlate, since the more words an individual provides, the higher the probability that a subset of these will not coincide with those provided by the other speakers. This correlation results from the availability of each term to the individual, as more accessible terms will be provided first, leading these terms to occur most frequently throughout the sample (note that the ILD reflects the decentralization of the speaker's vocabulary irrespective of its size, whereas the ILA is strongly size dependent, representing the overall number of words provided by a speaker for all the stimuli).

As shown in Figure 1, a positive, strong and significant correlation was observed between the two variables (Rho = 0.951, R^2 = 0.904, sig. = 0.000, level of sig. = 0.01, N = 72). This figure is in fact a statistical reflection of the above-mentioned well-established qualitative constant in linguistics: cognitive structures, or prototypes, contain a nucleus of lexical elements that are interrelated as well as closely related to the concept of reference (such as *arm* and *mouth* in connection with the human body, or *eagle* and *sparrow* in connection with birds); as we distance ourselves from the center of the lexical spectrum and, thus, move away from frequently used, very characteristic elements, the elements become

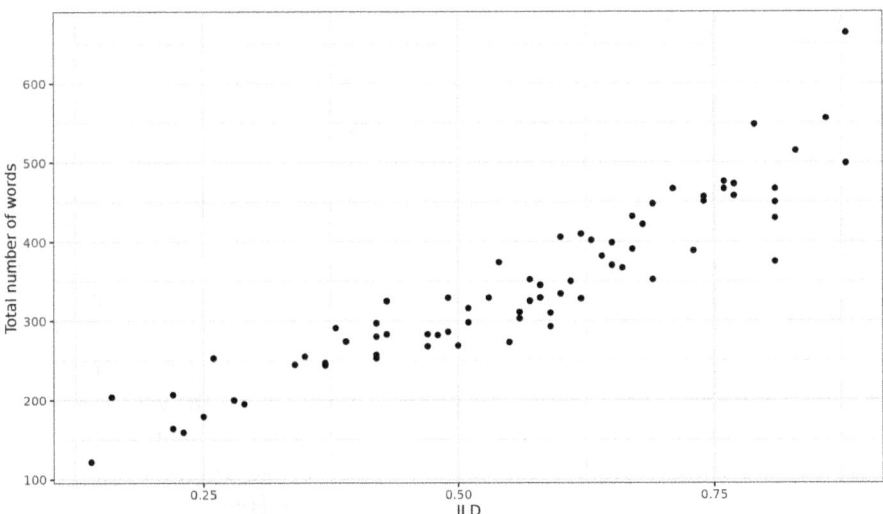

Figure 1: Correlation between the number of words provided and their decentralization (R^2 = 0.904).

less frequent in use and therefore less prototypical and increasingly decentralized (such as *steatopygia* and *lipodystrophy* in connection with the human body, or *ostrich* and *gannet* in connection with birds).

4.3 Corrected lexical values: The gradation of nuclearity

The two lexical variables discussed thus far are considered adequate with regard to our second objective – obtaining objective measures of lexical breadth. However, their calculation does not account for the internal structure of the vocabulary provided by a speaker for a stimulus and, thus, only serves as a quantitative measure of their lexical breadth. Considering the individual lists, it is reasonable to assume that, when a stimulus is proposed to an informant during the test, they will move through their lexical network, picking up nuclear words first and progressively moving away from the nucleus along paths produced by various associations. Hence, the speaker moves away from the access point explicitly proposed by the prototype label.

Within this assumption, the underlying problem emerges relating to distance to the prototype. On the one hand, a particular word may be closely related to the prototype but not generally accessible (e.g., due to its technical specificity), meaning it will indicate a high degree of lexical breadth. On the other hand, association processes will likely lead to the non-provision of words that form part of the nucleus, with words that are only indirectly related being provided instead, which are hence irrelevant in the determination of the individual's lexical breadth for the category of reference.

Though the problem is irrelevant when quantifying the lexical availability of a particular word, clearly identifying and distinguishing both situations is vital for the expression of a speaker's lexical breadth through their degree of decentralization (ILD). We have not yet found a way to address this problem without adding more information to the model, i.e., by considering the researchers' assessment of the compatibility of each word with the prototype of reference.

Beyond the constants deduced from the individuals' lexical structures and the fact that the Index of Lexical Decentralization (ILD) builds on the concept of gradation of compatibility – as described above in Section 1 –, the vocabulary provided by the speakers is quite varied, consisting of nuclear elements (N-1) and the following three types of elements, each group distanced progressively further from the nucleus: denotational associations (N-5), derivatives, which are simply repetitions of already mentioned elements (N-25), and individual associations (N-0) (see Ávila-Muñoz and Villena-Ponsoda 2010: 183–201).

The nucleus consists of the elements that are most available to the speakers in the sample – i.e., the terms appearing most frequently throughout and most often in the first positions of the lists. These elements likely belong to the collective prototype from the point of view of semantics, which means it is highly probable that they will be provided by the speakers (the human body: *head, leg, hand*). Thus, they may be defined as nuclear elements (N-1), irrespective of their individual degree of decentralization. Although associations (N-5) do form part of the prototype, they are not considered nuclear and stem rather from connotations (evocations, associations, etc.) of the denotations of nuclear elements. They are therefore common to the group of speakers and not individual (the human body: *taste, touch, amylase, lipase*). Derivatives (N-25) imply a quantitative or qualitative increase in already mentioned vocabulary (the kitchen and kitchenware: *spoon, wooden spoon, dessert spoon, baby spoon*). Although these words belong to the nucleus, they are an effect, or rather, an artefact of the test and contribute little to an individual's degree of lexical breadth. Finally, individual associations (N-0) are elements that are neither included in the nucleus nor directly related to the prototype. They are the product of evocations or associations stemming from the references of nuclear elements and not their denotations (for connotations of references see Cruse 1986). The relevance of individual associations in the study of the available lexicon for a conceptual category and individual lexical breadth is highly debatable, though they may well be of great interest in the analysis of psycholinguistic processes.

In this manner, the vocabulary provided by each speaker can be divided into four groups corresponding to this classification: nuclear elements (N-1), communal associations (N-5), derivatives (N-25) and individual associations (N-0). Each denomination corresponds to its importance in the constitution of the individual lists and, thus, to the value that should be given to the lexical elements in each group: 1, 0.5, 0.25 and 0.0, respectively.

The calculation of the two indexes described above in Section 2 should therefore be modified – based on the researchers' own assessment of each word and by assigning them one of the four values: 1.0, 0.5, 0.25, 0.0 – to account for the effects of these differences both on quantity (ILA) and degree of decentralization (ILD). This results in two new measures, the Corrected Index of Lexical Amplitude (COILA) and the Corrected Index of Lexical Decentralization (COILD). The COILA can be calculated via the following addition:

$$COILA = N1 + (N5 * 0.5) + (N25 * 0.25) + (N0 * 0)$$

More specifically, if $n(x)$ is the value of compatibility (1, 0.5, 0.25, 0, as assigned by the researcher) of a certain word x with the prototype, the corrected degree of specificity of this word can be calculated as the intersection of the word's decentralization and the assigned relevance. In fuzzy set theory, this intersection can be computed as a compatibility value of

$$(1 - m_c(x)) \cdot n(x)$$

Therefore, a word will suggest high specificity when it shows non-nuclearity (i.e. when $m_c(x)$ is near 0) but is still closely related to the prototype (i.e. when $n(x)$ is near 1). Through a process such as the one described above, specificity can easily be integrated for each speaker

$$\text{COILD} = 1 - \prod (1 - k \cdot n(x) \cdot (1 - m_c(x)))$$

and then normalized with a suitable value of k.

Table 3 shows a classification of the speakers' production according to their scores in the four lexical measures discussed. Two groups are indicated based on the speakers' scores of decentralization – group 0 (IDL > COILD) and group 1 (ILD < COILD). Group 0 is highlighted in gray. Inversely, as expected, ILA is always higher than COILA.

Table 3: Initial and corrected lexical variables organized in increasing order of COILD.

Speaker	N-0	N-25	N-5	N-1	ILA	COILA	ILD	COILD
64	5.00	5.00	1.00	111.00	122	112.750	.14	.21
72	0.00	6.00	12.00	149.00	164	156.500	.22	.26
66	12.00	4.00	16.00	127.00	159	136.000	.23	.28
56	7.00	2.00	2.00	193.00	204	194.500	.16	.28
61	20.00	11.00	6.00	163.00	200	168.750	.28	.31
58	5.00	5.00	12.00	185.00	207	192.250	.22	.32
48	14.00	1.00	15.00	149.00	179	156.750	.25	.32
98	8.00	12.00	17.00	158.00	195	169.500	.29	.33
35	3.00	3.00	5.00	242.00	253	245.250	.26	.40
50	20.00	7.00	21.00	197.00	245	209.250	.34	.41
69	15.00	1.00	6.00	269.00	291	272.250	.38	.43
60	117.00	.00	40.00	172.00	329	192.000	.49	.44
2	6.00	16.00	16.00	209.00	247	221.000	.37	.45
65	3.00	3.00	21.00	217.00	244	228.250	.37	.46
97	17.00	11.00	21.00	234.00	283	247.250	.43	.48
51	11.00	.00	20.00	224.00	255	234.000	.35	.49
1	25.00	3.00	20.00	232.00	280	242.750	.42	.49
39	6.00	11.00	7.00	229.00	253	230.250	.42	.50
26	8.00	5.00	7.00	254.00	274	258.750	.39	.51
3	12.00	.00	18.00	227.00	257	236.000	.42	.51

Table 3 (continued)

Speaker	N-0	N-25	N-5	N-1	Iʟᴀ	Cᴏɪʟᴀ	Iʟᴅ	Cᴏɪʟᴅ
59	13.00	23.00	13.00	219.00	268	231.250	.47	.51
30	58.00	10.00	30.00	205.00	303	222.500	.56	.53
29	4.00	8.00	17.00	268.00	297	278.500	.42	.53
4	.00	7.00	15.00	303.00	325	312.250	.43	.55
36	14.00	5.00	16.00	247.00	282	256.250	.48	.56
37	15.00	3.00	29.00	222.00	269	237.250	.50	.56
75	14.00	11.00	18.00	273.00	316	284.750	.51	.57
40	8.00	2.00	15.00	258.00	283	266.000	.47	.57
9	45.00	.00	22.00	206.00	273	217.000	.55	.57
42	7.00	8.00	9.00	262.00	286	268.500	.49	.58
53	13.00	5.00	37.00	243.00	298	262.750	.51	.59
47	10.00	7.00	31.00	263.00	311	280.250	.56	.60
63	51.00	8.00	28.00	263.00	350	279.000	.61	.60
8	20.00	23.00	20.00	266.00	329	281.750	.53	.61
32	37.00	12.00	19.00	257.00	325	288.500	.57	.61
46	14.00	31.00	20.00	245.00	310	262.750	.59	.61
45	19.00	11.00	31.00	267.00	328	285.250	.62	.63
67	11.00	2.00	40.00	321.00	374	341.500	.54	.64
71	14.00	2.00	32.00	245.00	293	261.500	.59	.64
74	3.00	35.00	12.00	279.00	329	293.750	.58	.64
41	18.00	17.00	19.00	280.00	334	293.750	.60	.65
28	12.00	13.00	22.00	298.00	345	312.250	.58	.66
55	12.00	4.00	26.00	310.00	352	324.000	.57	.67
70	32.00	13.00	14.00	351.00	410	361.250	.62	.67
52	26.00	15.00	38.00	291.00	370	313.750	.65	.68
24	10.00	22.00	28.00	307.00	367	326.500	.66	.69
77	26.00	6.00	21.00	349.00	402	361.000	.63	.69
33	38.00	26.00	29.00	296.00	389	317.000	.73	.70
76	20.00	109.00	27.00	219.00	375	259.750	.81	.70
49	20.00	4.00	52.00	306.00	382	333.000	.64	.70
22	16.00	19.00	17.00	347.00	399	360.250	.65	.70
34	9.00	1.00	19.00	377.00	406	386.750	.60	.72
99	21.00	23.00	20.00	288.00	352	303.750	.69	.72
6	20.00	6.00	18.00	388.00	432	398.500	.67	.74
27	10.00	2.00	17.00	362.00	391	371.000	.67	.75
31	13.00	8.00	28.00	399.00	448	415.000	.69	.75
96	60.00	7.00	60.00	349.00	476	380.750	.76	.76
38	10.00	4.00	19.00	389.00	422	399.500	.68	.76
5	18.00	18.00	31.00	400.00	467	420.000	.71	.77
68	38.00	49.00	50.00	313.00	450	350.250	.81	.77

Table 3 (continued)

Speaker	N-0	N-25	N-5	N-1	Ila	Coila	Ild	Coild
73	56.00	41.00	69.00	301.00	467	345.750	.81	.79
25	29.00	27.00	41.00	333.00	430	360.250	.81	.79
21	11.00	17.00	25.00	398.00	451	414.750	.74	.79
23	12.00	21.00	31.00	394.00	458	414.750	.77	.80
13	24.00	34.00	36.00	379.00	473	405.500	.77	.81
43	13.00	2.00	20.00	422.00	457	432.500	.74	.82
62	6.00	12.00	27.00	422.00	467	438.500	.76	.83
15	20.00	20.00	28.00	480.00	548	499.000	.79	.84
14	57.00	20.00	52.00	427.00	556	458.000	.86	.85
10	70.00	36.00	49.00	344.00	499	377.500	.88	.85
19	27.00	5.00	36.00	447.00	515	466.250	.83	.87
12	44.00	5.00	49.00	566.00	664	591.750	.88	.91
Average	20.6	12.8	24.38	285.9	343.7	301.5	0.56	0.61
Group 0	54.0	30.3	43.2	292.2	420.4	322.1	0.74	0.71
Group 1	14.6	9.7	21.0	284.6	330.0	298.0	0.52	0.59
Sig.	0.000	0.000	0.000	No sig.	0.007	No sig.	0.000	0.032

Note: Mean differences between both groups for each variable are shown. Speakers whose ILD > COILD are highlighted in gray.

It is to be recalled, firstly, that the two indexes of decentralization (ILD, COILD) are calculated for each informant on the basis of the aggregation of the degree of decentralization of each word provided and, secondly, that communal associations (N-5), derivatives (N-25) and individual associations (N-0) are either associations that are common to the sample or simply repetitions or variants of elements already included in the nuclear group (N-1).

After the normalization process, the ILD should therefore generally be lower than the COILD, since the former assigns all the terms provided by a speaker the same value, i.e. $N = 1$, whereas the latter considers only the nuclear elements (N-1) in full, and assigns the other elements their respective lower values (N-5, N-25, N-0). In other words, the ILD includes the vocabulary from the groups N-5, N-25 and N-0, considering them as singular units equivalent in weight and relevance to the nuclear vocabulary in N-1, whereas the COILD does not consider these non-nuclear elements as singular units, since they are simply associations, repetitions or variants of previously mentioned words.

As a consequence, ILD is likely to oversize the speaker's lexical breadth due to the impossibility of ascertaining the relative centralization of the vocabulary provided, i.e. its relative proximity to the nucleus, since speakers who mention a high number of words marked as N-0 will obtain incorrect higher scores. Conversely, COILD is able to overcome this problem through the adjustment process that assigns lower values to these elements, thus causing an increase in the scores of the other speakers during the normalization process.

As described above, the consideration of the N-1, N-5, N-25 and N-0 sets results in the Corrected Index of Lexical decentralization (COILD) by modifying the original measure for decentralization (ILD), scaling the four groups by factors 1, 0.5, 0.25 and 0 as a previous step to the aggregation. In this way, it is possible to distinguish between words closely related to the nucleus and words less closely related. With this simple addition to the calculation, the individual's lexical spectrum can be adjusted.

For individuals whose ILD > COILD, it is assumed that they will have provided elements in the non-nuclear N-5, N-25 and N-0 groups that are truly distinct from those included in the nuclear N-1 group. This may serve as an indication of a special ability in the individual to provide original lexical associations for the proposed stimuli, although it should be noted here that – as explained above and specifically in Section 3.1 – the index itself (the ILD and, thus, its correction, the COILD) also assigns elements different scores depending on their compatibility with their set.

4.4 Nuclearity and displacement

The lexical variables discussed show a positive correlation, as shown in Table 4. Table 5 shows Euclidean similarity and distance, providing an idea of the extent of the distance between the variables: the higher the bilateral coefficient is in the cells, the less distance there is between them and the stronger is their relation, and vice versa. The behavior of the variables shows the connection between the COILA and N-1 as well as the advantages of using the corrected indexes.

Table 4: Spearman correlation between the initial and corrected lexical variables (N = 72).

	ILA	N-1	N-5	N-25	N-0	ILD	COILD
N-1	.926						
N-5	.655	.457					
N-25	.404	.278	.242				
N-0	.484	.240	.619	.266			
ILD	.951	.831	.710	.494	.544		
COILD	.965	.910	.640	.424	.419	.973	
COILA	.952	.993	.511	.324	.289	.874	.940

Note: All correlations are significant. In bold: $p = 0.01$, rest: $p = 0.05$.

In line with expectations, the original (ILD) and corrected (COILD) indexes of decentralization are strongly related (0.974), yet their relationship varies with the measures describing the size of the provided lists (ILA, COILA). As stated above (21–22), it would be logical for the ILD to be lower than the COILD, due to adaptation of centrality to decentralization for each word and the subsequent normalization. However, as also shown in Figure 2, some speakers record higher values in the original index (ILD) than in its corrected version (COILD). This means that these speakers ($n = 11$; highlighted in gray in Table 3; also refer to Table 6) constitute the most productive group of individuals, since they do the least to limit their capacities of lexical association, derivation and variation.

Table 5: Euclidean similarity between the lexical variables.

	ILD	COILD	COILA	ILA	N-1	N-5	N-25
ILD							
COILD	.974						
COILA	.844	.919					
ILA	.926	.942	.966				
N-1	.801	.891	1.000	.940			
N-5	.684	.599	.473	.639	.399		
N-25	.407	.272	.065	.220	.000	.207	
N-0	.363	.204	.094	.335	.039	.584	.061

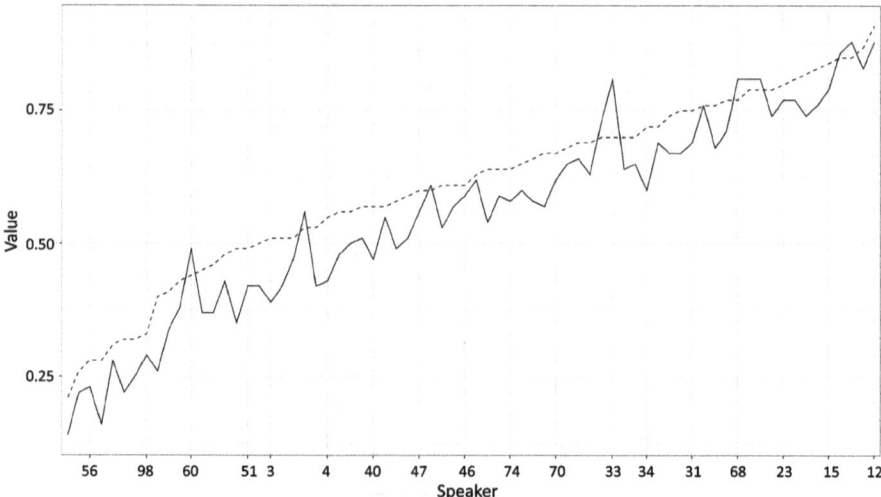

Figure 2: A comparison of the values of decentralization recorded for each speaker, showing both the original (ILD) and the corrected (COILD) indexes.

The speakers who proved most productive are shown in Table 6. Though they provided a high quantity of terms per stimulus, many of these were associations or derivatives, leading to a lower COILD than expected. It is interesting that these speakers not only expand their lists by providing associations or derivatives, but that they also belong to the group of speakers mentioning the most nuclear elements, with only four individuals recording values below the average (highlighted in gray in Table 6). These four speakers provide a relatively low number of nuclear elements and compensate by providing a higher number of non-nuclear elements (see Figures 3 and 4 below).

Table 6: Speakers whose ILD > COILD.

Speaker	N-0	N-25	N-5	Non-Nuclear	N-1	Ila	CoilA	Ild	Coild
60	117.00	0.00	40.00	157	172.00	329	192.000	.49	.44
30	58.00	10.00	30.00	98	205.00	303	222.500	.56	.53
63	51.00	8.00	28.00	87	263.00	350	279.000	.61	.60
76	20.00	109.00	27.00	156	219.00	375	259.750	.81	.70
33	38.00	26.00	29.00	93	296.00	389	317.000	.73	.70
96	60.00	7.00	60.00	127	349.00	476	380.750	.76	.76
68	38.00	49.00	50.00	137	313.00	450	350.250	.81	.77
25	29.00	27.00	41.00	97	333.00	430	360.250	.81	.79
73	56.00	41.00	69.00	166	301.00	467	345.750	.81	.79
10	70.00	36.00	49.00	155	344.00	499	377.500	.88	.85
14	57.00	20.00	52.00	129	427.00	556	458.000	.86	.85

Note: *Non-Nuclear* is the sum of the non-nuclear word sets (N-5, N-25, N-0) mentioned by an informant

The COILD thus discerns non-nuclear speakers, who produce a high number of the non-nuclear N-5, N-25 and N-0 elements (Figure 3, x axis) independent of their ILD (Figure 3, y axis), with the individual lists becoming more repetitive in line with the decrease in COILD.

These results corroborate the hypothesis regarding the existence of non-nuclear speakers (group 0, marked with black squares in Figure 3). They are characterized by the provision of associations and derivatives (N-5, N-25, N-0) but differ in terms of total number of words provided. Nuclear speakers, on the other hand, (group 1, marked with white dots in Figure 3) limit their associative and/or derivative capacities and focus on providing nuclear elements (N-1).

The relationship between the COILD and non-nuclearity is, in fact, not linear but curved. At first it is positive: the COILD rises in line with the provision of non-nuclear elements up to a score of around 0.75. However, the relationship levels

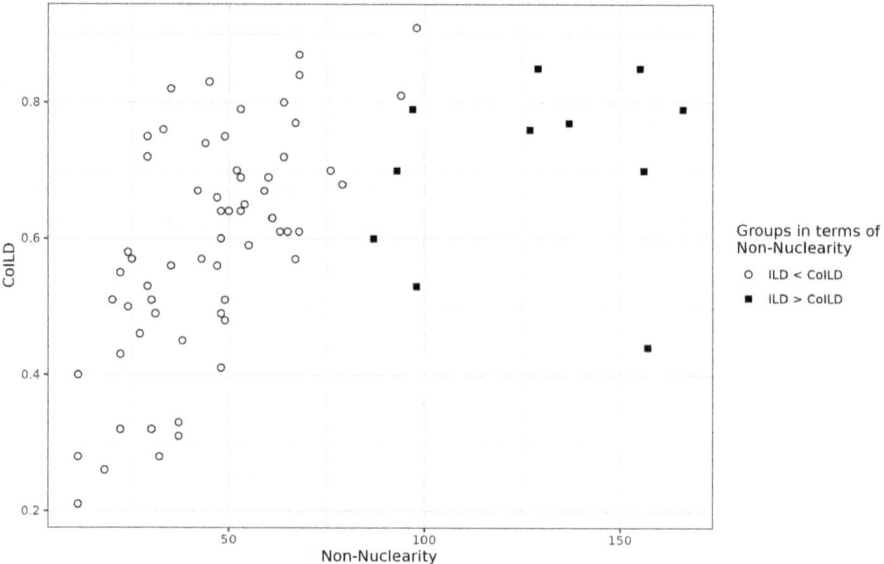

Figure 3: Dispersion of the subjects in terms of non-nuclearity (N-0 + N-25 + N-5).

Table 7: A curve fit estimate of the correlation between the COILD and non-nuclearity. Summary of the model and estimations of the parameters.

Equation	Summary of the model					Estimations of the parameters			
	R^2	F	df1	df2	Sig.	Constant	b1	b2	b3
Linear	.272	26.175	1	70	.000	.470	.002		
Cubic	.436	17.552	3	68	.000	.209	.013	−9.63E-005	2.28E-007
S	.456	58.792	1	70	.000	−.237	−12.158		

off at this point and remains constant, showing a tendency to decrease (S-curve). Table 7 shows a comparison of the linear and the alternative curved models.

The Scurve model accounts for 45.6% of the relationship between the two variables, as opposed to the linear model, which only accounts for 27.2%. Figure 4 compares the fit of the three curves.

The number of words provided by a speaker for a given stimulus during an association test increases exponentially over the time spent on that stimulus. Initially, the speaker provides only nuclear elements. However, at a certain point, this process is discontinued and either looped displacement (N5 + N25 + N0) or deviation (N25 + N0) can be observed, as depicted in Figure 5.

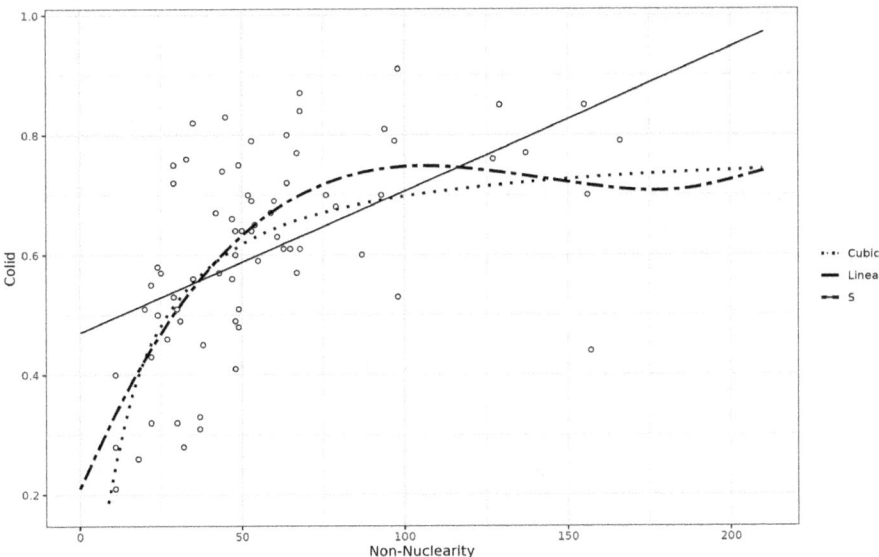

Figure 4: A comparison of the linear, cubic and S-shaped fits between the COILD and non-nuclearity.

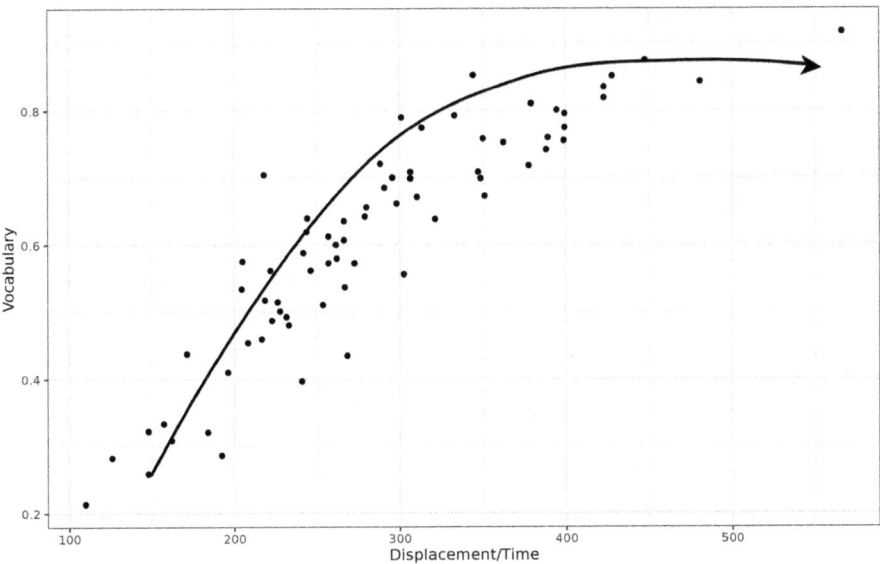

Figure 5: A model of the displacement of nuclear vocabulary during a test.

This model produces results that can be considered from different perspectives. For example, the relationship between the COILD – the most representative variable of the four developed – and the degree of non-nuclearity of a lexical production is curvilineal, the reason being explained by the above model of displacement.

The notion is that speakers who display a notable degree of lexical breadth (by providing both general and specialized terms) develop the tendency to associate elements to the nuclear vocabulary of each category. The extent of the relationship of these elements with the nucleus varies (see Figure 6); some do relate and are connotations or associations of the denotations of nuclear elements (N5), whereas others are simply digressions or derivatives stemming from nuclear elements (N25) or individual associations that have no denotational relation to the stimulus (N0). During the test, some speakers do indeed develop this tendency towards providing nonnuclear elements (i.e., displacement). A number of these speakers persists in this way and displays high values on the *y* axis as a result (i.e. displacement through deviation; see Figure 6). Others correct this displacement at some point and return to providing nuclear elements (i.e. looped displacement). The hypothesis is that, during displacement, (a) the first group of speakers provides derivatives or individual associations (N25, N0), whereas the second also provides communal associations (N5), and (b) the second group puts a stop to the displacement, independent of its content, and returns to providing nuclear elements.

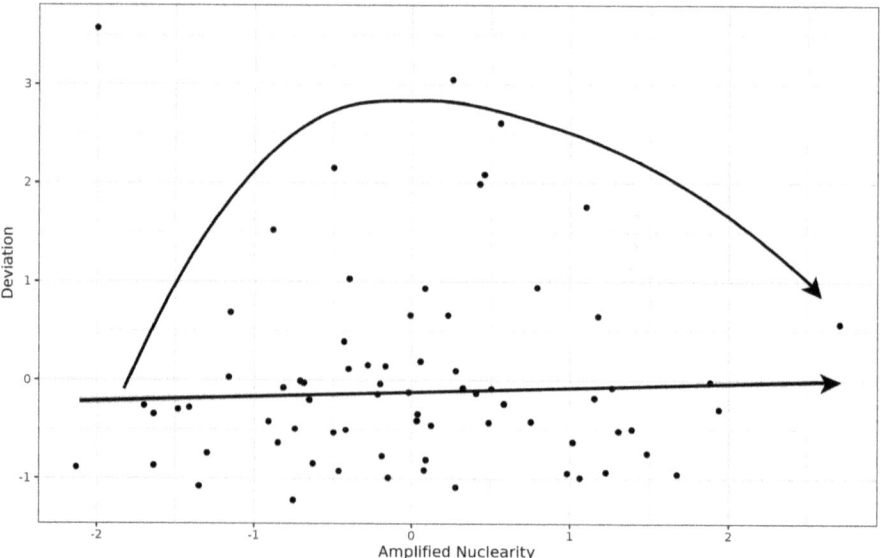

Figure 6: A model of deviation and amplified nuclearity regarding lexical variation in the speech community's available lexicon.

Figure 6 considers this difference. Deviation (vertical axis) measures only derivatives and individual associations (N25, N0), while nuclearity (N-1; horizontal axis) is amplified to include denotational associations (N5).

The hypothesis that relates deviation and amplified nuclearity is corroborated, as shown in Table 8. Speakers with the highest deviation provide the most deviating elements (N-25, N-0) relative to the quantity of nuclear vocabulary (N-1) and the total number of words provided (ILA).

Table 8: A comparison of speakers showing displacement and deviation.

Speaker	ILA	N-1	N-5	N-25	N-0	Nuclear.	Displac.	Dev.	Vertical Axis
25	430	333	41	27	29	374	97	56	.97076
63	350	263	28	8	51	291	87	59	.75594
33	389	296	29	26	38	325	93	64	1.19530
96	476	349	60	7	60	409	127	67	.70239
30	303	205	30	10	58	235	98	68	1.23573
14	556	427	52	20	57	479	129	77	.98101
68	450	313	50	49	38	363	137	87	2.20044
73	467	301	69	41	56	370	166	97	2.34446
10	499	344	49	36	70	393	155	106	2.46100
60	329	172	40	0	117	212	157	117	2.34428
76	375	219	27	109	20	246	156	129	4.71905

Note: Vertical Axis refers to values of deviation in the model in Figure 7.

We have now established a new model capable of generating mathematical indexes that can be used – in addition to those existing already – to determine individual lexical richness in a more appropriate and precise manner. The four indexes used in this study to measure a speaker's lexical breadth provide an easily understandable framework that can be interpreted in two complementary ways: as a methodological model – i.e., a model of the method – and as a real model – i.e., a model of the speech community.

With the aim of clarifying the concepts and measures presented above, they are detailed and described individually in Table 9.

Table 9: Summary of concepts and measures.

Concept/Measure		Description/Calculation	Features/Comments
Center of Interest	CI	A given concept (the human body, clothing, etc.) as the stimulus for an association test	A fuzzy set of lexical elements whose distance from the prototype's center is a matter of element/set compatibility
Lexical Availability Index	LAI	Weighted index of lexical size and rank order in a list of available vocabulary	Disregards re-entering processes observed in some informants during an association test
Index of Centrality	IC	For a word in a CI: a measure of its estimated compatibility with the CI based on its position in the lexical network For a word in a test: the aggregate of its IC for every CI	Modulated as a fuzzy set; expresses the compatibility of the word with the stimulus
Fuzzy Expected Value	FEV	A fuzzy set theory tool that allows characteristic degrees of element/set compatibility to be obtained	Allows for the characterization of limits for a word's degree of belonging to a set and provides parameters to identify these (i.e. x is very, hardly, etc. characteristic of a set)
Lexical Amplitude	LA	Total number of words in an individual's word list associated with n CIs	Expressed through the ILA
Index of Lexical Amplitude	ILA	Total number of words in an individual's word list associated with n CIs	Overall number of words provided by an individual for n stimuli, regardless of their degree of centrality
Stimulus Index of Lexical Amplitude	SILA	Number of words in an individual's word list associated with a particular CI	Number of words provided by an individual for a particular stimulus, regardless of their degree of centrality
Corrected Index of Lexical Amplitude	COILA	Weighted number of words based on researchers' assessment of their centrality	Weighted ILA measure; considers each word's rank order; prevents oversized ILA scores

Table 9 (continued)

Concept/ Measure		Description/Calculation	Features/Comments
Lexical Decentralization	LD	Degree of a word's compatibility with the set of words for a particular CI	Based on the word's distance to the set's center as established by the words provided by a sample of n speakers
Index of Lexical Decentralization	ILD	Weighted index of lexical specificity, reflects decentrality and compatibility of an individual's production with the set, irrespective of vocabulary size	Measures the accumulated relative decentralization of a speaker's vocabulary, i.e., the number of words provided in the test that are not common to the community
Stimulus Index of Lexical Decentralization	SILD	Weighted index of lexical specificity for a particular CI	Measures the relative decentralization of a speaker's vocabulary for a particular stimulus
Corrected Index of Lexical Decentralization	COILD	Corrected ILD based on researchers' assessment of the relevance of words	Corrected specificity of an individual word; can be calculated as the intersection of the word's decentralization and the assigned relevance

5 Discussion and conclusions

In view of the results obtained, we can conclude that association tests are an efficient method of accessing individual lexical breadth, and, although limitations were observed, we have succeeded in developing a set of measures that appropriately describe lexical breadth. For more immediately interpretable results, we propose that the instructions given at the beginning of an association test should require participants to provide fewer individual associations (N-0) and, especially, fewer derivatives, which simply constitute repetitions of already mentioned elements (N-25). If the aim of a study, however, is to obtain the available lexicon of a speech community and to analyze the differences between various groups – by determining the fields of experience occurring most frequently in speakers' daily lives, rather than representing conceptual networks by describing the nature of the lexical connections –, methodologically limiting the provision of nuclear vocabulary (N-1) and denotational associations (N-5) would seem advisable. By avoiding such deviation, an association test would result in a more precise measurement of the concept we call decentralization, meaning the models developed for this study would be more likely to provide accurate predictions of individual lexical breadth.

Thanks to the model presented here, the notion of "lexical richness" now no longer simply refers to a general idea of how many words a certain speaker passively knows or is actively capable of using in a specific context, whenever a certain topic arises. Instead, the proposed conceptualization of "lexical breadth" intends to capture the idea of a vocabulary with weighted size or extension. From this perspective, the relevance of each word does not depend on its frequency or its position in a rank list but is determined by its relative distance from the center of the prototype corresponding to the center of interest (CI) for which it was provided.

In order to construct the proposed conceptualization of "lexical breadth," lexical availability measures (ILA, COILA) have been traditionally used. These two measures are based on the individual average of the words provided during the test and allow for the calculation of the degree of coincidence between the words provided by an individual and by the rest of the informants in a sample. In the model proposed here, indexes of decentralization are used (ILD, COILD), which are built on concepts and tools from fuzzy set theory. A model computing a speaker's lexical decentralization shows the amplitude of his or her available vocabulary (i.e., the vocabulary ready to be used when a particular topic arises in conversation), since, as proved in this chapter, the concepts of decentralization, specificity and breadth are closely related.

Regarding the fuzzy operators proposed here (the compliment operator, probabilistic sum and product), these allow for model complement, union and intersection operations and facilitate a more precise calculation of both decentralization and specificity. Due to a lack of further research on the subject, simply the most straightforward and usual operators were chosen. Thorough research on the models underlying this study will have to be conducted in future in order to determine which are the most adequate operators.

References

Aitchinson, Jean. 2012. *Words in the mind. An introduction to the mental lexicon*. 4th edn. Oxford: Wiley and Blackwell.

Ávila, Raúl. 1988. Lengua hablada y estrato social: un acercamiento lexicoestadístico. *Nueva Revista de Filología Hispánica* 36(1). 131–148. doi:10.24201/nrfh.v36i1.668.

Ávila-Muñoz, Antonio-Manuel. 2016. Can speakers' virtual lexical richness be calculated? Individual and social determining factors. *Spanish in Context* 13(2). 285307. doi:10.1075/sic.13.2.06avi.

Ávila-Muñoz, Antonio-Manuel & Juan-Andrés Villena-Ponsoda (eds.). 2010. *Variación social del léxico disponible en la ciudad de Málaga*. Malaga: Sarriá.

Ávila-Muñoz, Antonio-Manuel & José-María Sánchez-Sáez. 2011. La posición de los vocablos en el cálculo del índice de disponibilidad léxica: procesos de reentrada en las listas del léxico disponible de la ciudad de Málaga. *Estudios de Lingüística. Universidad de Alicante (ELUA)* 25. 45–74. doi:10.14198/ELUA2011.25.02.

Ávila-Muñoz, Antonio-Manuel & José-María Sánchez-Sáez. 2014. Fuzzy sets and prototype theory. Representational of cognitive community structures based on lexical availability tests. *Review of Cognitive Linguistics* 12(1). 133–159. doi: https://doi.org/10.1075/rcl.12.1.05avi

Ávila-Muñoz, Antonio-Manuel, Inmaculada Santos-Díaz & Ester Trigo-Ibáñez. 2020. Análisis léxico-cognitivo de la influencia de los medios de comunicación en las percepciones de universitarios españoles ante la COVID-19. *Círculo de Lingüística Aplicada a la Comunicación* 84. 85–95. http://dx.doi.org/10.5209/clac.70701.

Ávila-Muñoz, Antonio-Manuel, José-María Sánchez-Sáez & Nina Odishelidze. 2021. *Dispocen*. Mucho más que un programa para el cálculo de la disponibilidad léxica. *Estudios de Lingüística de la Universidad de Alicante (*ELUA) 35. 9–36. doi: 10.14198/ELUA2021.35.1.

Bowles, Melissa A. 2011. Measuring implicit and explicit linguistic knowledge: What can heritage language learners contribute? *Studies in second language acquisition* 33(2). 247–271.https:// doi:10.1017/S0272263110000756.

Bowles, Melissa A., Rebecca J. Adams, & Paul D. Toth. 2014. A comparison of L2–L2 and L2–heritagelearner interactions in Spanish language classrooms. *The Modern Language Journal* 98(2). 497–517. https://doi.org/10.1111/modl.12086

Castañeda-Jiménez, Gabriela &Scott Jarvis. 2013. Exploring lexical diversity in second language Spanish. In Kimberly L. Geeslin (ed.), *The handbook of Spanish second language acquisition*, 498–513. Hoboken, NJ: Wiley-Blackwell.

Checa-García, Irene & Laura Marqués-Pascual. 2020. Where are Heritage Learners of Spanish relatively positioned when it comes to the lexicon? Lexical Richness Measures in Spanish heritage, native, and L2 learners. *Paper presented at the 49th Annual LASSO (Linguistic Association of the SouthWest) Meeting*. Virtual Meeting.

Craig, Colette (ed.). 1986. *Noun Classes and Categorization*. Amsterdam/Philadelphia: John Benjamins Publishing Company.

Cruse, David A. 1986. *Lexical semantics*. Cambridge: Cambridge University Press.

Cutillas, Laia,Liliana Tolchinsky, Elisa Rosado, E. & Joan Perera. 2014. Indicators of lexical growth throughout age, genre and modality for a Catalan L1 corpus. In Ana Díaz Negrillo & Francisco Javier Díaz Pérez (eds.), *Specialization and variation in language corpora*, 161–188. Bern: Peter Lang.

Daller, Helmut, James Milton, & Jeanine Treffers-Daller (eds.). 2007. *Modelling and assessing vocabulary knowledge*. Cambridge: Cambridge University Press.

Davies, Mark. 2006. *A Frequency Dictionary of Spanish: Core Vocabulary for Learners*. London: Routledge.

Dell, Gary S. & Padraig G. O'Seaghdha. 1992. Stages of lexical access in language production. *Cognition* 42(1–3). 287–314. doi: 10.1016/0010-0277.

Ellis, Rod 1994. *The study of second language acquisition*. Oxford: Oxford University Press.

Fairclough, Marta & Anel Garza. 2018. The lexicon of Spanish heritage language speakers. In Kim Potowski & Javier Muñoz-Basols (eds.), *The Routledge Handbook of Spanish as a Heritage Language*. London: Routledge. https://doi.org/10.4324/9781315735139.

Goldfield Beverly A. & J. Steven Reznick. 1990. Early lexical acquisition: rate, content, and the vocabulary spurt. *Journal of Child Language* 17. 171–183.

Gougenheim, Georges, René Michéa, Pierre Rivenc & Aurélien Sauvageot. 1954. *L'élaboration du français élémentaire. Étude sur l'établissement d'un vocabulaire et d'une grammaire de base*. Paris: Didier.

Hernández-Muñoz, Natividad, Cristina Izura & Andrew W. Ellis. 2006. Cognitive aspects of lexical availability. *European Journal of Cognitive Psychology* 18(5). 730–755. DOI: 10.1080/09541440500339119.

Holland, Dorothy & Naomi Quinn (eds.). 1987. *Cultural Models in Language and Thought*. Cambridge: Cambridge University Press.

Hüllen, Werner & Rainer Schulze (eds.). 1988. *Understanding the Lexicon. Meaning, Sense, and World Knowledge in Lexical Semantics*. Tübingen: Max Niemeyer Verlag.

Jarvis, Scott. 2002. Short texts, -fitting curves and new measures of lexical diversity. *Language Testing* 19. 1–15. doi:10.1191/0265532202lt220oa.

Jarvis, Scott. 2013. Defining and measuring lexical diversity. In Scott Jarvis & Michael Daller (eds.), *Vocabulary Knowledge. Human ratings and automated measures*, 13–44. Amsterdam: John Benjamins.

Jarvis, Scott & Michael Daller (eds.). 2013. *Vocabulary Knowledge: Human Ratings and Automated Measures*. Amsterdam/N.Y.: John Benjamins

Koizumi, Rie, & Yo In'nam. 2012. Effects of text length on lexical diversity measures: Using short texts with less than 200 tokens. *System* 40(4). 554–564. https://doi:10.1016/j.system.2012.10.012

de Kock, Josse. 1983. *Elementos para una estilística computacional*. Madrid: Coloquio.

Lakoff, George. 1987. *Women, Fire, and Dangerous Things. What Categories Reveal about the Mind*. Chicago: University of Chicago Press.

Langacker, Ronald W. 1987. *Foundations of Cognitive Grammar I*. Stanford: Stanford University Press.

Laufer, Batia &Paul Nation. 1995. Vocabulary Size and Use: Lexical Richness in L2 Written Production. *Applied Linguistics* 16. 307–322

Lehmann, Winfred P. (ed.). 1988. *Prototypes in Language and Cognition*. Ann Arbor: Karoma.

Levelt, Willen J. 1989. Lexical Access in Speech Production. In Eric Reuland & Werner Abraham (eds.), *Knowledge and Language*, 241–251. Netherlands: Kluer Academic Publishers.

Levelt, Willen J. 1993. *Speaking: From intention to articulation*. Massachusetts: The MIT Press.

Levelt, Willen J. 2001. Spoken word production: a theory of lexical access. *Proc Natl Acad Sci* 98(23). 13464–13471. doi: 10.1073/pnas.231459498.

Lonsdale, Deryle & Yvon Le Bras. 2009. *A Frequency Dictionary of French: Core Vocabulary for Leaners*. London: Routledge.

López-Chávez & Strassburger-Frías. 1987. Otro cálculo del índice de disponibilidad léxica. *Presente y perspectiva de la investigación computacional en México. Actas del IV Simposio de la Asociación Mexicana de Lingüística Aplicada*. México: UNAM.

López-Morales, Humberto. 1999. *Léxico disponible de Puerto Rico*. Madrid: Arco Libros.

Malvern, David & Bryan James Richards. 2000. Investigating accommodation in language proficiency interviews using a new measure of lexical diversity. *Language Testing* 19. 85–104. doi:10.1191/0265532202lt221oa.

Malvern, David, Bryan James Richards, Ngoni Chipere & Pilar Durán. 2004. *Lexical Diversity and Language Development: Quantification and Assessment*. Hampshire, United Kingdom: Palgrave Macmillan.

Díez-Villoria, Emiliano, Begoña Zubiauz de Pedro, & María Ángeles Mayor Cinca (coords.) 2005. *Estudios sobre la adquisición del lenguaje*. Salamanca: Universidad de Salamanca.

Medin, Douglas & Edward Smith. 1984. Concepts and concept formation. *Annual Review of Psychology* 35. 113–138

Mervis, Carolyn & Eleanor Rosch. 1981. Categorization of natural objects. *Annual Review of Psychology* 32. 89–115.

McCarthy, Philip & Scott Jarvis. 2010. MTLD, vocd-D, and HD-D: A validation study of sophisticated approaches to lexical diversity assessment. *Behavior research methods* 42(2). 381–392.

Montrul, Silvina 2016. Dominance and proficiency in early and late bilingualism. In Carmen Silva-Corvalán & Jeanine Treffers-Daller (eds.), *Language Dominance in Bilinguals: Issues of Measurement and Operationalization*, 15–35. Cambridge: Cambridge University Press. https://doi:10.1017/CBO9781107375345.002.

Neisser, Ulrich. 1987. *Concepts and Conceptual Development. Ecological and Intellectual Factors in Categorization*. Cambridge: Cambridge University Press.

Rosch, Eleanor. 1973. On the internal structure of perceptual and semantic categories. In T. E. Moore (ed.), *Cognitive Development and the Acquisition of Language*, 111–144. New York: Academic Press.

Rosch, Eleanor. 1975. Cognitive representations of semantic categories. *Journal of Experimental Psychology General* 104(3). 192–233.

Rosch, Eleanor. 1977. Human categorization. In N. Warren (ed.). *Studies in Cross-cultural Psychology I*, 1–49. New York: Academic Press.

Rosch, Eleanor. 1978. Principles of categorization. In E. Rosch & B. B. Lloyd (eds.), *Cognition and Categorization*, 27–48. Hillsdale: Lawrence Erlbaum.

Rosch, Eleanor. 1988. Coherences and categorization: a historical view. In F. Kessel (ed.), *The Development of Language and Language Researchers. Essays in Honor of Roger Brown*, 373–392. Hillsdale: Lawrence Erlbaum.

Rosch, Eleanor & Carolyn B. Mervis. 1975. Family resemblances: Studies in the internal structure of categories. *Cognitive Psychology* 7(4). 573–605.

Rosch, Eleanor, Carolyn B. Mervis, Wayne D. Gray, David Johnson & Penny Boyes-Braem. 1976. Basic objects in natural categories. *Cognitive Psychology* 8(3). 382–439.

Rudzka-Ostyn, Brygida. 1988. Semantic extensions into the domain of verbal communication. In B. Rudzka-Ostyn (ed.), *Topics in Cognitive Linguistics*, 507–553. Amsterdam/Philadelphia: John Benjamins Publishing Company.

Samper-Padilla, Juan-Antonio. 1998. Criterios de edición del léxico disponible. *Lingüística* 10. 311–333.

Šifrar-Kalan, Marjana. 2017. La universalidad de los prototipos semánticos en el léxico disponible de español. *Verba Hispanica* 24. 147–165. DOI: 10.4312/vh.24.1.147-165.

Silva-Corvalán, Carmen & Jeanine Treffers-Daller (eds.). 2015. *Language Dominance in Bilinguals: Issues of Measurement and Operationalization*. Cambridge: Cambridge University Press. https://doi:10.1017/CBO9781107375345.002.

Smith, Eduard & Douglas Medin. 1981. *Categories and Concepts* Cambridge: Harvard University Press.

Strassburger-Frías, Carlos & Juan López Chávez. 2000. El diseño de una fórmula matemática para obtener un índice de disponibilidad léxica confiable. *Anuario de Letras: Lingüística y filología* 38. 227251.

Taylor, John. 1989. *Linguistic Categorization. Prototypes in Linguistic Theory*. Oxford: Clarendon Press.

Tsohatzidis, Savas L. (ed.). 2014. *Meanings and Prototypes. Studies on Linguistic Categorization*. London: Routledge.

Verhoeven, Ludo, Jan van Leeuwe, J. & Anne Vermeer. 2011. Vocabulary Growth and Reading Development across the Elementary School Years. *Scientific Studies of Reading* 15(1). 825. doi:10.1080/10888438.2011.536125.

Vermeer, Anne. 2004. The Relation between Lexical Richness and Vocabulary Size in Dutch L1 and L2 Children. In Paul Bogaards & Batia Laufer (eds.), *Vocabulary in a Second Language: Selection, Acquisition, and Testing*, 173–189. Amsterdam: John Benjamins.

Wierzbicka, Anna. 1985. *Lexicography and Conceptual Analysis*. Ann Arbor: Karoma.

Zadeh, Lotfi. 1965. Fuzzy sets. *Information and Control* 8. 338–353. doi:10.1016/S0019-9958(65)90241-X.

Zimmermann, Hans Jirgen. 2001. *Fuzzy Set Theory and its Applications*. Boston: Kluwer Academic Publishers.

Irene Checa-García, Austin Schafer
Chapter 5
L1 to L2 lexical development transfer? A within subjects study on lexical richness measures

1 Introduction

The area where researchers as well as instructors can probably most easily see transfer from a first language to a second one is the lexicon. It is also the area of language where this possibility is addressed most often in textbooks, in the form of false cognates, explanations of lexical fields that work differently in different languages, or warnings about non-corresponding polysemy. Most of the approaches, as Jarvis (2009: 106) mentions, are in fact focused on error sources, explanation, and a negative view of transfer. In this paper we explore the possibility of a positive lexical transfer: the transfer of lexical richness, a complex construct that includes lexical density, lexical diversity, lexical sophistication, and lexical accuracy (Henriksen and Danelund 2015). We will look at the first three components as those are the three that speak of a positive transfer: a transfer of certain characteristics of lexical production. Our hypothesis is that there can be positive transfer of these characteristics when they exhibit high values in the L1 and in more advanced levels of L2. A learner who uses the lexicon in such a way that produces more lexical diversity, density and sophistication in their L1 may feel the need to acquire L2 vocabulary to match this kind of production abilities in their L1, while a learner who does not have such characteristics in their native language lexical production will not have that need. Likewise, since L2 ability mediates to what extent L1 abilities and strategies can be transferred (Karim and Nassaji 2013), transfer of lexical production characteristics dependent on lexical richness is more likely to appear only once a certain level of lexical proficiency is achieved.

Assuming this ability can be transferred, at least once vocabulary knowledge has a certain depth and breadth, it could then be beneficial for the L2 learner to increase the L1 lexical richness, if possible, prior to L2 instruction. This is because lexical characterization of L2 discourse, particularly written discourse, has often been associated with its quality or with overall writer's proficiency (Engber 1995;

Irene Checa-García, University of Wyoming
Austin Schafer, University of Wisconsin

https://doi.org/10.1515/9783110730418-005

Lemmouh 2008; Vögelin et al. 2019), and hence, its development is viewed as key in advancing L2 knowledge and performance.

In order to research this possibility, we have analyzed the productions of L2 learners of Spanish both in Spanish and English, studying the correlation between 3 key lexical richness features. In what follows, we first present these main lexical features and some key findings about them in L2. Next, we discuss the possibility of lexical transfer in L2 and end that section with our research questions. After presenting our methods and results, we discuss some possible explanations as well as some pedagogical suggestions that can be derived from this study's results.

2 Lexical richness measures and L2 results

Measures of lexical development can be classified into production and comprehension measures. In this section we will focus on production measures. There are two different types of productive lexical measures, those based on general lexical characteristics of subjects' productions collected in a corpus, and those consisting in prompting lexical items, typically lists of words on a topic such as those of lexical availability (Jiménez Catalán 2017). For studies examining production data, such as the present study, the focus has been on one or more of four measures: lexical diversity, lexical density, lexical sophistication, and lexical accuracy (Lindqvist et al. 2011), either working at the word level, lemmas, word families, or collocations. In the study reported here we use the first three measures. We did not analyze lexical error correlation between L1 and L2 because this type of error is infrequent in L1 and has different causes than in L2 and because the main interest of our study is to clarify if there is a positive transfer of lexical abilities. Next, we present each of the lexical richness features included in this study.

2.1 Lexical density

Lexical density consists of the proportion of content words for total words.

Although not the most frequently used measure, it was proposed as a substitute for lexical diversity that was not affected by the sample's length like diversity is. Johansson (2008) found a significant growth of both diversity and density in the late adolescent years of her L1 Swedish data, as well as a correlation between the indexes. However, Johansson explains the difference between the two and how no one measure can substitute the other, as other authors have expressed (Jarvis 2013; Malvern et al. 2004; Read 2000). More recently, Gregori-Signes and Clavel-Arroitia (2015) found a decrease in lexical density in their English L2 (Spanish L1) data at the university level, but there is no study of its statistical significance and the authors believe this decrease is mainly due to task differences rather than time between samples. Zheng (2016) analyzed longitudinal data for English L2 (from college level Chinese L1 students) and found a significant increase in lexical density early in time, but not so much on the later measurements. A few studies involving heritage speakers of Spanish also showed lexical density to be a sensitive measure. Marqués-Pascual and Checa-García (in press) found that lexical density increased after a study abroad experience for heritage speakers and the effect size was large. Reznicek-Parrado, Patiño-Vega and Colombi (2018) also found an increase over time in diversity, although their calculation of diversity eliminates most common words, in effect mixing it with the notion of sophistication (see 2.3. below). However, when studying the correlation between lexical density and holistic scores in English L2, Engber (1995) did not find a significant correlation between the two. Finally, lexical density has been used to measure readability in texts (To, Fan and Thomas 2013) and has been studied in relation to its impact on word and sentence retention and working memory (Borges Mota 2003; Perfetti 1969).

Given what density consists of, we could expect that initially it is high in an L2, as students still must learn how to use function words, then they may stabilize or decrease, as more function words are integrated. Finally, as sentences become more complex and compressed, students may need less function words, but also know and use more of them, resulting in an increase and maybe a subsequent plateau, showing a U shape in their development. Previous results showed an increase in lexical density at middle points or initial points in the development, and not so much at the highest or lowest levels. If the development of lexical density does happen in a U shape, we could expect the density used in the L1 to transfer only to the L2 in upper levels and less so in lower levels due to greater command of grammatical words in advanced speakers and knowledge of specific constructions rather than more lexical knowledge in beginning speakers. Of all the lexical measures, this is the one that is notionally more connected to grammatical competence.

2.2 Lexical diversity

Lexical diversity has been the most used measure in lexical research, to the point of even being taken as a synonym for "lexical richness" (Castañeda-Jiménez and Jarvis 2014). It measures the variety and quantity of vocabulary used (McCarthy and Jarvis 2010). Lexical diversity is generally considered a measure of the quality of a text. Like density, it has been found to be higher in writing than speech (Johansson 2008), and to be characteristic of academic writing (Fairclough and Belpoliti 2015).

In terms of its calculations, the proposals have varied. Initially, and given its definition, it was calculated as the ratio between non-repeated words and total words (TTR) and its value ranges between 1 (all words different) and almost 0 (all the same word). Although its interpretation is easy, this calculation presents a problem: it depends on text length, that is, number of words in the sample being analyzed. There are two ways to avoid this correlation: to keep all samples for all subjects the same size, or to take sufficiently long samples from each subject (in a register study by García-Cardona and Checa-García [2019] the correlation decrease of lexical diversity by increase of text extension seemed to stop after 8000 words, so a minimum sample would have to be at least 8000 words per participant). Most researchers cannot collect samples of this length, so alternative calculations have been proposed for lexical diversity with both Jarvis (2013) and Castañeda-Jiménez and Jarvis (2014) offering their diachronic evolution. Two measures have proved not to correlate with text extension: Measure of Textual Lexical Diversity (MTLD) by McCarthy and Jarvis (2010) and Moving Average of Type-Token Ratio (MATTR) by Covington and McFall (2010) for smaller samples. In addition, previously, Jarvis (2002) designed a study to compare the different diversity measures empirically and found that for written production, the Uber U measure was best, provided it was applied only to content words (as grammatical words are the ones most often repeated in a more extended text). On the other hand, Guiraud's (possibly the most used calculation) and D indexes were better suited to measure lexical diversity in oral production without a strong correlation with text length, although checking for such correlation is always advisable. Because our study deals with written compositions, we will use the Uber U measure applied to content words.

Regardless of the measure applied, results on lexical diversity are mixed and not all research has tested for correlation between lexical diversity and text extension (measured in words or lemmas). Johansson (2008), Crossley et al. (2013), and Zheng (2016) found significant increases by proficiency levels and Engber (1995) found a correlation with overall scores using the simple measure and no collinearity study with text extension. In contrast, Booth (2014), and Serrano et al. (2012) found no significant increases over time in this measure. However, the ability, or habit, of including diverse vocabulary into one's writing is perhaps the lexical ability most generally tested and the one most commonly identified with lexical richness. For these reasons, lexical diversity was included in the study calculated through the Uber index as recommended by Jarvis (2002) for written language.

2.3 Lexical sophistication

Impressionistic/qualitative evaluations of vocabulary diversity and depth, the kind instructors may have when reading and evaluating the vocabulary of their students' productions, may be influenced by at least one other aspect, perhaps even more so than any of the other lexical richness measures: lexical sophistication. This aspect refers to how many unusual or sophisticated words the writer uses. Thus, lexical sophistication is a key aspect in the perception of vocabulary development in L2. There are reasons for sophistication being an important factor in judging vocabulary development. Words that are more unusual are harder to acquire and remember, but also more characteristic of advanced users of the language. In order to assign a sophistication score to lexical items, each item is paired with its frequency in a frequency list of words of the language, in which they are ranked according to their occurrences in a reference corpus. From here, how the sophistication score is calculated has also varied among different studies. Some studies have calculated sophistication using the Advanced Guiraud's index of lexical richness: a proportion of words beyond a certain frequency threshold: either beyond the most frequent 2000 words, (Kalantari and Gholami 2017), beyond the 100 most frequent words (Waldvogel 2014),[1] or beyond the 1000 most frequent items (González-López and López-López 2015). Other studies have divided the frequencies in bands, typically in ranges of a thousand, to yield the number of words in 1–1000 most frequent, 2000–3000 most frequent, etc. (Fairclough and Belpoliti 2015; Tracy-Ventura 2017; Berton and Sánchez, in this volume). Finally, others have simply used the log-transformed frequency in the corpus to avoid Zipfian effects (Kyle and Crossley 2015). Those measures that opted for bands of frequencies have the disadvantage of losing information, by grouping together values that could potentially be different. Also, by using the position in the frequency list rather than the frequency itself, items that could in fact be very far apart in frequency but consecutive in the ranking will be considered equally as close as those that are in fact only one unit apart. Crossley, Cobb and McNamara compared the band methods and the frequency count method to calculate sophistication. Their study showed that the score method is better at detecting differences between groups. In this study we have calculated sophistication with the count-based method used by Kyle and Crossley (2015) for two reasons: because of more quantitative information being preserved, and because of its increased sensitivity according to the results in Kyle and Crossley (2015). The calculation is explained later in section 3.3.

---

1 It is worth noting that when the margin of words considered "frequent" is so narrow, it mostly contains function words, which means that there may be a possible collinearity with density.

The diversity of calculations once again makes it difficult to compare results across studies, but most studies have found a progression in sophistication, correlation with other lexical richness indexes or group differences, oftentimes significant (González-López and López-López 2015 for L2 Spanish; Kalantari and Gholami 2017 for L2 English; Kyle and Crossley 2015 for L1 and L2 English; Tracy-Ventura 2017 for L2 Spanish; Waldvogel 2014 for lower levels of L2 Spanish; and Zheng 2016 for L2 English).

2.4 Lexical units for lexical richness analysis

There is not only a myriad of forms to calculate these indexes, but also a set of possible lexical units that they could be applied to (Jarvis and Hashimoto 2021). The most obvious unit, the word, presents several issues: are words like *buy* and *buying* separately stored and different items in terms of diversity, for instance? Furthermore: are *boy* and *boys* to be considered different? A unit that avoids this type of problem is the lemma. A lemma is the constant root in different words that consists of that root and inflectional morphemes attached to it and may be closer to what may be a lexical unit in the speaker's or writer's mind. Another possibility is to consider a whole family of words, including those formed by derivational morphemes, like *seller, unsaleable, sale,* etc. Here things get fuzzier in terms of what is reasonable to expect a second language learner to recognize as part of the same family. For instance, the meaning 'short' in Spanish, *corto*, is related to the verb *cortar*, 'to cut', this may or may not be transparent to the L2 learner, and sometimes these relationships are not even transparent to native speakers. An added problem is that it is very hard to identify members of the same family, even if we thought the speaker identifies them as part of an entry as well, requiring complete lists of families, not available in most languages. In this study, we have opted to use lemmas rather than words or word families for the problems these two options posit as exposed above. We explain how we extracted lemmas in 4.3., in the methods sections.

Regardless of the units and of the indexes, we have found only one work that compares L1 and L2 lexical diversity in a within subject design (Ströbel, Kerz and Wiechmann 2020) and none that incorporate the three lexical richness measures that could show positive transfer. A within-subjects design is crucial to study transfer possibilities (Jarvis 2000) as discussed earlier, and therefore we include it in this study.

3 Transfer in L2: Positives and negatives

Initially, traditional views of transfer suggested the presence of separate lexicons for each language learned within the mind of a user (Singleton 2006). The processes by which learners acquired and stored vocabulary in the L1 was thought to be fundamentally different from the L2 (Laufer 1989). This different access between the two languages was taken to imply that little transfer occurred. However, evidence of transfer and its systematic study soon revealed that in fact, transfer, in all areas of non-native language acquisition (phonetics, lexical semantics, syntax, and pragmatics) is not just frequent, but pervasive (Jarvis and Pavlenko 2008). Hence, traditional views have started to account for transfer as a common factor in language acquisition. More specific to the present study, a growing body of evidence points out, at the end of the last century (William and Hammarberg 1998), the influence of language activation on a particular kind of transfer, lexemic transfer, and how multiple languages can be activated at the same time, thus more easily allowing for transfer (Dewaele 1998).

In addition to prior views hypothesizing little transfer occurrence between languages, until recently, all forms of transfer were seen as interference when acquiring another language, and both terms, transfer, and interference, were used interchangeably (Jarvis and Pavlenko 2008; Singleton 2006). Consequently, transfer was a source of error and something to be avoided. Even if seen as negative, transfer was still an important locus for L2 acquisition research, and in particular its role in the formation of the interlanguage and its insight into language storage and processing for both L1 and L2, as well as issues of accessibility between the two. More recently, research in language transfer has shifted to explore potential positive transfer in the bilingual and multilingual brain as a way of building on one's L1 lexicon foundation to aid L2 development, but the way in which languages interact and how much interaction exists is still debated (Jarvis 2009; Singleton 2006).

Evidence of the existence of L1 to L2 transfer is overwhelming in current literature. Many recent studies (Jarvis, Castañeda-Jiménez and Nielsen 2012; Murakami 2013; Shum et al. 2016; Sparks et al. 2019; Vulchanova et al. 2014; Ben-Yehuda et al. 2019; Fuster and Neuser 2020; Hohenstein, Eisenberg and Naigles 2006) find evidence of many forms of transfer between a variety of languages and areas.

Recent discoveries in transfer have also made researchers wonder about its directionality. Although traditionally, and still, the focus is on the L1 to L2 transfer, it is unclear whether all types of transfer can happen in all directions. Hohenstein, Eisenberg and Naigles (2006) found evidence of lexical bidirectional transfer in a sample of English and Spanish adult speakers while only unidirectional grammatical transfer from the L1 to the L2. Results from these types of studies suggest transfer is not only motivated by lack of knowledge in the target language, but it is rather a multifactorial phenomenon that can be due to advantages in processing, and that can therefore have a processing motivation. For instance, an L2 learner may insert a lexical item from their L2 into their L1 because this learner perceives the item to better or more accurately describe a certain reality. This transfer from the L2 lexicon to the dominant L1 may point to users experimenting with a broader range of vocabulary to better describe situations or even a preference of a language's lexicon in favor of the current language in use. More broadly, this evidence signals a more fluid relationship between L1 and L2 than previously thought, going in both directions (Cook 2003; shown in the lexicon by Laufer 2003), and including effects on metalinguistic awareness (Atar 2018).

In addition to directionality and effect in learning, transfer can be classified by its intentionality, as intentional or accidental (Fuster and Neuser 2020). Following Jarvis and Pavlenko's proposal (2008), they define an intentional transfer as: "an action that is done on purpose and of which the doer is aware" (Fuster and Neuser 2020: 518). Thus, intentional transfer involves using conscious effort in bringing parts of one language to the other language. For example, using a word that the speaker knows to be from their dominant language during the production of the L2 language would be intentionally transferring language ability. Accidental transfer involves transferring abilities without knowing that the transfer is occurring. For example, unknowingly using a false cognate as a real cognate. Most of the research has been on non-intentional transfer, which is classified itself into two types: processing interference and crosslinguistic association. However, intentional use of L1 into L2 (or vice versa) is possible as well. The existence of intentional non-automatic transfer implies that such transfer can be interpreted as pragmatically positive by its users, and it would be an instance of a non-negative transfer. In their empirical study Fuster and Neuser categorized instances of transfer in the L1 and the L2 while labeling each instance as intentional or unintentional to see just how frequent each type was. They found intentional transfer occurs at rates (44%) only slightly lower than unintentional transfer (56%). The existence of moderately high rates of intentional transfer support the idea that users have a variety of reasons, both intentional and unintentional, for language transfer and these cases of transfer can have both negative and positive effects on production. Examples of positive and negative lexical transfer include cognates and false cognates that can either help an L2 learner to acquire vocabulary quickly, or create an obstacle due to vocabulary appearing similar, but having a different meaning. Additionally, Jarvis (2009) suggest that words can form connections between languages and can, therefore, create instances of positive transfer when two words have a strong connection that is readily available, or create a negative instance of transfer when a strong connection might cause an L1 word to be substituted for an L2 word erroneously.

As we can see, the phenomenon of transfer is due to multiple factors and not merely a strategy to supply with knowledge from the L1 when the L2 one is absent in the interlanguage (IL). It can have both negative and positive effects, it can be intentional or accidental, and it can work in both directions, from the L1 to the L2 and vice versa, or come for any language the speaker comes in closer contact with (Odlin 1989). For the present study, a learner could be used to be able to show a certain level of L1 lexical richness and wanting to transfer this characteristic of their production to their L2, motivating them to learn more vocabulary to be able to do so, whether that occurs consciously or not. Here, we would like to investigate the possibility of transfer of lexical abilities, rather than lexical items, and explore which abilities transfer more clearly or in a significant way and if they do so at both levels or more at one of them. Below we show how some findings support the idea that such a transfer is to be possible.

3.1 Can there be lexical ability transfer from L1 to L2?

The evidence for transfer has been shown for different areas of languages, in different directions and with different effects. In the area of lexical development, lexemic and lexical transfer has been studied more extensively, particularly concerning cognates and the influence of the distance between L1 and L2 in their frequency of occurrence and positive or negative effects (Poulisse 1999; Ringbom 2007; Sánchez-Casa and García-Albea 2005 for a summary). For instance, Iniesta et al. (2021) showed how bilingual coactivation of cognates whose spelling was incongruent (such as "v" in one language, but "b" in the other, as in *government* vs. *gobierno*), had an effect in bilinguals' processing so that their processing speed and accuracy was lower than in typing congruent words dictated to them. This effect was also bigger in their weaker language. Such effects were not observed in monolinguals. Phonological similarity also plays a similarly significant role in bilingual naming latencies in oral tasks, with higher effects than frequency of the lexical items (Sadat et al. 2016). However, there is less research on transfer of lexical abilities specifically between L1 and L2. Would it be reasonable then to expect that abilities reflected in production, in the form of the theoretical construct "lexical richness" can be affected by transfer as well? That is, can we expect that, for instance, L2 learners with high lexical diversity in their L1 would also tend to show higher lexical diversity in their L2? Or perhaps more clearly the other way around: is it reasonable to expect that learners who do not exhibit a high lexical diversity in their production will exhibit it in their L2? Or is this ability in their L1 a pre-condition to be able to develop it in an L2? If we believe these are linguistic abilities, it is reasonable to think that transfer of them, at least if they reached a certain level in their L1, could happen. It could be, as it happens with "lexical items transfer", that such transfer is affected not only by L1 degree of the ability, but also perhaps metalinguistic knowledge of L1 and possibly relationships between L2 and L1, as well as other factors. Evidence from other linguistics areas, and specifically syntactic complexity, has shown that transfer of general linguistic abilities does seem to happen from L1 to L2 at least at higher levels of L2 competence (Schafer 2020; Ströbel et al. 2020).

While there is an abundance of studies employing lexical richness measures to assess language development in either L1, L2, or comparing the two in a between subjects design (Booth 2014; Collentine 2004; Jarvis 2009, 2013; Kyle and Crossley 2015; Lindqvist, Bardel, and Gudmundson 2011; Serrano et al 2012; Zheng 2016), so far there has been very few studies, to our knowledge, that explore the possibility of transfer between the two, and in particular from the L1 to the L2. There are a few studies that investigated this directly while other studies have investigated transfer of abilities in a more general way or have used L1 lexical styles to predict L2 ones, providing more indirect evidence for this relationship. For example, a study performed by Jarvis, Castañeda-Jiménez, and Nielsen (2012) demonstrates how one's L1 can be predicted based on L2 lexical style by using machine learning techniques to classify writing samples. The classifier the authors developed correctly identified a participant's L1 background with an overall accuracy of 76.9%. The L1 backgrounds were predicted based on word choice (what particular words were used in their productions) in each participant's writing. These results point towards similar L2 tendencies based on the influence of one's L1 background, that is, word choices in the L2 are similar if the L1 is the same one. Other studies such as Sparks, Patton, and Luebbers (2019) found significant predictors to future general L2 success based on skill levels in the students' L1 abilities during primary school. For instance, vocabulary in L1 and L2 were mildly (0.37) but significantly correlated, while phono-orthographic memory in the L1 and linguistic analysis in the L1 were the best predictors for success in their L2. Sparks, Patton, Ganschow and Humbach (2009) found similar evidence in an earlier longitudinal study. Karim and Nassaji (2013) summarize the body of research at the time in transfer of L1 writing strategies to L2 writing, including more or less literal translation. There are a few studies (Kubota 1998; Uzawa and Cumming 1989; Beare 2000; Wang and Wen 2002, as cited in Karim and Nassaji 2013) that were able to compare L1 and L2 writing strategies for the same subjects using think aloud protocols, although the number of participants was very low, and the studies were fundamentally case studies rather than quantitative ones. In general, participants benefited from using L1 general strategies, mostly at the pre-writing and editing phases. Interestingly, some strategies were picked from their L1 language writing, planning, ideas brainstorming, but the editing postwriting strategies were mostly those students had seen used in their L2 courses.

Looking specifically at linguistic abilities in the L1 transfer into the L2 similar abilities, Vulchanova et al. (2014) discovered correlations between Norwegian L1 and English L2 skills in Norwegian children. Specifically, they found correlations between the results of vocabulary size standardized tests and English oral skills general tests and overall score in a Norwegian L1 oral ability test. The authors posited that the abilities may be similar due to their common dependence on memory measures, specifically phonological and short-term memory. The study by Ströbel et al. (2020) did look at each linguistic ability correlation in German learners of English. They studied the relation between 7 lexical, 4 syntactic and 1 overall measures of complexity in the compositions of 80 participants at college level. Their results indicated that all measures in the L1 but word length contributed to those in the L2, particularly the overall complexity measure (Kolgomorov index) and several lexical diversity measures. There are at least two other studies concerned with lexical diversity in L1 and L2, although none of them addresses the possible transfer of this kind of lexical competence from L1 to L2. Laufer (2003) investigates L1 lexical diversity change due to prolonged contact with an L2. Her participants included Russian L1 speakers now living in Israel who learned Hebrew as an L2. The study suggests that extended contact with an L2 results in decreased L1 lexical diversity. In the same volume, Dewaele and Pavlenko (2003) find that individual language differences such as lexical diversity norms in Russian and English can be emulated by L2 speakers when accustomed to the norms. The authors also find that bilinguals do not transfer L2 norms in lexical diversity to their L1 production, indicating little influence from L2 to L1. These studies contribute to further research of lexical diversity between languages, but either focus on L1 lexical diversity change over an extended period due to L1 skill loss (Laufer 2003; Schmid and Jarvis 2014) or maintaining language norms when using different languages (Dewaele and Pavlenko 2003) rather than researching individual lexical diversity skill transfer.

Other investigations have looked at other measures of lexical richness, such as sophistication. Palfreyman and Karaki (2019) focused on comparing the sophistication of a group of students in L1 Arabic and L2 English. Their results indicated big differences between the sophistication of the languages, as one would expect, but a positive, though not significant, correlation between the sophistication scores in the two languages. Because the non-significance could be due to two big outliers, the authors suggest that it could be possible to find a significant correlation with a bigger sample of students and more extensive writing pieces.

Finally, when it comes to lexical density, we have not found studies addressing its potential transfer between languages in any direction. However, we will include results in this study on lexical density transfer for various reasons. First, precisely because it has not been studied and it forms part of the triad of lexical richness measures excluding accuracy more focused on errors. Second, there is evidence that density may in fact be a good measure to differentiate lexical ability levels, characterize lexical development, and show significant differences among different types of language acquisition: dominant L1, heritage L1, and L2 (Checa-García and Marqués-Pascual 2020).

In sum, at this broader skill level, both positive and negative skill transfer may occur between languages allowing educators and students to predict areas of strength and weakness before learning an L2 (Shum et al. 2016; Sparks, Patton and Luebbers 2019). Cummins (1979; 1991) proposed earlier that the development of L2 was conditioned by the L1 previous development in two ways: through the Linguistic Interdependence Hypothesis (L1 and L2 share underlying competences) and through the Threshold Hypothesis (some aspects of L2 development can then be capped at their L1 levels of attainment). Shum et al. (2016) predicted deficiencies in English as an L2 from Chinese L1 learners for areas such as word fluency (speed to recover a word from memory into production). Additionally, Sparks, Patton and Luebbers (2019) found similar results for Spanish as an L2 with English L1 participants. This research highlights how transfer may occur at granular levels, affecting individual lexical items such as cognates, and at broader levels such as word fluency. Most importantly, these results support Cummins' Hypotheses, which means that as high as possible L1 development is desirable before or during L2 acquisition. All in all, previous studies show a relationship between L1 lexical ability and L2 lexical development. However, they did not look at sophistication, density or other measures of lexical richness and their direct relation in L1 and L2 compositions in a controlled production environment. This study will look into the possible transfer of these features of lexical richness.

In order to decide whether there is an L1 transfer into an L2, Jarvis (2000) suggests working with a heuristic tentative definition of transfer: "L1 influence refers to any instance of learner data where a statistically significant correlation (or probability-based relation) is shown to exist between some feature of learners' IL performance and their L1 background" (p. 252). In addition, he offers three comparisons that can indicate transfer. One of them is "L1-IL congruities", which is said to be "the strongest type of evidence for L1 influence" (p. 258). In our particular study, this means to search for a correlation between the L1 lexical richness measures and those in the L2 -in similar tasks-. Even if this type of evidence is the strongest, Jarvis points out two possible scenarios where additional evidence would be needed: (i) if L1 influence is obscured because of differences in proficiency in the L2 language and (ii) if the L1 influence is susceptible of being language-specific (so different L1s should be checked to see if the influence does not happen in those other L1s with the same L2). The first of the problems is solved in two ways: by using a within-subjects study and by keeping level constant or converting it into another explanatory (independent) variable. Thus, this study has been designed taking into account both solutions (see the methods section later). The second of the problems cannot be said to apply when the linguistic transfer is of a very general skill, such as those involved in lexical richness (lexical diversity, lexical sophistication and lexical density). In fact, we should expect, in this particular case, that the effect would be sustained with different L1s.

Our research questions for this study are therefore: (i) are there any correlations between L1 lexical diversity, density and sophistication scores and L2 scores? And (ii) do correlations vary according to L2 level (intermediate vs. advanced)?

4 Methods

4.1 Participants

We recruited all participants through current enrollment in Spanish courses and known connections from previous participation in the Spanish program at a flag state university in the Western United States. Participation was voluntary with some instructors of currently enrolled students offering small extra credit incentives. The subjects completed the entire study in designated locations agreed upon with the one of the researchers. Forty participants completed the study and were divided into two groups (intermediate or advanced) based on their language experience.

The intermediate group (n=20) consisted of students currently completing or having completed at least a third semester college level Spanish course and a maximum of a fourth semester. Participants with greater academic experience were placed in the advanced group (n=20) along with any participants with greater than two months experience abroad in a Spanish-speaking country. Levels were decided based on course experience at the university and abroad experience. The intermediate group consisted of students who had completed the first year of Spanish at the college level and were enrolled in the 3rd or 4th semester, roughly corresponding to the Intermediate level of the ACTFL standards. We decided on this cut at the 4th semester Spanish class due to the composition of classrooms above and below this level. At the university where the study was conducted, the first four semesters of Spanish consist of a smaller number of majors and minors in Spanish and considerably more students from other majors that require Spanish course credit. After the fourth semester in the program, majors and, to a lesser extent, minors of Spanish contribute to the majority of class enrollments. In addition, students could not have an abroad experience longer than 2 months to be classified in this group.

The advanced group was more heterogeneous in terms of previous background but had completed the fourth semester of Spanish instruction (so they were at least at the Intermediate High level according to ACFTL standards). The experience abroad for this group was also more heterogenous and ranging between zero months and seven years. This later highest value resulted in a high overall average abroad experience (6.5 months), but the median was lower, at less than 2 months abroad.

Around 70% of participants selected female as their gender with one participant choosing not to answer. Two participants chose not to answer a question asking for the subject's age, but the rest of the sample was on average 21.68 years old with a minimum age of 18 and maximum age of 33.

4.2 Procedure

Participants first agreed upon a time and location with the researchers to complete the study. Each subject was required to first read and sign a consent form. Next, they completed a survey containing questions about their age, gender, highest Spanish course enrolled in or completed, and time spent abroad in Spanish-speaking countries. Finally, each participant wrote two essays, one in English and the other in Spanish. Each essay contained a different, but similar prompt[2] to ensure different content with similar information, structure and style, as prompt topic and discourse type has been shown to influence at least diversity results (Fernández-Mira et al. 2021) as well as sophistication results (Berton and Sánchez, in this volume). Both essays were descriptive as this type of essay we determined suited both intermediate and advanced groups because it can incorporate both basic and advanced vocabulary skills. Furthermore, prompts and order of language testing were randomized so that there was no effect of either topic nor order of testing of languages. The participants completed the study without computers or translators and were allowed as much time as necessary to write, which was typically between 30 and 45 minutes, but could use more if needed.

---

[2] The prompts were: (a) Describe the area in which you were born with detail. Include the best and worst aspects, personal experiences, or places that you enjoy visiting, and (b) Compare XXXXX (university town) and your life style here with the place where you used to live before. If you have always lived here, compare XXXX with other big cities you know and the life style in those cities. (XXXXX is a smaller town, although much bigger than the rest of towns in the state).

4.3 Analysis

As previously mentioned, we processed the data to obtain a measure of lexical diversity, lexical density, and lexical sophistication for each subject and composition (in English and Spanish), which rendered six dependent variables: L1 diversity, L2 diversity, L1 density, L2 density, L1 sophistication, and L2 sophistication. To extract and count types and tokens, all writing samples were coded in the CHAT format for the Computerized Language Analysis (CLAN) program (MacWhinney 2000). The transcripts were later morphosyntactically tagged using the Spanish MOR3, which is provided as part of the CLAN program. The tagged files were used for the lexical diversity analysis based on lemmas. We extracted the lemma category and the lemma itself and created a database with the subject number, lemmas produced and part of speech of each lemma. This helped disambiguate most homonym cases, but we also used the POST command to help with disambiguation in CLAN. The parts of speech in the frequency lists included four categories of content words: noun, adjective, adverb, and verb, and the labeling was modified to match precisely those tags used by MOR in CLAN.

We calculated the lexical diversity for each subject at each time by dividing the total number of unique content lemmas (our types) by the total number of content lemmas (our tokens). We decided to use only content words for lexical diversity because it is the non-content words that are mostly responsible for the correlation between text length and lexical diversity, as they repeat more often the longer the language sample is, and because Jarvis (2002) and Zheng (2016) demonstrated this computation to be best for written data. We then transformed the data with the Uber transformation (Jarvis 2002). The variables 'Uber-transformed content diversity' and 'extension in number of words' were then studied for correlation. Correlation was low in both cases (Pearson = −0.01 for the English compositions and Pearson = 0.3 for the Spanish composition, only the later statistically significant $p < 0.001$). As for the calculation of lexical density, we used CLAN again to compute the type and token count for content lemmas and all other categories, and find their proportion to each other, rendering a lexical density measure for each subject at each point in time.

In the case of sophistication, a frequency score from a frequency list is needed to be assigned to each lemma since we are calculating count-based sophistication for the reasons mentioned in 2.3. In the case of Spanish, we used the frequency list by Mark Davies (2006) and in the case of English we used the list extracted by Adam Kilgarriff found at his website (http://www.kilgarriff.co.uk/bnc-readme.html#lemmatised) and explained in Kilgarriff (1997). Since Kilgarriff's list only has the first 6300 words, we only took the first 6300 words from Davies's as well. This gave us multiple sophistication scores for each subject, one per lemma used. Since we wanted to be able to explore the possible correlation of the indexes among themselves and since there were many more values for the L1 than for the L2, almost double, we had to find a way to summarize sophistication in one value per subject. Following Crossley, Cobb, and McNamara (2013) we obtained one lexical sophistication score for each subject by calculating the mean of all lemmas' sophistication score for that subject. To do so, we assigned a frequency to each lemma based on the frequency list compiled by Davies (2006) from his *Corpus del Español*. Next, following Kyle and Crossley (2015), the frequencies in each list were transformed with a 10th logarithm to avoid a Zipfian effect, and those items which did not have a frequency in the Davies corpus were eliminated. A script was created in the R programming language to match each lemma and part of speech combination with its transformed frequency in the frequency list. This allowed matching each lemma produced with its frequency in a count-based fashion and rendered several sophistication measures for each subject, one per lemma produced, so the average of those was the measurement used to represent sophistication per subject. That average represents a mean of the frequency, and hence, the higher it is, the lower the sophistication. To avoid this anti-intuitive measure, the inverse of this score was used to represent sophistication, so the higher the number, the higher the sophistication. A summary of the measures analyzed in this study is provided in Table 1 below.

Table 1: Summary of lexical measures used.

Measure	Description
Diversity	Uber transformation of content lemma types/content lemma totals Log(tokens)^2/ log(tokens)-log(types)
Density	Content lemma types/all types
Sophistication	1/Mean lemma log10 frequency

Once the measures were obtained, we first explored the data graphically to observe relationships between the indexes themselves, between and within languages, using scatter plots and the Pearson correlation. Next, we performed a linear regression study to model each of the L2 lexical indexes (density, diversity, sophistication) based on their L1 equivalent measure and the level, as well as the interaction of L1 lexical ability index and level. In a stepwise backwards selection fashion, we eliminated variables and/or interactions to arrive at the minimal model that predicts most the dependent variable.

5 Results

5.1 Summary descriptive measure for the three lexical richness indexes

Table 2 shows the main centrality and dispersion measures for all the lexical indexes in L1 and L2 for the total population and for each level, intermediate and advanced.

Table 2: Centrality and dispersion measures for all lexical richness indexes total and by group.

	mean	sd	median	min	max	range	se
All Groups							
L1 Diversity	21.02	3.00	20.13	16.80	28.29	11.48	0.67
L2 Diversity	14.45	1.80	14.12	11.89	18.08	6.20	0.40
L1 Density	0.61	0.04	0.62	0.54	0.67	0.13	0.01
L2 Density	0.48	0.08	0.49	0.31	0.60	0.29	0.02
L1 Sophistication	0.28	0.02	0.27	0.24	0.33	0.08	0.00
L2 Sophistication	0.26	0.01	0.26	0.24	0.29	0.05	0.00
Intermediate							
L1 Diversity	21.57	2.70	21.23	16.11	27.76	11.65	0.60
L2 Diversity	18.53	2.49	18.98	13.52	23.99	10.47	0.56
L1 Density	0.63	0.04	0.63	0.56	0.69	0.13	0.01
L2 Density	0.56	0.04	0.56	0.50	0.62	0.12	0.01
L1 Sophistication	0.27	0.02	0.27	0.25	0.31	0.06	0.00
L2 Sophistication	0.27	0.04	0.27	0.13	0.32	0.19	0.01
Advanced							
L1 Diversity	21.30	2.83	21.17	16.11	28.29	12.17	0.45
L2 Diversity	16.49	2.98	16.11	11.89	23.99	12.11	0.47
L1 Density	0.62	0.04	0.62	0.54	0.69	0.15	0.01
L2 Density	0.52	0.07	0.53	0.31	0.62	0.31	0.01
L1 Sophistication	0.28	0.02	0.27	0.24	0.33	0.08	0.00
L2 Sophistication	0.27	0.03	0.27	0.13	0.32	0.19	0.00

In terms of centrality, we can observe a tendency across all indexes for the L1 values to be higher, although much less so for sophistication. Comparing the two groups, these tendencies are similar, but although the L1 values are comparable, the L2 values are higher for diversity for the intermediate group, while density and sophistication remain similar between the two groups. As for the dispersion, looking at range and standard deviation, not only sophistication, but also density show higher values generally for the L2 compositions. The dispersion measures are higher for the advanced group, except for sophistication, where the two groups show similar values.

The picture that emerges from these values is that there is not a big impact of group or language over sophistication, there are some differences in terms of density, and the biggest differences occur in diversity. In the next sections we look at each index separately and see whether the differences found are significant and which variable or interaction can explain them better.

5.2 Regression study for each lexical richness index in Spanish L2

A multiple linear regression was performed for lexical density incorporating L1 density, group level, and their interaction in the initial model. The simplest model included only the group level, which significantly predicted L2 density scores ($t\ value$ = 4.299, $p < .001$). However, level explained only an intermediate proportion of variance in L2 density (*adjusted R^2* = .31, $F[38]$ = 18.48, $p < .001$).

The multiple linear regression performed for lexical diversity rendered a model that included level and L1 diversity, but not their interaction. Level significantly predicted L2 diversity scores ($t\ value$ = 0.62, $p < .0001$). L1 diversity also significantly predicted L2 diversity scores ($t\ value$ = 0.111, $p < .01$). Together, level and L1 diversity explained a relatively high proportion of variance in L2 diversity (*adjusted R^2* = .57, $F[37]$ = 26.94, $p < .0001$). However, since there was no interaction between level and L1 diversity it does not seem that only participants at certain level and with a certain L1 diversity would have higher L2 diversity. Instead, having a higher Spanish level/proficiency and higher L1 diversity seems to result in higher L2 diversity.

The multiple linear model calculated for lexical sophistication did not meet the normality and homoscedasticity for the residuals, so it was replaced by a robust linear regression. However, none of the variables or interactions significantly predicted the L2 sophistication scores.

In sum, only one of the lexical measures in the L1, diversity, in conjunction with level, predicted the scores in its equivalent in the L2, and in a relatively high proportion. Both density and diversity were affected by level, with the advanced group exhibiting higher scores. Sophistication did not seem affected by either level or the L1 ability scores.

5.3 Correlation among lexical richness measures in the two acquisition types: L1 and L2

Although it may seem more intuitive to think that it would be a certain ability in the first language affecting the same ability in the second language, it is possible to imagine that an ability may affect other abilities, either in the first or the second language. For instance, a more diverse vocabulary may lead to a more sophisticated score, or a denser vocabulary with more content words could lead to more varied words or more sophistication, since grammatical words tend to be the most frequent and repeated words. In order to explore these potential relationships, we performed a correlation analysis among our six dependent variables. Figure 1 presents scatter plots of the dependent variables pairwise and Table 3 shows the correlations between all six lexical scores, with significant correlations in bold case.

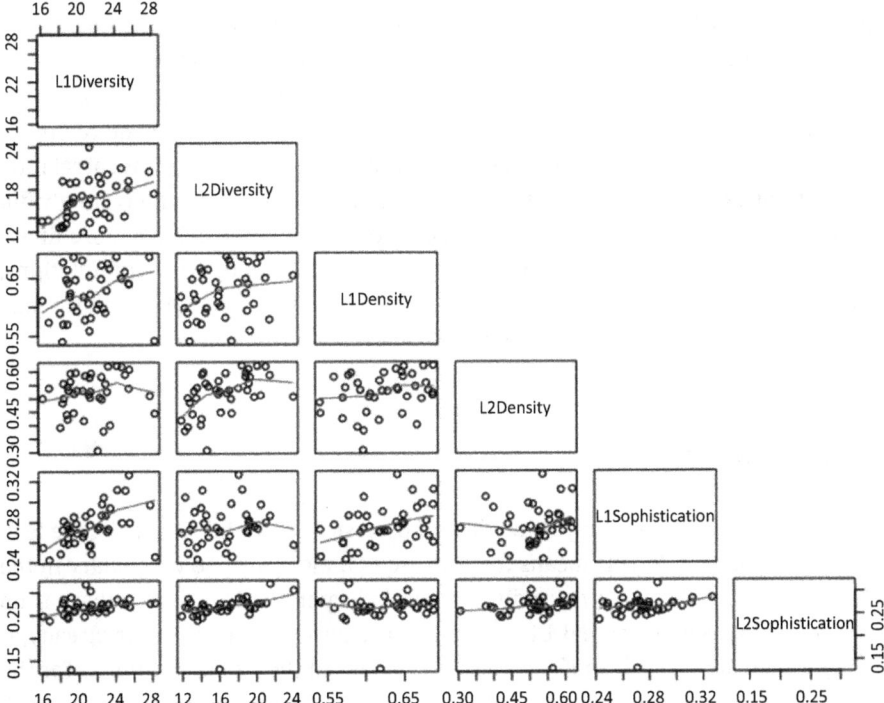

Figure 1: Pairwise scatter plots of all six lexical measures.

Table 3: Correlations between all six lexical measures.

	L1 diversity	L2 diversity	L1 density	L2 density	L1 sophistication	L2 sophistication
L1 diversity	1.000	0.400	0.226	0.126	0.495	0.299
L2 diversity	**0.400****	1.000	0.303	0.517	0.124	0.365
L1 density	0.226	0.303	1.000	0.296	0.423	0.041
L2 density	0.126	**0.517*****	0.296	1.000	0.150	0.128
L1 sophistication	**0.495*****	0.124	**0.423****	0.150	1.000	0.177
L2 sophistication	0.299	0.365*	0.041	0.128	0.177	1.000

0.5*, 0.01**, 0.001***

As the regression study already showed, the only lexical measure in L1 correlated with the L2 measure is diversity. In addition, lexical diversity in L1 is correlated to lexical sophistication in L1, as it could be expected. However, this is not the case in L2, where the diversity may not be high enough to be reflected in the sophistication scores. There is also a significant correlation between L1 density and L1 sophistication, also as we could expect since it is in content words where sophistication can occur more easily and with more density there is more opportunity for content words to occur. Finally, there is one final significant correlation between indexes in the L2, between diversity and density, which interestingly did not happen in the L1. Within grammatical words it is harder to have more diversity, although not impossible. However, it is typical to not vary conjunctions, prepositions or such words as much in an L2 where the inventory of those may grow proportionally more slowly than the inventory of content words.

6 Discussion

The main finding of this study is that lexical diversity in an L1 does predict the lexical diversity in the L2. This means that the use of a more diverse vocabulary in the L1 does have an effect of a more diverse vocabulary in the L2. Because there is no interaction between level and L1 diversity, this transfer seems to occur already at the intermediate level, even if the scores are lower in the L2 but not the L1 for the intermediate group. Nonetheless, scores were much higher for the L1 than the L2 for both levels, indicating that in both cases there is still room for lexical diversity to increase in the L2 with hopefully more positive transfer and pending vocabulary acquisition in the L2. These results are similar to those found for English L2 and German L1 by Ströbel, Kerz and Wiechmann (2020). In addition, diversity in the L1 was also significantly correlated with L1 sophistication, even though sophistication values did not appear very dispersed between or within groups and levels. Also, interestingly, L1 sophistication was correlated with higher density, not too surprisingly since rarer words tend to be content words rather than grammatical ones. In the L2, there was also a correlation between diversity and density, probably because diversity is mostly achieved through content words in L2, as diversity in grammatical words is harder to achieve, requiring both sophisticated grammatical words and the grammatical knowledge that accompanies them. Therefore, it seems possible to transfer lexical diversity to the L2 and increase density by doing so. Sophistication seemed more dependent on task, since scores in this index were too similar for both groups and levels and even in both languages, despite using a more sensitive calculation for it. There are still some questions to answer, for instance why sophistication is correlated with diversity in L1, but with density in L2. A combination of the quantitative results with a fine qualitative analysis could shed light on this issue.

Our results are consistent with those of Ströbel et al. (2020) in the presence of correlation between diversity in L1 and L2. However, they differ in terms of density (they did not study sophistication). While we did not find a correlation between L1 and L2 density, they found density to be the most correlated index, followed by different measures of diversity. One thing to take into account is that English and German are closer language, which could potentially make it easier to transfer certain function words. In any case, L2 learners with a higher L1 diversity seem to be at an advantage for the transfer of this ability into their L1. Thus, at least for lexical diversity, and perhaps for other abilities as well (Ströbel, Kerz and Wiechmann did find lexical complexity, measured in characters length, to correlate between L1 and L2 although the least among the significantly contributing indexes), a better commanding in the L1 does seem to favor a better development in L2, in consonance with Cumming's hypothesis of linguistic interdependence.

7 Conclusions

The idea that the degree of lexical richness achieved in the L1 may condition the degree achieved (and possibly achievable) in the L2 found some grounding in the results of this study. However, this is not equally so for each of the lexical richness indexes. Diversity seems the most L1 conditioned lexical property, while sophistication seems the least affected. It seems that for sophistication to be affected (and more correlated with other richness measures even within L2), a wider L2 lexicon may be needed. Another possible reason is that sophistication is affected for order of instruction of vocabulary, so that more sophisticated vocabulary for native speakers could sometimes be instructed earlier, while more "mundane" vocabulary would be taught later. For instance, Marqués-Pascual and Checa-García (in press) found that L2 learners of Spanish did not improve their lexical sophistication significantly after a semester abroad; in fact, it decreased. One possible explanation is that students may not learn the most common words through classroom instruction, and not so frequent words that are cognates to their L1 are favored (for example *oficina* instead of *despacho* or *horas de oficina* instead of *tutorías*), as well as words that are considered easier for some other reason (shorter words, regular verbs, etc.). Only a rigorous study of the input students receive could help clarify this issue.

As regards why diversity of lexical items would transfer into the L2, it would be because it needs to exist to a certain degree in the first place (in the L1) so that it can be transferred into the L2. Students who normally write more lexically diverse essays in their native language, may try to do so, or automatically do that, in their L2. Our hypothesis that this transfer would be mediated by level, being higher at more proficient levels, was rejected, however. Perhaps at the basic level there is no transfer of the ability, but it was present already at the intermediate level. Although at first sight it may seem that differences in diversity will only be due to lexical breadth (size of the lexicon), it seems that already at the vocabulary size that we may find at the intermediate level, there is a different individual display of diversity.

The findings of this study have some pedagogical implications. With the knowledge that lexical diversity ability can transfer from one's first language to the second, language educators can help students be in a better position to develop L2 lexical diversity by ensuring instruction specifically devoted to L1 vocabulary development is built into the L1 language curriculum, in an intentional and specific manner, rather than mere incidental learning through reading. Given that it seems easier for students with already built in diversity in their L1 to go the extra length of learning more diverse words, it could be easier to estimate this interest and ability earlier on in their lives and have the students already motivated to diversify their vocabulary, perhaps adding learning techniques that are specific to L1 to their repertoire so their learning is made more efficient. However, only further research in L1 lexical development transfer can help determine if it is best to stimulate future L2 lexical diversity by first focusing on L1 lexical diversity abilities before learning the L2 or if additional L1 instruction is best used after identifying students struggling to develop L2 lexical diversity. Though the present study does not identify other areas of transfer, it also does not rule out the possibility of transfer of other lexical skills at later stages of the development or with different tasks. It is also possible that working on L2 skills may improve L1 skills in return (Gonca 2016).

In the future, studies should continue to focus on identifying areas of lexical skills transfer. To best build on the findings of the present study, we suggest using the same indexes of lexical diversity, density, and sophistication. Lexical density and sophistication should not be excluded based on the fact that this study did not find transfer between these areas. Further studies using the same indexes could include additional groups of participants with a wider range of proficiency levels. This would allow to better capture the development in language ability depending on L1 previous ability. In addition, subjects should be classified into different groups according to a general proficiency test rather than previous learning experience or using both sources of information. Additional modifications to future studies could include randomly assigning writing prompts to participants from a sample of preselected prompts. This strategy would minimize the effect of a single prompt failing to expose a participant's true lexical ability. However, it would require extensive sampling, which could be difficult to obtain for a within-subjects study, and researchers would need to ensure that the topics/prompts would be similar in L1 and L2. Finally, future studies may want to determine sophistication using frequency lists that are genre specific, rather than a frequency list coming from all sorts of genres and modes (oral and written) in the language.

As mentioned earlier, previous studies (Borges Mota 2003; Perfetti 1969; Vulchanova et al. 2014) have found a relationship between general working memory, phonological working memory and word retention as well as sentence understanding/retention. It would be extremely interesting to research what effects those relationships have in the indexes studied here and, in the case of phonological working memory, how the effect could differ between the L1 and the L2. Transfer studies have found that similarities in the linguistic form are very influential factors in triggering specific lexemic transfer (Sánchez-Casas and García-Albea 2005). Finding a way to determine if this kind of transfer may enhance other types, such as lexical diversity, could further illuminate the process of transfer, for instance by comparing lexical diversity transfer between languages closer to each other and more phonetically dissimilar, even if sharing several cognates.

References

Atar, Cihat. 2018. The effects of learning a second language on the first: The case of increased metalinguistic awareness. *Journal of Language and Linguistics* 14(1). 242–260.
Beare, Sophie. 2000. *Differences in content generating and planning processes of adult L1 and L2 proficient writers*. Ottawa, Canada: University of Ottawa.
Ben-Yehudah, Gal, Elizabeth A. Hirshorn, Travis Simcox, Charles A. Perfetti & Julie A. Fiez. 2019. Chinese-English bilinguals transfer L1 lexical reading procedures and holistic orthographic coding to L2 English. *Journal of Neurolinguistics* 50. 136–148. https://doi.org/10.1016/j.jneuroling.2018.01.002 (accessed 15 February 2021).

Booth, Paul. 2014. The variance of lexical diversity profiles and its relationship to learning style. *International Review of Applied Linguistics in Language Teaching* 52(4). 357–375. https://doi.org/10.1515/iral-2014-0015 (accessed 15 February 2021).

Borges Mota, Mailce. 2003. Working memory capacity and fluency, accuracy, complexity, and lexical density in L2 speech production. *Fragmentos: Revista de Língua e Literatura Estrangeiras* 24. 69–104.

Castañeda-Jiménez, Gabriela & Scott Jarvis. 2014. Exploring Lexical Diversity in Second Language Spanish. In Geeslin, K. (ed.), *The Handbook of Spanish Second Language Acquisition*. New York, NY: John Wiley and Sons, Inc.

Checa-García, Irene & Laura Marqués-Pascual. 2020. *Where are relatively positioned Heritage Learners of Spanish when it comes to the lexicon? Lexical Richness Measures in Spanish heritage, native, and L2 learners*. Paper presented at the 49th Annual LASSO (Linguistic Association of the SouthWest) Meeting. Virtual Meeting.

Collentine, Joseph & Barbara F. Freed. 2004. Learning context and its effects on second language acquisition: Introduction. *Studies in second language acquisition* 26(2). 153-171. https://doi.org/10.1017/S0272263104262015

Cook, Vivian J. (ed.). 2003. *Effects of Second Language on the First*, 1–19. Clevedon, Avon: Multilingual Matters.

Covington, Michael A. & Joe D. McFall. 2010. Cutting the Gordian knot: The moving-average type–token ratio (MATTR). *Journal of quantitative linguistics* 17(2). 94–100.

Crossley, Scott A., Tom Cobb & Danielle S. McNamara. 2013. Comparing count-based and band-based indices of word frequency: Implications for active vocabulary research and pedagogical applications. *System* 41. 965–981. https://doi:10.1016/j.system (accessed 5 February 2021).

Cummins, James. 1979. Linguistic interdependence and the educational development of bilingual children. *Review of Educational Research* 49. 222–251.

Cummins, James. 1991. Interdependence of first-and second-language proficiency in bilingual children. In Ellen Bialystok (ed.), *Language processing in bilingual children*. 70–89. Cambridge, UK: Cambridge University Press.

Davies, Mark. 2006. *A frequency dictionary of Spanish: Core vocabulary for learners*. New York, NY: Routledge.

Dewaele, Jean M. 1998. Lexical inventions: French interlanguage as L2 versus L3. *Applied linguistics* 19(4). 471–490.

Dewaele, Jean M. & Aneta Pavlenko. 2003. Productivity and lexical diversity in native and non-native speech: A study of cross-cultural effects. *Effects of the second language on the first* 3. 120.

Engber, Cheryl A. 1995. The relationship of lexical proficiency to the quality of ESL compositions. *Journal of second language writing* 4(2). 139–155.

Fairclough, Marta & Flavia Belpoliti. 2015. Emerging literacy in Spanish among Hispanic heritage language university students in the USA: a pilot study. *International Journal of Bilingual Education and Bilingualism* 19(2). 185–201.

Fernández-Mira, Paloma, Emily Morgan, Sam Davidson, Aaron Yamada, Agustina Carando, Kenji Sagae & Claudia Sánchez-Gutiérrez. 2021. Lexical diversity in an L2 Spanish learner corpus: The effect of topic-related variables. *International Journal of Learner Corpus Research* 7(2). 230–258. https://doi.org/10.1075/ijlcr.20017.fer

Fuster, Carles & Hannah Neuser. 2020. Exploring intentionality in lexical transfer. *International Journal of Multilingualism* 17(4). 516–534. https://doi.org/10.1080/14790718.2018.1559845 (accessed on 2 February 2021).

García-Cardona, Juan & Irene Checa-García. 2019. La coloquialidad en la adaptación cinematográfica del texto teatral: una propuesta de estudio interdisciplinario con el ejemplo de "Bajarse al moro". *Trasvases entre la literatura y el cine* 1. 129–150.

Gonca, Altmısdort. 2016. Do L2 Writing Courses Affect the Improvement of L1 Writing Skills via Skills Transfer from L2 to L1? *Educational Research and Reviews* 11(10). 987–997.

González-López, Samuel & Aurelio López-López. 2015. Lexical analysis of student research drafts in computing. *Computer Applications in Engineering Education* 23(4). 638–644. https://doi.10.1002/cae.21638 (accessed on 5 February 2021).

Gregori-Signes, Carmen & Begoña Clavel-Arroitia. 2015. Analysing lexical density and lexical diversity in university students' written discourse. *Procedia-Social and Behavioral Sciences* 198. 546–556.

Henriksen, Birgit & Lise Danelund. 2015. Studies of Danish l2 learners' vocabulary knowledge and the lexical richness of their written production in English. In Päivi Pietilä (ed.), *Lexical issues in L2 writing*, 29–56. Cambridge, UK: Cambridge Scholars Publishing.

Hohenstein, Jill, Ann Eisenberg & Letitia Naigles. 2006. Is he floating across or crossing afloat? cross-influence of L1 and L2 in Spanish-English bilingual adults. *Bilingualism* 9 (3).249. https://doi.org/10.1017/S1366728906002616 (accessed on 15 February 2021).

Iniesta, Antonio, Daniela Paoleri, Francisca Serrano & María Teresa Bajo. 2021. Bilingual writing coactivation: lexical and sublexical processing in a word dictation task. *Bilingualism: Language and Cognition* 24(5). 1–16. https://doi.org/10.1017/S1366728921000274

Jarvis, Scott. 2000. Methodological rigor in the study of transfer: Identifying L1 influence in the interlanguage lexicon. *Language learning*, 50(2), 245–309. https://doi.org/10.1111/0023-8333.00118

Jarvis, Scott. 2002. Short Texts, Best-Fitting Curves and New Measures of Lexical Diversity. *Language Testing* 19(1). 57–84. https://doi.org/10.1191/0265532202lt220oa

Jarvis, Scott. 2009. Lexical transfer. In A. Pavlenko (ed.), *The Bilingual Mental Lexicon*, 99–124. Bristol, Blue Ridge Summit: Multilingual Matters.

Jarvis, Scott. 2013. Defining and Measuring Lexical Diversity. In Scott Jarvis & Michael Daller (eds.), *Vocabulary Knowledge: Human Ratings and Automated Measures*, 13–44. Amsterdam/N.Y.: John Benjamins.

Jarvis, Scott, Gabriela Castañeda-Jiménez & Rasmus Nielsen. 2012. Detecting L2 writers' L1s on the basis of their lexical styles. In Scott Jarvis & Scott Crossley (eds.), *Approaching Language Transfer through Text Classification: Explorations in the Detection-Based Approach*, 34–70. Bristol, Blue Ridge Summit: Multilingual Matters.

Jarvis, Scott & Brett James Hashimoto. 2021. How operationalizations of word types affect measures of lexical diversity. *International Journal of Learner Corpus Research* 7(1). 163–194. https://doi.org/10.1075/ijlcr.20004.jar

Jarvis, Scott & Aneta Pavlenko. 2008. *Crosslinguistic influence in language and cognition*. New York, London: Routledge.

Jiménez Catalán, Rosa María. 2017. Estudios de disponibilidad léxica en español y en inglés: revisión de sus fundamentos empíricos y metodológicos. *Revista Nebrija de Lingüística Aplicada a la Enseñanza de Lenguas* 22. 16–31.

Johansson, Victoria. 2008. Lexical diversity and lexical density in speech and writing: A developmental perspective. *Working papers/Lund University, Department of Linguistics and Phonetics* 53. 61–79.

Kalantari, Reza & Javad Gholami. 2017. Lexical Complexity Development from Dynamic Systems Theory Perspective: Lexical Density, Diversity, and Sophistication. *International Journal of Instruction* 10(4). 1–18.

Karim, Kahled & Hossein Nassaji. 2013. First Language Transfer in Second Language Writing: An Examination of Current Research. *Iranian Journal of Language Teaching Research* 1(1). 117–134.

Kilgarriff, Adam. 1997. Putting Frequencies in the Dictionary. *International Journal of Lexicography* 10(2). 135–155.

Kubota, Ryuko. 1998. An investigation of L1–L2 transfer in writing among Japanese university students: Implications for contrastive rhetoric. *Journal of Second Language Writing* 7(1). 69–100.

Kyle, Kristopher & Scott A. Crossley. 2015. Automatically Assessing Lexical Sophistication: Indices, Tools, Findings, and Application. *TESOL Quarterly* 49(4). 747–786. https://doi.org/10.1002/tesq.194 (accessed on 15 February 2021)

Laufer, Batia. 1989. A factor of difficulty in vocabulary learning: Deceptive transparency. *International Association of Applied Linguistics Review* 6(1). 10–20.

Laufer, Batia. 2003. The influence of L2 on L1 collocational knowledge and on L1 lexical diversity in free written expression. Vivian Cook (Ed.) *Effects of the second language on the first*, 19–31. Bristol: Multilingual Matters.

Lemmouh, Zakaria. 2008. The relationship between grades and the lexical richness of student essays. *Nordic Journal of English Studies* 7(3). 163–180.

Lindqvist, Christina, Camilla Bardel & Anna Gudmundson. 2011. Lexical richness in the advanced learner's oral production of French and Italian L2. *IRAL – International Review of Applied Linguistics in Language Teaching* 49(3). 221–240.

MacWhinney, Brian. 2000. The CHILDES Project: Tools for Analyzing Talk. 3rd edn. Mahwah, NJ: Lawrence Erlbaum Associates

Malvern, David, Brian Richards, Ngoni Chipere & Pilar Durán. 2004. *Lexical diversity and language development: quantification and assessment*. New York: Palgrave Macmillan.

Marqués-Pascual, Laura & Irene Checa-García. 2023. Lexical development of Spanish heritage and L2 learners in a study abroad setting. *Study Abroad Research in Second Language Acquisition and International Education* 8(1). 115–141. https://doi.org/10.1075/sar.21012.mar

McCarthy, Phillip M. & Scott Jarvis. 2010. MTLD, vocd-D, and HD-D: A validation study of sophisticated approaches to lexical diversity assessment. *Behavior Research Methods* 42. 381–392. https://doi:10.3758/BRM.42.2.381 (accessed on 3 February 2021).

Murakami, Akira. 2013. Cross-linguistic influence on the accuracy order of L2 English grammatical morphemes. In Sylviane Granger, Gaëtanelle Gilquin & Fanny Meunier (eds.), *Twenty years of learner corpus research: Looking back, moving ahead*, 325–334. Louvain-la-Neuve: Presses universitaires de Louvain.

Odlin, Terence. 1989. *Language transfer*. Cambridge: Cambridge University Press.

Palfreyman, David M. & Suha Karaki. 2019. Lexical sophistication across languages: a preliminary study of undergraduate writing in Arabic (L1) and English (L2). *International Journal of Bilingual Education and Bilingualism* 22(8). 992–1015.

Perfetti, Charles A. 1969. Lexical density and phrase structure depth as variables in sentence retention. *Journal of Verbal Learning and Verbal Behavior* 8(6). 719–724.

Poulisse, Nanda. 1999. *Slips of the Tongue: Cross-linguistic Influence in Language Learning*. Cambridge: Cambridge University Press.

Read, John. 2000. *Assessing vocabulary*. Cambridge: Cambridge University Press.

Reznicek-Parrado, Lina M., Melissa Patiño-Vega & Cecilia M. Colombi. 2018. Academic peer tutors and academic biliteracy development in students of Spanish as a heritage language. *Journal of Spanish Language Teaching* 5(2). 152–167. https://doi.10.1080/23247797.2018.1538358 (accessed on 15 February 2021).

Ringbom, Håkan. 2007. *The Importance of Cross-linguistic Similarity in Foreign Language Learning: Comprehension, Learning and Production*. Clevedon: Multilingual Matters.

Sadat, Jasmin, Clara D. Martin, James S. Magnuson, François-Xavier Alario & Albert Costa. 2016. Breaking down the bilingual cost in speech production. *Cognitive Science* 40(8). 1911–1940. https://doi.10.1111/cogs.12315.

Sánchez-Casas, Rosa & José E. García-Albea. 2005. The representation of cognate and noncognate words in bilingual memory. In Judith Kroll & Annete B. De Groot (eds.), *Handbook of bilingualism: Psycholinguistic approaches*, 226–250. Oxford: Oxford University Press.

Schafer, Austin. 2020. *First language syntactic complexity ability and its influence on second language syntactic complexity ability*. Laramie, WY: University of Wyoming MA Thesis.

Schmid, Monika S. & Scott Jarvis. 2014. Lexical access and lexical diversity in first language attrition. *Bilingualism: Language and Cognition* 17(04). 729–748. http://dx.doi.org/10.1017/S1366728913000771 (accessed on 29 January 2021).

Serrano, Raquel, Elsa Tragant & Ángels Llanes. 2012. A longitudinal analysis of the effects of one year abroad. *The Canadian Modern Language Review* 68(2). 138–163.

Shum, Kathy K., Connie S. Ho, Linda S. Siegel & Terry K. Au. 2016. First-language longitudinal predictors of second-language literacy in young L2 learners. *Reading Research Quarterly* 51(3). 323–344. https://doi.org/10.1002/rrq.139 (accessed on 28 January 2021).

Singleton, David. 2006. Lexical transfer: Interlexical or intralexical. In Jasnusz Arabski (ed.), *Cross-Linguistic Influences in the Second Language Lexicon*, 130–143. Bristol, Blue Ridge Summit: Multilingual Matters.

Sparks, Richard L., Jon Patton, Leonore Ganschow & Nancy Humbach. 2009. Long-term crosslinguistic transfer of skills from L1 to L2. *Language Learning* 59(1). 203–243.

Sparks, Richard L., Jon Patton, & Julie Luebbers. 2019. Individual differences in L2 achievement mirror individual differences in L1 skills and L2 aptitude: Crosslinguistic transfer of L1 to L2 skills. *Foreign Language Annals* 52(2). 255–283. doi:10.1111/flan.12390 (accessed on 28 January 2021).

Ströbel, Marcus, Elma Kerz & Daniel Wiechmann. 2020. The relationship between first and second language writing: Investigating the effects of first language complexity on second language complexity in advanced stages of learning. *Language Learning* 70(3). 732–767. https://doi.org/10.1111/lang.12394 (accessed on 15 June 2021).

To, Vinh, Si Fan & Damon Thomas. 2013. Lexical density and readability: A case study of English textbooks. *Internet Journal of Language, Culture and Society* 37. 61–71.

Tracy-Ventura, Nicole. 2017. Combining corpora and experimental data to investigate language learning during residence abroad: A study of lexical sophistication. *System* 71. 35–45. https://doi.org/10.1016/j.system.2017.09.022.

Uzawa, Kozue & Alister Cumming. 1989. Writing strategies in Japanese as a foreign language: Lowering or keeping up the standards. *Canadian Modern Language Review* 46(1). 178–194.

Vögelin, Cristina, Thorben Jansen, Stefan D. Keller, Nils Macts & Jens Möller. 2019. The influence of lexical features on teacher judgements of ESL argumentative essays. *Assessing Writing* 39. 50–63. https://doi.org/10.1016/j.asw.2018.12.003

Vulchanova, Mila, Camilla H. Foyn, A. Nilsen & Hermundur Sigmundsson. 2014. Links between phonological memory, first language competence and second language competence in 10 years-old children. *Learning and Individual Differences* 35. 87–95. https://doi.org/10.1016/j.lindif.2014.07.016 (accessed on 15 February 2021).

Waldvogel, Dieter A. 2014. An analysis of Spanish L2 lexical richness. *Academic Exchange Quarterly* 18(2). 17–25.

Wang, Wenyu & Qiufang Wen. 2002. L1 use in the L2 composing process: An exploratory study of 16 Chinese EFL writers. *Journal of second language writing* 11(3). 225–246.

Williams, Sarah & Bjorn Hammarberg. 1998. Language switches in L3 production: implications for a polyglot speaking model. *Applied Linguistics* 19(2). 295–333.

Zheng, Yongyan. 2016. The complex, dynamic development of L2 lexical use: A longitudinal study on Chinese learners of English. *System* 56. 40–53. https://doi.org/10.1016/j.system.2015.11.007 (accessed 5 February 2021).

Judith Borràs, Àngels Llanes, Goretti Prieto Botana
Chapter 6
Development of lexical deployment as a result of a short-term study abroad experience in Costa Rica

1 Introduction

The importance of vocabulary knowledge in second language (L2) learning cannot be understated. For many decades, there has been an agreement among vocabulary researchers that lexical knowledge is something learners cannot go without (Milton 2009). As an example, Wilkins (1972: 111) stated that "without grammar very little can be conveyed, without vocabulary nothing can be conveyed". Furthermore, it seems that vocabulary can be a strong predictor of proficiency and development of other aspects of language such as reading (Grabe 2009). Overall, it seems that having a certain control over the L2 lexicon can aid students to have a better command of the L2.

Different studies have come upon various suggestions as to what can help L2 learners enhance their vocabulary knowledge, and it seems that many acknowledge that what fosters vocabulary learning is having opportunities to use the L2 in different contexts, with different interlocutors and for different purposes (Foster 2009). That is, being able to use their L2 in a place other than their formal classroom. Accordingly, it seems that learning context is key when learning an L2 (Collentine 2009), and it could have a great impact on L2 vocabulary development (Zaytseva, Pérez-Vidal and Miralpeix 2018). Consistent with this belief, Llanes and Muñoz (2013) established that context is decisive when learning an L2 given that it will determine factors like the quantity and quality of the input students receive, the opportunities they will have to practice the language, and the type of formal instruction, among others.

The study abroad (SA) setting is believed to provide many opportunities for L2 practice and development. Learners in situations of immersion will use their L2 vocabulary inside the target language environment and in different contexts beyond the L2 classroom which, as Foster (2009: 93) suggested, provides learners the possi-

---
Judith Borràs, UDIT: University of Design and Technology
Àngels Llanes, Universitat de Lleida
Goretti Prieto Botana, University of Southern California

bility "to build more authentic networks of L2 word associations." Consequently, it seems that participating in a SA experience could be of paramount importance when learning an L2 and, in particular, in order to increase the students' vocabulary knowledge. Nonetheless, most of the studies on the topic examine vocabulary from a receptive perspective, that is, the ability to recognize a word when heard or seen (Dewey 2004; Milton and Meara 1995). Therefore, these studies usually investigate the number of words over which learners have at least some superficial knowledge (Schenker 2018). On the other hand, productive vocabulary, which consists of the learners' abilities to use this vocabulary effectively, has not been studied to the same extent (but see Arvidsson 2019; Leonard and Shea 2017).

Moreover, the few studies on the topic investigate rather long experiences abroad (Pérez-Vidal and Joan-Garau 2011; Zaytseva 2016). In fact, despite short summer SA experiences being one of the most popular types of international experiences, especially among North American undergraduates (Institute of International Education 2020), only a handful of studies investigate the impact of short SA experiences on L2 gains (but see Borràs and Llanes 2020; Schenker 2018; Rodrigo 2011). Finally, another gap within the SA literature is related to the fact that most of the existing research investigates groups of students whose L2 is English (Serrano, Tragant and Llanes 2012; Ife, Vives-Boix and Meara 2000), and the number of studies investigating groups of L2 Spanish learners is much smaller (but see Jiménez Jiménez 2010; Mitchell, Tracy-Ventura and McManus 2017; Tracy-Ventura 2017).

Altogether, with the purpose of determining whether SA plays a role in the students' L2 vocabulary development, this chapter examines the productive lexical development of a group of North American undergraduates, learners of Spanish as an L2, who spent five weeks in Costa Rica. Contrary to the norm, this study also has the potential of yielding valuable information to the question at hand in that 1) it focuses on a short-term stay and 2) it examines productive vocabulary rather than receptive vocabulary.

2 Previous studies on language and vocabulary learning in the SA context

Before the pandemic caused by covid-19, travelling abroad had become a reality for many undergraduates, and every year thousands of students participated in an experience abroad. Certainly, it seemed that overseas travel was the new norm at many universities around the world (and hopefully it will be again in the near future), and this was especially true across North American institutions (Farrell 2007). Researchers that have investigated vocabulary development across different contexts seem to agree that the SA is one of the most beneficial settings, possibly because it offers many opportunities to encounter L2 words, consequently, allowing learners to create L2 word associations (Milton 2009; Zaytseva, Pérez-Vidal and Miralpeix 2018). The Output Hypothesis outlined the importance of output learning an L2 when stating that producing L2 output makes students aware of their linguistic gaps and helps them reflect and analyze these issues with the objective of improving their output (Swain 1995). Consistent with her hypothesis, more recent studies suggest that language learning is facilitated by producing output (e.g., Elgort et al. 2018; Pichette, de Serres and Lafontaine 2012). Arguably, output production opportunities are greater in a SA situation because students will need to use their L2 more often than in their L1 setting. Therefore, it seems reasonable to believe that learners will enhance their vocabulary skills after spending some time in the target country.

Furthermore, the value of peer-to-peer dialogue on aspects of L2 learning has been demonstrated by various researchers who claim that talking and discussing language issues with other L2 learners allows students "to consolidate and reorganize knowledge of the L2 in structural and rhetorical aspects and to make this knowledge explicit for each other's benefit" (De Guerrero and Villamil 2002: 65). This, again, provides support to the idea that completing a stay in a foreign country could possibly enhance the students' L2 vocabulary, given that learners will be constantly exposed to the L2 and they will receive feedback from their peers when using the L2. As Vygotsky (1986) argued, for learning to occur, what is needed is the presence of a person with more knowledge of the L2 who will help the learner to use the L2 independently and with ease. Hence, it is possible that SA contexts foster learning because of the immersion in the L2 it provides. Altogether, it seems that a SA setting could provide the perfect combination between informal learning (opportunities to use the L2 in a real context, talks with native speakers) and formal learning (L2 instruction with other L2 learners).

According to some researchers, whereas other aspects of language such as grammar will depend on the students' meta-cognitive abilities and may benefit from formal instruction, exposure alone may suffice in order to increase receptive L2 lexical knowledge (Towell, Hawkins and Bazergui 1996). In other words, per previous research, while morphosyntactic development may require levels of attention that are generally not yielded by exposure alone, lexical development "thrives more on wider and more varied exposure to the target language" (Foster 2009: 93). This belief also aligns with DeKeyser's (1997) Skill Acquisition Theory, which suggests that for learning to occur, learners need to convert their declarative knowledge into procedural knowledge, and after massive hours of practice and exposure *automatization* occurs. Therefore, it seems plausible to believe that the SA context will have a positive impact on the learners' L2 vocabulary since it will provide a great amount of opportunities for L2 practice. However, DeKeyser (2007) claims that the SA experience will be influenced by the participants' previous preparation in their home country and that students should be ready for fluency improvement (linguistically speaking). DeKeyser (2007) suggests that the transition from the AH context to the SA one should coincide with the automatization, and hence puts forward that before going abroad participants should have gone through the proceduralization stage. Additionally, the author claims that, ideally, SA participants should receive some feedback from their (NS) interlocutors, and this is often not the case. Finally, what is important to note here is that vocabulary has many different dimensions and, consequently, it is very difficult to investigate all vocabulary aspects within one study (see Zyzik and Marqués-Pascual, this volume). Therefore, defining how vocabulary improves after a SA experience will depend on the objectives of each individual study.

Importantly, studies have many times made a distinction between receptive and productive vocabulary, with the former generally improving after a SA experience, and the latter seemingly needing more time to develop (Briggs 2015; Borràs and Llanes 2021). That is, typically, SA participants learn new words when they go abroad (arguably because of the different activities in which they participate, formal and informal). However, this doesn't necessarily manifest itself in writing due to its highly complex nature. Most studies within the SA literature only include measures of receptive lexical knowledge, that is, the ability to recognize a word when heard or seen (Ife, Vives-Boix, and Meara 2000; Milton and Meara 1995). Thus, findings on this point are limited to SA impact on passive lexical knowledge. Productive vocabulary, on the other hand, has not received the same amount of attention and, as when studied at all, findings have been far from conclusive (Borràs and Llanes 2020). In short, productive control of the L2 lexicon (i.e., the ability to use vocabulary effectively when speaking or writing), may well take require longer SA stays to ensue (Briggs 2015). In fact, given the vast amounts of practice involved its development, some authors have claimed that spending at least two semesters abroad will be necessary to observe gains inlearners' productive lexicon (Ife Vives, Vives-Boix and Meara 2000; Laufer and Paribakht 1998; Pérez-Vidal and Juan-Garau 2011; Serrano, Tragant and Llanes 2012). In sum, while it is fairly uncontroversial that passive knowledge of vocabulary can be expected as a result of shorter sojourns, the impact of shorter SA experiences over that aspect of acquisition is yet unclear (Fitzpatrick 2012).

Some examples of studies investigating L2 productive vocabulary development as a result of a SA experience are those by Marqués-Pascual and Checa-García (in press), Serrano, Tragant, and Llanes (2012), Pérez-Vidal and Juan-Garau (2011), Tracy-Ventura (2017) and Zaytseva (2016). Pérez-Vidal and Juan-Garau

(2011) examined a group of 55 Catalan/Spanish bilinguals after a 6-month period of formal English instruction at home (AH) and after a 3-month SA experience in an English-speaking country in terms of fluency, accuracy, grammatical complexity, and lexical complexity. During their stay, most participants lived in residence halls, some lived in shared flats, and a few decided to stay with a host family. Moreover, it is important to note that their participants attended content classes in English while abroad. Given that participants were majoring in translation and interpreting, the subjects they took while abroad included translation, literature, and cultural studies. The authors found that SA was beneficial for the participants (who did not show any significant gains after the period they spent learning English AH). The greatest gains were found in the participants' oral fluency, oral accuracy, grammatical complexity, use of formulaic language, written fluency, and written lexical complexity. Moreover, the authors used a pre-departure questionnaire from which they learnt that those students with higher post-stay gains exhibited high values in the following variables: hard work at learning English, a great desire to learn, and a low level of anxiety when speaking. Therefore, the authors stated that the attitudes that students have towards their English learning and the SA experience in general are a predictor of success.

Serrano, Tragant and Llanes (2012) investigated the oral and written skills of a group of Spanish undergraduates (n= 14) in terms of L2 English fluency, accuracy, syntactic complexity, and lexical diversity after spending the whole academic year in the UK. The authors found that some gains in the students' oral skills appeared during the first semester, but that positive changes in the students' written skills did not start emerging until the second semester. Hence, Serrano, Tragant and Llanes (2012) suggested that students would benefit from short stays abroad in terms of oral fluency and oral lexical diversity, but that such stays would not be as advantageous for the rest of the measures under examination. The main conclusion that arose from Serrano, Tragant and Llanes' (2012) study was that length of stay in the foreign country was an important predictor of oral and written gains and that productive measures need longer periods abroad in order to develop (which was particularly true in relation to the written productive measures).

Another objective of Serrano et al.'s (2012) study was to examine what could possibly have affected the development of high or low-achievers, and it was found that there was a relationship between the students' perceptions of English people and their gains or lack thereof. This finding aligned with Pérez-Vidal and Juan-Garau (2011), who found that positive attitudes towards the native speakers positively impacted learner outcomes when British were perceived to be as sociable (rather than unsociable) or humble (rather than snobbish). Therefore, it seems that the attitudes toward the L2 and its speakers and the students' willingness to learn and use the L2 while abroad can have a facilitative effect. Another important finding in Serrano Tragant and Llanes (2012) is that those students who did not have many interactions with other Spanish co-nationals were the ones who experienced more gains in terms of lexical richness. Therefore, it seems that making an effort to interact using the L2 rather than with peers with the same L1 is also beneficial (in light with DeKeyser 1997). Importantly, Serrano, Tragant and Llanes (2012) featured learners majoring in vastly different disciplines, such as science, languages, or history. Furthermore, participants also differed with respect to their academic year, that is, some of them were studying their second year at university when they departed to the UK, and others were in their third or fourth year. It is reasonable to assume that these differences could have had some impact on the final results.

Another example of a study investigating productive vocabulary is that by Zaytseva, Miralpeix and Pérez-Vidal (2019). These authors examined the development of 30 Catalan/Spanish undergraduates after a 6-month period of formal instruction AH and after a 3-month SA experience in the UK (93.3%) or the USA (6.7%). Participants were Translation and Interpretation majors for whom it was a requirement to participate in an international experience at least once during their undergraduate studies. During their stay, they were part of the Modern Languages and Humanities departments of their host universities and took content classes in English. In terms of accommodation, most of them lived in residence halls (60.7%), shared apartments with other students (25%), or stayed with host families (14.3%). According to the self-reports students completed after the stay, they had had much contact with native speakers and other international students, which is important because as it has been stated, using the L2 and having contact with other L2 users can have a significant impact on the students' development. Zaytseva, Miralpeix and Pérez-Vidal (2019) investigated the students in terms of their oral and written development as measured by density, accuracy, diversity, and sophistication and they found gains in all the measures but one (namely lexical sophistication). Their findings revealed the largest and most significant changes in lexical diversity and lexical accuracy. These results lend credence to the claim that different aspects of vocabulary develop at different paces, with some measures needing longer periods of time abroad and much more L2 practice in order to develop (Ife, Vives-Boix and Meara 2000; Laufer and Paribakht 1998). Specifically, it seems that lexical fluency, accuracy, and diversity are more sensitive to cater for gains, while lexical density and sophistication may take longer to develop. In line with this, Zaytseva, Miralpeix and Pérez-Vidal (2019) attributed their lack of gains in lexical sophistication to the demanding nature of argumentative writing and to the fact that, many times, this type of task is not practiced much in SA contexts.

Interestingly, in a longer-term SA study, Tracy-Ventura (2017) did find gains in lexical sophistication after a year-long SA period. In her study, she examined a group of 27 British undergraduate learners of L2 Spanish who participated in a longer experience in Spain or Mexico. On the one hand, she investigated the students' knowledge of words from different frequency bands by means of the X-lex test. That is, she used a receptive vocabulary task to examine the number of words that participants in her study had learnt in relation to their frequency (the 1000 most frequent, words in Spanish, the 2000 most frequent words, etc.). Therefore, this test provided an estimation of the knowledge students had of words from different frequencies (with 1000 being the most frequent, simpler words). Moreover, she also examined the students' productive use of more sophisticated words through an oral and a written task (productive vocabulary sophistication). A profiler of lexical sophistication was created, and it provided the total lemmas produced in the first five frequency bands (1–1000, 1001–2000, 2001–3000, 3001–4000, 4001–5000). The objective was to investigate whether students stopped using simple vocabulary (first frequency bands) and started using more difficult, or sophisticated vocabulary (higher frequency bands) after their SA experience. Tracy-Ventura (2017) found significant gains in both the students' receptive knowledge of infrequent words and in their productive use of such words. Hence, this study was one of the first to reveal that improvement in lexical sophistication as a result of staying abroad is possible, provided that the stay abroad is long-enough, and students receive sufficient writing practice.

Overall, the duration of the sojourn seems to have an impact on the changes that will emerge in the students' productive development, with stays lasting one term sometimes not being long enough for learners to increase their productive vocabulary knowledge. However, Borràs and Llanes (2020) investigated the receptive and productive vocabulary development (through writing) of a group of Spanish students who travelled to Ireland for only three weeks. Participants in their study were teenagers, and their experience consisted of living with a host Irish family (with whom they spent their evenings and weekends) and attending some language classes during the weekdays. In their study, Borràs and Llanes (2020) included a total of five measures of vocabulary: receptive vocabulary (raw scores), lexical fluency, lexical accuracy, lexical density, and lexical sophistication, and they found that their participants improved their receptive vocabulary, their lexical accuracy, and their lexical fluency (although gains were only significant for the first two measures). In other words, they learnt a significant number of new words and they used such words more accurately in their post-stay texts. Moreover, learners in their study wrote longer texts after their stay.

Hence, a 3-week experience was enough for participants in Borràs and Llanes (2020) to improve three of the five measures under investigation. It is important to note that participants in their study were teenagers, whose proficiency level was rather low at the beginning of the stay (A1–B1) and this could have influenced the lack of gains in lexical density and lexical sophistication. As previous research suggests, argumentative writing is very demanding and having a high proficiency level may be needed in order to have a good command of the different lexical measures (Tracy-Ventura 2017; Zaytseva 2016; Zaytseva, Miralpeix and Pérez-Vidal 2019). Moreover, investigations on the topic have also provided evidence that what is important when being abroad is to use the L2 and practice the different skills in order for them to develop (Serrano, Tragant, Llanes 2012). Although participants in Borràs and Llanes (2020) used their L2 to a large extent because they lived with host families (who only spoke English and had no knowledge of Catalan or Spanish), and attended classes in a language school, when triangulating the data, the authors realized that students mostly used their L2 in oral conversations and activities. Therefore, their written practice was almost inexistent, which could partially explain the lack of gains in the rest of the productive vocabulary measures.

All in all, the previous literature on productive vocabulary development after a SA experience is rather contradictory, which makes it difficult to draw any robust conclusions on this topic. Moreover, this gap in research is particularly notorious for learners of Spanish as an L2. Overall, it seems that despite the fact that L2 Spanish has received attention within the SA literature, there is still much to learn about the impact that participation in a stay abroad has over the L2 Spanish lexical deployment of the participants.

An additional problem is the fact that most studies examine semester- or yearlong experiences, whereas short (<8 weeks) SA experiences have been underresearched. Even though the previous literature on the topic seems to point out that short periods abroad will not be as beneficial for some aspects of productive vocabulary acquisition, some investigations have found gains in this aspect of the language even when the experience is short (Borràs and Llanes 2020; Zaytseva, Miralpeix and Pérez-Vidal 2019). Moreover, previous research suggests that if written skills are practiced while abroad, participants might be able to improve their productive vocabulary significantly (Tracy-Ventura 2017). Given that short (<8 weeks) SA experiences are the most common types of SA experience (Institute of International Education 2020) and that one of the goals of participants engaging in such SA programs is to improve fluency and proficiency (Allen 2002), and none of these is achieved without an improvement in vocabulary, it is of paramount importance that the role of short SA experiences on L2 vocabulary development is examined.

Additionally, the fact that short SA experiences have not been investigated to the same extent as longer ones neglects a great part of the SA population given the popularity of short SA programs, especially among students in the United States (Sanz and Morales-Front 2018). The latest report by the US Open Doors (Institute of International iEducation 2020) on the duration of SA programs shows that the number of participants in summer SA experiences lasting from two to eight weeks (30.5% in 2016/17 and 29.9% in 2017/18) is almost equal to that of participants who study abroad for a semester during the academic year (30.3% in 2017/18). Moreover, high percentages of students (up to 26% in 2017/18) participate in short experiences during the year (8 weeks or less and January term), whereas the number of people who take part in a yearlong SA experience is remarkably low (2.2% in 2017/18).

Altogether, given the limited number of studies investigating the impact of short SA experiences vis-à-vis the importance of the SA modality, it seems relevant to investigate whether participating in a short SA experience can have a positive effect on the students' L2. To that end, the present study set out to examine whether a short stay abroad would have a positive impact on L2 vocabulary development by a group of Spanish L2 learners. Accordingly, the following research question guided the investigation:

RQ: Does a 5-week SA experience have a significant impact on the productive lexical development of a group of L2 Spanish learners in terms of lexical diversity, accuracy, and sophistication?

3 Methods

3.1 Participants and SA program

A total of ten learners of Spanish (L2) participated in the present study. All of them had completed at least the equivalent of six semesters of college Spanish at their home institution in the United States before departure, their ages ranged between 19 and 23 and they were completing a major in Spanish. Most of them (n=7) were English native speakers who had studied Spanish since high school. Another two were heritage speakers of Spanish, and one participant was a native speaker of Chinese, but all of them reported English as their dominant language. Since heritage speakers sometimes have a higher proficiency (as compared to L2ers) and they often exhibit different motivations to travel abroad, the option of omitting the two heritage speakers of Spanish was considered for the present study. Nonetheless, after comparing their initial ratings to those of the other participants in the database (by examining their first written task), it was deemed that their performance did not appear qualitatively different. Further, data were analyzed both including and excluding heritage speakers with results remaining unchanged. Finally, it must be noted that their Spanish teacher in the North

American institution declared that they all had the same proficiency level. All things considered, it was decided to include them for the present study.

Participants enrolled in a 5-week SA program in Costa Rica, which was offered by their home university. During their stay, the students lived with local, Spanish monolingual families from Costa Rica and took part in two courses, an upper-level culture course (intended for students in their last stages of the major, and who had completed all least six semesters of college Spanish) and an intermediate level writing and language course, which were taught by Spanish native teachers. This is of particular importance given that, as stated in the literature review section, traditionally, SA participants lack practice of their written skills during their SA experience. However, participants in the present study enrolled in a language course that targeted writing in particular. They spent a total of 42 days in the target country, and during 24 of them they received formal instruction for three hours a day (total of 72 hours of instruction). In general, instruction took place during the week (Monday-Friday), except for planned trips and other activities, all of which involved interaction with Spanish speakers. Finally, the students were asked to complete different weekly assignments that usually required visits to nearby facilities to obtain information from local people.

3.2 Procedure and instruments

Participants were tested at four points in time during their stay in Costa Rica. All data collections happened in-situ at the host institution where participants were taking a 200-level writing and language course. The lessons were planned around four different topics that changed weekly, i.e., the students dealt with the same theme for a week. During that time, all learning activities evolved around the same topic and there was a weekly outing aimed at providing the students with a deeper insight on that given subject. Learners read various authentic texts relevant to the local area and proceeded to analyze their macro and micro-organization so as to scaffold students toward the production of a text of similar characteristics. Text content also received focus by way of comprehension questions. New vocabulary items were featured in these texts but were never the focus of instruction, which revolved around comprehension only in as much as it was needed to gauge the quality of the writing. As such, acquisition of vocabulary would have resulted from increased exposure to content pertaining to local issues that were featured in the syllabus, but was never an overt goal for student. At the end of each week, students had to write a formal composition on the topic they had covered that week. Thus, at the end of the stay the students had completed four formal written pieces on four distinct topics, three of which were subsequently analyzed to examine their lexical development. Despite the implications for data comparability that might stem from the differences in prompts and based on previous work by Llanes (2019), it was deemed that comparing the essays would yield a robust, yet small corpus comprised of thirty pieces of writing and a total of 14,368 words.

As mentioned before, out of the four compositions, only the first three were used for the purposes of the present study, to control for task difficulty. In other words, although all assignments instructed students to compose a formal piece of writing, the first three written tasks involved argumentation, which is generally considered more cognitively demanding (Rahimi 2019; Ruiz-Funes 2015). By contrast, the last piece of writing was descriptive, and therefore less likely to involve development of their own arguments for the purpose of persuading a reader, which would presumably demand a higher level of reasoning processing (Ruiz-Funes 2015). Altogether, it was believed that the last piece of writing would lend itself to confounding complexity and SA-related vocabulary gains. It is important to note that the writings had a minimum and maximum length that required students to create a piece of writing of about 400, but lengths varied depending on each of the prompts (See Table 1 for information about the length of the three prompts).

Table 1: Information about texts' length.

Text n°	Minimum	Maximum	Average length	SD
1	400	670	528.30	70.79
2	463	812	585.00	117.62
3	241	507	323.50	77.00

Students received feedback in the form of metalinguistic explanations and reformulations on their writing and, subsequently, they were asked to write a second version of the composition implementing the teacher's suggestions. Given the nature of the course, feedback was heavily focused on text organization and adherence to the genre, although occasional comments regarding grammatical accuracy were also included. Naturally, students received feedback with respect to their vocabulary use, but these received considerably less attention, with comments mostly offered on account of register issues. These second versions have not been used for investigation purposes; however, they might have raised awareness to lexical items and their appropriate use (DeKeyser 2007).

3.3 Measures and data analysis

Five measures of lexical deployment were examined from the written tasks in order to examine whether there was any development in the participants' L2 lexical development. In order to analyze the data, first of all the writings were transcribed into the Computerized Languages Analysis (CLAN) software (MacWhinney 2000), which provided information about T-units, total number of words, different types of words, and number of lexical errors. Once all this information was gathered, it was transferred into the Statistical Package for the Social Sciences (SPSS) program through which measures of lexical fluency and accuracy were computed.

The measures of lexical diversity, lexical accuracy, and lexical sophistication were calculated to account for the students' L2 vocabulary development. Two measures were used in order to examine lexical accuracy: lexical errors per total number of words (lexerr/W) and lexical errors per T-unit (lexerr/T). T-unit is defined as 'one main clause with all subordinate clauses attached to it' (Hunt 1965: 20). Following Zaytseva's (2016) error scheme, Table 2 below exemplifies the different types of errors that were taken into account for the present study: L1 transfer, word choice, non-words, and fixed expressions.

The command "vocD" available within the CLAN program was employed to examine lexical diversity (D). Although previous SA research has repeatedly used the Guiraud's Index of lexical richness when examining changes in the students' lexical diversity (Pérez-Vidal and Juan-Garau 2011; Serrano, Tragant and Llanes 2012; Zaytseva 2016), vocabulary researchers have often declared that GUI provides poor models of Type/token ratios because it is still correlated with extension and that the most reliable way of gauging gains in the students' lexical diversity is to use the D formula (Jarvis 2002; Malvern and Richards 1997; Meara and Miralpeix 2017). Consequently, it was decided to use the vocD command in CLAN because it avoids innate flaws in raw type/token ratios. Moreover, the CLAN program offers the option of examining texts in languages other than English, which was necessary within the present project given the L2 of the participants.

Finally, an added objective was to determine whether students had become more lexically sophisticated in their use of the L2. That is, whether they stopped using "simple" vocabulary and started using "rare" or "more sophisticated" words, which provides an illustration of the participants' command of high- and low-frequency vocabulary. Overall, lexical sophistication consists of distinguishing the students' competence to use simple, more frequent words or advanced, less frequent vocabulary (Tracy-Ventura 2017). In this study, lexical sophistication was examined by comparing the students' use of words from different frequency bands (from 1K to 5K). Therefore, in order to examine lexical sophistication, the present study adopted a band-based method involving lexical frequency profiling. The

Table 2: Lexical errors: types and examples.

Type	Description	Examples
L1 transfer	"Literal translation or direct borrowings of L1 words; false friends"	"*. . . para lograr nuestros **goles**"* meaning "goals" (correct form = *objetivos/metas*) "*el albergue **foca** mucho en sostenibilidad*" meaning "focuses" (correct form = *se centra*) "*se hace uso de una **machina**"* meaning "machine" (correct form= *máquina*)
Word choice	"Wrong or inappropriate lexical choice; mistakes with commonly confused words"	"*Pienso que puede **trabajar** porque hay muchos animales . . .*" meaning "it can work" (correct form = *funcionar/servir*) "*. . . es esencial para **guardar** la diversidad*" meaning "save/keep" (correct form= *proteger, salvar, mantener*) "*los campesinos **saben** sus tierras mejor*" meaning "know them better" (correct form= *conocen*)
Non-words	"Non-existent words based on L1 forms or resulting from erroneous morphology"	"He noticiado que . . ." meaning "I've noticed" (correct form= me he dado cuenta)
Fixed expressions	"Problems with formulaic language and idioms"	"*Por años a venir*" meaning "in years to come" (correct form= *en los proximos años/en el futuro*) "*la sostenibilidad es **un estado de mente**"* meaning "state of mind" (correct form= una manera de vivir) "*estas prácticas **hacen una diferencia**"* meaning "make a difference" (correct form= hacen o marcan la diferencia)

small corpus gathered from the students' writings through the CLAN program was formatted in CHAT. The transcripts were morphosyntactically tagged using the Spanish MOR grammar provided by CLAN. A separate program based on lemmas was used to determine the total amount of lemmas produced in the five frequency bands to compute sophistication. This script uses the frequency list provided in Davies (2006), a frequency dictionary listing the most frequent lemmas in the *Corpus del Español* which includes around 20 million words of spoken and written Spanish from Latin America and Spain. The script that has been used in the present study is the same as in Tracy-Ventura (2017: 40). It offered a list of the words from different frequency levels that students had used in their compositions, and it was created because no other publicly available option exists to match lemmas to their frequencies. Although band-based methods have received criticism for being less sensitive to group than count-based ones and lose information (Marqués-Pascual and Checa-García, in press; Checa-García and Schafer, this volume) both types of analyses have their advantages and disadvantages and frequency-band methods have been frequently deployed (Berton and Sánchez this volume). Higher values were expected for lexical diversity in the post-test for an amelioration to have taken place. Concerning lexical accuracy, lower values were expected since this would mean that participants made fewer lexical errors in their post-stay writings and, consequently, became more lexically accurate. With regard to lexical sophistication, a lower use of words from low frequency levels and a higher of words from the 4000-frequency level and above would mean that participants had become more sophisticated in their L2 word use.

The written data were coded by two applied linguists, both Spanish native speakers. Subsequently, codings were compared to calculate inter-rater reliability and they reached an agreement of 98.86%. Intra-rater reliability was also calculated by having the reviewer of the initial coding code a random 10% of the excerpts, coming to an agreement of 96.59%. Finally, the normality of the data was calculated, and it was found that all the measures were normally distributed. Hence, parametric tests were used for all measures under-study.

4 Results

The research question that guided this paper asked whether a 5-week SA experience would have a positive impact on the lexical deployment development of a group of L2 Spanish undergraduates in terms of lexical accuracy, diversity, and sophistication. The descriptive statistics in Table 3 show that, to some extent, students improved their accuracy, both in terms of Lexerr/W and Lexerr/T, and their lexical diversity over time.

All the measures that showed initial positive changes were normally distributed; hence, a repeated measures(RM) ANOVA was run in order to see if these differences in time were significant. The RM ANOVA with a Greenhouse-Geisser correction determined that mean lexical diversity (D) did not differ significantly from time points (F (1.903,17.127) = 1.370, $p < .28$). Finally, mean lexical accuracy did differ statistically significantly between time points both when measured in terms of lexerr/W (F (1.913, 17.213) = 14.543, $p < .000$, $d = 1.98$) and in terms of and lexerr/T (F (1.899, 17.088) = 12.788, $p < .000$, $d = 1.75$). The d values indicate that the difference between T1 and T3 was large for both Lexerr/W and Lexerr/T. Post hoc

Table 3: Descriptive statistics.

	Time 1		Time 2		Time 3	
	M	SD	M	SD	M	SD
VocD	66.62	7.17	71.92	8.00	73.07	11.20
Lexerr/W	.032	.009	.023	.008	.016	.007
Lexerr/T	.563	.204	.362	.138	.252	.146
1K	109.00	13.816	127.20	13.105	79.40	11.881
2K	21.00	5.538	24.50	5.503	13.40	3.340
3K	11.50	3.308	11.50	3.567	5.60	2.503
4K+	9.00	3.333	10.60	3.307	6.30	1.252

tests using the Bonferroni correction revealed that differences in lexical accuracy as measured by lexerr/W were significant from T1 to T3 ($p < .001$, $d = 1.98$), but neither from T1 to T2 ($p < 0.54$) nor from T2 to T3 ($p < 0.161$). Similarly, post hoc tests using Boferroni correction revealed that differences in lexical accuracy as measured by lexerr/T were only significant from T1 to T3 ($p < .002$, $d = 1.75$), but not from T1 to T2 ($p < 0.51$) nor from T2 to T3 ($p < .257$).

5 Discussion and conclusion

The main objective of the present study was to determine whether a short SA experience would have a positive impact on the lexical development of a group of learners of Spanish as a L2, as measured by lexical diversity, accuracy, and sophistication. Results showed that, following a 5-week stay in Costa Rica, participants improved significantly in terms of lexical accuracy only.

Per our findings, learners became significantly more accurate in their vocabulary (i.e. they made significantly fewer lexical mistakes over time) following their short stay abroad. This was true for both accuracy measures featured in the study (Lexerr/W and Lexerr/T). These results could very well originate in the immersive component of stay abroad, however, in the case of the present data, they could also owe to the fact that learners were enrolled in a writing-specific course that required written production and provided feedback. The present study does not make it possible to tease apart what portion of the recorded gains may have resulted from exposure alone. Thus, while initially, our findings seem to contradict previous SA research reporting null effects of short sojourns over lexical deployment (e.g., Serrano, Tragant and Llanes 2012), further research will be necessary to determine how much of those gains may come from exposure-related elements. All in all, however, it remains a possibility that our findings are tied to the additional interactional opportunities brought by SA environment, as well as our participants' willingness to capitalize on them (Zaytseva, Miralpeix and Pérez-Vidal 2019).

Our findings with respect to accuracy are also consistent with a subset of the existing SA literature, which suggests that studying abroad will increase the learners' capacity to use L2 words correctly (Zaytseva 2016). Specifically, previous research has generally suggested that being abroad will boost the participants' learning of L2 words (Ife, Vives-Boix and Meara 2000; Jiménez-Jiménez 2010), with this enhancement in receptive vocabulary potentially resulting in greater lexical accuracy, as well (Borràs and Llanes 2020). This seems plausible for our own results, too. It would be interesting for future short-term SA studies to feature accuracy, as well as receptive measures to try and determine any differential contribution of those two elements. Moreover, it seems reasonable to assume that improvements in accuracy may also stem from the greater chances for communication present in naturalistic learning environments (Borràs and Llanes 2020). As the Interaction Hypothesis, (Long 1985; 1996), points out, negotiation of meaning and the negative feedback that is conducive to, appear to trigger learners' awareness of their own shortcomings, which in turn makes them more receptive to subsequent input, and yields greater accuracy in the longer term. Our participants stayed with seasoned host-families who were used to having exchange students living with them. Given the living arrangements in the SA program reported here, it seems highly likely that some degree of feedback may have been present in our learners' daily homestay environment. Moreover, as part of their coursework, students were also consistently tasked with having conversations with other native speakers within the community, which may reasonably have included recasts and other forms of positive feedback. Finally, our participants also received frequent formal feedback as part of their instruction.

Constant and consistent feedback provision of any kind is certainly contingent upon the quality of the SA sojourn and any accompanying curricular goals, and not always a given. In this respect, it may be necessary to limit our findings to SA as we conceive of it in educational environments. It remains an empirical question whether these gains would result from immersion situations that exclude factors such as homestays and instructional practice, or other components that increase the likelihood for interaction.

Despite the positive findings in lexical accuracy, no significant gains were found in any of the other measures under exploration. Upon visual examination of the results, participants in this study appeared to become slightly more diverse after their 5-week stay in Costa Rica (in line with Pérez-Vidal and Barquin 2014 and Zaytseva 2016) but these gains failed to reach statistical significance. Considering that previous studies generally establish that lexical diversity are measures that benefit the most from SA experiences (Barquin 2012; Foster 2009; Zaytseva 2016), these findings were unexpected.

Our results could be partially explained in light of the topic that was used in the written tasks of the project. It could be that having to write compositions on different topics prevented participants from developing lexical breath, having to tap on a new and unrelated semantic field each time, instead. This might have been particularly so in T3, which required writing about *voseo*, that is, "the use of the *vos* pronoun together with its associated verbal forms" (translation from Benavides 2003: 612). The prompt in T3 may have, theoretically, asked that students compose a text featuring argumentation but was probably more informative in nature, as compared to prompts in T1 and T2, and this may have led to differing lexical needs. Moreover, the topic in T3 was also more technical, which means that learners may have needed to rely heavily on the same jargon-oriented vocabulary. Consequently, even though students composed three formal pieces of writing, and all three were argumentative and formal, it could be the case that the first two writings demanded a higher level of reasoning processing and use of L2 words, with this influencing the students' use of a variety of L2 words in the different texts (Ruiz-Fuentes 2015). One of the few studies that compared the extent to which using the same or different tasks is related to the participants' L2 gains (Llanes 2019) detected that differences were only significant for one of the five measures that were under-study (namely lexical diversity). In other words, it seems that using different tasks had an impact on the participants in Llanes (2019) in terms of lexical diversity examined through Guiraud's Index. Therefore, we could conclude that when measures such as lexical diversity or lexical fluency are under-study, using the same prompt each testing time might lead to more accurate results.

Finally, no statistical improvement emerged in relation to lexical sophistication. While our results with respect to sophistication are hardly exciting, they are rather illuminating. Only one study so far has reported positive findings in relation to lexical sophistication and SA (Tracy-Ventura 2017). Tracy-Ventura 2017 found gains both in students' learning of "sophisticated" words and their use of such words in production. As mentioned earlier, this study reported on a longer-term SA experience, and thus our findings appear to lend further credence to the claim that gains in this area only ensue as a result of longer stays. Another explanation to this finding could, again, be related to the topics used in the weekly writings. The fact that the third topic does not seem to be as demanding as those employed in times 1 and 2 may have limited the use of more advanced vocabulary in the last writing activity performed during the stay. Altogether, it seems that limitations in the design featured in the present study could account for some of its findings, too. Therefore, a conclusion from this is that prompts in this line of research must be carefully controlled to ensure that they are different yet comparable since keeping practice effects at bay calls for different prompts across testing times, but it would appear that controlling that variable might obscure certain types of gains.

Likewise, the effect of classroom practice needs to be controlled for, for instance by having two SA groups, one attending and one not attending such practices and studying their differences. Clearly, any gains reported in this study may have partially resulted from instruction, with the exact contribution of that variable remaining unknown. While vocabulary was not the focus of either of the classes in the sojourn this study reports on, and language was used as a vehicle to content rather than as the object of study, input sources learners were asked to engage with inevitably exposed them to new vocabulary within a setting conducive to learning. Due to the more advanced nature of the courses, arguably, both classes offered ample opportunities to encounter instances of vocabulary in the lower frequency bands, and in more erudite registers. Written assignments and subsequent feedback have increased exposure to vocabulary related to the topics of the courses, with this contributing to greater noticing of similar items in outings related to the courses, or in the community in general. It seems reasonable that more diverse and accurate production may have emerged as a result. Whether similar results might be expected from instruction alone is an understandable question in this respect, and yet one that pertains to whether SA is worthier, rather than whether SA is indeed effective. While admittedly an important question for appropriate resource allocation, assuming SA to be important only if it offers greater gains than an at-home class obviates the fact that learners may well decide to study languages for the opportunity to take part in SA, rather than for any extra benefits it may offer.

Further, at this point, study abroad research is no stranger to this confound. This is so much so that it is questionable whether SA that includes instruction should be considered confounded, as opposed to a strand of SA research in and of itself. Pairing instruction with a stay abroad is certainly very common for L2 learners, and comparability of groups who stay in the home institution versus those who travel tends to be ill-advised on account of the hardly avoidable socioeconomic variables that generally accompany those groups. While there is no question that studying the effect of a stay abroad in isolation would be most valuable to this area of research, instruction and the increased exposure it may result in are, at this point, arguably one more aspect of the SA experience. As such, we contend that it should be described in detail so as to try to better understand its potential impact, much like we do with variables like the amount or quality of interaction that purely naturalistic learners may engage in with host families or the local populations. In this vein, perhaps our most interesting finding is the absence of improvement in lexical sophistication. While gains in diversity and accuracy are perhaps understandably in part accounted for by instruction, the advanced level of courses, their required tasks and any related activities would have exposed learners to higher register elements (which, presumably day-to-day interaction in the community would not). Is it particularly telling, then, that no change was captured in this area, as it suggests that input richness may not immediately influence learning as much as input duration.

In light of the fact that only one of the measures examined in the present study showed significant development, our findings appear to lend credence to the notion that some aspects, such as accuracy, may be more susceptible to gains than others (Briggs 2015). Clearly, the brevity of the sojourn in the present study may be an important contributor to the general absence of improvement. It seems reasonable to argue that greater lexical accuracy may not always be accompanied by changes in lexical sophistication or diversity. While increased exposure to input and repeated opportunities for retrieval may result in more accurate use, arguably, it is possible that the SA environment still offers too little exposure to lower frequency and analogous forms for learners to notice, or that automaticity may be substantially affected. Similarly, it is possible that attentional limitations may not allow learners to make good on the limited opportunities to notice synonyms or lower-frequency words present in the input.

Previous studies establish that, for lexical deployment to improve significantly, learners need to spend at least two semesters abroad. In other words, the SA literature suggests that even one semester abroad may not be enough for learners to improve their lexical sophistication or some aspects of lexical fluency. As an illustration of this, studies like those by Jensen and Howard (2014), and Serrano et al. (2012), which investigated semester-long (or longer) experiences suggest that spending a term or less in the target country would not render any changes in the students' L2 vocabulary development, which is particularly true when it comes to lexical sophistication. Zaytseva (2016), for example, examined a group of students who only spent 3 months abroad and found improvement on some aspects of their productive vocabulary (namely, fluency, diversity, density, and accuracy). Our results also lend credence to the findings in these studies in as much as only some measures recorded a difference and the stay of the program we report on was, by all accounts, much shorter than a semester or a term.

In sum, this paper is positive in that some of the measures improved after spending only 5 weeks abroad. However, more emphasis should be placed on practicing our students' written skills because if there is something in common in the papers examining lexical deployment (as measured through written tasks), it is that what learners need is extensive practice. Further, our findings call for more research on the effects of task-type over learner production, to better understand the impact of using identical prompts, versus different prompts within the same genre, in gauging development of different aspects of lexical deployment. Future research needs to spin the fine details that emerge from SA investigations and continue to observe whether aspects such as lexical sophistication are impervious to exposure or if a longer experience or different instruments would produce gains.

Notwithstanding, these results must be taken with caution given the limitations of the present study. First, the sample size of participants was small, so results cannot be generalized; in other words, future investigations should set out to conduct research with a larger sample of participants. Additionally, another limitation of the present paper is that the topic of the essays was different, and this may have had an impact on the development of certain measures that were under-study. Finally, even though it was not an objective in the present study, it would be interesting to examine the impact (if any) of receiving vocabulary feedback after the first draft of the compositions by examining the results of the second versions.

Despite its limitations, the present study makes a significant contribution to the field in that it has found that 5 weeks abroad are enough for significant gains in lexical accuracy (lexerr/W and lexerr/T). Therefore, students, teachers and program organizers should be made aware of the fact that SA participants need to receive much practice in all L2 areas in order for them to develop all the aspects of the L2 in order to fully realize the gains that may arise from the experience.

References

Allen, Heather Willis. 2002. *Does study abroad make a difference? A study of motivational and linguistic outcomes* (Doctoral dissertation, Emory University, 2002). Dissertation Abstracts International 63. 1279.

Arvidsson, Klara. 2019. Quantity of target language contact in study abroad and knowledge of multiword expressions: A Usage-Based approach to L2 development. *Study Abroad Research in Second Language Acquisition and International Education* 4(2). 145–167. https://doi.org/10.1075/sar.18001.arv

Barquin, Elisa L. 2012. *Writing development in a study abroad context*. Barcelona: Universitat Pompeu Fabra dissertation.

Benavides, Carlos. 2003. La distribución del voseo en Hispanoamérica. *Hispania* 86(3). 612–623.

Borràs, Judith & Àngels Llanes. 2019. Re-examining the impact of study abroad on L2 development: a critical overview. *The Language Learning Journal* 49(5). 527–540. https://doi.org/10.1080/09571736.2019.1642941

Borràs, Judith & Àngels Llanes. 2020. L2 reading and vocabulary development after a short Study Abroad experience. *VIAL: Vigo International Journal of Applied Linguistics* 17. 35–55. https://doi.org/10.35869/vial.v0i17.1464

Borràs, Judith & Àngels Llanes. 2021. Investigating the impact of a semester-long study abroad program on L2 reading and vocabulary development. *Study Abroad Research and Second Language Acquisition and International Education*. https://doi.org/10.1075/sar.21015.bor

Borràs, Judith & Àngels Llanes. 2023. Investigating the impact of a semester-long study abroad program on L2 reading and vocabulary development. *Study Abroad Research in Second Language Acquisition and International Education* 6(2). 277–298. https://doi.org/10.1075/sar.21015.bor

Briggs, Jessica G. 2015. Out-of-class language contact and vocabulary gain in a study abroad context. *System* 53. 129–140. https://doi.org/10.1016/j.system.2015.07.007

Collentine, Joseph. 2009. Study Abroad Research: Findings, Implications, and Future Directions. In Michael H. Long & Catherine J. Doughty (eds.), *The Handbook of Language Teaching*, 218–233. New Jersey: John Wiley and Sons.

Davies, Mark. 2006. *A frequency vocabulary for Spanish: Core vocabulary for learners*. New York: Routledge.

De Guerrero, Maria C. M. & Olga S. Villamil. 2002. Activating the ZPD: Mutual Scaffolding in L2 Peer Revision. *The Modern Language Journal* 84(1). 51–68.

DeKeyser, Robert M. 1997. Beyond explicit rule learning: Automatizing second language morphosyntax. *Studies in second language acquisition* 19. 195–221.

DeKeyser, Robert M. 2007. *Practice in a second language: Perspectives from applied linguistics and cognitive psychology*. New York: Cambridge University Press.

Elgort, Irina, Sarah Candry, Thomas J. Boutorwick, June Eyckmans & Marc Brybaert. 2018. Contextual word learning with form-focused and meaning-focused elaboration. *Applied Linguistics* 39(5). 646–667. https://doi.org/10.1093/applin/amw029

Dewey, Dan. 2004. A comparison of reading development by learners of Japanese in intensive and domestic immersion and study abroad contexts. *Studies in Second Language Acquisition*, 26, 303–327.doi: https://doi.org/10.1017/S0272263104262076

Farrell, Elisabeth. 2007. Study Abroad Blossoms Into Big Business. *Chronicle of Higher Education* 54. https://www.chronicle.com/article/study-abroad-blossoms-into-big-business/. Accessed 18/05/2022

Fitzpatrick, Tess. 2012. Tracking the changes: Vocabulary acquisition in the study abroad context. *The Language Learning Journal* 40(1). 81–98. https://doi.org/10.1080/09571736.2012.658227

Foster, Pauline. 2009. Lexical diversity and native-like selection: the bonus of studying abroad. In Brian Richards, Michael Daller, David D. Malver, Paul Meara, James Milton & Jeanine Treffers-Daller (eds.), *Vocabulary studies in first and second language acquisition*, 91–106. Hampshire: Palgrave Macmillan.

Grabe, William. 2009. *Reading in a second language: Moving from theory to practice*. Cambridge: Cambridge Applied Linguistics.

Hunt, Kellog W. 1965. *Grammatical structures written at three grade levels*. Illinois: National Council of Teachers of English Research report 3.

Ife, Anne, Gemma Vives Boix & Paul Meara. 2000. The impact of study abroad on the vocabulary development of different proficiency groups. *Spanish Applied Linguistics* 4(1). 55–84.

Institute of International Education. 2020. Duration of Study Abroad. https://opendoorsdata.org/data/us-study-abroad/duration-of-study-abroad/ Accessed: 23/01/2021

Jarvis, Scott. 2002. Short texts, best-fitting curves and new measures of lexical diversity. *Language Testing* 19. 57–84.

Jensen, Julia and Martin Howard. 2014. The effects of time in the development of complexity and accuracy during study abroad: A study of French and Chinese learners of English. In EUROSLA

Yearbook (14) ed.L. Roberts, I. Vedder and J. H. Hulstijn, 31–64. John Benjamins Publishing Company: Amsterdam/Philadephia.

Jimenez, Jimenez, Antonio F. 2010. A comparative study on second language vocabulary development: Study abroad vs. classroom settings. *Frontiers: The Interdisciplinary Journal of Study Abroad* 19. 105–123.

Laufer, Batia & T. Sima Paribakht. 1998. The relationship between passive and active vocabularies: Effects of language learning context. *Language Learning* 48(3). 365–391.

Leonard, Karen Ruth. & Christine Shea. 2017. L2 Speaking Development During Study Abroad: Fluency, Accuracy, Complexity, and Underlying Cognitive Factors. *The Modern Language Journal*. https://doi.org/10.1111/modl.12382

Llanes, Àngels. 2019. Study abroad as a context for learning English as an international language: An exploratory study. In Martin Howard (ed.), *Study abroad, second language acquisition, and interculturality*, 88–106. Bristol: Multilingual Matters.

Llanes, Àngels & Carmen Muñoz. 2013. Age effects in a study abroad context: children and adults studying abroad and at home. *Language Learning* 63(1). 63–90. https://doi.org/10.1111/j.1467-9922.2012.00731.x

Long, Michael H. 1985. Input and second language acquisition theory. In Susan M. Gass & Carolyn G. Madden (eds.), *Input in second language acquisition*, 377–393. Rowley, MA: Newbury house.

Long, Michael H. 1996. The role of the linguistic environment in second language acquisition. In William C. Ritchie & Tej K. Bahtia (eds.), *Handbook of second language acquisition*, 413–468. New York: Academic Press.

MacWhinney, Brian. 2000. *The CHILDES project: Tools for analyzing talk*. 3rd edn. Mahwah: Lawrence Erlbaum Associates.

Malvern, David & Brian Richards. 1997. A new measure of lexical diversity. In Ann Ryan & Alison Wray (eds.), *Evolving models of language: papers from the annual meeting of the British Association for Applied Linguistics held at the University of Wales, Swansea, September 1996*, 58–71. Clevedon: Multilingual Matters.

Marqués-Pascual, Laura, & Irene Checa-García. 2023. Lexical development of Spanish heritage and L2 learners in a study abroad setting. *Study Abroad Research in Second Language Acquisition and International Education*, 8(1), 115–141.

Meara, Paul and Imma Miralpeix. 2017. *Tools for Researching Vocabulary*. Bristol: Multilingual Matters.

Milton, James. 2009. *Measuring second language vocabulary acquisition*. Bristol: Multilingual Matters.

Milton, James and Paul Meara. 1995. How periods abroad affect vocabulary growth in a foreign language. *ITI Review of Applied Linguistics* 107(8). 17–34.

Mitchell, Rosamond, Nicole Tracy-Ventura and Kevin McManus. 2017. *Anglophone students abroad: Identity, social relationships and language learning*. New York: Routledge.

Pérez-Vidal, Carmen & Elisa Barquin. 2014. Comparing progress in writing after formal instruction and study abroad. In Carmen Pérez-Vidal (ed.), *Language acquisition in study abroad and formal instruction contexts*, 217–234. Amsterdam: John Benjamins.

Pérez-Vidal, Carmen & Maria Juan-Garau. 2011. The effect of context and input conditions on oral and written development: A study abroad perspective. *International Review of Applied Linguistics in Language Teaching* 49(2).157–185. https://doi.org/10.1515/iral.2011.008

Pichette, François, Linda de Serres & Marc Lafontaine. 2012. Sentence reading and sentence writing for second language vocabulary acquisition. *Applied Linguistics* 33(1). 66–82.

Rahimi, Mohammad. 2019. A comparative study of the impact of focused vs. comprehensive corrective feedback and revision on ESL learners' writing accuracy and quality. *Language Teaching Research* 23(5). 633–654. https://doi.org/10.1177/1362168819879182

Rodrigo, Victoria. 2011. Contextos de instrucción y su efecto en la comprensión auditiva y los juicios gramaticales: ¿Son comparables cinco semanas en el extranjero a un semestre en casa? *Hispania* 94(3). 502–513. http://www.jstor.org/stable/23032123

Ruiz-Funes, Marcela. 2015. Exploring the potential of second/foreign language writing for language learning: The effects of task factors and learner variables. *Journal of Second Language Writing* 28. 1–19. https://doi.org/10.1016/j.jslw.2015.02.001

Sanz, Cristina & Alfonso Morales-Front. 2018. *The handbook of study abroad research and practice*. New York: Routledge.

Schenker, Theresa. 2018. Making short-term study abroad count – Effects on German language skills. *Foreign Language Annals* 51. 411–429.

Serrano, Raquel, Elsa Tragant, & Àngels Llanes. 2012. A longitudinal analysis of the effects of one year abroad. *The Canadian Modern Language Review*, 68, 138–163. doi: https://www.muse.jhu.edu/article/476509

Swain, Merrill. 1995. Three functions of output in second language learning. In Widdowson, H.G., Cook, G., & Seidlhofer, B. (Eds.), *Principle and practice in applied linguistics: Studies in honour of HG Widdowson* (pp. 125–144). OUP: Oxford.

Towel, Richard, Roger Hawkins, & Nives Bazergui. 1996. The development of fluency in advanced learners of French. *Applied Linguistics*, 17, 84–119

Vygotsky, Lev S. 1986. Thought and Language. Cambridge, MA: MIT Press.

Wilkins, David. 1972. Linguistics in language teaching. London: Arnold.

Zaytseva, Victoria, Carmen Pérez-Vidal, & Imma Miralpeix. 2018. Vocabulary acquisition during study abroad: A comprehensive review of the research. In Sanz, C., & Morales-Front, A. (Eds.), *The Routledge handbook of study abroad research and practice* (pp. 210–224). Routledge: London.

Zaytseva, Victoria. (2016). *Vocabulary acquisition in study abroad and formal instruction: An investigation on oral and written lexical development* (Unpublished doctoral dissertation). Universitat Pompeu Fabra, Barcelona.

Zayteva, Victoria, Imma Miralpeix, & Carmen Pérez-Vidal. 2019. Because words matter: Investigating vocabulary development across contexts and modalities. *Language Teaching Research*.doi: https://doi.org/10.1177/1362168819852976

Marco Berton and Laura Sánchez
Chapter 7
Effects of passive vocabulary knowledge and task type on lexical sophistication in L2 Spanish writing

1 Introduction

The dichotomy between passive and active vocabulary has been widely employed in second language acquisition studies, as it mirrors the distinction between comprehension and production common to many aspects of language performance (Nattinger 1988). The interest in the relationship between passive vocabulary knowledge and active vocabulary use arises from the fact that successful word storage in the mental lexicon does not guarantee word retrieval and usage as the need arises. The study presented here aims at further inquiring into the likelihood of a relationship between passive and active vocabulary, by exploring the effects of passive vocabulary knowledge on the active vocabulary used in writing by Swedish learners of Spanish as a foreign language in a university setting. Moreover, these effects are investigated in two cognitively different tasks, namely a narrative and a decision-making task, in order to determine whether task type has an effect on lexical sophistication, and whether there might be an interaction between these two factors.

In what follows, Section 2 offers a broad overview of the core construct investigated in the present study, that is, lexical sophistication, together with a brief summary of how it has been operationalized in empirical studies. Section 2.1 reports and discusses the main findings of the studies that have investigated the relationship between passive vocabulary knowledge and lexical richness (sophistication and diversity) in L2 writing. Finally, Section 2.2 accounts for the effects of task type on lexical richness. The research questions guiding the study are presented in Section 3, while the methodology followed in the data collection and the analysis is reported in Section 4. The results of the study are reported in Section 5. To conclude, the results are discussed in light of previous studies in Section 6, and some conclusions, including pedagogical implications and some limitations, are offered in the discussion.

Marco Berton, Karlstad University
Laura Sánchez, Stockholm University

2 Literature review

An increasing number of scholars have started to draw attention to the acquisition and teaching of vocabulary in Spanish as a foreign language, and a few overviews of the topic have recently been published (cf. Sánchez Rufat and Jiménez Calderón 2015; Barcroft and Muñoz-Basols 2021). However, lexical richness is among the most understudied constructs within studies on Spanish vocabulary, though lexical availability has arisen some interest in recent years (Jiménez Catalán 2017). Lexical richness is often used as a cover term for a number of features that tap into the different lexical characteristics of a text (Read 2000; Kyle 2020). In the present study, active vocabulary use is operationalized in terms of the feature commonly referred to *lexical sophistication*. Lexical sophistication relates to the ability to use relatively infrequent words. The distinction between basic and sophisticated words is traditionally established according to their frequency of appearance in a given corpus, which is often built on the basis of a considerable number of texts. In other words, lexical sophistication does not directly relate to the corpus upon which the frequency list is built, even though it is calculated by contrasting the texts to be analyzed with the frequency list in the corpus. Thus, lexical sophistication can be considered an extrinsic vocabulary measure (Meara and Bell 2001) or a word-list-based approach (Daller and Xue 2007).

Lexical sophistication has scarcely been investigated in studies on the acquisition of Spanish as a foreign language. The seminal work by Waldvogel (2014) is perhaps the first attempt to empirically investigate lexical richness in a pilot study based on a small sample of conversations that aimed at examining potential differences in the lexical sophistication and diversity of intermediate to advanced learners of Spanish. His results showed that the participants in the intermediate-high proficiency group outperformed those in the intermediate-low group, but no significant differences were found among the intermediate-high and the advanced-mid groups. However, the measure of lexical sophistication used in Waldvogel (2014) correlated very highly ($r=.922$) with the lexical diversity measure. Thus, the measurement of the two features of lexical richness in his study might be problematic, as sophistication and diversity are measured in rather similar ways. Moreover, the bar for sophistication is set at a quite low level, which may be the reason for such high correlation. In general, even though some low to moderate correlation is to be expected, these two constructs do not normally follow exactly the same path, as will be explained in this section.

Indeed, lexical richness involves both sophistication and diversity, and lexical diversity seems to be a more commonly investigated feature of lexical richness. The lexical diversity feature can be defined as the ability to use a varied lexical repertoire rather than repeatedly rely upon a limited set of words (Read 2000). As it involves solely the words contained in the language sample under analysis, it can be characterized as an intrinsic vocabulary measure (Meara and Bell 2001) or a word-list-free approach (Daller and Xue 2007). Even though the focus of the present study is not on lexical diversity, relevant results concerning such construct will be eventually discussed in order to compare and contrast sophistication with this other feature of lexical richness.

Generally speaking, the use of infrequent words (that is, sophistication), along with the use of a broader range of both frequent and infrequent words (that is, lexical diversity), is commonly considered to be a characteristic of the written and oral production of more proficient learners (e.g., Laufer and Nation 1995; Jarvis 2002). Nevertheless, the role played by a much more specific type of proficiency, i.e., passive vocabulary knowledge, in written production is still unclear. The following section discusses the effects of passive vocabulary knowledge on lexical richness in studies on L2 writing. In addition, as passive vocabulary knowledge might play a different role depending on the type of task at hand, previous studies investigating the effect of task type on vocabulary use in an L2 are discussed in a separate section.

2.1 Effects of passive vocabulary knowledge on lexical richness in L2 writing

A few authors hold that the distinction between passive and active vocabulary knowledge oversimplifies the conception of vocabulary knowledge. In Melka's view, for instance, this distinction is considered instead as an indivisible continuum that ranges from comprehension to use (Melka 1997). Nonetheless, this distinction is a common and useful way to operationalize and investigate vocabulary knowledge in L2 studies. Passive and active vocabulary knowledge have also been referred to as merely passive and active vocabulary (Laufer 1998) or receptive and productive vocabulary (Nation 2013; Zhong 2018). Most studies adopting this distinction make use of controlled tests of active vocabulary knowledge (Waring 1997; Fan 2000; Nemati 2010; Zhong 2018), in which specific lexical items are elicited. In turn, fewer studies have focused on the relationship between passive vocabulary knowledge and lexical richness in free production.

Regarding lexical sophistication, it has traditionally been calculated by establishing a cutting point in a frequency list and comparing language samples with the words included in the list of most frequent words. The words in the language samples not included among the most frequent ones in the frequency list are used as an indicator of the sophistication of the samples (Laufer 1995). In order to avoid dependence on text length, sophistication is frequently calculated as a proportion (or percentage) of sophisticated words over the total number of different words (word types) in a text (Read 2000: 204). A further development in lexical sophistication consists in the use of frequency bands, which aim at providing a more nuanced picture of the lexical sophistication in a language sample in the form of a lexical frequency profile (e.g., Laufer and Nation 1995). However, its condensed version (Laufer 1995), which works as a traditional cutting-point measure, is often preferred to the more complex lexical profile.

A study on the effects of passive vocabulary knowledge on lexical sophistication is Laufer (1998). This study investigates the written production of adolescent learners of English as a foreign language. In this case, passive vocabulary knowledge was measured by means of a test in which learners had to choose the synonym of a given set of words, while lexical sophistication was calculated on the basis of data from argumentative texts. In Laufer's study, no significant correlation was found between passive vocabulary knowledge and lexical sophistication. Further insight into the relationship between passive vocabulary knowledge and lexical sophistication is provided by Laufer and Paribakht (1998), Lemmouh (2010) and Sanhueza, Ferreira and Sáez (2018), which are discussed in more detail in what follows.

The study by Laufer and Paribakht (1998) relied on data from Israel and Canada, collected using the same instruments and procedure as in Laufer (1998). To be more specific, the participants in this study wrote an argumentative essay of their choice based on the prompt whether governments should be allowed to limit the number of children in families or whether technology can technology replace traditional face-to-face teaching in the classroom. The Israeli data were elicited from both high-school and university learners of English as a foreign language, while the Canadian data were collected exclusively among university learners of English as a second language. As far as the learners' linguistic background is concerned, those in Israel had Hebrew, Russian or Arabic as their L1, whereas the learners in Canada had a much wider variety of L1s. Contrary to the results in Laufer (1998), those in Laufer and Paribakht (1998) showed moderate (in the Canadian group) and high (in the Israeli group) correlations between passive vocabulary knowledge and lexical sophistication in argumentative writing. Moreover, since Laufer and Paribakht (1998) grouped their participants according to their scores in the passive vocabulary knowledge test, it is possible to see a clear trend consisting in a progressively greater lexical sophistication displayed by the learners with increasing passive vocabulary knowledge (i.e., wider passive vocabulary knowledge). Thus, one possible way to explain the incongruity of the results in the methodologically consistent studies by Laufer (1998) and Laufer and Paribakht (1998) is the different age, and therefore cognitive maturity, of the learners in both studies.

Relying on the same test as Laufer (1998) and Laufer and Paribakht (1998), Lemmouh (2010) measured the passive vocabulary knowledge of Swedish university learners of English. However, the texts he used in order to calculate lexical sophistication were academic essays on literature and linguistics that the learners wrote as a home assignment. Lemmouh (2010) found no significant correlations between passive vocabulary knowledge and lexical sophistication in the written production of these learners. Compared to the learners in Laufer and Paribakht (1998), these different results might be due to the more specific topics (such as close readings of various literature genres) Lemmouh's learners wrote about, and the possibility to use any kind of aid and tool while performing the task at home. Indeed, the learners in Lemmouh (2010) widely outperformed even the most lexically proficient learners in Laufer and Paribakht (1998).

Another relevant study is the one by Sanhueza et al. (2018), where the effects of vocabulary learning strategies on gains in passive vocabulary knowledge and lexical sophistication were investigated. The tests and methodology for data collection and analysis are similar to those in the other studies on lexical sophistication reported in this section. These authors compared the performance of an experimental group with that of a control group in a pre- and post-test, with the experimental group being explicitly instructed in the use of vocabulary learning strategies for a period of fourteen weeks. All the participants were university learners studying English as a foreign language at a Chilean university. Their results showed that the passive vocabulary knowledge of both the participants in the experimental group and the in the control group increased over the period under investigation. However, while the control group improved significantly in the knowledge of words belonging to only one frequency band, the experimental group improved with respect to three frequency bands.

As regards active vocabulary use, measured by lexical sophistication, the two groups in Sanhueza et al. (2018) showed different patterns. On the one hand, the control group failed to significantly develop, and also revealed a decrease in two measures related to the words included in the second frequency band (words comprised between the first 1000 and 2000 in the corpus). These results suggest that one term of study (i.e., eighteen weeks) is not enough to improve lexical sophistication in argumentative writing, but it is likely to allow learners to expand their passive vocabulary knowledge. On the other hand, the experimental group showed an increase in the total number of words produced and in three measures related to the most basic frequency bands. These results may suggest some development in the learners' vocabulary that the authors were not explicitly investigating, such as a potentially greater lexical diversity within such bands, though not a higher lexical sophistication overall, as the English word families that are normally considered sophisticated are not included among the first 2000. This interpretation of their findings, apart from confirming the lack of improvement in lexical sophistication of the control group, might indicate that the learning strategies implemented in the study might have had a positive effect on lexical diversity instead even if this feature of lexical richness was not explicitly measured. The findings by Sanhueza et al. (2018) seem to largely disagree with Laufer and Paribakht (1998), while supporting Laufer's (1998) and Lemmouh's (2010) absence of significant increases in lexical sophistication. It is worth mentioning that the studies reported so far investigated passive vocabulary knowledge and lexical richness in L2 English.

A recent publication focusing on lexical sophistication in Spanish as a foreign language is the study by Tracy-Ventura (2017). The main purpose of her investigation was to analyze the effects of study abroad on passive vocabulary knowledge and lexical sophistication. The data collection took place at two points, before and towards the end of the participants' study abroad period. The participants under investigation, most of them having English as their L1, had studied for nine months in a Spanish speaking country (either Spain or Mexico) by the time the second data collection took place. Passive vocabulary knowledge was assessed by testing the recognition of words from different frequency bands based on L1 corpora. In order to calculate lexical sophistication in writing, the participants were asked to perform an argumentative task, for which they were given three minutes to organize their thoughts and fifteen to write a text of approximately 200 words. Furthermore, lexical sophistication was also assessed in two oral tasks (an interview and a picture-based narrative), performed at the same points in time as the passive vocabulary test and the argumentative essay writing. Lexical sophistication was calculated by comparing the participants' linguistic production with five frequency bands. Both for passive vocabulary knowledge and active vocabulary use in writing and speaking, comparisons were made on the basis of the words belonging to the three lowest-frequency bands. It is worth noting that Tracy-Ventura (2017) analyzed the written production of her participants together with the spoken samples obtained in the two oral tasks. With respect to passive vocabulary knowledge, the results showed a significant improvement as far as the recognition of less frequent words is concerned. Regarding lexical sophistication in free writing and speaking, the results pointed towards a significant rise of low-frequency words in their texts. In short, this pioneering study on passive vocabulary knowledge and lexical sophistication in L2 Spanish indicated that an increased general proficiency derived from a long stay abroad in an immersion context can lead to a significant improvement in the proportion of low-frequency words that the learners are able to both recognize and produce. Consequently, it seems plausible to hypothesize that there might be a positive relationship between passive vocabulary knowledge and lexical sophistication in vocabulary use, as also revealed by Laufer and Paribakht (1998). Nonetheless, given that the results for lexical sophistication in Tracy-Ventura (2017) mix oral and written data and different types of task, caution is necessary when comparing them to results from other studies.

None of the studies discussed so far investigated the relationship between passive vocabulary knowledge and lexical sophistication in narrative texts. Given the relevance of narrative tasks in the empirical study that will be presented in Section 3, where narrative and argumentative tasks are compared, a study addressing the effects of passive vocabulary on lexical diversity is now discussed. Jarvis (2002) investigated the relationship between a word recognition test and lexical diversity in narrative writing by 140 Finnish speaking and 70 Swedish speaking adolescent learners of English. His results showed moderate correlations between passive vocabulary knowledge and lexical diversity, pointing at the existence of a positive relationship between the two constructs. In other words, drawing on these results it is plausible to expect that learners having a wider passive vocabulary may be able, to some degree, to employ a more varied vocabulary in foreign language writing.

In a nutshell, the scarce evidence available in previous research has shown that passive vocabulary knowledge seems to occasionally correlate moderately and positively with lexical sophistication in argumentative writing tasks (Laufer and Paribakht 1998), as they appear to follow similar developing patterns (Tracy-Ventura 2017). However, the development of lexical sophistication in L2 writing seems to require more time in comparison with passive vocabulary knowledge (Sanhueza et al. 2018). In terms of narrative tasks, whereas no evidence of the effects of passive vocabulary on lexical sophistication is available, it appears that passive vocabulary knowledge would correlate moderately and positively with lexical diversity (Jarvis 2002).

Based on the evidence presented in this section, it seems that a considerable increase in passive vocabulary knowledge is needed in order to affect lexical sophistication. In turn, relatively smaller differences in passive vocabulary knowledge can already result into a more diverse lexical repertoire of basic words. Nevertheless, none of the studies discussed in this section has investigated the relationship between passive vocabulary knowledge and lexical sophistication in L2 narrative writing, being argumentative tasks the only type of task investigated. The difference between the two task types may depend on the different degree of complexity that any task type entails, as they require a specific kind and number of mental operations. More precisely, an abstract relationship that involves reasoning oriented towards the formulation of arguments for or against a given issue is considered a more complex task than a narration. Along similar lines, Skehan's (1996; 2015) account of cognitive complexity translates into the idea that coping with less concrete and less familiar information is cognitively more demanding, which may have a bearing on performance (Sánchez 2019). This would include, for instance, justifying decisions, which is at the core of a decision-making task such as the one employed in the present study. General considerations about task complexity and the ways in which it can affect lexical richness in writing are provided in the following section.

2.2 Effects of task type and complexity on lexical richness in L2 writing

Task complexity is conceived as the intrinsic cognitive demands (Robinson 2011; 2015) of a pedagogical task. In short, it refers to an objective difficulty that can be more easily appreciated when comparing different types of tasks, or different versions of the same task in which some features have been somehow manipulated. The adjective 'cognitive' draws attention to the fact that a more demanding task would require a greater amount of cognitive resources, namely working memory and attention, for a learner to successfully complete it (Foster and Skehan 1996; Skehan 1998; also Robinson 2003). As stated above, the inherent cognitive complexity of a task is largely dependent on task type. Even early studies on cognitive task complexity already acknowledged that different task types pose different cognitive demands on the learner (e.g., Brown et al. 1984). Notwithstanding, only a few studies to date have compared the lexical richness elicited by different types of writing tasks. More importantly, these studies have investigated only on one aspect of lexical richness, namely, lexical diversity. Hence, the following paragraphs discuss only this aspect of lexical richness, yet with a focus on finding out potential differences across different types of tasks.

One such study is Castañeda-Jiménez and Jarvis (2014), which analyzed the written production of 112 university learners of Spanish as a foreign language in the United States. Every learner wrote both a narrative and an argumentative text, from which the authors calculated several measures of lexical diversity. Their comparison between the two task types showed that the argumentative texts were more lexically diverse than the narrative texts, and this was true in spite of the fact that the narrative texts were, on average, longer than the argumentative ones. These results clearly point towards the existence of an effect of task type on lexical diversity in foreign language writing.

Similar results were obtained in Frear and Bitchener (2015), a study that analyzed the written production of adult learners of English as a second language in New Zealand. Data were elicited using a less complex task (a description), and two versions of a more complex task (a decision-making task). The less complex task consisted in writing a letter in which the learners had to provide information about the country in which they were living at the time. In one of the decision-making tasks the learners had to choose a restaurant on the basis of a fictitious friend's tastes and needs, comparing them to the information provided about two restaurants. In turn, in the more complex task, the learners still had to choose a restaurant, but having to cope with more restaurants and further needs, which complicated the decision. The results showed that both versions of the decision-making task elicited a higher lexical diversity than the descriptive task, even though the differences were statistically significant only in the comparison between the most complex version of the decision-making task and the descriptive task. Thus, once again the higher inherent complexity in the decision-making task (in comparison with other task types) seems to lead to greater lexical diversity. It is worth mentioning that in Frear and Bitchener's study the tasks contained instructions in the target language, which may have played a role in the higher lexical diversity, as the decision-making tasks contained increasingly extensive instructions such as descriptions of the restaurants among which the learners had to choose.

In sum, the findings in these studies point at a tendency for argumentative essays to be more lexically diverse than narratives (Castañeda-Jiménez and Jarvis 2014), and for decision-making tasks to elicit a more diverse vocabulary compared to descriptive tasks (Frear and Bitchener 2015). From a research perspective, more importantly, the effects of task type on lexical sophistication are still unknown, and therefore worth investigating so as to have a more comprehensive view of its effects on lexical richness in writing. Summing up, the overall picture given in Sections 2.1 and 2.2 suggests a shortage of studies that specifically address the relationship between passive vocabulary knowledge and lexical sophistication in general, and in L2 Spanish in particular. In addition to this, the inconclusive results in the evidence assembled point at a need to more deeply investigate and understand the way in which passive vocabulary knowledge affects lexical sophistication when performing different types of written tasks that differ in their inherent cognitive complexity.

3 Research questions

With the empirical gap identified above as the point of departure, the goal of the study presented here is two-fold. On the one hand, it sets out to investigate the contribution of passive vocabulary knowledge in active vocabulary use, by asking whether passive vocabulary knowledge affects the development of lexical sophistication. If so, on the other hand, the study tries to ascertain whether the effects of passive vocabulary knowledge on the development of lexical sophistication are mediated by the inherent complexity of two different types of tasks. In other words, the effects of task type on lexical sophistication are also investigated, as well as the existence of a joint effect of task type and passive vocabulary knowledge. Bearing this in mind, the study is guided by the following questions:

RQ (1): Does passive vocabulary knowledge affect the development of lexical sophistication?

RQ (2): Does task type affect the development of lexical sophistication?

RQ (3): Is there an interaction of the effects of passive vocabulary knowledge task type?

4 Methodology

In order to answer the research questions guiding the study, data were used from a larger investigation (Berton 2020). The participants in the study were 62 Swedish university learners of Spanish as a foreign language (47 females and 15 males), whose profile is described below. This description is followed by an explanation of the instruments selected to elicit data from the participants. Next, the procedure followed in the process of data gathering is presented. After that, the data analysis section gives an account of how the data were coded, how lexical sophistication was calculated, and the statistical treatment of the data.

4.1 Participants

Spanish is the most studied foreign language in Sweden (Ministerio de Educación y Formación Profesional 2020) after English. In spite of this, Österberg (2021: 12) reports a relative lack of interest in this language within the Swedish society, which may affect motivation to learn and cause the high incidence of abandonment and poor learning achievement among upper secondary school pupils. Nevertheless, Spanish is also a common choice among learners in higher education. As for teaching at a university level, Swedish universities do not follow any shared syllabus, as they organize credit distribution and course content independently. Likewise, because teaching at this level is not regulated by the department of education, vocabulary is sometimes mentioned in the syllabi for beginner courses, but no specific guidelines are given as to how its teaching should be implemented in the classroom.

Participants were recruited from four universities in Sweden, and their participation was voluntary. As Table 1 below shows, most of them were in the first term of their university studies in Spanish (83.9%), and around 20 years old at time of testing. Upon entry in the Spanish program, learners at Swedish universities need to have at least an A2 level according to the Common European Framework of Reference (CEFR, henceforth; Council of Europe 2001), which is roughly equivalent to a low, non-beginner proficiency level. For this reason, such participants are described in the table as having a low proficiency level. In subsequent terms, the proficiency level of the courses progresses towards approximately lower-intermediate and intermediate (B1 in CEFR), and high intermediate (B2 in CEFR). Finally, the participant who was studying Spanish at a master level when the data was collected can be considered an advanced user of this language (C1 in CEFR). Table 1 offers an overview of the participants' age and term of study. All but seven of the 62 participants were between 19 and 23 years old. The remaining seven were more than 50 years old. The presence of mature learners is quite common in Sweden, as people often decide to interrupt their working activities to continue their education in a related or different field. Public financial support makes it feasible for all learners to support themselves while studying, and it is worth noting that university education is completely free of charge.

Table 1: Overview of the participants' age and term.

	1st Term (Low)	2nd Term (Low-Int)	3rd Term (Int)	4th Term (High-Int)	Master (Advanced)
Minimum	19	20	21	–	–
Maximum	71	68	68	–	–
Mean	26.50	35.40	39.33	23	24
Standard Deviation	11.469	20.169	25.146	–	–
n	52 (83.9%)	5 (8.1%)	3 (4.8%)	1 (1.6%)	1 (1.6%)

The participants were all native speakers of Swedish, while four of them were bilingual in Swedish and another language and four were even trilingual.[1] It is important to note, though, that potential candidates with Spanish or any other Romance language as their additional L1 were excluded from the working sample to prevent linguistic similarities across languages from conceding an advantage to these participants and biasing the results.

4.2 Instruments

The battery of tests used in the present study relied on various tests of linguistic proficiency and writing tasks. First and foremost, in order to assess the partici-

---

[1] The terms 'bilingual' and 'trilingual' are used in this study to refer to the simultaneous acquisition of two or three L1s during childhood.

pants' passive vocabulary knowledge, a visual word recognition test was employed, namely, the Lextale-Esp test (Izura, Cuetos and Brysbaert 2014). In this test, which consists of 90 sequences of letters out of which only 60 are existing words in Spanish, participants were asked to identify these 60 words leaving out the sequences of non-words that functioned as distractors. The existing words included in this test were chosen from a series of frequency bands established by Izura et al., and they represent a range of proficiencies from beginning to more competent speakers. Table 2 shows the descriptive statistics of the learners' performance in this test. The distractors in this test were punished with −2 points, which justifies the negative punctuation displayed in the table. All in all, 3 participants obtained a negative punctuation. Scores are expressed in percentages.

Table 2: Passive vocabulary knowledge test descriptive statistics.

n	Mean	Stand. Dev.	Min.	Max.	Range
62	25.19	19.49	−20	75	95

Secondly, in order to confidently tease apart the effects of passive vocabulary knowledge from those of overall proficiency, a general proficiency test was administered. This test was based on a 25-item cloze test (Muñoz 2006), and was used as an indicator of overall proficiency. The results of this test proved to significantly (p=.000) correlated with the passive vocabulary test, with an effect size that can be interpreted as moderate to high (r=.676). For the sake of transparency, the descriptive statistics of the learners' performance are presented in Table 3, even though its effects are not investigated in the present study.

Table 3: Overall proficiency test descriptive statistics.

Profic.	n	Mean	Mode	Stand. Dev.	Min.	Max.	Range
Low	26	4.73	5.00	1.218	1	6	5
High	36	10.00	9.00	3.406	7	19	12

In order to answer RQ2, it was necessary to compare different types of writing tasks. To this aim, task complexity was operationalized in terms of inherent cognitive difficulty, and so two different genres were selected that differed in terms of their inherent complexity and that have been frequently investigated in research on second language acquisition. To be more precise, a *narrative* task and a *decision-making* task were used, in the understanding that a narrative is expected to be cognitively easier (i.e., less complex) and less demanding than a decision-making task, as discussed in Section 2.2. As pointed out above, the study presented here is part of a larger investigation into the development of lexical richness in writing, and into the constraining effects of task complexity on this development (Berton 2020). In the study by Berton (2020), task complexity was also operationalized by means of the manipulation of complexity within the same type of task. In particular, two versions (+ simple vs. + complex) of each writing task were used. Even though this specific operationalization of task complexity is not the focus of the present study, to be able to analyze a larger pool of data it was decided to include data from both the simple and complex versions of each task type.

The narrative tasks, adapted from Tavakoli and Foster (2008), were based on a visual stimulus and consisted of a strip cartoon with various pictures. They differed from each other in terms of structure and in the presence or absence of background events. The simple version of the narrative task was *Football* (Heaton 1966), which shows only foreground information and has a fix, easily identifiable structure that makes the events depicted less difficult to process. In turn, the complex version of the narrative task was *Walkman* (Jones 1979). The events in this task are developed both in the foreground and the background and do not follow a specific chronological order, which would make the task more difficult to process. As for the decision-making task, the task was adapted from Levkina and Gilabert (2012), and it consisted in writing a letter to a friend recommending him or her a vacation destination based on his or her preferences and needs. The main difference between the simple and complex versions of this task was the number of elements to be considered. Thus, whereas the simple version of the task included two possible destinations, the complex version of the task included six. Table 4 summarizes the characteristics of the tasks employed in the study:

Table 4: Task features across writing tasks.

	Narrative Task	Decision-Making Task
Complexity feat. Manipulated	± structure ± background events	± many elements
Less complex version (n=31)	tight structure & only foreground events	2 elements (destinations)
More complex version (n=31)	loose structure & background events	6 elements (destinations)

Additional information on the instruments employed in the present study, as well as the tasks themselves including visual stimuli and instructions in Swedish, can be found in Berton (2020).

4.3 Procedure

To maximize the representativity of the sample, data were gathered from four different universities in different sessions, with Swedish as the language of communication to make sure the participants would not be exposed to additional target language input. With the purpose of avoiding an undesired task effect on performance, the order of administration of the tests was counter-balanced in each session. The participants had 15 minutes to complete the vocabulary task, 15 minutes to fill-out the cloze test, and then 20 minutes for each writing task. All participants wrote both a narrative and a decision-making task. However, they wrote different versions. Specifically, half the participants wrote the simple version of each task, whereas the other half wrote the complex version of each task. The effects of the manipulation of task complexity within the same task type are beyond the scope of this chapter, as they would also involve other linguistic aspects not directly related to vocabulary, which is the focus of the present edited volume. The participants were not allowed to use any online resources (including dictionaries, orthographic correction, etc.), and they were explicitly asked to handwrite a text about 120–200 words long to guarantee comparability across texts. The instructions provided together with the written tasks, in Swedish, included information about the expected length, the impossibility of relying on any kind of pedagogical support or electronic device, and, most importantly, what the participants were supposed to do within the timeframe awarded for the tasks.

4.4 Data Analysis

In order to answer the three research questions, linear mixed models were implemented for every measure of lexical sophistication (explained in more detail in the next paragraph) using passive vocabulary knowledge and task type as fixed-effect independent variables and 'subject' as a random-effect variable. Passive vocabulary knowledge was operationalized by means of the passive vocabulary knowledge test by Izura et al. (2014), and computed into the model as the percentage of right answers, that is, as a continuous variable.

Data processing and analysis were conducted by means of various software tools. The texts written by the participants were first transcribed and converted to Word file documents. The measurement of lexical sophistication in the texts was based on the calculation of five measures. More specifically, the measurement was made by comparing participants' texts with the frequency list SUBTLEX-ESP (Cuetos et al. 2011). The choice of this frequency list was motivated by the assertion that this list had been employed in the construction of the Lextale-Esp test (Izura et al. 2014).

Besides, given that the frequency list is based neither on word families nor on lemmas, it makes it possible to make direct comparisons with the words contained in texts without having to code. Apart from this practical advantage, working with single words avoids the potential information loss caused by grouping all inflected and derived forms, as is the case for word families. As Crossley et al. (2013: 967) point out, grouping words in lemmas or word families would imply assuming that a learner who can produce *go* and another one who can produce *gone* are assessed in the same way even though the latter produced a much more sophisticated word according to frequency lists. However, this choice could also be perceived as having the disadvantage of assessing both lexical and morphological knowledge, as in every case where no lemmatization is applied.

In the absence of a generally accepted measure for Spanish (as 'Beyond 2000' for English, Laufer 1995), it was necessary to establish a cut-off point so as to determine which words would be considered sophisticated. Five different cut-off points were chosen, to establish how lexical sophistication would change while setting the cut-off point to an increasingly higher level. The cut-off points were set at 4.000, 6.000, 8.000, 10.000 and 12.000 most frequent words in the chosen frequency corpus. The comparisons were made using the online tool Text Lex Compare v.3 (Cobb 2013). The output given by the tool consisted in the number of words in the texts not included in the list it had been compared with. This number was then divided by the total number of words in the texts in order to transform it into the proportion of relatively sophisticated words in the text. For instance, a value of 0.1 for the 4.000 cut-off point for would correspond to a 10% of words in a text not belonging to the first 4.000 most frequent words in the main frequency list. This procedure was repeated for each text and for each list obtained from the frequency list by changing the cut-off points between sophisticated and non-sophisticate words. Working with proportions instead of absolute values would allow the comparison among different texts.

The process of data analysis proceeded along two steps. The first step was the assessment of proficiency, both in terms of passive vocabulary knowledge and of overall proficiency, as described earlier. After that, the second step was the analysis of lexical sophistication in written production. The results of these analyses were transferred to the software SPSS (Statistical Package for the Social Sciences, version 27) and submitted to statistical treatment. For the statistical treatment of the data, the mixed linear model was chosen. This test makes it possible to examine the effects of the independent variables (i.e., passive vocabulary knowledge and task type) on the dependent variables (i.e., lexical sophistication for each cut-off point) and also any interaction between the two independent variables, which might imply that the effect of one of them is mediated by the other. Finally, Cohen's *d* effect sizes were calculated for the factors whose effect on lexical sophistication proved to be significant.

Such effect sizes aim at quantifying the magnitude of the significant effects, thereby completing the information provided by *p* values.

5 Results

The study was guided by three research questions, one on the effects of passive vocabulary knowledge on the development of lexical sophistication, one on the effects of task type, and another one asking whether there was an interaction between passive vocabulary knowledge and task type. This section presents the results of the mixed linear models conducted to find out the significance of the factors passive vocabulary knowledge and task type, and their interaction. Before delving into the results of the mixed linear models, Table 5 below presents the descriptive statistics (mean and standard deviation) corresponding to the overall lexical sophistication for the narrative task and the decision-making task.

Table 5: Lexical sophistication in the narrative task and in the decision-making task.

Measure	4k	6k	8k	10k	12k
Narrative (*n*=62)					
Mean	.09742	.05992	.04665	.03782	.03077
Stand. Dev.	.038687	.031279	.026395	0.22967	.020733
Decision-making (*n*=62)					
Mean	.11624	.09284	.07587	.05773	.04427
Stand. Dev.	.043384	.036094	.033693	.028725	.027048

As expected, the proportion of infrequent words becomes smaller when the cut-off point is raised, that is, the frequency of the words considered sophisticated is lower. Likewise, it seems that texts elicited using the decision-making task were more sophisticated in comparison to those elicited by the narrative task. For example, when the words not included among the first 4000 in the frequency list are regarded as sophisticated, they roughly account for the 9,7% in the narrative and the 11,6% in the decision-making task, respectively. The results of the mixed linear models measuring the effects of passive vocabulary knowledge and task type on lexical sophistication are presented in Table 6. Significant effects ($p<.05$) are marked with an asterisk.

Table 6: Effect of passive vocabulary knowledge and task type on lexical sophistication.

Measure	Factor	Sig.	F Value
4k	PVK	.301	1.170
	TT	.058	3.769
	PVK*TT	.988	.481
6k	PVK	.322	1.148
	TT	.000*	21.946
	PVK*TT	.980	.516
8k	PVK	.520	.979
	TT	.000*	17.703
	PVK*TT	.995	.432
10k	PVK	.307	1.163
	TT	.001*	12.043
	PVK*TT	.966	.557
12k	PVK	.270	1.203
	TT	.015*	6.317
	PVK*TT	.957	.576

PVK= Passive Vocabulary Knowledge; TT= Task Type

The results provided in Table 6 show no significant effect of passive vocabulary knowledge on lexical sophistication, irrespective of the measure used to operationalize lexical sophistication. In contrast, task type turned out to have a big impact on lexical sophistication. To be more precise, all the models considering lexical sophistication as the proportion of types beyond the the first 6000 words in the frequency corpus reached statistical significance. Finally, no significant interaction was found between the independent variables passive vocabulary knowledge and task type. To have a better understanding of the magnitude of the effect of task type on lexical sophistication, repeated t-tests for paired samples were run. The descriptive statistics regarding group means and standard deviations for the two task types have already been reported in Table 5. In Table 7, the *p*-values obtained in the t-tests, the correlation coefficients r and Cohen's d values are provided.

According to the standards in the field of second language acquisition (Plonsky and Oswald 2014), these effect sizes are considered small. The scale proposed for paired samples accounts for the high intragroup correlations normally found in this type of design (p. 889). In other words, an effect size of .7 would still be considered small when regarding paired-samples, but medium in independent-samples, where

Table 7: Paired-samples t-test and power analysis.

Measure	6k	8k	10k	12k
p	.000	.000	.000	.002
r	.020	.023	.061	.122
Cohen's d	.696	.691	.558	.422

correlations are expected to be low or nonexistent. However, as can be appreciated in Table 7, no correlation proved to be statistically significant in the present comparisons, which might allow for the highest effect sizes, i. e., those related to the measure 6k and 8k, to be regarded as medium.

In order to provide a clearer view of these results, Figure 1 shows scatter plots for passive vocabulary knowledge (reported on the Y axis) and lexical sophistication (on the X axis) for each cut-off point analyzed. Blue dots are used for the narrative task, while green dots represent the decision-making task. The pattern that emerged in the data suggests a significant effect of task type on lexical sophistication, while no effect was found for passive vocabulary knowledge. First, lexical sophistication was higher in the more complex task type. Secondly, and perhaps more importantly, this was so irrespective of passive vocabulary knowledge. This can be seen in the lack of interaction between passive vocabulary knowledge and task type, but also by examining the scatterplots provided in Figure 1, in which the distribution of the dots representing lexical sophistication in the decision-making task, in general, show that they are often to be found on the right side, compared to those related to the narrative task. Such a pattern holds for all the four sophistication measures analyzed with significant results. The homogeneity of the effect of task type along the vertical axis, representing passive vocabulary knowledge, visually confirms the absence of any interaction between the two independent variables in the study. Regarding the measures 6k, 8k and 10k, it is interesting to notice how even the two participants who displayed the lowest passive vocabulary knowledge, represented by the four dots closest to the bottom of the graphics, managed to use a more sophisticated vocabulary when performing the decision-making task.

The results section closes with a few examples of learners' performance. These examples are meant to illustrate different levels of lexical sophistication, as well as differences across task types. More precisely, (1) illustrates a low level of sophistication in the simple version of the narrative task, whereas (2) illustrates a higher level of sophistication in the complex version of another participant's decision-making task. The examples are accompanied by a word-for-word translation into English, which often results in ungrammatical constructions in this language.

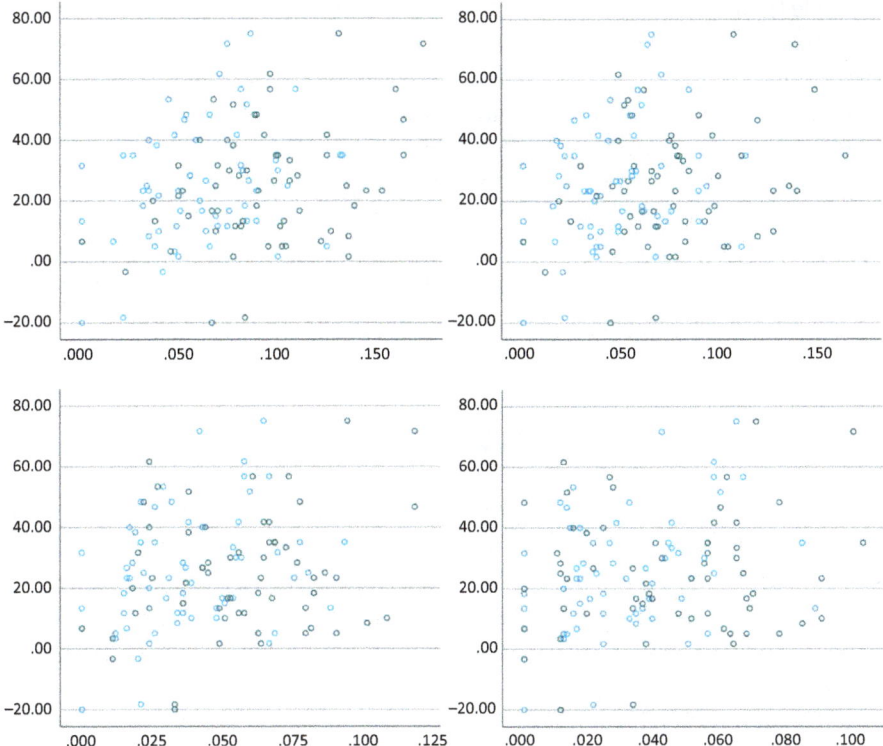

Figure 1: Scatter plots for the measures 6k, 8k, 10k and 12k (clockwise orientation).

(1) "Los hijos juegan fútbol en el *courto* de un escuela. El viene en un cosa al lado de un árbol. Los hijos no saben cómo hacer porque no pueden tomar. Un hijo toma agua, mucho agua y pone en la cosa y un otro hijo puede tomar el fútbol y todos los hijos serán feliz." [The sons play football in a school's court. He comes in a thing on the side of a tree. The sons do not know how to do because they cannot take. A son takes water, much water and puts in the thing and another son can take the football and all the sons will be glad]

(2) "Sé que me pediste que revisara los paquetes de viaje que te recomendó la agencia de viaje. Teniendo en cuenta la cuestión de la financiación, las opciones que tienes son la I, IV y V." [I know that you asked me to revise the travel packages that the agency recommended to you. Keeping in mind the funding issue, the options you have are I, IV and V.]

Example (1) above shows a sentence with a low level of lexical sophistication. As can be seen, the learner used almost only basic words, especially in terms of verbs (*jugar, saber, tomar, poner*) and lexical strategies such as adapting a foreign word (*courto* from 'court') and using a similar word to the one needed, such as sons (*hijos*) instead of children (*niños*). On the contrary, example (2) illustrates a higher level of lexical sophistication. This can best be seen in the use of a more elaborated vocabulary, as required also by the type of task he was performing, i.e., a decision-making task, or its topic. In this example more nuanced verbs are used, such as revise (*revisar*) and recommend (*recomendar*), as well as more sophisticated nouns like travel agency (*agencia de viajes*) and funding (*financiación*).

6 Discussion and conclusions

The results presented in the preceding section allow us to confidently answer the research questions guiding the study. First, the data clearly showed no effect of passive vocabulary knowledge on the lexical sophistication of the learners investigated (RQ1), at least in the tasks examined. Secondly, a clear effect of task type was found (RQ2), and this effect did not seem to interact with passive vocabulary knowledge (RQ3).

The absence of effects related to passive vocabulary knowledge on lexical sophistication might be explained in several ways. In the first place, it should be remembered that most of the participants in the study were learners in their first semester of Spanish. Thus, it could be hypothesized that participants with lower passive vocabulary knowledge did not know part of the vocabulary necessary to carry out the tasks. Another possibility could be that these participants with lower passive vocabulary knowledge might have relied on a wider range of high-frequency words and therefore using a proportion of sophisticated words not much lower than those of their peers. As Laufer and Paribakht (1998) point out, a narrower passive vocabulary knowledge is formed by more frequent words, whereas a larger passive vocabulary knowledge includes more infrequent words. As stated in the introduction of this chapter, word storage in the mental lexicon does not automatically ensure its recovery for active use in writing. In other words, it seems plausible that, in order for passive vocabulary knowledge to significantly affect lexical sophistication, the difference in passive vocabulary knowledge among the learners (or groups of learners) under investigation needs to be considerable. The hypothesis according to which small differences in passive vocabulary knowledge are sufficient to affect lexical diversity while a major difference is needed for it to affect sophistication is worth investigating in future studies.

These results are consistent with those in Laufer (1998), who analyzed the written production of adolescent learners and found no correlation between passive vocabulary knowledge and lexical sophistication. The author claimed that the population investigated in her study was rather homogeneous in terms of proficiency, which also seems to be the case in the present study. This narrow gap in proficiency among the participants, which would reflect also on similar levels of passive vocabulary knowledge, might have prevented the emergence of differences in their lexical sophistication. On the other side, the study by Laufer and Paribakht (1998), who did show a positive and moderate correlation between lexical sophistication and passive vocabulary knowledge in the argumentative texts of adult foreign language learners, focused on a more diverse population in terms of proficiency in the target language.

The results in the present study are also consistent with another study with adults that did not find a correlation between passive vocabulary knowledge and lexical sophistication (Lemmouh 2010). In turn, Sanhueza et al. (2018) found changes in lexical sophistication regarding solely high-frequency words (that is, not sophisticated), whereas the improvements in passive vocabulary knowledge regarded low-frequency (that is, more sophisticated) words. Unfortunately for cross-comparison purposes, Tracy-Ventura (2017) analyzed the written production of her participants together with the spoken samples. Therefore, it would be problematic to compare the results from her study with the ones obtained here, which are based solely on L2 Spanish writing. In any case, the overall picture emerging from Tracy-Ventura's results indicated a positive relationship between passive vocabulary knowledge and lexical sophistication, as they showed a joint increase after a relatively long study abroad period. Hence, length of residence and the increase in proficiency that it might have produced is, in all likelihood, the factor which made possible for the author to detect changes in lexical sophistication.

In this line of reasoning, it would be wise to contend that a narrative and a decision-making task might differ from each other when it comes to their dissimilar cognitive load. The general impression, contrary to the narrative task (which restricts the type and amount of vocabulary that the participants could use), is that the inherent features of the decision-making task call for the use of a broader and more sophisticated vocabulary range. Hence, the cognitive load imposed by the mental operations involved in decision-making is higher than in the telling of events. This contention echoes Brown et al.'s (1984) assessment of task complexity in terms of the relationship between the elements involved, over and beyond the number of elements. The abstract reasoning required for formulating arguments in a decision-making task, as explained in Section 2, poses considerably high demands on cognitive resources, which might affect performance (Sánchez 2019). In a narrative task, however, the demands may be lower because this task calls for a relative more basic and limited vocabulary use, given the number and nature of the events in the strip cartoon. Notwithstanding, participants with low passive vocabulary knowledge would seem to be less equipped to satisfy those demands.

These results have pedagogical implications for foreign language teaching when it comes to informing teachers' choice and sequencing of tasks. Knowing that tasks constructed upon an argumentation (as the decision-making task in this study) may increase the lexical sophistication of adult learners of Spanish, teachers may want to make a wider selection of text types when working with vocabulary. Moreover, they may want to do so at a point in instruction when learners' vocabulary knowledge is sufficiently developed to carry out more complex tasks successfully. Instead of employing generic statements as a prompt for argumentative writing, the foreign language instructor might decide to use a decision-making task constructed around a number of different options, such as the holiday destinations in the decision-making task used in this study. The number of requirements on the fictional friend's side could also be manipulated, and other similar tasks could easily be created, such as the selection of a restaurant given someone's tastes, allergies and budget to be compared against restaurants placed in different locations and serving different dishes at different prices, as in Frear and Bitchener (2015). Cognitive complexity can easily be manipulated also in narrative tasks, for example by providing unrelated pictures involving the same characters instead of a clear sequence of events, or deleting some crucial pictures in order to stimulate reasoning on what might have happened based on the previous and the following picture.

A future development of the present study might include an assessment of lexical sophistication by means of count-based indexes, i.e., indexes "that calculate word frequency as a function of word incidences as found in large-scale corpora" (Crossley et al. 2013: 966). A count-based index is used, as for instance in Checa-García and Schafer (this volume) and in Marqués-Pascual and Checa-García (this volume). In comparison with band-based indexes, count-based indexes proved to predict the proficiency level of L2 English learners more accurately (Crossley et al. 2013). They are also considered to reflect more closely the real average frequency of a language sample, as no grouping by frequency bands is involved. Notwithstanding the common disadvantage of band-based indices, consisting in grouping words into lemmas or word families, could not affect the results presented here, as the lexical unit employed lies on the word level. Besides, the results obtained by means of count-based methods are difficult to understand and interpret, while band-based indexes give an intuitive and clear picture of lexical sophistication in a text (Crossley et al. 2013: 968). Another possible path would be treating lexical sophistication as a multi-dimensional construct and developing a tool capable of analyzing aspects such as word range, n-gram frequency, psycholinguistic word information, academic language, polysemy, and hypernymy (Kyle and Crossley 2016). Finally, it would be interesting to compare the results obtained with respect to lexical sophistication with indexes of lexical diversity, the other main feature of lexical richness.

References

Barcroft, Joe & Javier Muñoz-Basols (eds.). 2021. *Spanish Vocabulary Learning in Meaning-Oriented Instruction*. London: Routledge.
Berton, Marco. 2020. *Riqueza léxica y expresión escrita en aprendices suecos de ELE*. Doctoral dissertation, Stockholm University.
Brown, Gillian, Anne Anderson, Richard Shilcock, & George Yule. 1984. *Teaching talk: Strategies for production and assessment*. Cambridge: Cambridge University Press.
Castañeda-Jiménez, Gabriela &Scott Jarvis. 2014. Exploring lexical diversity in second language Spanish. In Kimerly Geeslin (ed.), *The handbook of Spanish second language acquisition*, 498–513. Chichester: Wiley-Blackwell.
Cobb, Tom. 2013. Text Lex Compare v.3. Available at https://www.lextutor.ca/cgi-bin/tl_compare/
Council of Europe. 2001. Common European Framework of Reference for Languages: Learning, Teaching, Assessment. Cambridge: Cambridge University Press.
Crossley, Scott, Tom Cobb & Danielle McNamara. 2013. Comparing count-based and band-based indices of word frequency: Implications for active vocabulary research and pedagogical applications. *System* 41. 965–981.
Cuetos, Fernando, María González-Nosti, Analia Barbón & Marc Brysbaert. 2011. SUBTLEX-ESP: Spanish word frequencies based on film subtitles. *Psicológica* 32(2). 133–143.
Daller, Helmut & Huijuan Xue. 2007. Lexical richness and the oral proficiency of Chinese EFL learners. In Helmut Daller, James Milton, J. & Jeanine Treffers-Daller (eds.), *Modelling and Assessing Vocabulary Knowledge*, 150–164. Cambridge: Cambridge University Press.
Fan, May. 2000. How big is the gap and how to narrow it? An investigation into the active and passive vocabulary knowledge of L2 learners. *RELC journal* 31(2). 105–119.
Foster, Pauline & Peter Skehan. 1996. The influence of planning and task type on second language performance. *Studies in Second Language Acquisition* 18(2). 299–323.
Frear, Marc & John Bitchener. 2015. The effects of cognitive task complexity on writing complexity. *Journal of Second Language Writing* 30(1). 45–57.
Heaton, John. 1966. *Composition through pictures*. Harlow: Longman.
Izura, Cristina, Fernando Cuetos & Marc Brysbaert. 2014. Lextale-Esp: A test to rapidly and efficiently assess the Spanish vocabulary size. *Psicológica* 35(1). 39–66.
Jarvis, Scott. 2002. Short texts, best-fitting curves, and new measures of lexical diversity. *Language Testing* 19(1). 57–84.
Jiménez Catalán, Rosa María. 2017. Estudios de disponibilidad léxica en español y en inglés: revisión de sus fundamentos empíricos y metodológicos. *Revista Nebrija de Lingüística Aplicada a la Enseñanza de Lenguas* 22. 16–31.
Jones, Leo. 1979. *Notions in English*. Cambridge: Cambridge University Press.
Kyle, Kristopher. 2020. Measuring lexical richness. In Webb, Stuart (ed.), *The Routledge Handbook of Vocabulary Studies*, 454–476. London: Routledge.

Kyle, Kristopher & Scott Crossley. 2016. The relationship between lexical sophistication and independent and source-based writing. *Journal of Second Language Writing* 34. 12–24.

Laufer, Batia. 1995. Beyond 2000: a measure of productive lexicon in second language. In Larry Eubank, Larry Selinker & Michael Sharwood-Smith (eds.), *The current state of Interlanguage*, 265–272. Amsterdam: John Benjamins.

Laufer, Batia. 1998. The Development of passive and active vocabulary in second language: Same or different? *Applied linguistics* 19(2). 255–271.

Laufer, B. & Paul Nation. 1995. Vocabulary size and use: Lexical richness in L2 written production. *Applied Linguistics* 16. 307–322.

Laufer, Batia & Sima Paribakht. 1998. The relationship between passive and active vocabularies: Effects of language learning context. *Language Learning* 48(3). 365–391.

Lemmouh, Zakaria. 2010. *The Relationship among Vocabulary Knowledge, Academic Achievement and the Lexical Richness in Writing in Swedish University Learners of English*. Doctoral Dissertation. Stockholm University.

Levkina, Maya &Roger Gilabert. 2012. The effects of cognitive task complexity on L2 oral production. In Alex Housen, Folkert Kuiken & Ineke Vedder (eds.), *Dimensions of L2 Performance and Proficiency: Complexity, Accuracy and Fluency in SLA*, 171–197. Amsterdam: John Benjamins.

Meara, Paul & Huw Bell. 2001. P_Lex: a simple and effective way of describing the lexical characteristics of short L2 texts. *Prospects* 16. 5–19.

Meara, Paul & Imma Miralpeix. 2017. *Tools for Researching Vocabulary*. Bristol: Multilingual Matters.

Melka, Francine. 1997. Receptive versus productive aspects of vocabulary. In Norbert Schmitt & Michael McCarthy (eds.), *Vocabulary: Description, Acquisition, and Pedagogy*, 84–102. Cambridge: Cambridge University Press.

Ministerio de Educación y Formación Profesional. 2020. *El mundo estudia español*. Madrid: Secretaría General Técnica.

Muñoz, Carmen (ed.). 2006. *Age and the Rate of Foreign Language Learning*. Clevedon: Multilingual Matters.

Nation, Paul. 2013. *Learning Vocabulary in Another Language*. 2nd edn. Cambridge: Cambridge University Press.

Nattinger, James. 1988. Some current trends in vocabulary teaching. In Ronald Carter & Michael McCarthy (eds.), *Vocabulary and Language Teaching*, 62–82. London: Longman.

Nemati, Azadeh. 2010. Active and Passive Vocabulary Knowledge: The Effect of Years of Instruction. *Asian EFL Journal* 12(1). 30–46.

Österberg, Rakel. 2021. Perfil laboral y formativo del profesorado de español como lengua extranjera o segunda (ELE/EL2) en Suecia. *Journal of Spanish Language Teaching* 8(1). 1–15.

Plonsky, Luke & Frederick Oswald. 2014. How Big Is "Big"? Interpreting Effect Sizes in L2 Research. *Language Learning* 64(4). 878–912.

Read, John. 2000. *Assessing Vocabulary*. Cambridge: Cambridge University Press.

Robinson, Peter. 2003. Attention and memory during SLA. In Catherine Doughty & Michael Long (eds.), *Handbook of Second Language Acquisition*, 631–678. Oxford: Blackwell.

Robinson, Peter. 2011. Second language task complexity, the Cognition Hypothesis, language learning, and performance. In Peter Robinson (ed.), *Second language task complexity: Researching the cognition hypothesis of language learning and performance*, 3–38. Amsterdam: John Benjamins.

Robinson, Peter. 2015. The Cognition Hypothesis, second language task demands, and the SSARC model of pedagogic task sequencing. In Martin Bygate (ed.), *Domains and Directions in the Development of TBLT*, 87–121. Amsterdam: John Benjamins.

Sanhueza, Cristián, Anita Ferreira & Katia Sáez. 2018. Desarrollo de la competencia léxica a través de estrategias de aprendizaje de vocabulario en aprendientes de inglés como lengua extranjera. *Lexis* 42(2). 273–326.

Sánchez, Laura. 2019. Weighing up the effects of working memory and cognitive abilities in CLIL learning. *English Language Teaching* 12(1). 113–126.

Sánchez Rufat, Anna & Francisco Jiménez Calderón. 2015. New perspectives on the acquisition and teaching of Spanish vocabulary/Nuevas perspectivas sobre la adquisición y la enseñanza del vocabulario del español. *Journal of Spanish Language Teaching* 2(2). 99–111.

Skehan, Peter. 1996. A framework for the implementation of task-based instruction. *Applied Linguistics* 17(1). 38–62.

Skehan, Peter. 1998. *A Cognitive Approach to Language Learning*. Oxford: Oxford University Press.

Skehan, Peter. 2015. Limited Attention Capacity and Cognition. In Martin Bygate (ed.), *Domains and Directions in the Development of TBLT*, 123–155. Amsterdam: John Benjamins.

Tavakoli, Parvaneh & Pauline Foster. 2008. Task Design and Second Language Performance: The Effect of Narrative Type on Learner Output. *Language Learning* 58(2). 439–473.

Tracy-Ventura, Nicole. 2017. Combining corpora and experimental data to investigate language learning during residence abroad: A study of lexical sophistication. *System* 71(1). 35–45.

Waldvogel, Dieter. 2014. An Analysis of Spanish L2 Lexical Richness. *Academic Exchange Quarterly* 18(2). 17–25.

Waring, Rob. 1997. A Comparison of the Receptive and Productive Vocabulary Sizes of some Second Language Learners. *Immaculata, The occasional papers at Notre Dame Seishin University* 1. 53–68.

Zhong, Hua. 2018. The relationship between receptive and productive vocabulary knowledge: a perspective from vocabulary use in sentence writing. *The Language Learning Journal* 46(4). 357–370.

Section III: **Attitudes and emotions in the lexicon**

Elisabet Llopart-Saumell
Chapter 8
"Learn the rules like a pro, so you can break them like an artist": On the emotional effects of breaking word-formation rules

1 Introduction

In our daily lives, when we talk to each other, read the newspaper, use social networks, watch television, or listen to the radio, we encounter new words, that is, recently created or infrequent in use. In this sense, the lexicon of a language is characterized by a tendency towards stability, to ensure communication, and a tendency to adapt to new realities and communicative situations (Guilbert 1975). Consequently, it is safe to say that lexical change is a linguistic phenomenon attached to any living language. These types of lexical units, which are called neologisms or lexical innovations, do not belong to the speakers' mental lexicon (Aitchinson [1987] 1994: 10), because they present formal, semantic, or syntactic changes in regard to the words that they already know. However, receivers usually understand these new words, even if it is the first time that they hear them or see them in written form (Aitchinson 1994: 147). Thus, "speakers understand and form not only 'real' words that occur in their language, but also potential words which are not instantiated in use in utterances" (Katamba 1993: 65). Nevertheless, it is true that since lexical innovations are not part of the mental lexicon, they have a higher processing cost (Llopart-Saumell and Freixa 2014).

Lexical creativity is considered one of human beings' inherent abilities, but in order for it to work, a mutual understanding of new lexical items is needed. The fact that this mutual understanding between the members of a linguistic community exists can only be explained by positing that words are not created randomly, but according to a set of rules and lexical items. Consequently, most neologisms follow word-formation rules (Dressler 1981) and are not considered new at all, but

---

Note: This is an English translation of the quotation "Aprende las reglas como un profesional, para que puedas romperlas como un artista" from the Spanish painter and sculptor Pablo Picasso.

I would like to thank the editors for their highly valuable suggestions and comments on an earlier version of this paper.

Elisabet Llopart-Saumell, Universitat Pompeu Fabra

https://doi.org/10.1515/9783110730418-008

"simply additions to existing words or recombinations of their components" (Aitchinson 1994: 159). However, there are some exceptions. What happens if neologisms break the word-formation rules? Such is the case of new words that show a morphological, syntactic, semantic, or pragmatic transgression or deviation. Rainer (2002: 283) indicates that there are no systematic studies on "neological propensity", although some researchers study different features of lexical creativity. For this reason, in order to affirm that, indeed, neologisms deviate from a particular word-formation rule, reliable linguistic descriptions that enable comparisons should be provided.

Speakers create new words to either refer to new realities, to be more precise, to attract the attention of the receiver, or in the interest of the economy of language (Cabré 2015: 93). Where the attention of the speaker is concerned, in some neologisms Jacokbson's (1984) emotional or aesthetic function prevails. Thus, neologisms that break word-formation rules tend to present a higher degree of originality, since they are not based on common and productive structures (Guilbert 1975: 41–43). For this reason, the deliberate transgression of linguistic norms is considered a form of "estrangement" and poeticism (García-Page 2003: 311) because the resulting forms are only partially expected or not at all (Martín Camacho 1994). This produces specific effects on the receiver, such as a surprise (Koestler 1975: 83), or humorous (Bernal and Sinner 2013: 493) and pragmatic effects (Bernal and Milà-García 2021).

The main objective of this article is to study the emotional effects of lexical innovations that break word-formation rules on the basis that communicative intention (Escandell-Vidal 2014) guides linguistic selection. For this reason, I hypothesize that transgressive neologisms are motivated by stylistic and subjective functions and especially by a playful and ironic value. To verify this hypothesis, a psycholinguistic study was conducted. Native speakers of Spanish evaluated a set of formal transgressive neologisms created by suffixation and neoclassical compounding[1] that had been previously registered in the Spanish press. In particular, they were asked to evaluate the stimuli using the Self-Assessment Manikin (SAM) (Bradley and Lang 1994), a pictorial technique that measures affective effects of word processing according to three dimensions: valence, arousal, and dominance. In this case, only two of the three dimensions were included: valence and arousal, but not dominance. The expected results are that breaking word-formation rules produces an emotional effect on the receiver reflected in higher values of valence and arousal. Therefore, this would be one of the reasons why word-formation rules are broken instead of

---

[1] In neoclassical compounding at least one of the elements of the compound is a root borrowed from Greek or Latin (Booij 2007: 86).

following the norms shared by the linguistic community, since this type of neologism is perceived as surprising and tends to be used in marked contexts.

1.1 Neologisms and word-formation rules

New words or neologisms are not an uncommon lexical phenomenon, since they appear repeatedly in everyday language. In this sense, neology is conceived as a sign of vitality, as dead languages do not have any speakers who use them on a spontaneous daily basis (Cabré 2006). Due to lexical change and variation, some words disappear or coexist with some variants, while other words that did not exist in an earlier stage. In short, language, especially its lexical component, evolves steadily as a reflection of the changes experienced by society. As mentioned above, morphological word-formation rules allow individuals within a linguistic community who share this linguistic knowledge to produce new words that other speakers can understand, even if they are not acquainted with the new lexical item. In order to distinguish neologisms from existing words, Rey (1976) establishes three different criteria: the temporal criterion, whereby a word is considered a neologism according to the first record of said lexical item in a text; the lexicographic criterion, based on the lack of evidence in a lexicographic corpus; and the psycholinguistic criterion, which considers its perception by the speakers. In practice, the lexicographic criterion is the one used more widely, since it offers a coherent and systematic methodology, although it presents some limitations, since dictionaries do not register all the words that are part of the speakers' mental lexicon. Following such a criterion, here are some examples of neologisms recorded in the Spanish press of 2021 and created by different word-formation mechanisms: prefixation (*antivoto* 'anti- + vote'; *prepandemia* 'pre-pandemic'), suffixation (*sanchista* '(Pedro) Sánchez + -ist'; *sinhogarismo* 'without + [home + -ism]'), native compounding (*vendeburras* 'sells + female donkey', that is, 'snake-oil salesman'; *todocamino* 'all + roader'), neoclassical compounding (*ecoamigable* 'ecofriendly'; *gordofóbico -ca* 'fat + -phobic'), syntagmatic compounding (*gel hidroalcohólico* 'gel + hydroalcoholic', that is, 'hand sanitizer'), clipping (*antifa* 'antifa(cist)'), blending (*vacunagate* 'vaccine + -gate'), semantic change (*bizum*, originally a proper noun to refer to a Spanish payment service provider), syntactic change (*perimetrar* 'perimeter + -ize'), and loanwords (*brexiter*, from English; *parkour*, from French).

There are, however, some lexical innovations (or neologisms) that break these word-formation rules. These words are considered transgressive neologisms, or, in the words of Hanks (2013: 212), they could be conceived of as *creative exploitations* of the lexical norm established by usage. Speakers can usually understand these innovations, although they may require more attention, more time, and effort to infer their meaning. That begs the question, why would someone choose to break word-formation rules if communication is at risk or, at the very least, might be affected by a lower processing speed? The hypothesis that guides this proposal is that creative exploitations of the lexical norm satisfy a communicative intention that goes beyond the referential function (i.e., to inform) with the aim to cause a surprising, humorous, or pragmatic effect on the receiver. In this sense, this type of word seems to fulfill a stylistic or expressive need. How are these neologisms distinguished from norm-conforming ones?

A dividing line cannot be clearly drawn between norms and exploitations because they represent two opposite poles of the same axis rather than two clearly separated categories (Hanks 2013). In any case, Hanks (2013) emphasizes that this fact does not invalidate the category, because most linguistic categories have undefined/unclear limits. To state that a word or, in this case, a neologism, deviates from the norm – that is, from word-formation rules –, it can be said that "word-formation rules (WFRs) typically undergo a number of general constraints or more specific restrictions conditioning or limiting their productivity" (Gaeta 2015, 2: 859). In this sense, Gaeta (2015), following Rainer (2005), distinguishes constrictions, of a more general nature, from restrictions, which are more specific. For the latter, the author differentiates six domain-specific restrictions: phonological, morphological, syntactic, lexical, semantic, and pragmatic (Gaeta 2015).

The transgressive neologisms selected for this study deviate from morphological and semantic restrictions. Morphological restrictions are challenged because the syntactic category of the base form does not agree with the ones selected by the added suffix. This could also be classified as a syntactic restriction (Gaeta 2015), although it is usually interpreted as a morphological restriction (Bauer 2001). The following instance in Gaeta (2015: 870) serves as an example: the suffix -*able* combines with transitive verbs, as in the case of *visitable* or *observable*; hence, constructions like *goable and *lookable, despite having a similar meaning to *visitable* and *observable*, are not possible, since *go* and *look* are intransitive. Semantic restrictions, that is, "when highly specific meaning aspects of the base domain are required in order to delimit the input of a WFR" (Gaeta 2015: 871), are also challenged in other units. According to Gaeta (2015), semantic restrictions may also include world knowledge in addition to word-meaning. In this sense they would be related to pragmatic restrictions as well, which includes encyclopedic knowledge (Bauer 2001) in context and it involves the register in which the base is used (Gaeta 2015). For instance, the combination form -*(o)logy* forms nouns with the sense 'the science or discipline of (what is indicated by the first element)' (Oxford English Dictionary), such as in *biology* (*bio-* + -*logy*), understood as 'the branch of science that deals with living organisms [. . .]' (OED), or *musicology* (*music* + -*ology*), which refers to 'the branch of knowledge that deals with music [. . .]' (OED). However, *rumorology* (*rumor* + *-ology*) is used ironically with the sense 'to gossip and spread rumors'; hence, the English neologism *rumorology* does not refer to a science or discipline.

1.2 The emotional effects of words and lexical creativity

The study of the affective effects of words is also the focus of experimental research in general, and of psycholinguistics, since it has been proven that emotion influences word recognition and word processing. Consequently, the emotional effects of words are now a linguistic variable that is considered when designing linguistic experiments, such as lexical decision tasks or other cognitive tasks (Kousta, Vinson, and Viglioco 2009; Kuperman, Estes, Bysbaert and Warriner 2014: 1066). For instance, emotion words have a processing effect that neutral words do not (Kousta, Vinson, and Viglioco 2009). Thus, valence has a beneficial effect on word recognition, both in positive and negative words, while increasing arousal slows down lexical decisions, mostly among infrequent words (Kuperman et al. 2014).[2]

These results are not clearly observed when the words are already established in use, but they are observed during language acquisition, both of first and second languages (Altarriba and Basnight-Brown 2011). In fact, the affective effects of words might help speakers acquire them, specifically regarding abstract concepts, which are harder to learn (Ferré, Ventura, Comesaña and Fraga 2015: 8) and may need of experiential information to form a word representation and aid its processing (Kousta, Vigliocco, Vinson, Andrews and del Campo 2011), since "it would be through emotionality that abstract words would become embodied" (Lang 1995; cited in Ferré et al. 2015: 3).

In a study by Ferré et al. (2015), participants attended two sessions. The first session began with a learning activity, in which the participants were presented a set of Basque words and their Spanish translation. By the end of the session, the participants had to carry out a decision-making task to recognize the learned Basque words and a translation task in which they had to provide the Spanish translation for each word. The second session took place a week later, and the participants were asked to do the same tasks once again. The results were very similar in both sessions, and they revealed that those words with emotional content facilitated the acquisition of abstract words in a new language. Thus, Ferré et al. (2015) conclude

---

2 Valence and arousal refer to two different emotional dimensions. While valence is used to evaluate a stimulus on a continuum from happy to sad, arousal is expressed as a continuum from high to low (specifically, activated to calm) (American Psychological Association 2022).

that the emotional load of a word has a positive impact on memory and facilitates word acquisition.

New lexical units of a particular language are not created randomly, but according to a set of word-formation rules and existing lexical bases. Morphology, understood as a branch of linguistics that studies the rules that regulate the internal structure of words, not only explains the structure of existing words, but also describes the word-formation rules needed to create new grammatically correct words according to the language system. However, a few neologisms deviate from these rules. In these cases, it seems that the motivation that underlies these types of creations is to call the attention of the receiver (Cabré 1989; Guerrero Ramos 1995; Guilbert 1975). Even though the transgression of word-formation rules is understood as a property of languages in general, neologisms have been given little attention in experimental studies and, consequently, transgressive neologisms have been far less explored from this perspective. Most studies on lexical processing tend to focus on the analysis of words or pseudowords that are not neologisms, but non-words.[3]

Nevertheless, there are some recent perception studies that analyze the effects of breaking word-formation rules: Bernal and Milà-García (2021) focus on the (un)marked uses of final combining forms, that is, a borrowing from Latin or Greek which appears only in the second or final part of a compound (i.e., *aerophobia* or *photopathy*), based on the theoretical framework of morphopragmatics, and Llopart-Saumell (2021) correlates the connotations of a set of neologisms with the linguistic characteristics of these units and their context of use. Both studies showed to a set of participants some Catalan neologisms in context to be classified according to different types of categories related to pragmatics and connotations. Among these neologisms, some followed the word-formation rules of Catalan language while others transgressed them. In Bernal and Milà-García (2021), speakers had to classify 20 neoclassical compounds according to two parameters: 1) the context, which could either be formal or neutral, or informal or colloquial, and 2) their pragmatic effects, in either neutral, on the one hand, or either affective, derogatory, humorous, and ironic, on the other hand. In Llopart-Saumell (2021), participants had to classify 20 neologisms created with different word-formation mechanisms in Catalan according to four couplets of opposing connotative features: 1) informal vs. formal register, 2) personal vs. general nature, 3) subjective

---

3 According to the *American Psychological Association (APA) Dictionary of Psychology* pseudowords are pronounceable non-words that are used in experimental studies because they 'do not already have meaning or associations with other information in memory' (APA2022). Thus, pseudowords are considered non-words, that is, 'an unrecorded or hitherto unused word; a word which has (or is regarded as having) no accepted meaning' (Oxford English Dictionary). Conversely, neologisms are recent or infrequent words attested in usage.

vs. objective opinion, and 4) ideological vs. neutral load; the questionnaire was structured in a 5-point Likert scale. The findings of these studies suggest that, on the one hand, breaking the rules has some pragmatic effects due to register, since these forms tend to appear in informal contexts, and they show additional nuances through ironic or derogative uses (Bernal and Milà-García 2021). Furthermore, neologisms classified as belonging to an informal register and manifesting personal nature, subjective opinion, and ideological load (that is, involving a connotation) present different marked linguistic features, on either a morphological, semantic, pragmatic, or discursive level (Llopart-Saumell 2021), because they deviate from some of the restrictions of word-formation rules or because some of the elements of the context of use are unexpected due to the genre of the text.

2 Methodology

2.1 Selection of transgressive neologisms

This section describes the word-formation rules from which the neologisms selected for this study derive. The transgressive neologisms chosen for this experiment are formal neologisms created by suffixation, either with the suffix *-ismo* '-ism', *-ez* '-ness' or *-itis*, or by neoclassical compounding with the combining form *-metro* '-meter'. They were selected on the basis of the transgression of either 1) the semantic domain of the base, for instance, in *dialoguitis* ('dialogue' + '-itis'), since the root does not designate a part of the anatomy; 2) the syntactic category regarding the suffix, as in *bigotez* ('moustache' + '-ness), because in Spanish the suffix *-ez* '-ness' only combines with adjectives, but *bigote* 'moustache' is a noun; or 3) the combining form that they combine with, for example, in *noviómetro* ('boyfriend' + '-meter'), since *-metro* '-meter' goes with the word *novio* 'boyfriend', which is not another combining form from Greek or Latin. In this case, all the words included in the study come from the Spanish newspapers *La Vanguardia* and *El País*, and they were obtained through the bank of neologisms of the Observatori de Neologia (BOBNEO),[4] which records neologisms from oral and written press in Spanish and Catalan. Below, the meaning and restrictions of these linguistic items are explained based on the information provided by dictionaries, grammars, and usage.

The Spanish suffix *-ismo* '-ism' is used to create words with five different meanings, but this study focuses on the first two according to the Royal Spanish Academy's *Diccionario de la lengua española* (DLE):

---

4 http://obneo.iula.upf.edu/bobneo/index.php

1. It creates nouns that tend to designate 'doctrine', 'system', 'school', or 'movement'. *Socialismo* 'socialism', *platonismo* 'Platonism', *impresionismo* 'impressionism'.
2. It creates nouns that designate 'attitude', 'tendency' or 'quality'. *Egoísmo* 'selfishness' (*selfish* + *-ism*), *individualismo* 'individualism', *puritanismo* 'puritanism'.

The transgressive neologisms selected for the study have bases that unexpectedly create these nouns, since they are typical of common and everyday language, as is the case with *buenismo* (Bernal and Sinner 2013, 3: 488), which was included in the DLE in 2017 with a derogatory sense.[5] Following this criterion, these were the neologisms that were included in the experiment:

(1) *chandalismo*: *chandal* 'tracksuit' + *-ismo* '-ism'
(2) *cualquiercosismo*: *cualquier cosa* 'anything' + *-ismo* '-ism'
(3) *facilismo*: *fácil* 'easy' + *-ismo* '-ism'
(4) *ninismo*: *nini* 'NEET' or 'neither + nor' + *-ismo* '-ism'
(5) *pedorrismo*: *pedorro -rra* 'dumb' + *-ismo* '-ism'
(6) *semaforismo*: *semáforo* 'traffic light' + *-ismo* '-ism'

As for the Spanish suffix *-ez* '-ness', it creates feminine abstract nouns that indicate the quality expressed by the adjective from which it derives (DLE), i.e., *altivez* 'haugthiness', *brillantez* 'brightness', and *lucidez* 'lucidity' (*lucid* + *-ness*). However, there are also instances of neologisms that take a noun as a base instead of taking an adjective and this was the criterion to select the following items:

(7) *bigotez*: *bigote* 'moustache' + *-ez* '-ness'
(8) *hijoputez*: *hijoputa* 'son of a bitch' + *-ez* '-ness'
(9) *pedorrez*: *pedorro -ra* 'dumb' + *-ez* '-ness'
(10) *tocinez*: *tocino* 'pig' + *-ez* '-ness'

Regarding the suffix *-itis*, it means 'inflammation', such as in *otitis* or *hepatitis* (DLE), but it also creates new words that do not refer to an inflammation, in which cases the suffix is used metaphorically. Julià (2015) differentiates between the specialized pattern and the colloquial and humorous pattern, which refers to "an exaggerated attitude towards a particular reality" (p. 151). Although this sense is not registered in the DLE, a few words created with this pattern are already registered in this dictionary. This is the case of *titulitis*, which contains the base *título* 'title', in the sense of

---

5 Nevertheless, some descriptive works point out that during the last decades *-ismo* '-ism' shows few productivity constraints and the resulting forms are used with a "whimsical nature" (Lang 1990: 135). Despite this fact, the baseline for this study was the *Diccionario de la lengua española* (DLE), since all the neologisms used come from newspapers, which generally belong to a formal register. Consequently, prescriptive sources, such as DLE, are taken into account.

'certificate', defined as the act of 'giving excessive importance to titles and study certificates to ensure someone's knowledge' (DLE) in a colloquial and derogatory sense. The transgressive neologisms that follow this pattern selected for the study are:

(11) *arquitecturitis*: *arquitectura* 'architecture' + *-itis*
(12) *catastrofitis*: *catástrofe* 'catastrophe' + *-itis*
(13) *dialoguitis*: *diálogo* 'dialogue' + *-itis*
(14) *festivalitis*: *festival* 'festival' + *-itis*

Finally, the combining form *-metro* '-meter' means 'measuring device', as in *pluviómetro* 'pluviometer', and *termómetro* 'thermometer' (DLE). Generally, *-meter* is attached to other neoclassical forms, as in the case of *barómetro* 'barometer' (*baro-*, which refers to the 'atmospheric pressure') or *cronómetro* 'chronometer' (*crono-* from Greek 'chrono-', which means 'time'), although it is also attached to other language bases, such as in *alcoholímetro* 'breathalyzer' (*alcohol*), *cremómetro* 'creamometer' (*crema* 'cream'), or *cursómetro* (*curso* in the sense of 'race'), a device that measures the speed of railroads. Regarding the productivity of *-meter* in Spanish, there are other neologisms that contain this combining form with the sense of a measuring instrument. Some have a technical nature, such as *aetalómetro* 'aethalometer' or *esfigmomanómetro* 'sphygmomanometer' (also known as *tensiómetro*), which are used to measure black carbon in the air and blood pressure, respectively. On the other hand, there are new designations that refer to usages that are not used in highly specialized contexts. For example, *manifestómetro* and *opinómetro*, from the base *manifestación* 'demonstration' and *opinión* 'opinion'. Finally, it is common to come across lexical innovations with a colloquial nature. This is the case of the last typology of neologisms selected for this study. As presented in the following examples (15–19), they do not refer to a real instrument or application, but rather they keep the sense of 'measurement' or 'scale':

(15) *abucheómetro*: *abucheo* 'to boo' + *-metro* '-meter'
(16) *aplausómetro*: *aplauso* 'applause' + *-metro* '-meter'
(17) *chutómetro*: *chut* 'shot (in soccer)' + *-metro* '-meter'
(18) *noviómetro*: *novio* 'boyfriend' + *-metro* '-meter'
(19) *odiómetro*: *odio* 'hate' + *-metro* '-meter'

2.2 Participants

The experimental study was carried out by 114 participants, 89 women and 25 men. The speakers that took part in the test were undergraduate and graduate students of Language Sciences and Linguistics in four Spanish universities (Pompeu Fabra University and Open University of Catalonia, in Barcelona; University of the Balearic Islands, in Palma de Mallorca; and Autonomous University of Madrid, in Madrid). The participants aged between 18 and 25 and were bilingual speakers of both Spanish and Catalan.

2.3 Materials

The study contained 56 stimuli of three types, as depicted in Table 1:

Table 1: List of lexical items and type.

Ending form	Type of word	Lexical units of the study (N = 56)
-ismo '-ism'	Bases (trans. neologisms)	*chandal* 'tracksuit' *cualquier cosa* 'anything' *fácil* 'easy' *nini* 'NEET' or 'neither . . . nor' *pedorro -rra* 'dumb' *semáforo* 'traffic light'
	Transgressive neologisms	*chandalismo* '(*chandal*) tracksuit + -*ism*' *cualquiercosismo* '(*cualquier cosa*) anything + -*ism*' *facilismo* '(*fácil*) easy + -*ism*' *ninismo* '(*nini*) NEET / neither . . . nor + -*ism*' *pedorrismo* '(*pedorro -rra*) dumb + -*ism*' *semaforismo* '(*semáforo*) traffic light + -*ism*'
	Non-transgressive neologisms	*articulismo* '(*artículo*) article + -*ism*' *comunitarismo* 'communitarianism' *informalismo* 'informalism' *secularismo* 'secularism' *tacticismo* '(*táctica*) tactic + -*ism*' *unilateralismo* 'unilateralism'
-ez '-ness'	Bases (trans. neologisms)	*biogote* 'moustache' *hijoputa* 'son of a bitch' *pedorro -rra* 'dumb' *tocino* 'pig'
	Transgressive neologisms	*bigotez* '(*bigote*) moustache + -*ness*' *hijoputez* '(*hijoputa*) son of a bitch + -*ness*' *pedorrez* '(*pedorro -rra*) dumb + -*ness*' *tocinez* '(*tocino*) pig + -*ness*'

Table 1 (continued)

Ending form	Type of word	Lexical units of the study (N = 56)
	Non-transgressive neologisms	*absurdez* 'absurdness' *horterez* '(*hortera*) tacky + *-ness*' *prematurez* 'prematureness' *sosez* 'dullness'
-itis	Bases (trans. neologisms)	*arquitectura* 'architecture' *catástrofe* 'catastrophe' *diálogo* 'dialogue' *festival* 'festival'
	Transgressive neologisms	*arquitecturitis* '(*arquitectura*) architecture + *-itis*' *catastrofitis* '(*catástrofe*) catastrophe + *-itis*' *dialoguitis* '(*diálogo*) dialogue + *-itis*' *festivalitis* '(*festival*) festival + *-itis*'
	Non-transgressive neologisms	*capsulitis* 'capsulitis' *esofaguitis* 'esophagitis' *osteocondritis* 'osteochondritis' *periodontitis* 'periodontitis'
-metro '-meter'	Bases (trans. neologisms)	*abucheo* 'boo' *aplauso* 'applause' *chut* 'shot' *novio* 'boyfriend' *odio* 'hate'
	Transgressive neologisms	*abucheómetro* '(*abucheo*) boo + *-meter*' *aplausómetro* '(*aplauso*) 'applause' + *-meter*' *chutómetro* '(*chut*) 'shot' + *-meter*' *noviómetro* '(*novio*) 'boyfriend' + *-meter*' *odiómetro* '(*odio*) 'hate' + *-meter*'
	Non-transgressive neologisms	*cardiómetro* 'cardiometer' *coagulómetro* 'coagulometer' *difractómetro* 'diffractometer' *etilómetro* '(*etilo*) ethyl + *-meter*' ('breathalyzer') *reflectómetro* 'reflectometer'

The study included as target items 19 neologisms created by suffixation (6 with the suffix *-ismo* '-ism', 4 with *-ez* '-ness', and 4 with *-itis*) and neoclassical compounding (5 with the combining form *-metro* '-meter') that break word-formation rules. In order to compare the effects of transgressive neologisms with non-transgressive neologisms, 19 additional neologisms with the same suffixes and combining forms, but with a base that follows word-formation rules were included.[6] Lastly, the bases of the first group of neologisms were included as fillers.

One example with the suffix *-ismo* '-ism' is *pedorrismo* 'dumb + -ism', which is considered a transgressive neologism, since it does not refer to a doctrine or movement; while *comunitarismo* 'communitarianism' is considered a non-transgressive neologism in Spanish because it is not registered in dictionaries yet, but it follows the word-formation rules. Finally, *pedorro -rra* 'dumb' is the base of the transgressive neologism. Regarding the suffix *-ez* '-ness', one example is *bigotez* 'moustache + -ness', which is considered a transgressive neologism, since this suffix can only be added to adjectival bases (DLE), but *bigote* 'moustache' is a noun. *Absurdez* 'absurdness' is considered a non-transgressive neologism created with the same suffix because in this case *-ez* 'ness' has been added to an adjectival base, *absurdo -da* 'absurd'; and *bigote* 'moustache' is the base of the transgressive neologism. One example of a transgressive neologism that contains the suffix *-itis* is *festivalitis* '(festival) festival + -itis', since it does not belong to the medical domain and the base (*festival*) does not refer to a part of the anatomy; *osteocondritis* 'osteochondritis', however, is considered a non-transgressive neologism, because it is perceived as new for the general public, but it follows the word-formation rules since it refers to a type of pathologyIn the case of the neoclassical compounds, one example is *odiómetro* '(odio) 'hate' + -meter', a transgressive neologism created with the combination form *-metro* 'meter' that does not designate a measuring device; *etilómetro* '(etilo) ethyl + -meter' ('breathalyzer') is a non-transgressive neologism because it refers to a device that measures the blood alcohol content, although the extended word to designate this device in Spanish is *alcoholímetro*; and *odio* is the base of the transgressive neologism. These examples are exposed in Table 2:

Table 2: An example of transgressive and non-transgressive neologism for each ending form.

Ending forms	Transgressive neologisms + base	Non-transgressive neologisms
-ismo '-ism'	pedor*rismo* (*pedorro -rra* 'dumb')	comunita*rismo* 'communitarianism'
-ez '-ness'	bigo*tez* (*bigote* 'moustache')	absur*dez* 'absurdness'
-itis 'itis'	festival*itis* (*festival* 'festival')	osteocondr*itis* 'osteochondritis'
-metro '-meter'	odió*metro* (*odio* 'hate')	etiló*metro* 'breathalyzer'

---

6 Taking into account that most of the participants were bilingual speakers of Spanish in Catalan, it is worth noting that while most of the non-transgressive neologisms have an equivalent that has been documented in Catalan, in the case of transgressive neologisms only some units are registered in use in Catalan, such as *chutómetro* 'xutometre' or *facilismo* 'facilisme'.

Participants were presented with a list of 28 words and were asked to rate each of the words according to three categories: valence, arousal, and familiarity. Valence and arousal are part of a three-dimension non-verbal pictorial technique designed by Bradley and Lang (1994) that measures the pleasure associated with a person's emotional reaction to different types of stimuli (images, words, products, etc.). Only valence and arousal, but not dominance, were used, since they are considered the most relevant affective variables for studying the emotional effects of word processing (Kousta et al. 2011; Ferré, Guasch, Moldovan, and Sánchez-Casas 2012; Kuperman et al. 2014; Ferré et al. 2015; Guasch, Ferré, and Fraga 2016). Dominance shows little variance, compared to valence and arousal (Bradley and Lang 2000), and the results tend to correlate with those of valence (Lang, Bradley, and Cuthbert 1999). Besides, the SAM instrument was adapted to include two opposite written categories related to valence and arousal: *triste* 'sad' / *alegre* 'happy', and *calmado* 'calm' / *activado* 'activated', which are based on the adjectives used in the instructions of the questionnaire, whereby *desactivado* 'unaroused' and *relajado* 'relaxed' relate to *calm*, and *despierto* 'aroused' and *excitado* 'excited' relate to *activated*, both for arousal. Participants evaluated these two categories using a 9-point semantic differential scale. Regarding familiarity, a 7-point Likert scale was chosen to be able to compare the results with other studies if needed (Guasch, Ferré, and Fraga 2016).[7]

Table 3: Categories and Likert scales for each of the variables under study.

Variable	Opposite categories	Likert scale
Valence	*triste* 'sad' / *alegre* 'happy'	9-points
Arousal	*calmado* 'calm' / *activado* 'activated'	9-points
Familiarity	*infrecuente* 'infrequent' / *frecuente* 'frequent'	7-points

For each item in the questionnaire participants were first shown a word in bold, followed by a context. In the sentence, the neologism was marked between asterisks (*), as seen in (20) below:

(20) festivalitis

Vivimos días de *festivalitis* y hay que sacar provecho.

---

7 This study provides affective ratings for 1,400 Spanish words for valence, arousal, and familiarity among other categories. The supplementary material is available online to authorized users.

'These are days of *festivalitis* and we have to make the most of them'. [English translation]

The participants were then instructed to assess the word in terms of valence, arousal and, lastly, in terms of familiarity (see the Figures 1 to 3). The instructions for the task were adapted from Ferré, Guasch, and Moldovan (2012), as shown below with their English translation followed by the differential scale for each item that contained the SAM (Bradley and Lang 1994):

> In this first category, you will have to assess each word in the dimension of valence. If the word makes you feel sad to a high degree, rate it with a value of 1. If it makes you feel happy to a high degree, rate it with a 9. If it does not make you feel sad nor happy, but neutral, rate it with a 5. You can use other values if the word makes you feel somewhat sad (3) or somewhat happy (7). You can also assess your level of sadness or happiness using the other values (2, 4, 6, and 8), located between the figures.

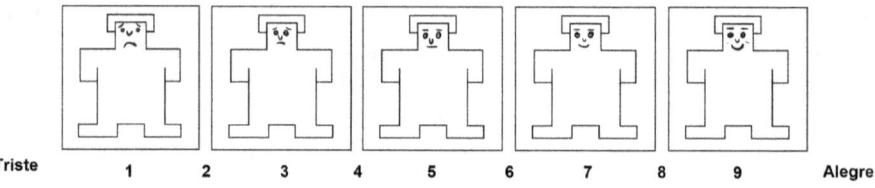

Figure 1: Adaptation of the SAM for valence dimension (triste 'sad' / alegre 'happy').

> The second category is used to assess each word according to the degree of arousal. If the word makes you feel calm to a high degree (that is, very unaroused or relaxed), rate it with a value of 1. If it makes you feel activated to a high degree (that is, very aroused or excited), rate it with a 9. If it does not make you feel calm nor activated, but neutral, rate it with a 5. You can also use the other values, as in the category above, to indicate different levels of calmness or activation.

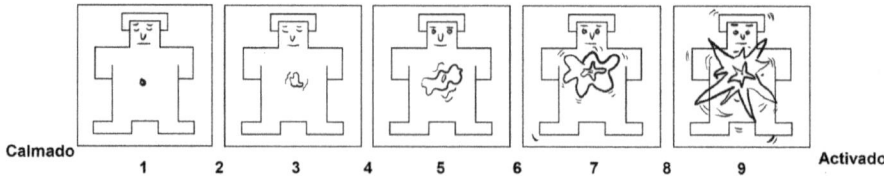

Figure 2: Adaptation of the SAM for arousal dimension (calmado 'calm' / activado 'activated').

> For the third category, you will have to assess the level of familiarity of each word. Rate how often you have encountered the word in everyday language, both in spoken and in written form. For example, in conversations, on the radio, on TV, in films, or in the press. If

you rarely come across the word in everyday language, you should rate it with a 1. If, on the contrary, you come across the word almost always, you should rate it with a 7. As in the questions above, you can use any of the other values according to the level of familiarity of the word.

Infrecuente	1	2	3	4	5	6	7 Frecuente

Figure 3: Familiarity rating (infrecuente 'infrequent' / frecuente 'frequent').

2.4 Procedure

The 56 items included in the experiment were divided into two questionnaires with 28 items each to avoid fatigue among the participants. To prevent priming effects, the bases of the transgressive neologisms and the corresponding transgressive neologisms were placed in different questionnaires. In doing so, the bases worked as fillers. For example, if one questionnaire contained the transgressive neologism *noviómetro*, the base *novio* did not appear in the same questionnaire, but in the other one. Regarding the sequence of the items, the order was fixed based on a randomized structure of transgressive and non-transgressive neologisms, and fillers. Each questionnaire could be answered in approximately ten minutes. The experimental study was anonymous and voluntary, and the participants were informed that they could stop answering the questionnaire whenever they felt like it without having to provide a justification. The two questionnaires were created and distributed online using Google Forms and the participants were only asked to answer one of them. Each survey was fully completed by 56 and 58 participants respectively, and no questionnaires needed to be discarded.

At the beginning of the survey, the participants read the instructions to complete the evaluation of the words in terms of valence, arousal, and familiarity. The instructions also contained two examples to practice the rating of the three categories for each of these two examples. Then, they could start the survey. For each of the 28 items they could read the instructions of each of the three categories again. Once participants had assessed all of the items, they had to complete a brief and anonymous sociolinguistic survey about their gender, age, mother tongue, country of origin, and level of education.

3 Results

In this section, the variation of the three dependent variables (that is, the emotional responses *valence, arousal,* and *familiarity*) is analyzed according to four independent variables. The first independent variable is the type of word, which includes the transgressive neologisms, their base forms, and the non-transgressive neologisms. Secondly, the type of transgression is considered, which can be semantic, syntactic, or zero transgression. The third independent variable is the type of word-formation that encompasses suffixation or neoclassical compounding.

According to the results obtained, the type of word can be considered the most relevant factor impacting the rating of the different words included in the study. Table 4 provides the descriptive statistics for each of the three dependent variables regarding centrality — related to average or middle values — for which median and mode are used, and dispersion — that focuses on the deviation from the average — expressed with minimum and maximum values.

Table 4: Descriptive statistics for the bases, and transgressive and non-transgressive neologisms.

Variable	Factor	Median	Mode	Min.	Max.
Valence	Bases (trans. neologisms)	6	5	1	9
	Transgressive neologisms	5	5	1	9
	Non-transgressive neologisms	5	5	1	9
Arousal	Bases (trans. neologisms)	6	5	1	9
	Transgressive neologisms	5	5	1	9
	Non-transgressive neologisms	5	5	1	9
Familiarity	Bases (trans. neologisms)	7	7	1	7
	Transgressive neologisms	1	1	1	7
	Non-transgressive neologisms	2	1	1	7

In this case, neither the analysis of the median nor the mode evidence differences on valence and arousal responses among transgressive and non-transgressive neologisms, but the median attests that the non-neological units, that is, the bases of transgressive neologisms, show more positive and arousing responses. This result is due to the fact that for the participants the bases are familiar words, as shown in the familiarity results (7 out of 7) and it is easier for the participants to classify familiar words further from the neutral zone, which corresponds to 5 in the 9-point semantic differential scale used. However, familiarity results corroborate that transgressive neologisms are perceived as less familiar than non-transgressive neologisms (with a median of 1 vs. a median of 2).

Descriptive statistics for each of the three dependent variables measuring emotionality in regards to the four independent variables in isolation are shown below. Table 5 shows the classification of positive, neutral, and negative words in terms of valence. The median of all the responses obtained for each neologism was considered. Thus, words with a median of 6 to 9 were considered positive, those with a median of 5 were classified as neutral, and words ranging from 1 to 4 were considered negative:

Table 5: Valence: positive, neutral, and negative words absolute and relative frequencies.

Classification		Transgressive neologisms		Non-transgressive neologisms	
		N (%)	Examples	N (%)	Examples
6–9	Positive	7 (36.84)	*chandalismo, festivalitis*	0	–
5	Neutral	10 (52.63)	*chutómetro, dialoguitis*	14 (73.68)	*horterez, informalismo*
1–4	Negative	2 (10.53)	*abucheómetro, odiómetro*	5 (26.32)	*capsulitis, prematurez*

As shown, transgressive neologisms and non-transgressive neologisms display different results if the line is set in the middle of the 9-point semantic differential scale used in the experiment, that is, 5. While 7 transgressive neologisms (36.84%) are placed in the upper side of the scale, none of the non-transgressive neologisms are located on this side of the axis. Yet, in both cases most of the neologisms are classified as neutral, with 10 (52.63%) and 14 units (73.68%), respectively. Two instances of transgressive neologisms that are considered positive are *chandalismo* 'tracksuit' + *-ism* and *festivalitis* 'festival + *-itis*'. The two transgressive neologisms classified as negative are *abucheómetro* 'boo + *-meter*' and *odiómetro* 'hate + *-meter*'. In the case of non-transgressive neologisms, the five remaining units that are considered negative are four units created with the suffix *-itis*, since it means 'inflammation', as in *capsulitis*, and the neologism *prematurez* 'prematureness'.

In order to study the correlation between each dependent variable and the independent variables selected, an ordinal regression analysis was carried out to examine which variable(s) had the strongest effect on each emotional response. Before applying this statistical test, the four assumptions related to ordinal regression test were checked. First, the dependent variables were ordered and that the independent variables were categorical. Secondly, a variance inflation factor test (VIF) was applied to check that there was no multi-collinearity. Since the VIF values obtained were lower than 10, it was concluded that there was no multi-collinearity in the dataset. Finally, proportional odds were analyzed conducting a test of parallel lines; this led to results that were integrated in the ordinal regression analysis and could be contrasted with the overall results from the regression analysis.

Table 6 shows the results of the ordinal regression test taking valence as the dependent factor. In more detail, it contains the four independent variables of this study: 1) *type of word*, which is divided into transgressive neologisms, non-transgressive neologisms, and bases of the transgressive neologisms; 2) *word-formation*, that can either be suffixation, neoclassical compounding, or none (this last category only affects the bases of the transgressive neologisms); and 3) *change*, which refers to the type of restriction transgressed by transgressive neologisms and which can either be related with the meaning of the base or with the syntactic and morphological category of the base.

Table 6: Results from ordinal regression analysis with valence as the dependent variable.

Valence	Chi-square	Sig	Test parallel lines
Type of word	10.911	.004	.337
Word-formation*	5.543	.063	.025
Change	.752	.686	.761

Note: Results for *word-formation* cannot be taken into account, since the result of the test of parallel lines is lower than .05 (*p* <.001).

The independent variable *type of word* shows statistically significant results for valence (*p* = .004), which means that the differences observed on this variable when rating the lexical items of this study according to valence are due to the characteristics of the words. It confirms that these results could not have been obtained randomly. The other independent variables, such as *word-formation* and *change*, related to the type of transgression, do not show significant results, which means that these characteristics do not have an impact on rating valence. Moreover, in this case the variable *word-formation* does not meet the last assumption of ordinal regression tests on proportional odds in the parallel lines test. Therefore, here it cannot be assumed that the relationship between these groups is the same.

Regarding the dependent variable arousal, Table 7 presents the classification results regarding the answers for this emotional response. In this case, the classification concurs with the one applied for valence, since answers ranging from 6 to 9 were considered arousing or exciting, the ones from 1 to 4 were classified as calming or relaxing, while the answers that correspond to 5 in this 9-point semantic differential scale were considered neutral.

As shown, transgressive neologisms are perceived as more arousing than non-transgressive neologisms. While 8 out of 19 transgressive neologisms (42.11%) were classified on the upper-side of the 9-point semantic differential scale, in the case of

Table 7: Arousal: exciting, neutral, and calming words absolute and relative frequencies.

Classification		Transgressive neologisms		Non-transgressive neologisms	
		N. (%)	Examples	N. (%)	Examples
6–9	Arousing	8 (42.11)	arquitecturitis, hijoputez	2 (10.53)	osteocondritis, unilateralismo
5	Neutral	11 (57.89)	facilismo, odiómetro	17 (89.47)	reflectómetro, sosez
1–4	Relaxing	0	–	0	–

non-transgressive neologisms this feature decreases to 2 units (10.53%). Some examples of transgressive neologisms are *arquitecturitis* 'architecture + -itis' and *hijoputez* 'son of a bitch + -ness', which contains a swear word. In the case of non-transgressive neologisms there is the case of *oseteocondritis* 'osteochondritis' and *unilateralismo* 'unilateralism'. On the lower side of the scale, no transgressive neologisms nor non-transgressive ones can be found. Therefore, none of these neologisms elicited a calming or relaxing emotional response from the participants.

Table 8 depicts the results of ordinal regression using arousal emotional responses as the dependent variable:

Table 8: Results from ordinal regression with arousal as the dependent variable.

Arousal	Chi-square	Sig	Test parallel lines
Type of word	12.933	.002	.613
Word-formation	8.112	.017	.620
Change	2.040	.361	.605

In this case, *type of word* also shows statistically significant results ($p = .002$). Another independent variable that has an impact on arousal is *word-formation* ($p = .017$). This suggests that the use of simple words in the study – base forms, words created by suffixation, or by neoclassical compounding – is a factor that affects this dependent variable. Finally, the type of transgression does not show significant results.

Regarding familiarity, Table 9 reports the classification of transgressive and non-transgressive neologisms.

This classification of familiarity clearly shows that all the 19 transgressive neologisms were considered unfamiliar (100%) while in the case of non-transgressive neologisms this result decreases to 13 units (68.42). Only 2 non-transgressive neologisms (10.53%), *absurdez* 'absurdness' and *cardiómetro* 'cardiometer' were considered familiar, and 4 lexical units (21.05%) were placed in a neutral zone among the two opposite poles (familiar-unfamiliar). This is the case of *informalismo* 'informal-

Table 9: Familiarity: familiar, neutral, and non-familiar words absolute and relative frequencies.

Classification		Transgressive neologisms		Non-transgressive neologisms	
		N. (%)	Examples	N. (%)	Examples
5–7	Familiar	0	–	2 (10.53)	*absurdez, cardiómetro*
4	Neutral	0	–	4 (21.05)	*informalismo, sosez*
1–3	Unfamiliar	19 (100)	*bigotez, facilismo*	13 (68.42)	*articulismo, esofaguitis*

Table 10: Ordinal regression taking familiarity as the dependent variable.

Familiarity	Chi-square	Sig	Test parallel lines
Type of word	66.194	<.001	.428
Word-formation*	62.936	<.001	<.001
Change	20.693	<.001	.223

Note: Results for *word-formation* cannot be taken into account, since the result of the test of parallel lines is lower than .05 (p <.001).

ism' and *sosez* 'dullness', for example. Table 10 shows the results from the ordinal regression test using familiarity as the dependent variable.

In this case the independent variables *type of word* and *change* (type of transgression) were significant (with p values below .001). When comparing the results of familiarity with the ordinal regression data of the two emotional responses reported above, valence and arousal, we can see that the correlation between the dependent and the independent variables is greater in the case of familiarity. We can assume that the familiarity of these lexical items can also have an impact on the emotional responses. Nevertheless, one would expect that words perceived as more familiar would show a higher variation on the 9-point semantic differential scales instead of a high incidence in neutral values, like in Table 2 in the case of the bases of transgressive neologisms (with a median of 6 both in valence and arousal while transgressive and non-transgressive neologisms show a median of 5 in both emotional responses).

Finally, a Kendall's W test for ordinal variables was conducted to measure the association of the dependent variables (valence, arousal, and familiarity). The result is statistically significant (Kendall's W = .231, p <.001), which represents a low association between the three variables in terms of emotional responses (valence and arousal) and familiarity.

4 Discussion

The results obtained in the different analyses and comparisons show that the hypothesis that guided this study was confirmed, since the type of word, divided into three categories (transgressive neologisms, non-transgressive neologisms, and the bases of transgressive neologisms) is the variable that has the strongest effect for both valence and arousal emotional responses. Although the median of transgressive and non-transgressive neologisms is the same in terms of valence and arousal, and corresponds to the neutral rating (5) in the 9-point semantic differential scale, they show some differences in the classifications reported: 14 out of 19 non-transgressive neologisms were evaluated with a median of 5, which corresponds to a 73.68%, while in the case of transgressive neologisms the results decreased to a total of 10 units, which represent 52.63%. From the affective valence perspective, the transgressive neologisms in the study were considered neutral-positive, since 7 units (36.84%) were rated with a median between 6 to 9, while non-transgressive neologisms were perceived as more neutral-negative, since 5 words had a median ranging in between 1 and 4, and none received a value higher than 5. At this point, it should also be noted that negative and positive stimuli can either be calming (e.g., *dirt* or *sleep*) or exciting (e.g., *snake* or *sex*) (Kuperman et al. 2014: 2). For this reason, I maintain that the fact that non-transgressive neologisms were considered more negatively than transgressive neologisms does not have an effect on the arousal dimension results.

The significant differences concerning the arousal dimension are accounted for when considering the classification results of the transgressive and non-transgressive neologisms. In this case, 8 transgressive neologisms (42.11%) were classified as arousing while in the case of non-transgressive neologisms only 2 words (10.53%) were classified as arousing. In this case, the word-formation type, which could be suffixation, for the suffixes *-ismo* '-ism', *-ez* '-ness', and *-itis*, neoclassical compounding, in the case of the combination form *-metro* '-meter', or simple, for the bases of the transgressive neologisms included, is also significant. However, considering the semantic and morphological restrictions (Gaeta 2015) transgressed by the lexical items of this study, no significant correlation could be attested since the domain of the base changes, or the base suffers from syntactic modification.

As for the results regarding familiarity, it is clear that the differences between transgressive and non-transgressive neologisms are statistically significant. This result can be explained from a double perspective. On the one hand, if one assumes that transgressive neologisms are the result of unproductive word-formation rules and, thus, more original, they can be perceived as newer and more infrequent, because speakers may become aware that the structures differ from the expected ones. On the other hand, since the motivation underlying most of the transgressive neologisms is related to a stylistic and subjective function, this can be translated as a low frequency rate as well, since this type of neologism does not tend to stabilize in use with time, but instead it is used to satisfy the expressiveness of a communicative situation at a particular time. The results on this dependent variable also show that the word-formation process of the words and the type of transgression have a significant result.

Lexical creativity is an ability that is shared by the speakers of a linguistic community, but stylistic or expressive neologisms are generally attributed to writers since they have a deeper knowledge and command of language (Guilbert 1975) due to their profession. Coseriu (1952: 52) adds that one of the objectives of poetry is discovering new meaningful associations (images) or formal associations (rhyme, alliteration, etc.), which are possible in the language system but unprecedented in use, since they do not follow the norm. However, the creative use of language could also be extended to text types other than literature, namely the media. Journalists and copywriters also share a strong command of language and, although the objectives may differ, breaking the rules could be desirable at some point. As a result, it would create a surprising effect on the receiver due to it being unexpected, which would be useful to attract readers' or listeners' attention. The interaction between language and emotion has also been analyzed in terms of grammar, and it also shows that some emotional effects such as surprise or emphasis can be achieved using an unexpected syntactic order (Martínez Caro and Downing 2016).

Using frequent words when writing a text benefits readability, such as with educational texts, which, according to a study by Kuperman et al. (2014), also contain boring or neutral words. In contrast, film and media subtitles contain more exciting words to draw and keep viewers' attention (p. 11). Indeed, frequent, calming, and shorter words are processed faster than infrequent, arousing, and longer words. For that reason, transgressive neologisms have a higher processing cost because they are infrequent and tend to be more arousing than non-transgressive words. Also, since they are complex words, they are usually longer than simple words. Concerning predictability, they may also take more time and effort to be recognized and understood, since they break word formation-rules. Despite having all these disadvantages by putting communication at risk and resulting in slow processing, it is important to highlight that they could be perceived as a positive challenge for receivers to respond to. Consequently, these words could be easier to memorize.

5 Conclusion

This study was set out to investigate the emotional effects of neologisms that break word-formation rules, since communicative intention guides linguistic selection. Consequently, this type of neologism is perceived as surprising and tends to be used in marked contexts.

The originality of this study on the emotional effects of words lies on the fact that two of the variables considered tested the effect of neologisms, since the words selected were either recent or infrequent in Spanish. Consequently, they could be considered as not belonging to the mental lexicon of the speakers. The results of the category devoted to the perception of familiarity confirmed, again, that the participants were not familiar with either type of neologism, both transgressive and non-transgressive. Moreover, the study is also innovative, since it analyzes the emotional effects of breaking word-formation rules according to the valence and arousal dimensions of the SAM (Bradley and Lang 1994). In particular, the participants were presented with the same type of formal neologisms, created by suffixation, with *-ismo* '-ism', *-ez* '-ness' and -itis, and neoclassical compounding, with the combining form *-metro* '-meter'. Half of these neologisms (19) followed the productivity constraints and restrictions of the selected suffixes or of the combining form, and the other half (19) deviated mainly from the morphologic and semantic restrictions of these linguistic items.

The results of the different descriptive and statistical analyses ratify the hypothesis that transgressive neologisms, that is, neologisms that break word-formation rules, cause stronger emotional effects on the receiver, regarding valence and arousal, than neologisms with the same pattern that can be considered non-transgressive since they are the result of productive and predictable word-formation rules. For this reason, breaking the rules can be considered a linguistic mechanism or strategy used with a particular communicative objective, which is to draw the reader or hearer's attention, and enhance memorization of what has been said. Finally, it would be interesting to test if, as shown in previous studies, the affective or emotional effects of infrequent words slow down word recognition but facilitate learning new vocabulary both in first and second language acquisition, especially in the case of abstract words.

References

Aitchinson, Jean. 1994 [1987]. *Words in the mind: an introduction to the mental lexicon*, 2nd edn. Oxford & Cambridge, MA: Blackwell.
Altarriba, Jeanette & Dana M. Basnight-Brown. 2011. The representation of emotion vs emotion-laden words in English and Spanish in the Affective Simon Task. *International Journal of Bilingualism* 15. 310–328.
[APA] American Psychological Association. 2022. *APA Dictionary of Psychology*. https://dictionary.apa.org/
Llopart-Saumell, Elisabet. 2021. The perception of connotations in lexical innovations. In Antonio Cortijo & Jordi Antolí (eds.), *Approaches to New Trends in Research on Catalan Studies*, 157–182. New York/Berlin: Peter Lang
Llopart-Saumell, Elisabet & Judit Freixa. 2014. La función de los neologismos: revisión de la dicotomía neología denominativa y neología estilística. *Neologica: revue internationale de néologie* 8. 135–156.
Bauer, Laurie. 2001. *Morphological Productivity*. Cambridge: Cambridge University Press.
Bernal, Elisenda & Carsten Sinner. 2013. Neología expresiva: la formación de palabras en Mafalda. In Emili Casanova & Cesáreo Calvo (eds.), *Actes del 26é Congrés de Lingüística i Filologia Romàniques (València, 6–11 de setembre de 2010)*, vol. 3, 479–496. Berlin: Walter de Gruyter.
Bernal, Elisenda & Alba Milà-García. 2021. Breaking the rules: speakers' perception on the pragmatic connotations of (un)marked uses of final combining forms. *Catalan Review* 35(1). 89–109
[BOBNEO] Observatori de Neologia. 2016. *Cercador BOBNEO*. http://obneo.iula.upf.edu/bobneo/index.php
Booij, Geert E. 2007. *The Grammar of Words*. Oxford: Oxford University Press.
Bradley, Margaret M. & Peter J. Lang. 1994. Measuring emotion: The Self-Assessment Manikin and the semantic differential. *Journal of Behavior Therapy and Experimental Psychiatry*. 25(1). 49–59.
Bradley, Margaret M. & Peter J. Lang. 2000. Measuring emotion: Behavior, feeling and physiology. In Richard D. Lane & Lynn Nadel (eds.), *Cognitive neuroscience of emotion*, 242–276. New York: Oxford University Press.
Cabré, M. Teresa. 1989. La neologia efímera. In Josep Massot (ed.), *Miscel·lània Joan Bastardas, 1 (Estudis de Llengua i Literatura Catalanes, XVIII)*, 37–58. Barcelona: Publicacions de l'Abadia de Montserrat.
Cabré, M. Teresa. 2006. Neologismes, observatoris i diccionaris [Neologisms, observatories, and dictionaries]. In Germà Colón & Luis Gimeno (eds.), *Els noms i els conceptes: noves tendències en l'estudi del lèxic*, 55–94. Castelló de la Plana: Publicacions de la Universitat Jaume I.
Cabré, M. Teresa. 2015. Bases para una teoría de los neologismos léxicos: primeras reflexiones. In Ieda Maria Alves & Eliane Simões Pereira (eds.), *Neologia das Línguas Românicas*, 70–110. Sao Paulo: Humanitas, CAPES.
Coseriu, Eugenio. 1952. *Sistema, norma y habla: con un resumen en alemán*. Montevideo: Universidad de la República.
[DLE] Real Academia Española. 2014. *Diccionario de la lengua española*, 23rd edn. Madrid: Real Academia Española, Espasa. http://dle.rae.es/
Dressler, Wolfang U. 1981. General Principles of Poetic License in Word Formation. *Logos Semantikos* 2. 423–431.
Escandell-Vidal, M. Victoria. 2014. *La comunicación: lengua, cognición y sociedad*. Madrid: Akal.

Ferré, Pilar, Marc Guasch, Cornelia Moldovan & Rosa Sánchez-Casas. 2012. Affective norms for 380 Spanish words belonging to three different semantic categories. *Behavior Research Methods* 44. 395–403.
Ferré, Pilar, David Ventura, Montserrat Comesaña & Isabel Fraga. 2015. The role of emotionality in the acquisition of new concrete and abstract words. *Frontiers in Psychology* 6(976). 1–10.
Gaeta, Livio. 2015. Restrictions in word-formation. In Peter O Müller, Ingeborg Ohnheiser, Susan Olsen & Franz Rainer (eds.), *Word-Formation. An International Handbook of the Languages of Europe*, vol. 2, 859–875. Berlin & New York: Mouton de Gruyter.
García-Page, Mario. 2003. Estructuras desviantes y discurso poético. In Agustín Vera Luján, Ramon Almela Pérez, José María Jiménez Cano & Dolores Anunciación Igualada Belchí (eds.), *Homenaje al profesor Estanislao Ramón Trives*, 311–336. Murcia: Universidad de Murcia. Servicio de Publicaciones.
Guasch, Marc, Pilar Ferré & Isabel Fraga. 2016. Spanish norms for affective and lexico-semantic variables for 1,400 words. *Behavior Research Methods* 48. 1358–1369.
Guerrero Ramos, Gloria. 1995. *Neologismos en el español actual*. Madrid: Arco Libros.
Guilbert, Louis. 1975. *La créativité lexicale*. Paris: Larousse.
Hanks, Patrick. 2013. *Lexical Analysis: Norms and Exploitations*. Cambridge, London: The MIT Press.
Jakobson, Roman. 1984. *Ensayos de lingüística general*. Barcelona: Ariel.
Julià, Carolina. 2015. Los patrones derivativos del sufijo *-itis* en español moderno: análisis de algunos ejemplos. In Janet de Cesaris & Elisenda Bernal (eds.), *Los afijos: variación, rivalidad y representación*, 147–156. Barcelona: Universitat Pompeu Fabra/IULA.
Katamba, Francis. 1993. *Morphology*. London: MacMillan.
Koestler, Arthur. 1975. *The Act of Creation*. London: Picador.
Kousta, Stavroula-Thaleia, David P. Vinson & Gabriella Vigliocco. 2009. Emotion words, regardless of polarity, have a processing advantage over neutral words. *Cognition* 112(3). 473–481
Kousta, Stavroula-Thaleia, Gabriella Vigliocco, David P. Vinson, Mark Andrews & Elena del Campo. 2011. The Representation of Abstract Words: Why Emotion Matters. *Journal of Experimental Psychology General* 140(1). 14–34.
Kuperman, Victor, Zachary Estes, Mark Bysbaert & Amy Beth Warriner. 2014. Emotion and language: valence and arousal affect word recognition. *Journal of Experimental Psychology General* 143(3). 1065–1081.
Lang, Mervyn Francis. 1990. *Spanish word formation: Productive derivational morphology in the modern lexis*. London-New York: Routledge.
Lang, Peter J. 1995. The emotion probe: Studies of motivation and attention. *American Journal of Psychology* 119. 46–65.
Lang, Peter J., Bradley, Margaret M. & Bruce N. Cuthbert. 1999. *International affective picture system (IAPS): Technical manual and affective ratings*. Gainesville: Center for Research in Psychophysiology, University of Florida.
Martín Camacho, José Carlos. 1994. Consideraciones sobre la creatividad léxica. El ejemplo de Juan Goytisolo. *Anuario de estudios filológicos* 17. 307–324.
Martínez Caro, Elena & Angela Downing. 2016. Grammar and emotion: emotion and syntax. MOOC course module. https://www.academia.edu/43126705/Grammar_and_emotion_Emotion_and_syntax_2016_by_E_Mart%C3%ADnez_Caro_and_A_Downing
Oxford University Press. 2021. *Oxford English Dictionary*. http://www.oed.com/

Rainer, Franz. 2002. Neologismos monstruarios. In Bernhard Pöll & Franz Rainer (eds.), *Vocabula et vocabularia. Études de lexicologie et de (méta-) lexicographie romanes en l'honneur du 60e anniversaire de Dieter Messner*, 283–302. Frankfurt: Peter Lang.

Rainer, Franz. 2005. Constraints on productivity. In Pavol Stekauer & Rochelle Lieber (eds.), *Handbook of Word-formation*, 335–352. Dordrecht: Springer.

Rey, Alain. 1976. Néologisme: un pseudo-concept? *Cahiers de lexicologie* 28(1). 2–17.

Stefan DuBois
Chapter 9
Do L2 Speakers sound strange when using slang? L1 attitudes toward L2 Use of peninsular Spanish colloquial lexical items

1 Introduction

The speech of L2 speakers varies not only according to what Mougeon et al. (2004) defines as Type 1 variation – that is, alternation between grammatical target forms and ungrammatical interference from the learner's L1 – but also according to Type 2 variation: forms where L1 speakers themselves exhibit variation due to sociostylistic factors. For example, an English learner might hear L1 speakers produce *y'all*, *yuns*, or *yous* depending on the region; a learner's decision to produce one of these nonstandard variations contrasting with the 'standard' form in the prestige variant of the target language would constitute Type 2 variation.

While language attitudes research has extensively documented the social effects of this second type of variation in L1 speakers (see Garrett 2010 for an overview), perceptions of nonstandard language use by L2 speakers have received far less attention. Historically, theoretical arguments such as that by Auger and Valdman (1999), specifically addressing French, have indicated that L1 listeners perceive nonstandard variation negatively when coming from L2 speakers:

> Naive native speakers do not expect foreign learners to speak as they do; they expect them to speak "better." That is to say, they do not view favorably the use by foreigners of colloquial speech forms and marked regional or social accents, especially by those who have acquired the language through formal instruction. Indeed, it seems that native speakers resent, as a form of intrusion, the appropriation of these forms by foreigners. (p. 409)

This conjecture about negative L1 reactions to L2 use of nonstandard language occurs repeatedly throughout several decades of literature up through the early 2000s, with similar generalizations in articles addressing English, French, and German implicating the view that this is a common trend (Christophersen 1973, Irujo 1986, Piller 2002, Thomas 1983, Valdman 1988, 2000, 2003). Andreasson (1994) sums up the paradoxical viewpoint that "a subtle double standard applies to the learner,

---

Stefan DuBois, University of Denver

https://doi.org/10.1515/9783110730418-009

who will be considered 'deficient' as far as acquisition is concerned when he or she imitates certain linguistic elements that nobody regards as deficiencies in the speech of native speakers . . . The general attitude towards foreign language learners is that they are supposed to learn to speak the 'right' way" (396).

Although the above articles imply that this attitude extends to all manner of variation, including phonological, morphosyntactic, and lexical, they do not substantiate their claims with empirical data. The small handful of studies which have investigated the issue from a quantitative angle have found inconsistent results: some support the conception that what may be perfectly acceptable – or even desirable, in accordance with the theory of covert prestige (Trudgill 1972) – for L1 speakers is paradoxically perceived negatively in L2 speakers (Prodromou 2007, Ruivivar and Collins 2018, Swacker 1976). In contrast, others indicate that L2 speakers stand to gain from this variation (Beaulieu 2016, George 2013b, 2014, 2017). Before moving on to the research questions of the present study, the specific findings of these existing empirical studies will be summarized.

With results supporting the existence of this 'double standard,' Swacker (1976) asked Texas residents to evaluate the speech of two L1 English speakers and two L1 Arabic speakers. One speaker from each group used a neutral variant of American English while the other employed "strong east-Texas pronunciation" and "such regional markers as multiple modals, 'y'all', and absence of adjectival morphemes." The two L1 speakers received similar ratings, although the one using regionalisms was rated slightly higher on trustworthiness and lower on leadership. The L2 speakers employing regionalisms received considerably more negative evaluations than the neutral variant, being perceived as untrustworthy, poorly informed, uneducated, and humorless. From this, Swacker concludes that "Certain dialectal markers may be perfectly acceptable even advantageous when coming from a native speaker but be quite offensive when spoken by a foreigner" (3), arguing that foreign speech which too closely approximates that of L1 speakers causes discomfort and the rejection of the very regional markers the listener uses in their own speech. This, Swacker continues, leaves learners with the paradoxical goal of seeking native competence without reproducing their target too faithfully.

More recently, Prodromou (2007) asked participants to evaluate an unusual phrasal verb collocation in English. Those who had been told that the sentence was produced by a native speaker overwhelmingly rated the collocation as acceptable, while responses were far more mixed when the speaker was identified as a non-native speaker. A participant comment sums up this double standard: "I must admit I'd be happier with this from a NS than a NNS!" (22). Prodromou therefore argues that L2 speakers do not have the same freedom when it comes to linguistic creativity as L1 speakers. Although license for innovation and non-standard language use are not one and the same, this study nevertheless supports the postulation that L1 speakers are afforded more leeway in their production than L2 speakers.

Ruivivar and Collins (2018) reached a similar conclusion. In a study examining the impact of foreign accentedness on the acceptability of nonstandard grammatical constructions, raters evaluated stimuli containing nonstandard language characteristic of spoken English grammar. The more strongly-accented the speaker, the less grammatical raters found the constructions, thereby indicating that L1 users are permitted more leniency in bending linguistic norms. The authors conclude that "It would appear that L2 speakers' use of these forms does not signal group membership; rather, L1 speakers appear to perceive it as a deviation from what the speaker is expected or able to say" (196).

Other studies have found opposite results. In George's (2013b, 2014) study on the acquisition of Spanish dialectal variants in study abroad students, L1 speakers rated the students' speech according to foreign-accentedness in samples designed to elicit local phonological variants. The study found that using these variants in at least 10% of possible environments correlated with lower foreign accent ratings; that is, the more students employed the variants, the less foreign-sounding their accent. George (2017) similarly found that the production of regional phonological features resulted in significantly less foreign-sounding accents than speakers who did not produce any. Whether these results are specific to Spanish – a language not explicitly addressed in the literature above – is unclear, but they nevertheless call into question the universality of negative reactions toward L2 nonstandard language use.

Beaulieu (2016) similarly brings this double standard into question with an investigation of the attitudes of French-speaking nursing patients in Canada toward stylistic variation of nurses who spoke French as an L2. The study compared informal phonological, grammatical, and lexical variants typically used by French L1 nurses to the formal variants recommended in textbooks for L2 nursing students. Participant interviews demonstrated largely negative reactions to the formal lexical variants, while responses to the informal sample were overwhelmingly positive. Praise centered around social qualities linked to positive bedside manner, attributing to the nurse characteristics such as "warmth, kindness, adaptability and trustworthiness" (281). Some patients even praised the informal guise for professionalism in their flexibility to adapt to patients by using informal words. Despite most participants responding positively, 17% found the nurse's accommodation to the local norm "patronising, condescending, and highly unprofessional" (281), evidencing the conflicting opinions of L1 speakers. Beaulieu therefore argues that a successful learner must control both formal and informal varieties.

L2 learners themselves have expressed ambivalence toward the adoption of nonstandard language and regional dialect features. Justifications for avoidance include accentuating their foreignness or to preserve their identity (Bley-Vroman 1989, Gatbonton et al. 2005, George 2013b, Ringer-Hilfinger 2012, LoCastro 1998, Lybeck 2002, Morley 1991, Ringer-Hilfinger 2012, Siegal 1996, Trosset 1986), because they find the variation in question inappropriate outside the target community (George 2013a, 2013b, 2014, Kang 2009, Ringer-Hilfinger 2012), and insecurity about implementing the relevant features correctly (French and Beaulieu 2016, Kinginger and Farrell 2004, Ringer-Hilfinger 2012). Others seek to adopt nonstandard variation out of a desire to acculturate (Dewaele 2004a, Ringer-Hilfinger 2012, Tarone and Swain 1995, Van Compernolle and Williams 2012) or recognition of its necessity for their linguistic repertoire (Dewaele 2004b).

The scarcity of studies examining whether L2 learners' positive and negative motivations are well-founded means that they must rely on intuition rather than academic consensus. The present study sought to address this gap by investigating the attitudes of L1 listeners toward L2 nonstandard variation via quantitative means, specifically focusing on the perception of L1 speakers of Peninsular Spanish toward L2 use of colloquial lexical variants. The following research questions were investigated:

1. How does the use of colloquial lexical items correlate with ratings of linguistic proficiency?
2. In terms of personality judgments, do L2 speakers benefit from the same advantages and suffer the same disadvantages of colloquial language use as L1 speakers?
3. Does the gender of the speaker play a role in either of the above issues?

2 Methods

Although nonstandard variation manifests itself in a variety of forms including phonological, morphosyntactic, and lexical variants, this study focuses on the latter. Specifically under investigation are mildly-marked, non-vulgar colloquial lexical items – that is, words typical of an informal register which differ from the standardized prestige norm, but not to the extent that they are stigmatized or considerably stratified according to social class or gender (Mougeon et al. 2004).

The investigation follows a variation on the matched guise methodology (Lambert et al. 1960), a format which aims to gather attitudes about speech characteristics by asking listeners to evaluate various audio recordings ("guises") prepared by the same speaker and differing only in the variables under investigation. Widespread throughout language attitudes research and most often applied to phonetic variables (see Garrett 2010 for an overview), the matched guise technique has been used to explore lexical variation as well (Cargile and Giles 1998) and facilitates the elicitation of quantitative data via an indirect manner. That is, rather than directly asking participants "What do you think of an L2 speaker using colloquialisms?", which may prompt responses influenced by social expectations, listener attitudes are inferred by comparing reactions to multiple different recordings.

Strictly speaking, the matched guise technique requires all recordings to be produced by the same individual to minimize the impact of speech characteristics outside the variables in question, while the verbal guise variation (e.g. Carrie 2017) permits multiple speakers in situations where a single individual is not capable of producing every guise. Because the L1 status of the speaker is central to this study's research questions, the authenticity gained by using both L1 and L2 speakers was deemed to outweigh any confounding influence introduced by variation between individuals' voice quality. As will be seen in the next section, each individual speaker still produced both neutral and colloquial guises, meaning that vocal qualities were held constant between guise pairs (as opposed to, for example, Swacker 1976 – the closest existing parallel to the present study – where a separate speaker produced the neutral and regional guises and one could argue that the effect of vocal qualities cannot be entirely separated from those of register). This hybrid between the matched and verbal guise techniques therefore sought to reduce the disadvantages inherent in both traditions.

2.1 Stimuli

Two scripts for the guises were prepared: one including 14 colloquial words, and the other consisting of that same script with each of the words replaced by their neutral equivalents (full scripts provided in Appendix A). The words used in the colloquial guise were selected using the Peninsular Spanish section of Fitch's (2011) *Diccionario de coloquialismos y términos dialectales del español* and then ranked according to data from the Peninsular Spanish portion of the Mark Davies *Corpus del Español: Web/Dialectos* (CdE) with the intention of selecting the colloquialisms which L2 speakers would most likely encounter and therefore acquire. This ranking was determined according to *DP* (deviation of proportions), a measure of dispersion which accounts not only for the number of times a word is attested in a corpus, but also for the different types of areas in which it appears, thereby serving as a more reliable indicator of a word's prevalence than raw frequencies alone (Gries 2008). A script for calculating *DP* (Gries, personal communication, April 3, 2018) was applied to the selected colloquial words within the CdE. The resulting 20 most frequent and widely-dispersed words from this list are provided in Table 1:

Table 1: Colloquial words with lowest DP and highest frequency.

Word	Translation	DP	Frequency Count	Neutral equivalent
tío	dude	0.8989	19263	persona
rollo	drag	0.9206	11058	cosa aburrida
pasta	cash	0.9248	14254	dinero
chaval	kid	0.9448	9160	niño
pasada	something incredible	0.9450	6524	cosa divertida
peli	movie	0.9494	17645	película
chorrada	nonsense	0.9582	4285	tontería
pega	problem	0.9629	4234	inconveniente
cabrear	to piss off	0.9660	3135	enfadarse
molar	to be cool	0.9665	4898	gustar
crack	whiz	0.9672	3993	experto
coco	head	0.9700	3766	cabeza
coña	joke	0.9740	2417	broma
guay	cool	0.9746	3016	bueno
majo	nice	0.9752	2327	simpático
curro	job	0.9757	3276	trabajo
afanar	snatch	0.9819	987	robar
finde	weekend	0.9825	2772	fin de semana
mosquear	annoy	0.9834	1134	enfadarse
cachondeo	joke	0.9837	1458	broma

Table 1 is sorted starting with the most well-dispersed words: *DP* theoretically ranges from 0 to 1, with values close to 0 representing even distribution throughout corpus parts, and values closer to 1 representing uneven distribution. The unsurprisingly high *DP* values of the words in Table 1 reflect the contextual restrictions applied to colloquial register.

From these 20 words, the 14 highlighted in blue were chosen for inclusion in the study in accordance with the ease of their incorporation into two scripts[1]

---

[1] While prepared scripts are not the most true-to-life, this study's research questions necessitated more careful control than would be possible in spontaneous speech. Ruivivar and Collins (2018) similarly chose prepared scripts for their study detailed in Section 1: "Although previous rating studies have used extemporaneous speech samples, and our target forms typically occur in such informal conversation, it was not possible to record extemporaneous speech while simultaneously ensuring

based on 3 authentic texts collected in a previous study (Marqués-Pascual 2020) and written by L2 Spanish speakers studying abroad in Spain. One of the two scripts contained the chosen colloquial words, and the other replaced those with their neutral equivalents (see the rightmost column of Table 1). Finally, a distractor stimulus was prepared which paraphrased the content of the neutral and colloquial scripts without using any of the involved lexical items.

2.2 Speakers

Five speakers between the ages of 22 and 33 recorded these stimuli as speech samples. Four produced experimental guises, while the fifth produced a distractor guise. Of the four speakers producing experimental speech samples, two were L1 speakers of Peninsular Spanish and two were advanced L2 speakers from the United States who had lived in Spain for at least a year and who had adopted many of the colloquialisms selected for the study into their own interlanguage. Each pair of speakers consisted of one male and one female. The speaker selected for the distractor was a female L2 speaker of Spanish. As summarized in Table 2, these five speakers produced a total of nine recordings: eight experimental guises and one distractor.

Table 2: Summary of guise characteristics.

Recording Number	Speaker Number	Speaker Nativeness	Speaker Gender	Speaker Register
1	1	L1	Female	Neutral
2	1	L1	Female	Colloquial
3	2	L1	Male	Neutral
4	2	L1	Male	Colloquial
5	3	L2	Female	Neutral
6	3	L2	Female	Colloquial
7	4	L2	Male	Neutral
8	4	L2	Male	Colloquial
9 (Distractor)	5	L2	Female	Distractor

Besides providing the opportunity to examine how gender impacts attitudes toward colloquial language, using both male and female speakers endowed the experimental design with some degree of redundancy: the principal drawback of the verbal

---

that the target forms were produced" (190). Likewise, George (2017) justifies the use of read samples with the rarity of the features under investigation in spontaneous speech.

vs. matched guise technique (i.e. several individuals producing the speech samples vs. just one) is the concern that variations in voice quality between speakers muddies the effects of target variables, and including two speakers of each L1 status meant that if evaluations of both speakers coincided, the result could more confidently be attributable to L1 status and not individual differences. Two speakers per gender would have been preferable to provide further clarity, but this would have unfortunately expanded the number of recordings beyond an amount feasibly analyzable for this study.

To further minimize the confounding influence of extraneous vocal factors, the speakers were asked to re-record their samples several times in order to eliminate false starts and repetitions as well as to ensure the rate of speech and tone remained relatively consistent between speakers. Each of the final recordings totaled roughly 1 minute in length.

2.3 Questionnaire

A questionnaire containing the nine guises was administered using Qualtrics survey software to 233 students enrolled in the Department of Catalan Philology at a prominent university in Spain. Thirteen students were excluded from the study on the grounds of demographic information (e.g., exchange students who had only recently arrived in the country). Of the remaining 220, 187 considered Spanish to be their native language or themselves to be balanced bilinguals,[2] and the rest were deemed to have sufficient familiarity with Peninsular Spanish to warrant inclusion (e.g., they considered Catalan their native language but had spent the majority of their lives speaking Spanish). The median age of the participants was 18; 172 of those included in the study were female, 46 were male, and 2 declined to provide their gender.

Each participant evaluated three of the nine guises: two experimental stimuli (one L1 and one L2) separated by a distractor. By presenting only three guises to each participant, more data could be collected per individual than by listening to a single stimulus, but without risking excessive fatigue effects from a larger number of samples. The first stimulus was randomly chosen from the 8 experimental guises articulated in Section 2.2, and the Qualtrics 'Evenly Present Elements' function ensured every guise was heard first by an equal number of participants. The second experimental stimulus was then assigned according to which guise

---

[2] It should be noted that participants' familiarity with other languages meant their attitudes likely differed from those in more monolingual regions. Even so, with the prominence of minority languages in Spain, these participants still represent a sizable portion of the Spanish population.

had the opposite level of every independent variable (*speaker register, speaker nativeness,* and *speaker gender*) as the first. That is, if a participant first heard the neutral L1 male guise, they would then hear a distractor followed by the colloquial L2 female speech sample. In this way, each participant responded to every level of each independent variable, albeit not every combination thereof.

Participants evaluated each guise with a rating of 1–7 on several semantic differential scales. Common in matched guise experimental design (Jaworski et al. 2012), these scales ask participants to provide ratings between semantically-opposed terms. For example, participants were asked to evaluate the *pronunciation* of the speaker with a rating between 1 ("Strong foreign accent") and 7 ("No foreign accent").[3]

In addition to *pronunciation*, two other metrics were used to evaluate participant attitudes toward the speakers' language proficiency: *global language competence* was intended as a more holistic evaluation of the speakers' language ability, while *comprehensibility* was included in consideration of research showing that foreign accentedness and the difficulty a listener has in understanding the speaker are not necessarily equivalent (Derwing and Munro 1997, Munro and Derwing 1995).

The same 7-point scale was applied to 12 personality traits divided into three dimensions common to language attitude investigations (Giles and Billings 2004): *status* (represented by the terms *successful, intelligent, educated,* and *competent*), *solidarity* (*pleasant, nice, sociable,* and *friendly*), and *dynamism* (*active, talkative, confident,* and *enthusiastic*). The individual terms for *status* and *solidarity* were taken from Dragojevic et al. 2017, while the terms for *dynamism* were adapted from Zahn and Hopper (1985). These questions were designed to measure whether ratings varied in the same manner for L2 speakers as L1 speakers: in comparison to standard language varieties, L1 speakers using nonstandard language are typically downgraded on *status* (Fuertes et al. 2012) and upgraded on *solidarity* (Giles and Billings 2004). Findings on *dynamism* – a dimension less frequently included in studies than the traditional *status/solidarity* dichotomy – are mixed, with some studies (Ohama et al. 2000) finding nonstandard accents upgrade *dynamism,* while others (Fuertes et al. 2012) have shown the opposite effect.

2.4 Statistical analysis

The three independent variables outlined in Table 2 (*speaker nativeness, speaker gender,* and *speaker register*) coupled with *stimulus position* (i.e., whether a given

---

[3] The Spanish wording provided to participants is available in Appendix B, although the English translations are provided directly for clarity.

recording was heard first or second, again recalling that all stimuli occurred an equal number of times in both positions) gave a total of four predictors for each rating of 1–7 produced by participants. Once the data was collected, it was analyzed via a linear mixed-effects model and type II ANOVAs. After 21 rounds of model selection, 8 significant higher-order interactions remained, the majority of which were 3- or 4-way and therefore quite difficult to draw clear conclusions from. Due to the complexity of these higher-order interactions, it was decided to continue the analysis with conditional inference trees.

Levshina (2015) describes conditional inference trees as "non-parametric tree-structure models of regression and classification that can serve as an alternative to multiple regression" (291). Based on binary recursive partitioning, this method of analysis is useful when numerous higher-order interactions are present (that is, when three or more independent variables have significant interactions on the dependent variable), as was the case in this investigation. The conditional inference trees predicted values for the dependent ordered factor variable rating (1–7), and a separate tree was generated for each dependent variable. The resulting trees provided a relatively easily-interpretable visualization, and are presented in the next section.

3 Results

This section will unpack in detail the five conditional inference trees generated to investigate the impact of colloquial language on linguistic proficiency (as measured by *global language competence, pronunciation,* and *comprehensibility* on 7-point semantic differential scales) as well as personality traits (grouped into *status, solidarity,* and *dynamism*). As the interpretation of conditional inference trees can be somewhat tedious for those unfamiliar with them, readers more interested in a summary of the results are encouraged to proceed directly to Section 4 for a discussion of the findings on this paper's research questions.

3.1 Global language competence

Figure 1 visualizes the conditional inference tree generated for the *global language competence* measure:

The conditional inference tree displays only those predictors which the algorithm used to generate the tree found to be significant, along with the predicted ratings for each combination thereof. Starting at the top of the tree, the data is di-

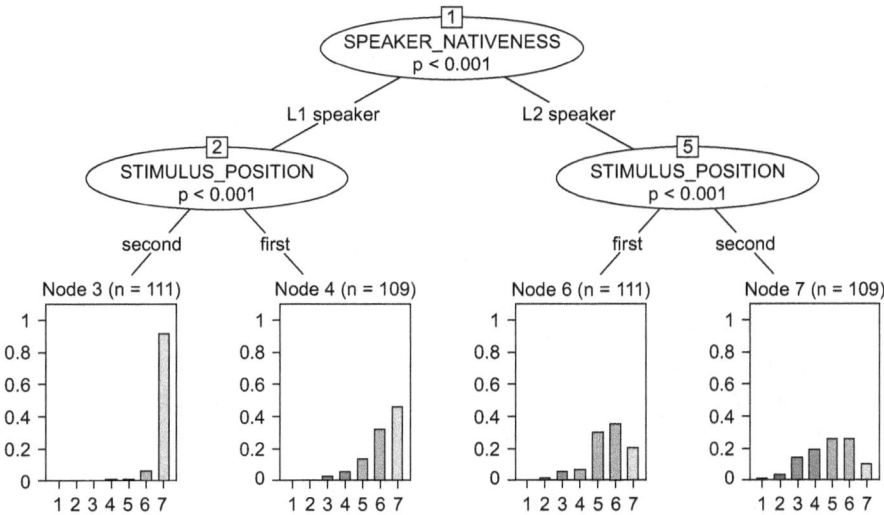

Figure 1: *Global language competence* conditional inference tree.

vided according to the most significant predictor (Node 1 in Figure 1). Each level of this predictor receives its own branch, which is further separated according to predictors of decreasing significance (Nodes 2 and 5). Predictors which did not meet the 0.05 significance threshold are not included in the visualization. Finally, the predicted values for each combination are displayed along the bottom row (Nodes 3–4, 6–7), with each bar representing the percentage of ratings corresponding to that number. The classification accuracy for the inference tree – that is, the percentage of predicted outcomes matching the observed data – was 50%, a substantial increase over the 14% (1/7) probability of assigning the correct rating by random chance.

Speaker nativeness is the most significant predictor of *global language competence*, followed by *stimulus position*. The inference tree predicted that L1 speakers (Nodes 3–4) would receive higher ratings than L2 speakers (Nodes 6–7), as evidenced by the high proportion of 7s predicted for L1 speakers (between 40–90% of total predictions) in comparison to L2 speakers (10–20%). This result is unsurprising, as L1 speakers should be expected to demonstrate greater language proficiency than L2 speakers.

The results of *stimulus position* provide a more interesting finding. Ratings of L1 speakers were substantially higher if heard second (Node 3) than if heard first (Node 4), while ratings of L2 speakers were slightly lower when heard second (Node 6 vs. Node 7). These results indicate that participants used the first stimulus as a frame of reference, and then adjusted their ratings of the second stimulus accordingly. That is, hearing an L2 speaker first set a lower baseline which L1 speakers vastly overperformed, while the opposite was true when setting an L1 baseline and subsequently hearing an L2 speaker (although a floor effect did seem to be at play in preventing 2nd-position L2 ratings from being evaluated as entirely devoid of linguistic proficiency). This tendency of second-stimulus ratings increasing for L1 speakers and decreasing for L2 speakers will be seen repeatedly throughout this section and will hereafter be referred to as the "comparison effect."[4] It should be remembered, however, that all 8 experimental stimuli were heard an equal number of times at each position, so this effect was evenly distributed.

More important than the impact of *speaker nativeness* and *stimulus position*, however, is the absence of *speaker register* as a significant predictor. Regardless of whether the speaker used colloquial or neutral language, neither L1 nor L2 speakers received significantly differing evaluations. In terms of *global language competence*, colloquial language did not offer any significant benefits, but it also did not seem to affect the speaker negatively.

3.2 Pronunciation

The inference tree for *pronunciation* ratings (Figure 2) correctly predicted the observed data 56% of the time, making it slightly more accurate than the 50% classification accuracy of the tree generated for *global language competence*.

As with *global language* competence, *speaker nativeness* was unsurprisingly the most significant predictor of *pronunciation* ratings (Node 1). Presumably due to the comparison effect discussed above, L1 speakers again received higher ratings if their sample came second (Node 3 vs. Node 4).

Node 5, however, demonstrates that *speaker gender* was a significant predictor for the L2 speaker, with the male (Node 9) receiving lower ratings than the female in either stimulus position (Nodes 7 and 8). Notably, many participants' debriefing comments of the male L2 speaker critiqued the lack of phonemic contrast between /θ/ and /s/, a distinction unique to most varieties of Peninsular Spanish.[5] Out of 7 possible environments for this distinction in each of the colloquial and neutral guises – 100% of which were produced by both L1 speakers –

---

4 This same effect was seen in the distractor clip. Also produced by an L2 speaker, the distractor was rated more negatively when preceded by an L1 sample, providing further evidence of the priming effect the first stimulus had on the second.
5 Local as well as national differences may be at play here: varieties lacking this phonological distinction include not only those outside Spain, but also several southern Peninsular regions whose varieties are typically perceived as less prestigious (see, for example, Santana Marrer 2018). This,

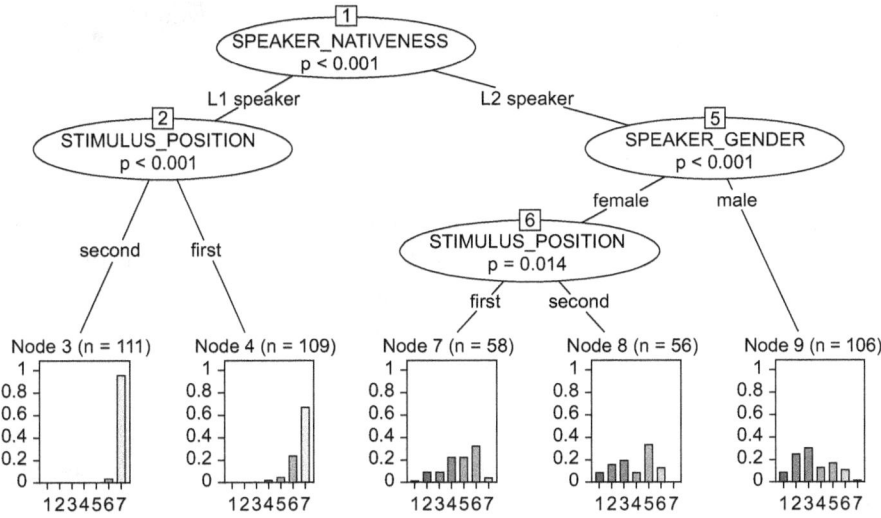

Figure 2: *Pronunciation* conditional inference tree.

the female L2 speaker realized /θ/ 5 and 4 times respectively, while the male L2 speaker did so 0 times in both. The male L2 speaker's omission of this highly salient regional marker might have played a role in negative evaluations of his *pronunciation*. This explanation corroborates the work of George (2013b, 2014, 2017), which found that the production of regional phonological variants improved evaluations of accent in L2 speakers.

The lack of this regional marker potentially explains why *stimulus position* proved a significant factor for the female L2 speaker, but not the male. The female exhibited the same trend explained above, receiving lower ratings when heard second (Node 8 vs. 7) due to comparison with an L1 baseline. Evaluations of the male, however, were not significantly affected by the ordering of stimuli. The absence of /θ/ possibly caused a floor effect such that it made little difference whether the speaker was compared to an L1 baseline.

While this difference in pronunciation between the two L2 speakers introduces an unfortunate confound as far as gender is concerned, it should be emphasized that even with the redundancy of two L2 speakers, the principle variable under investigation, *speaker register*, was once again entirely absent as a significant predictor. As was the case with *global language competence*, using colloquial

---

alongside the historical animosity between Catalonia and Andalusia, may have contributed to negative associations on the part of the participants who themselves were studying Catalan.

lexical items did not correlate either positively or negatively with evaluations of the speaker's *pronunciation*.

3.3 Comprehensibility

The conditional inference tree of *comprehensibility* had the highest classification accuracy, with predicted values matching the observed data 63% of the time.

Figure 3 demonstrates that *comprehensibility* followed the same tendencies as *global language competence* and *pronunciation*. Speaker nativeness once again was the most significant predictor, with the comparison effect repeating the tendency for the second stimulus to be rated higher when an L1 speaker (Node 4 vs. 3) and lower when an L2 speaker (Nodes 7 and 8 vs. 10 and 11, respectively). The L2 female (Nodes 7 and 10) received higher ratings than her male counterpart (Nodes 8 and 11) in both corresponding stimulus positions, which again may have resulted from more nativelike production on the part of the female speaker.

Finally, like *global language competence* and *pronunciation*, *speaker register* again had no significant effect on ratings of *comprehensibility*, which remained the same regardless of whether a speaker used colloquial language.

3.4 Status

Section 2.3 discussed how 12 personality traits were chosen for investigation according to three dimensions common in the literature. After collecting the data, a principal components analysis (a method for dimensionality reduction used to simplify data structures of multiple variables into a smaller handful of groups) was conducted to verify that the traits correlated with their expected dimensions. The results based on a correlation matrix for the 12 factors representing *status*, *solidarity*, and *dynamism* are shown in Table 3. PC1, PC2, and PC3 represent the top three principal components and cumulatively accounted for 76% of the variance in the data.

PC2 and PC3 demonstrated that the traits patterned according to the expected dimensions: *successful*, *intelligent*, *educated*, and *competent*, characteristics associated with the dimension of *status*, were the only factors to load negatively on PC2. *Pleasant*, *nice*, *sociable*, and *friendly* (representative of *solidarity*) loaded positively on PC3, although *sociable* was only slightly positive (0.0755) and *educated* (a *status* trait) was as well, albeit at a very low level (0.0189). PC3 therefore generally confirmed the expected tripartite division, but not as clearly as the two-way *status/solidarity* division suggested by PC2. Furthermore, PC3 represented only

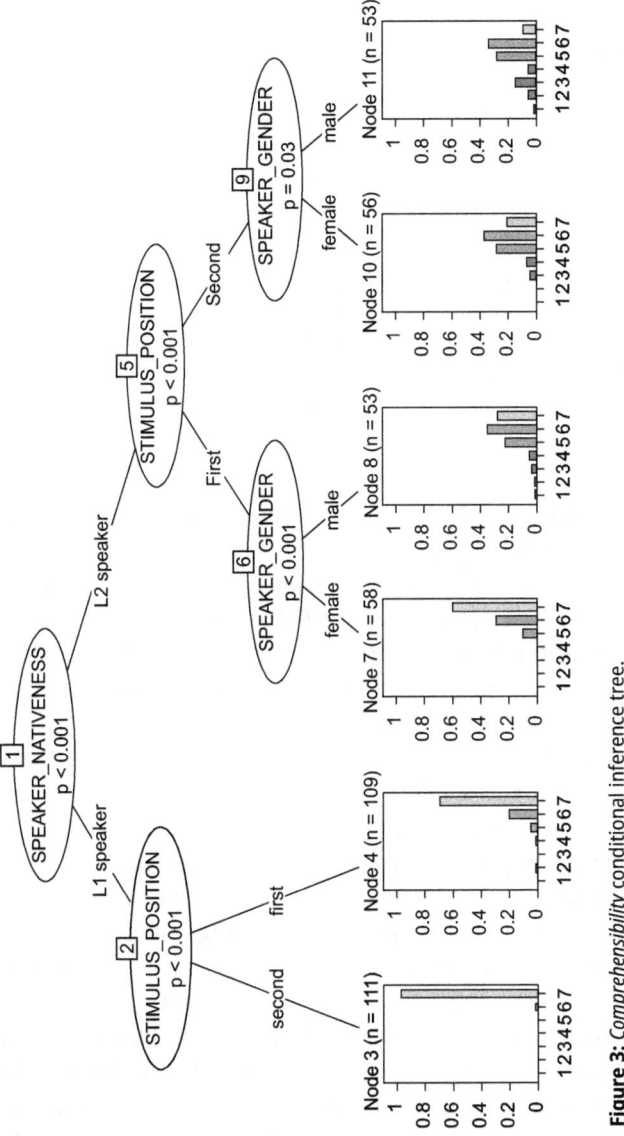

Figure 3: *Comprehensibility* conditional inference tree.

Table 3: Factor loadings for personality characteristics.

TRAIT	PC1	PC2	PC3
Successful	0.7508	**−0.3776**	−0.0901
Intelligent	0.6728	**−0.5794**	−0.0114
Educated	0.6032	**−0.6660**	0.0189
Competent	0.7304	**−0.3643**	−0.0451
Pleasant	0.7944	0.0274	**0.4100**
Nice	0.7957	0.2209	**0.3944**
Sociable	0.7902	0.3515	**0.0755**
Friendly	0.8240	0.2696	**0.2606**
Active	0.8028	0.1647	−0.0470
Talkative	0.7091	0.3810	−0.3805
Confident	0.7427	0.0849	−0.4607
Enthusiastic	0.7897	0.2257	−0.2120

7% of the overall variance, a relatively small number in comparison to PCs 1 and 2 (57% and 13%, respectively). In light of these reasons and in order to reduce overall degrees of freedom, the *solidarity* and *dynamism* traits were collapsed into one dimension. This decision was further justifiable due to the tendency to not distinguish *dynamism* in the literature (Zahn and Hopper 1985), as well as some indications that *solidarity* and *dynamism* pattern similarly with respect to the use of nonstandard language (Giles and Billings 2004).

This left the data from the twelve personality traits listed in Table 3 condensed into two groups: *status* and *solidarity/dynamism*. The conditional inference tree for *status* (Figure 4) had a classification accuracy of 32% and found *speaker register* to be the most important predictor (p<0.001). Although this classification accuracy was lower than those found above, it still represents an over twofold improvement beyond the 14% (1/7) chance of assigning ratings randomly.

Starting with the neutral level of *speaker register*, *stimulus position* once again had a significant effect: when presented first, L2 speakers (Node 7) actually received higher ratings of *status* than L1 speakers (Node 8). One possible explanation is that participants may have associated speaking a second language with increased social status or cognitive ability (Adesope et al. 2010) – the L2 speakers may have been perceived as more *successful, intelligent, etc.* because they performed the same task as the L1 speakers, but in a foreign language. The comparison effect otherwise shows itself to follow the typical pattern: when presented second in both registers, L1 speakers (Nodes 4 and 11) received higher ratings than L2 speakers evaluated in the same position (Nodes 5 and 12).

When comparing the neutral register to the colloquial one, L1 speakers exhibited the expected decrease from the literature in *status* ratings (compare Node 8 to

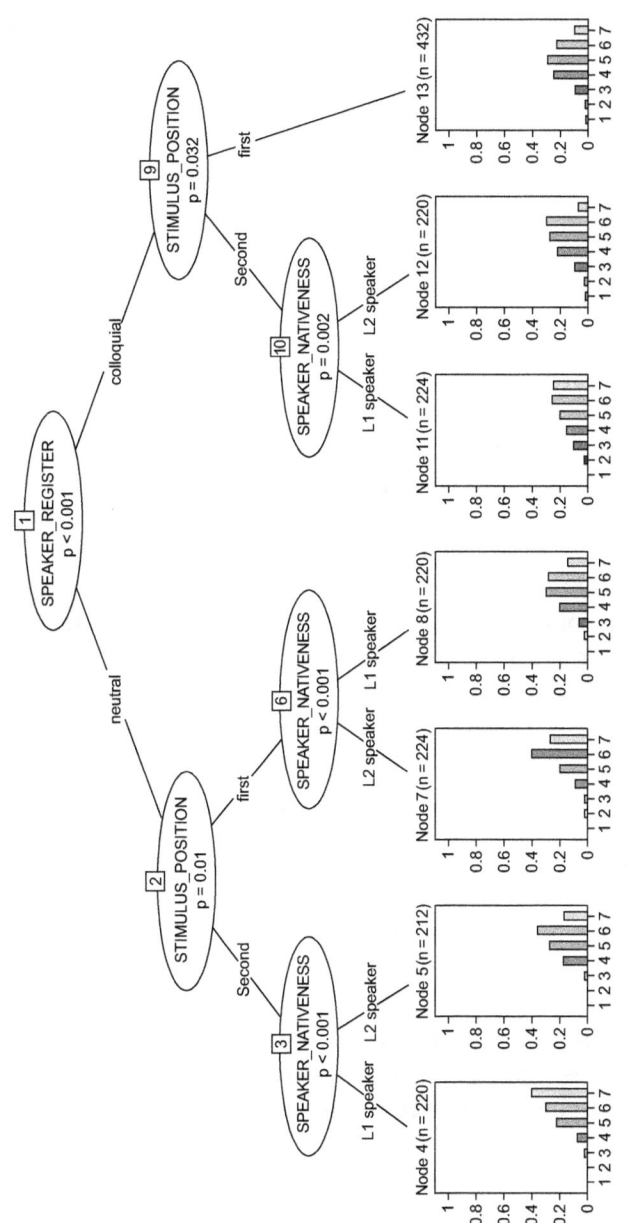

Figure 4: *Status* conditional inference tree.

13 and 4 to 11). L2 speakers experienced the same drop, although to a slightly larger extent (Node 7 to 13 and 5 to 12). Participants do not seem to associate knowledge of colloquialisms with *status* due to increased linguistic knowledge; instead, L2 speakers are subject to the same penalties as L1 speakers, but to a greater degree. Gender did not significantly affect the results for any level of *speaker nativeness* or *register*, meaning that neither differing attitudes toward language use by different genders nor the individual characteristics of any speaker played a significant role in the evaluation of *status*.

3.5 Solidarity/dynamism

In contrast, the conditional inference tree for *solidarity/dynamism* (Figure 5) found *speaker gender* to be the most significant predictor for participant ratings (p<0.001). The classification accuracy was nearly identical to that generated for *status*, at 33%.

For the female level of *speaker gender*, *stimulus position* once again was a significant predictor, with the comparison effect accounting for increased L2 ratings when presented first (Node 17 vs. 23) and mostly increased L1 ratings when presented second (Node 21 and 22 vs. 18). Interestingly, *speaker register* only played a significant role in participant ratings in the second stimulus for the L1 female, where ratings experienced the increase expected from the literature from colloquial to neutral language (Nodes 21 and 22). The L2 female, on the other hand, did not benefit from this same increase (Node 23). Nevertheless, it should be noted that she did not receive significantly worse evaluations when using colloquial language, either; as far as *solidarity/dynamism* is concerned, the female L2 speaker simply did not gain or lose anything from its use.

Whereas *speaker register* was only significant in one instance for females, it was the most significant predictor for males. For both registers, the comparison effect exhibited the now predictable trend of the second stimulus position increasing ratings of L1 speakers (Node 7 to 5 and 13 to 14) and decreasing ratings of L2 speakers (Node 10 and 11; this did not seem to have an impact on ratings between Nodes 7 and 6).

For both stimulus positions, the L1 speaker received the expected increase in ratings from colloquial language (Node 14 vs. 7 and 13 vs. 5) as expected from the literature (Giles and Billings 2004). While the L2 speaker saw no notable change in the first stimulus (Node 10 vs. 7), the second stimulus does show a marginal increase in comparison to the neutral guise (Node 11 vs. 6). Although this increase is not as substantial as that experienced by the L1 speaker in the same position (Node 13 vs. 5), it demonstrates that colloquial language did in fact increase rat-

Chapter 9 Do L2 Speakers sound strange when using slang? — 233

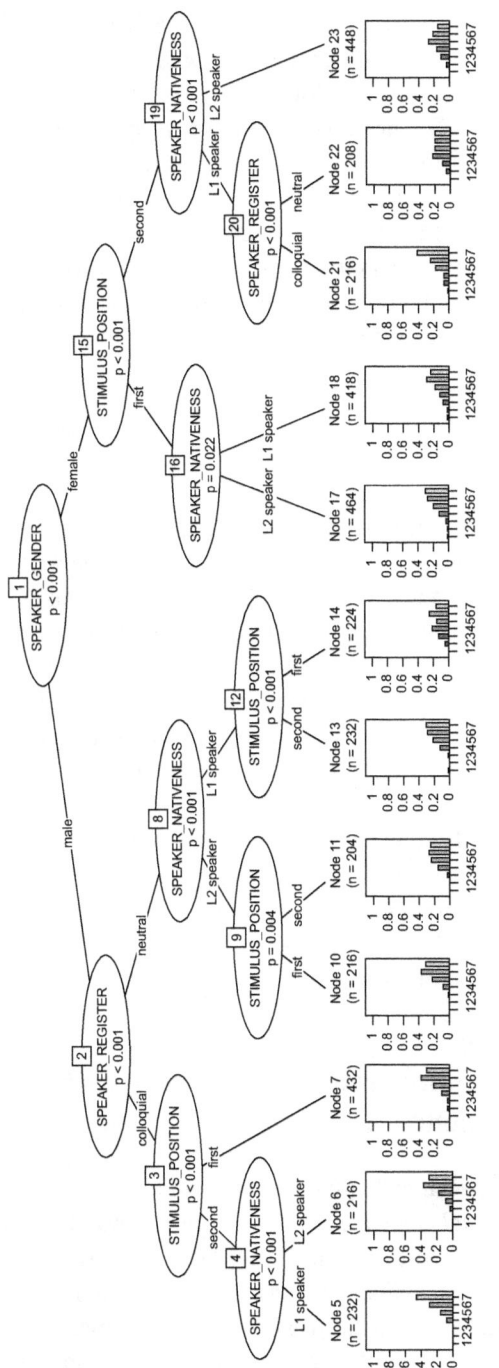

Figure 5: *Solidarity/dynamism* conditional inference tree.

ings for the male L2 speaker in terms of *solidarity/dynamism*; while these benefits were small in comparison to the L1 speaker and only observable in the second stimulus, this contrasts with the female L2 speaker, for whom colloquial language made no difference whatsoever. This difference according to *speaker gender* perhaps results from covert prestige from informal language being more typically associated with males (Trudgill 1972). Even so, this increase is small and certainly not proportional to that experienced by L1 speakers – L2 speakers simply do not seem to have access to the same benefits of *solidarity/dynamism* as L1 speakers. It should again be noted, however, that evaluations were not more negative in the colloquial guise, it merely did not have the positive effect as seen in L1 speakers.

4 Discussion

As outlined in Section 1, the scarce literature existing on L1 attitudes toward L2 use of nonstandard language falls into two conflicting camps. Older, theoretical arguments (e.g. Andreasson 1994, Auger and Valdman 1999) along with some empirical studies (Prodromou 2007, Ruivivar and Collins 2018, Swacker 1976) present the notion of a 'double standard,' where L2 speakers are evaluated negatively for the same linguistic forms deemed acceptable for L1 speakers. Other empirical studies (Beaulieu 2016, George 2013b, 2014, 2017) support the opposite view, namely that L2 speakers actually have the potential to benefit from producing this sort of language.

The results of this investigation fall somewhere in between these two camps, indicating that, at least in the case of Peninsular Spanish colloquial lexical items, benefits to L2 speakers are fairly minimal, but that any double standard which may exist does not appear to carry with it considerable penalties. Specific results in terms of each research question are summarized below.

4.1 How does the use of colloquial language correlate with ratings of linguistic proficiency? (RQ1)

The analysis found no correlation between colloquial language and ratings of linguistic proficiency, as measured by *global language competence, pronunciation,* and *comprehensibility. Speaker register* was not a significant predictor for any of the conditional inference trees modeling participant ratings. This indicates that L2 speakers suffer no penalties or benefits from the use of colloquial language in terms of linguistic proficiency, contrasting with the existing literature on both sides: participants in the present study did not respond positively as did George's (2013b, 2014), who evaluated accents as less foreign when using regional variation, but they also did not view L2 speakers to be "deficient" as predicted by Andreasson (1994). According to the results of the present study, the use of colloquial lexical items can hardly be considered a shortcut to vastly improved linguistic proficiency, but neither is it liable to automatically torpedo an L1 listener's impression of their capabilities.

4.2 In terms of personality judgments, do L2 speakers benefit from the same advantages and suffer the same disadvantages of colloquial language use as L1 speakers? (RQ2)

In accordance with the well-established literature (Fuertes et al. 2012, Giles and Billings 2004), L1 speakers using nonstandard language were downgraded on *status* and upgraded on *solidarity*. L2 speakers did suffer the same disadvantages on *status* as L1 speakers, perhaps even to a somewhat greater degree, but they did not benefit from the same advantages. Whereas *solidarity/dynamism* rose slightly for L1 speakers, these benefits were reduced or non-existent for L2 speakers: ratings of the male did increase marginally, but the female received the same ratings whether or not she employed colloquial language. Unlike one may have predicted from Beaulieu (2016), where many patients responded positively to L2 departures from the standardized norm, L2 speakers in the present study did not gain as much from colloquial language use as L1 speakers. Even so, participants were not penalized for its use in the same way found by Swacker (1976). The main disadvantage L2 speakers seem to face is therefore one of inaccessible benefits rather than outright penalties.

4.3 Does the gender of the speaker play a role in either of the above issues? (RQ3)

Gender had very little effect on the other research questions. In some cases, the male L2 speaker had a slight advantage in using colloquial language over females. This was seen in the ratings of *solidarity/dynamism*, where use of colloquial language by the male correlated with marginally increased evaluations, whereas ratings of the female speaker remained unchanged regardless of register. Overall, male and female use of colloquial language was perceived largely the same, with the possibility that males have slightly more access to its benefits – a finding which matches L1 trends of covert prestige (Trudgill 1972) being more readily accessible to males. It is worth reiterating that these results should be interpreted with the acknowledgement of a possible confound in the realization of regional phonemic contrast between /θ/ and /s/ by the female L2 speaker but not by the male. Interestingly, the results of George (2013b, 2014) suggest that this should have helped the female rather than hurt her; perhaps the female would have been evaluated lower or the male higher had the production of the contrast been reversed.

5 Conclusions

5.1 Implications for L2 learners: Is it safe to use colloquialisms?

These results do appear to suggest that listeners are slightly more critical of L2 speakers than of L1 speakers using the same lexical items. L2 speakers suffer the same negative consequences as L1 speakers, possibly to a greater degree, without having access to the same benefits. To this extent, a certain double standard does appear to exist against the use of colloquial language by L2 speakers, and one could argue that the absence of rewards along with increased risks validates the warnings against colloquial language use.

Nevertheless, while it is true that L2 speakers were judged more harshly on some measures when using the same colloquial language, the magnitude of this difference can hardly be considered so substantial as to argue that L2 speakers should never use it. Furthermore, L2 speakers did not necessarily have access to the same benefits as L1 speakers, but they did not experience additional drawbacks in these areas either. For example, although L2 speakers did not unilaterally receive the same *solidarity/dynamism* benefits as L1 speakers, their ratings in this category did not suffer in comparison to the neutral register, they simply remained the same.

For this reason, rather than unilaterally discouraging second language learners from using colloquial language or making the equally unreasonable assertion that it should dominate a learner's vocabulary, these results support a policy of careful consideration in its application. The conflicting findings of previous studies on the topic perhaps are an indication that opinions on the use of colloquial language vary substantially, and learners should keep this in mind. So long as an L2 speaker exercises caution in the context of its use, however, this study does not provide any strong reason to discourage them from doing so. Standard language may be a safer target, but the current findings did not give reason to avoid colloquial language *per se*.

5.2 Limitations and future directions

The present study attempted to address the literature gap on L1 perceptions of L2 nonstandard variant use, but more research is required on this complex issue. A variety of limitations emerging from this investigation's experimental design could be addressed by more targeted studies. For example, differences in production of /θ/ by the male and female L2 speakers introduced a confound as far as gender was concerned; future studies could investigate the impact of this variant, or even limit themselves to just one gender. Removing the gender variable entirely would allow for an increased number of speakers without prompting fatigue effects (thereby minimizing the effect of individual vocal qualities) or for the inclusion of other variables such as intermediate vs. advanced L2 proficiency. Moreover, this study's participant body, given their status as university students studying another language (particularly Catalan, in light of its tumultuous history with Spanish), likely held language attitudes differing from those which might be found in the general populace.

The lexical focus of this study leaves open the possibility for future studies regarding L1 attitudes toward L2 nonstandard phonological and morphological variation. The perception of any of these three variants could also be investigated outside the locale where they are common among L1 speakers. Ringer-Hilfinger (2012) recorded the reluctance of American study abroad students to adopt the Peninsular Spanish [θ] due to its absence inside the United States. Obviously, social pressures exist which encourage conformity with the local community, but because Peninsular Spanish is a prestige variety, L2 speakers who use it outside of Spain may experience some benefits. Knowledge of potential benefits available to them upon returning home might encourage students to be more willing to adopt the variant while studying abroad. Similar studies could be performed employing the same experimental design and stimuli as this investigation, but with a participant base from a non-Peninsular Spanish community. Finally, any of these attitudes could vary depending on the L1 of the listener; with so few studies covering a small subset of languages, it is clear that considerable research is required to gain insight on an issue with which so many L2 learners grapple.

Appendices

A. Experimental Scripts

The left word in each bolded pair was the one used in the neutral version of the script, and the right word was the one used in the colloquial version.

Este verano, yo fui a Hawái durante tres semanas con mi familia y mi abuela. Durante las vacaciones, jugué al golf muchas veces y fue **(increíble/una pasada)** porque podía ver el mar desde donde jugaba al golf. Jugamos con un **(hombre/ tío)** del **(trabajo/curro)** de mi padre, y ¡era un **(experto/crack)**! Siempre nos ganó fácilmente, pero no nos **(enfadamos/cabreamos)** porque era muy **(simpático/ majo)** y siempre estaba de **(broma/cachondeo)**. También, nosotros celebramos el cumpleaños de mi padre. Fuimos a un restaurante que tenía el bistec más delicioso del mundo. A todos en mi familia les **(gusta/mola)** la idea de cenar y pasar tiempo juntos durante una buena comida. Aunque me encantó el viaje, **(no me gustó/me mosqueó)** que pasáramos cada **(fin de semana/finde)** viendo **(películas/pelis)**. Fue **(aburrido/un rollo)** quedarnos dentro cuando habíamos gastado **(tanto dinero/tanta pasta)** en viajar a Hawái. Pero fueron unas vacaciones muy relajadas, lo cual fue la **(mejor parte/parte más guay)**.

B. Abridged Qualtrics Questionnaire

The below questions summarize the Qualtrics form provided to participants. The informed consent form, instructions, progress pages, demographic questions, and other question items not analyzed in this paper are not included. A series of 7 radio buttons were provided between the poles of each semantic differential scale; only the pole names are included below.

1. Items evaluating *global language competence, pronunciation,* and *comprehensibility*

    En términos generales, ¿cómo evaluaría el dominio global del español de esta hablante?

    (No competente en español / Muy competente)

    ¿Cómo evaluaría la pronunciación del hablante?
    (Fuerte acento extranjero / Sin acento extranjero)

    ¿Cómo evaluaría la dificultad de entender a el hablante?
    (Muy difícil de entender / Muy fácil de entender)

2. Items evaluating *status* and *solidarity/dynamism*

El hablante me parece una persona . . .
(Poco exitosa / Exitosa)
(Poco inteligente / Inteligente)
(Inculta / Culta)
(Incompetente / Competente)
(Desagradable / Agradable)
(Antipática / Simpática)
(Insociable / Sociable)
(Poco amigable / Amigable)
(Pasiva / Activa)
(Tímida / Habladora)
(Insegura / Segura de sí misma)
(Indecisa / Entusiasta)

References

Adesope, Olusola O., Tracy Lavin, Terri Thompson & Charles Ungerleider. 2010. A Systematic Review and Meta-Analysis of the Cognitive Correlates of Bilingualism. *Review of Educational Research* 80. 207–245. doi:10.3102/0034654310368803.

Andreasson, Anne-Marie. 1994. Norm as a pedagogical paradigm. *World Englishes* 13. 395–409. doi:10.1111/j.1467-971X.1994.tb00325.x.

Auger, Julie & Albert Valdman. 1999. Letting French Students Hear the Diverse Voices of Francophony. *The Modern Language Journal* 83. 403–412. doi:10.1111/0026-7902.00030.

Beaulieu, Suzie. 2016. Prescriptivism and French L2 instruction. *Journal of Multilingual and Multicultural Development* 37. 274–285. doi:10.1080/01434632.2015.1068786.

Bley-Vroman, Robert. 1989. What is the logical problem of foreign language learning? In Susan M. Gass & Jacquelyn Schachter (eds.), *Linguistic Perspectives on Second Language Acquisition*, 41–68. Cambridge University Press.

Cargile, Aaron Castelan & Howard Giles. 1998. Language attitudes toward varieties of English: An American-Japanese context. *Journal of Applied Communication Research* 26. 338–356. doi:10.1080/00909889809365511.

Carrie, Erin. 2017. 'British is professional, American is urban': attitudes towards English reference accents in Spain. *International Journal of Applied Linguistics* 27. 427–447. doi:10.1111/ijal.12139.

Christophersen, Paul. 1973. *Second language learning: Myth and reality*. Harmondsworth, U.K.: Penguin.

Derwing, Tracey M. & Murray J. Munro. 1997. Accent, Intelligibility, and Comprehensibility: Evidence from Four L1s. *Studies in Second Language Acquisition* 19. 1–16.

Dewaele, Jean-Marc. 2004a. Retention or Omission of the ne in Advanced French Interlanguage: The Variable Effect of Extralinguistic Factors. *Journal of Sociolinguistics* 8. 433–450.

Dewaele, Jean-Marc. 2004b. The acquisition of sociolinguistic competence in French as a foreign language: an overview. *Journal of French Language Studies* 14. 301–319. doi:10.1017/S0959269504001814.

Dragojevic, Marko, Howard Giles, Anna-Carrie Beck & Nicholas T. Tatum. 2017. The fluency principle: Why foreign accent strength negatively biases language attitudes. *Communication Monographs* 84. 385–405. doi:10.1080/03637751.2017.1322213.

Fitch, Roxana. 2011. *Diccionario de coloquialismos y términos dialectales del español*. Madrid, Spain: Arco-Libros.

French, Leif M. & Suzie Beaulieu. 2016. Effects of sociolinguistic awareness on French L2 learners' planned and unplanned oral production of stylistic variation. *Language Awareness* 25. 55–71. doi:10.1080/09658416.2015.1122024.

Fuertes, Jairo N., William H. Gottdiener, Helena Martin, Tracey C. Gilbert & Howard Giles. 2012. A meta-analysis of the effects of speakers' accents on interpersonal evaluations. *European Journal of Social Psychology* 42. 120–133. doi:10.1002/ejsp.862.

Garrett, Peter. 2010. *Attitudes to Language*. Cambridge University Press.

Gatbonton, Elizabeth, Pavel Trofimovich & Michael Magid. 2005. Learners' Ethnic Group Affiliation and L2 Pronunciation Accuracy: A Sociolinguistic Investigation. *TESOL Quarterly* 39. 489–511.

George, Angela. 2013a. The development of /θ/, a variable geographic phonetic feature, during a semester abroad: The role of explicit instruction | University of Calgary Contacts. http://contacts.ucalgary.ca/info/sllc/research/publications/view/1-7608038.

George, Angela. 2013b. The Development of Castilian Dialectal Features During a Semester Abroad in Toledo, Spain. United States – Minnesota: University of Minnesota. http://search.proquest.com/docview/1702712476/abstract/EC623DCDE4784046PQ/1.

George, Angela. 2014. Study Abroad in Central Spain: The Development of Regional Phonological Features. *Foreign Language Annals* 47. 97–114. doi:10.1111/flan.12065.

George, Angela. 2017. Effects of listener and speaker characteristics on foreign accent in L2 Spanish. *Journal of Second and Multiple Language Acquisition – JSMULA*, 5(4), 127–148. https://www.academia.edu/38075656/Effects_of_listener_and_speaker_characteristics_on_foreign_accent_in_L2_Spanish.

Giles, Howard & Andrew C. Billings. 2004. Assessing Language Attitudes: Speaker Evaluation Studies. *The Handbook of Applied Linguistics*, 187–209.

Gries, Stefan Th. 2008. Dispersions and adjusted frequencies in corpora. *International Journal of Corpus Linguistics* 13. 403–437. doi:10.1075/ijcl.13.4.02gri.

Irujo, Suzanne. 1986. Don't Put Your Leg in Your Mouth: Transfer in the Acquisition of Idioms in a Second Language. *TESOL Quarterly* 20. 287–304. doi:10.2307/3586545.

Jaworski, Adam, Nikolas Coupland & Dariusz Galasinski. 2012. *Metalanguage: Social and Ideological Perspectives*. Walter de Gruyter.

Kang, Okim. 2009. ESL Learners' Attitudes toward Pronunciation Instruction and Varieties of English. In John Levis & Kimberly LeVelle (eds.), *Proceedings of the 1st Pronunciation in Second Language Learning and Teaching Conference*, 105–118. Ames, IA: Iowa State University.

Kinginger, Celeste & Kathleen Farrell. 2004. Assessing Development of Meta-Pragmatic Awareness in Study Abroad. *Frontiers: The Interdisciplinary Journal of Study Abroad* 10. 19–42.

Lambert, Wallace E., Richard C. Hodgson, Robert C. Gardner & Samuel Fillenbaum. 1960. Evaluational reactions to spoken languages. *The Journal of Abnormal and Social Psychology* 60. 44–51. doi: http://dx.doi.org/10.1037/h0044430.

Levshina, Natalia. 2015. *How to do Linguistics with R: Data exploration and statistical analysis*. John Benjamins Publishing Company.

LoCastro, Virginia. 1998. Learner Subjectivity and Pragmatic Competence Development. Paper presented at the Annual Conference of American Association for Applied Linguistics, Seattle, WA. https://files.eric.ed.gov/fulltext/ED420201.pdf.

Lybeck, Karen. 2002. Cultural Identification and Second Language Pronunciation of Americans in Norway. *The Modern Language Journal* 86. 174–191.

Marqués-Pascual, Laura. 2020. Los hablantes de español como lengua de herencia en programas de estudios en el extranjero. In P. Taboada-de-Zúñiga Romero & R. Barros Romero (eds.), *Perfiles, factores y contextos en la enseñanza y el aprendizaje de ELE/EL2*, 703–720. Santiago de Compostela, Spain: Santiago de Compostela University Press.

Morley, Joan. 1991. The Pronunciation Component in Teaching English to Speakers of Other Languages. *TESOL Quarterly* 25. 481–520.

Mougeon, Raymond, Katherine Rehner & Terry Nadasdi. 2004. The learning of spoken French variation by immersion students from Toronto, Canada. *Journal of Sociolinguistics* 8(3). 408–432. doi:10.1111/j.1467-9841.2004.00267.x.

Munro, Murray J. & Tracey M. Derwing. 1995. Foreign Accent, Comprehensibility, and Intelligibility in the Speech of Second Language Learners. *Language Learning* 45. 73–97. doi:10.1111/j.1467-1770.1995.tb00963.x.

Ohama, Mary Lynn Fiore, Carolyn C. Gotay, Ian S. Pagano, Larry Boles & Dorothy D. Craven. 2000. Evaluations of Hawaii Creole English and Standard English. *Journal of Language and Social Psychology* 19. 357–377. doi:10.1177/0261927X00019003005.

Piller, Ingrid. 2002. Passing for a native speaker: Identity and success in second language learning. *Journal of Sociolinguistics* 6. 179–208. doi:10.1111/1467-9481.00184.

Prodromou, Luke. 2007. Bumping into creative idiomaticity. *English Today* 23. 14. doi:10.1017/S0266078407001046.

Ringer-Hilfinger, Kathryn. 2012. Learner Acquisition of Dialect Variation in a Study Abroad Context: The Case of the Spanish [θ]. *Foreign Language Annals* 45. 430–446. doi:10.1111/j.1944-9720.2012.01201.x.

Ruivivar, June & Laura Collins. 2018. The Effects of Foreign Accent on Perceptions of Nonstandard Grammar: A Pilot Study. *TESOL Quarterly* 52. 187–198. doi:10.1002/tesq.374.

Santana Marrer, Juana. 2018. Creencias y actidudes de los jóvenes universitarios sevillanos hacia las variedades cultas del español. *Boletín de Filología* 53. doi:http://dx.doi.org/10.4067/S0718-93032018000200115.

Siegal, Meryl. 1996. The Role of Learner Subjectivity in Second Language Sociolinguistic Competency: Western Women Learning Japanese. *Applied Linguistics* 17. 356–382.

Swacker, Marjorie. 1976. When [+Native] Is [-Favorable]. Lektos: Interdisciplinary Working Papers in Language Sciences, Special Issue. https://eric.ed.gov/?id=ED135254.

Tarone, Elaine & Merrill Swain. 1995. A Sociolinguistic Perspective on Second Language Use in Immersion Classrooms. *The Modern Language Journal* 79. 166–178. doi:10.2307/329617.

Thomas, J. 1983. Cross-Cultural Pragmatic Failure. *Applied Linguistics* 4. 91–112. doi:10.1093/applin/4.2.91.

Trosset, Carol S. 1986. The Social Identity of Welsh Learners. *Language in Society* 15. 165–191.

Trudgill, Peter. 1972. Sex, Covert Prestige and Linguistic Change in the Urban British English of Norwich. *Language in Society* 1. 179–195. doi:10.2307/4166683.

Valdman, Albert. 1988. Classroom foreign language learning and language variation: the notion of pedagogical norms. *World Englishes* 7. 221–236. doi:10.1111/j.1467-971X.1988.tb00233.x.

Valdman, A. 2000. Comment gérer la variation dans l'enseignement du français langue étrangère aux États-Unis. *The French Review*, 73(4), 648–666.

Valdman, A. 2003. The acquisition of sociostylistic and sociopragmatic variation by instructed second language learners: The elaboration of pedagogical norms. In The sociolinguistics of foreign language classrooms: Contributions of the native, the near-native, and the non-native speaker, ed. C. Blyth, 57–78. Boston: Heinle Thomson.

Van Compernolle, Remi A. & Lawrence Williams. 2012. Reconceptualizing Sociolinguistic Competence as Mediated Action: Identity, Meaning-Making, Agency. *The Modern Language Journal* 96. 234–250.

Zahn, Christopher J. & Robert Hopper. 1985. Measuring Language Attitudes: The Speech Evaluation Instrument. *Journal of Language and Social Psychology* 4. 113–123. doi:10.1177/ 0261927X8500400203.

Section IV: **Approaches to teaching L2 lexicon**

Claudia Helena Sánchez-Gutiérrez, Pablo Robles-García,
César Hoyos Álvarez

Chapter 10
Vocabulary in the L2 Spanish classroom: What students know and what their instructors believe they know

1 Introduction

Second language (L2) teachers need to decide on a daily basis which specific words to teach in their classes, and this task, though trivial at first sight, is far from being easy. Contrary to the clear grammatical learning goals that can be found in L2 course syllabi and textbooks, vocabulary goals tend to remain vague. For example, mastering the communicative task of *sharing a story from your past* would require that students learn the uses of both the imperfect and the preterit tenses. This makes it easy to establish a set of clearly defined grammatical goals that will allow students to fulfill the task. For this same task, however, which are the specific words that would allow students to complete it? The answer is not as obvious, as it will depend on the story each student wants to share. A student who wants to tell a story about their family may find the word *abuela [grandma]* extremely useful, while a student who would want to share one of their sport team's successes, may need to learn the word for *baseball bat* in Spanish. Even in cases where a task requires a specific thematic set of words, such as *buying food at the supermarket*, many questions arise. After all, is the word *zucchini* more relevant than *eggplant* when it comes to completing the task? Or is it the other way round? If we were to ignore this question, and all the similar ones that would necessarily come about, and we decided to include all the food-related words we could recall, the glossary for that particular task could amount to hundreds, if not thousands, of words, thus setting an unachievable goal for L2 learners. Due to the virtually limitless nature of any language's lexicon and the limited class time available to teach these many words, making choices about which words to teach and which to dismiss is necessary but challenging.

When making those decisions, instructors could rely on lexical frequency information, a criterion that has been acknowledged and promoted by the research

---

Claudia Helena Sánchez-Gutiérrez, César Hoyos Álvarez, University of California, Davis
Pablo Robles-García, University of Toronto, Mississauga

https://doi.org/10.1515/9783110730418-010

community for decades now. Indeed, the 3,000 most frequent words in a language provide approximately 95% of vocabulary coverage in most oral and written texts (Davies 2005; Nation 2006; Schmitt and Schmitt 2014), which has been set as the minimal threshold for acceptable comprehension (Laufer 1989; Laufer and Ravenhorst-Kalovski 2010; Van Zeeland and Schmitt 2013), and represent the cut-off point for most L2 learner dictionaries (Schmitt and Schmitt 2014). Consequently, vocabulary researchers often invite language practitioners to prioritize this high-frequency vocabulary during the early stages of language instruction (Horst 2013; Meara 1980; Nation 2013; Stæhr 2008). In the *zucchini* vs. *eggplant* case, *eggplant* has 56 occurrences in SUBTLEX-US (Brysbaert and New 2009), a corpus of subtitles in US English, as opposed to the 49 of *zucchini*. Following a purely frequency-based decision-making process, *eggplant* should be prioritized over *zucchini*.

At this point, though, one may wonder how these research-based recommendations are followed in real classes and whether students are adequately exposed to high-frequency words in L2 courses. Namely, are students more exposed to *eggplant* than *zucchini* in their L2 classes due to the higher frequency of the former? In the absence of large-scale generalizable corpora of teacher talk in L2 classrooms, textbooks can function as proxies of actual vocabulary use in the classroom and offer insights into learners' lexical exposure, as they are "powerful indicators of prevalent pedagogical paradigms, and the content analysis of published titles can provide a snapshot of established practices and perspectives on language teaching and learning" (Cubillos 2014: 206). In terms of high-frequency vocabulary in L2 textbooks, Lipinski (2010) found that out of all the words in the glossaries of the three L2 German textbooks that she analyzed, only 32% pertained to the first 1,000 most frequent words, 17% to the second 1,000 frequency band, and 10% to the third. More than 35% of the words introduced in these textbooks did not fall within the 4,000 most frequent words. Similar findings have been reported in English (Alcaraz Mármol 2009; Criado and Sánchez 2009; Donzelli 2007; Martini 2012; Sun and Dang 2020; Yang and Coxhead 2020) and Spanish (Davies and Face 2006; López Bastidas and Sánchez-Gutiérrez 2020). Recently, Sánchez-Gutiérrez, Marcos Miguel and Olsen (2018) found that the 16 Spanish L2 textbooks that they studied included, on average, only 27% of the words from the first 1,000-word band, 17% from the second 1,000-word band, and 11% from the third.

Considering the vagueness of lexical learning goals in the syllabi and the fact that textbook glossaries do not systematically favor high-frequency words over less frequent ones, teachers are ill-equipped and left alone when it comes to determining which words to teach in their classes (McCrostie 2007). In this context, two sources of information can drive their vocabulary selection decisions: (1) lexical frequency data that they would need to retrieve from corpora or frequency lists, and (2) their own intuition. So far, research indicates that teachers' decision-making relies mostly on the latter instead of on empirical data (Creighton 2007; Earl and Katz 2006; Sánchez-Gutiérrez, Robles-García and Pérez Serrano 2022; Vanlommel et al. 2017), and that these intuitions are primarily based on teachers' experiences and subjective feelings of knowledge (Epstein 2008). Since teachers' intuitions play such a crucial role in their pedagogical decisions, there is a logical need to assess their accuracy with regard to lexical frequency, an aspect that is so critical in L2 vocabulary teaching/learning. Basically, do teachers know that *eggplant* is more frequent than *zucchini*?

Most research on native speakers' accuracy in determining word frequency is based on comparisons with non-native speakers (Aizawa, Mochizuki and Meara 2001; Alderson 2007; McCrostie 2005; Ringeling 1984; Schmitt and Dunham 1999), but few studies have specifically focused on L2 teachers. To the best of our knowledge, only McCrostie (2007) has analyzed L2 English teachers' assessments of word frequency to date. In this two-fold study, the author (1) compared the word frequency judgments of 21 EFL teachers and 11 native English speakers who were not involved in language teaching, and (2) examined both groups' abilities to estimate the frequency ranks of high-frequency (i.e., words among the 2,000 most frequent) and mid frequency words (i.e., words in the 4,000 to 10,000 frequency bands). Results showed that teaching experience did not play a significant role in word frequency judgements and that participants were all much more accurate when ranking words at the extremes of the frequency bands (i.e., the most frequent and infrequent ones), while displaying notable difficulties when classifying mid frequency words.

These results suggest that, even though teachers have relatively accurate intuitions when it comes to very high frequency words, such intuitions rapidly become insufficient when moving beyond the first 2,000 most frequent words. Therefore, given the importance of teaching mostly frequent words (but not only the first 2,000), the limited guidance in syllabi, and the excessively large amount of low frequency words presented in L2 textbooks, it would be advisable for teachers to complement their intuitions with objective data from frequency corpora when selecting vocabulary for teaching purposes (McCrostie 2007). However, as was mentioned earlier, teachers do rely more on their intuition than on corpus-data, a fact that is further evidenced in Dang and Webb (2020). In their survey of 16 Vietnamese L2 English teachers, corpus-based wordlists, research-based vocabulary tests, and lexical profilers (all grounded in corpus-based computations of frequency) were considered the least useful tools when deciding which words to teach. Conversely, language instructors listed textbooks and their own linguistic experience as their main sources of information for vocabulary selection. These data confirm the complicated situation currently in place: language teachers do not actively use corpus-based lexical frequency data due to lack of familiarity with the tools or overall distrust for such data. Furthermore, their own intuitions are not to be trusted either when it comes to word frequencies past the 2,000 most frequent, and the textbooks they use do not offer a systematic coverage of high-frequency words.

In an interesting turn of events, though, recent literature has advocated for vocabulary wordlists creation practices that transform teachers' role from passive "consumers" of corpus-based frequency lists – which they are not anyway – to active contributors to wordlists that better address the needs of students in real classrooms (He and Godfroid 2019; Stein 2017). While frequency lists, if actually used, have the potential of helping teachers identify words that provide greater lexical coverage in most texts, recent studies have demonstrated that this information may not be directly transferable into the classroom unless *usefulness* is taken into consideration (Dang, Webb and Coxhead 2020; Garnier and Schmitt 2015; Laufer and Nation 2012). The introduction of this additional criterion may contribute to closing the distance between researchers, who focus on objective corpus-based measures to determine whether a word needs to be taught or not, and teachers, who base those decisions on their daily experience with actual students in the classroom. In addition to this call for a greater involvement of teachers in the creation of wordlists, through their providing usefulness ratings, other authors have also advocated for a more bottom-up approach in establishing the lists of words that should be taught at different proficiency levels. Concretely, Brysbaert, Keuleers, and Mandera (2020) have recently published vocabulary lists based on the words that real L2 English students actually know, thus establishing current students' word knowledge as a criterion to decide which words should be taught at each proficiency level to future students.

In a similar line of inquiry, which unites the calls for both teachers' and instructors' experiences to be considered when creating wordlists, Dang, Webb, and Coxhead (2020) examined the usefulness of different wordlists as evidenced in teachers' perceptions and students' actual vocabulary knowledge. A total of 973 non-overlapping headwords were selected from two different corpora: 545 from the Nation's (2012) BNC/COCA2000 (British National Corpus/Corpus of Contemporary American English 2000) and 428 from the Brezina and Gablasova's (2015) New-General Service List (New-GSL). 78 English language teachers rated the usefulness of each of the headwords on a five-point Likert scale (1 being the least useful and 5 being the most useful) based on how these words would help their students perform basic functions in English. In parallel, 135 Vietnamese learners of English took *yes/no* tests that included the same 973 words, as well as 408 pseudowords, thus providing reliable information about students' reported knowledge of the words. Words from the BNC/COCA2000 – which relies both on corpus frequency and subjective usefulness ratings – were considered more useful by the teachers and were better known by the students than the words from the New-GSL, which only computes corpus-based frequency with no subjective ratings of usefulness. These data reinforce the idea that wordlists need to be developed through a balanced approach that takes into account objective measures of lexical frequency, student's lexical knowledge, and teachers' considerations about words' usefulness.

These considerations will be helpful in designing future wordlists and textbooks but the very real and immediate problem that Spanish language instructors face in their current classes is that, while such lists and textbooks do not yet exist, they still need to make daily decisions about which words to teach. As was stated above, said decisions could draw on (1) corpus-based word frequency data, (2) teachers' perception of usefulness, and (3) students' actual vocabulary knowledge or, (4) ideally, a combination of those three criteria. Concerning lexical frequency, studies have proved that teachers tend not to make active use of corpus-based frequency lists (Dang and Webb 2020) and have relatively poor intuitions about specific word frequencies beyond the 2,000 most frequent ones (McCrostie 2007). With respect to usefulness, it has mostly been conceptualized in terms of a words' relevance to fulfill functions that are specific to the L2 classroom (Dang, Webb and Coxhead 2020; Garnier and Schmitt 2015; He and Godfroid 2019; Laufer and Nation 2012; Stein 2017). For instance, a word such as *adjective* may not be frequent in a corpus of native speakers, but it is definitely useful when first discovering the notion of gender and number agreement in a beginner Spanish course. However, there is an aspect of a word's usefulness that has yet to be explored and that connects points (2) and (3) of the list of vocabulary selection criteria presented earlier: teachers' intuitions about L2 learners' lexical knowledge at different levels of proficiency. Indeed, a teacher will naturally find that it is more useful to spend time explicitly teaching and practicing a given word if they believe that most of their students do not already know it.

Coming back to the *zucchini* vs. *eggplant* conundrum, if a pure frequency criterion was used, only *eggplant* would be taught but, really, who would believe that not one student in the class would actually prefer to learn *zucchini* (or would want to learn both)? If, instead, a usefulness criterion was favored, there would be no way to make a reasonable decision, as a preference for *zucchini* over *eggplant*, or vice versa, would depend more on the recipes that students have in mind when learning how to buy food at the supermarket than on any inherent level of usefulness of either vegetable. In this example, the last criterion, namely students' actual knowledge of the word may seem like the most reasonable option for vocabulary selection. Since both words can be just as useful depending on each student's culinary goals in performing the *buying food at the supermarket* task, the word that would actually be more useful to focus on explicitly in class would be the one that students do not yet know.

Although this criterion may seem sound, if no systematic vocabulary tests are completed by the students to provide evidence of their learning process, it completely relies on teachers' intuitions about their students' lexical knowledge. And inaccurate intuitions may result in inefficient teaching decisions, where some words are dismissed due to the erroneous belief that students know them, and conversely others that are already mastered are taught over and over again. If these types of errors were to happen often in a same language course, students could feel overwhelmed while flooded with unknown words or, alternatively, bored and unchallenged in a class where no new words are introduced. The present study aims to explore whether teachers are good judges of students' lexical knowledge or not by addressing these specific research questions (RQs):

RQ1: How accurate are teachers' intuitions about L2 students' reported lexical knowledge?

RQ2: Are teachers' intuitions more, or less, accurate at different course levels?

RQ3: In course levels where teachers tend to have less accurate judgments of their students' reported lexical knowledge, are teachers' intuitions more, or less, accurate for words in different frequency ranks?

RQ4: Does the amount of teaching experience at a particular course level impact the accuracy of teachers' judgment accuracy in that level?

2 Methods

2.1 Participants

Participants in this study came from two pools: (1) 421 students enrolled in one of the three courses of a First-Year Spanish program at a large public West Coast University (i.e., SPA 1, 2 and 3), and (2) 38 instructors who taught those courses at the same institution. The First-Year Spanish program is designed for students who start learning Spanish with no previous experience with the language. Given that there was only one instructor per each class of approximately 25 students, and that those instructors were the same across academic terms (i.e., 11-weeks long quarters), the number of participants in the student pool is significantly larger than that in the instructors' pool. Nevertheless, those instructors represent 100% of the teacher population for those courses during the time of data collection.

From the 421 participants in the student pool, 216 were enrolled in SPA 1 (i.e., the first course in the program), 138 in SPA 2 (i.e., the second course in the series), and 117 in SPA 3 (i.e., the third course in the program). Of those, 70.2% were female, 18.1% male and 1.7% selected the "Other" option when asked about their gender identity. The mean age of the student participants was 20.32, ranging from a minimum of 17 to a maximum of 58. Concerning their L1s, 80.1% declared that English was their first language, 11.6% chose Mandarin and the other 8.3% had a variety of other L1s, such as Vietnamese, Hmong or Japanese.

When it comes to the 38 instructors who participated in this study, 13 were teaching SPA 1, 10 were teaching SPA 2, and 15 were teaching SPA 3. 68.4% of them were female and 28.9% were male. One instructor did not respond to the question about gender identity, which explains the missing 2.6%. The mean age of the instructors was 31.03, ranging from a minimum of 22 to a maximum of 51. 65.8% of the instructors reported that Spanish was their first language, whereas 28.9% declared that it was English. The remaining 5.3% (N=2) wrote another language as their L1. On average, they had taught the course they were offering at the time 2.18 times, with a minimum of 1 and a maximum of 6.

2.2 Items

Both students and instructors were presented the full list of real words included in 3K-LEx,[1] (Robles-García 2020a), a *yes/no* lexical decision test in which participants indicate whether or not they know the meaning of these words by saying *yes* or *no*, respectively. The complete test contains 108 real words (36 words pertaining to each of the three first 1,000-frequency bands) which were randomly selected from Davies and Davies (2017) Spanish lemmatized frequency dictionary, as well as 54 pseudowords, which were not used in this study. 3K-LEx measures the written recognition (Nation 2013) of nouns, verbs, and adjectives. Reflecting the actual percentage of these word classes within the 3,000 most frequent words in Spanish, 3K-LEx follows a 60 (noun): 28 (verb): 20 (adjective) ratio.

2.3 Data collection

The test for the students was administered during the last two weeks of the course to ensure highest levels of vocabulary knowledge. Likewise, instructors were also

---

[1] 3K-LEx can be downloaded for free from the following link: https://github.com/problg00/3K-LEx. While the full 3K-LEx also includes a set of pseudowords, destined to be used in a penalization matrix to calculate the total scores in the test, this study only uses data from the 108 real words in the test.

asked to take the test during the same period of time. Data collection took place during the three academic terms of the academic year 2018–2019. Both groups of participants completed the corresponding tests on Qualtrics (2002), but students did so during scheduled class time while teachers could complete the questionnaire on their own time. Figure 1 illustrates the format of two items from the test:

Suerte	
Yes	No
Pisar	
Yes	No

Figure 1: Example of 3K-Lex Test Items.

Before administering the test, all participants responded to a short demographic questionnaire and signed a consent form in which information about the nature of the test and their rights as participants were explained in detail. Students were again orally reassured that their data would be de-identified upon their receiving the corresponding extra credit that was approved on the IRB protocol and that their instructors would not have access to their results.

Students were told that they would see a series of words on the screen, and they would have to decide whether or not they knew the meaning of each of them by pressing *yes*, if they did, or *no*, if they did not. They were encouraged to select *no* whenever they were unsure about the meaning of any given word and to limit their *yes* responses to words for which they would easily give a translation or a definition. Students were not given any time restriction in completing the test – other than finishing during class time, which amounted to 50 minutes. They all finished within 12 minutes.

Instructors were told that they would see a series of words and would have to decide whether or not they thought students at the course level they were teaching at the time of testing knew the meaning of the word. If they thought most students did know the word, they were asked to select *yes*, and if they thought they did not, they were asked to respond *no*. If they were unsure, we asked them to select *no*, and to reserve their *yes* responses strictly for words that they were convinced most students in their course level would know. Since teachers were explained how the students were taking the test (i.e., responding *yes* when they recognized the word, and *no* when they did not), they were asked to think about word knowledge in terms of word recognition, which was the type of knowledge assessed in the students' test. They were allowed to complete the test any time within the last two weeks of the academic term, and all of them took less than 17 minutes to complete the test.

2.4 Measurements

A total of 108 scores was obtained for the student dataset, and another 108 for the teacher dataset, one score per word in the test (see Appendix 1). Each score represents the percentage of *yes* responses per item.[2] Concretely, a score of 0 for a given item means that 0% of the participants responded *yes* to this item, whereas a score of 1 indicates that 100% of the participants responded *yes*. For example, a score of 0.6 in the students' dataset for a given item would mean that 60% of the students who participated declared knowing the word. A score of 0.4 for that same item in the teachers' dataset would mean that 40% of the teachers thought that the students enrolled in the same course level they were teaching would know that word. In sum, the unit of analysis for each item is the percentage of participants in each dataset (i.e., students vs. teachers) who responded *yes* to that particular item. Exploratory comparisons between groups were thus carried out by item and not by subject, given the great difference in sample size between groups.

It is important to note that since responses were anonymous in both datasets (i.e., students and teachers), it was impossible to match a teacher's response and the responses of the students enrolled in their own class at the times of testing.

3 Results

Since the data in both groups were not normally distributed, as assessed through Kolmogorov-Smirnov tests, and were skewed towards 0 (i.e., there were more words that students declared to not know than to know, and that teachers thought their students did not know than know), only non-parametric analyses were carried out in this study.

Results are presented in three steps. First, teachers' and students' results were assessed through a correlational analysis. This initial step aimed to respond to RQ1. The second step examined students' and teachers' responses further, through a series of non-parametric tests and visual examinations of response distribution graphs. This step aimed to answer RQ2 and RQ3. Finally, another correlational anal-

---

[2] Even though our data are not normally distributed since there are many more words that beginner students do not know than words that they know, resulting in a high kurtosis and data that are skewed left, we did not carry out the analyses utilizing median values. The median of series of 1 and 0 responses results in a median of either 1 or 0 per item, thus not providing enough distribution to carry out any statistical analysis. Instead, the percentage of *yes* responses is a measure that, although imperfect, makes results easy to interpret.

ysis was carried out, which explored the relationship between teachers' experience and the accuracy of their intuitions regarding students' reported vocabulary knowledge, thus responding to RQ4.

3.1 RQ1: How accurate are teachers' intuitions about L2 students' reported lexical knowledge?

One Spearman correlation was run using (1) the percentage of *yes* responses per item across the 421 student participants, and (2) the percentage of *yes* responses per item across the 38 teacher participants. Results indicate that the correlation was very high and significant, $r=.811$, $p <.001$, which is also visually confirmed in Figure 2.

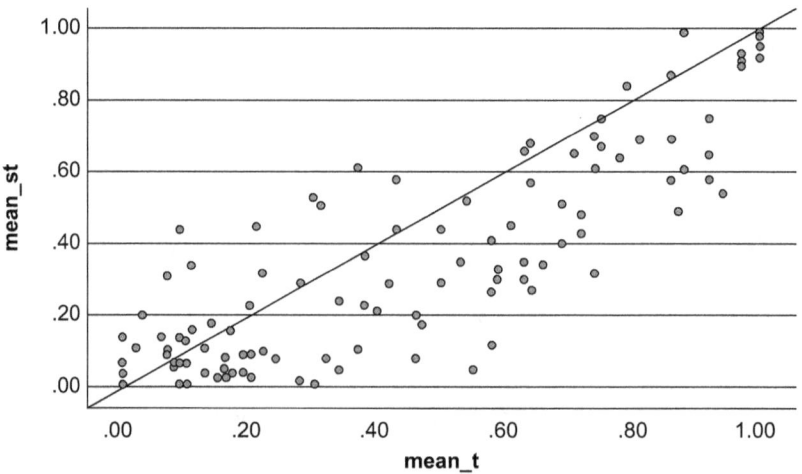

Figure 2: Scatter Plot of Percentage of Yes Responses in Teachers (Mean_t) and Mean Percentage of Yes Responses in Student Responses (Mean_st).

Even though data from students and teachers seem to be highly correlated, it is important to know whether student' and teachers' responses show similar distributions across course levels. This will be further explored in the next section, where the distribution of teachers' and students' responses will be compared at each course level.

3.2 RQ2: Are teachers' intuitions more, or less, accurate at different course levels?

Three Mann-Whitney U tests were run, one per each course level, to compare students' and teachers' percentage of *yes* responses to each of the words in the test. Table 1 presents the summary of results for each of the tests and reveals that the distribution of percentages of *yes* responses between groups is only significantly different in SPA 2, with an almost medium effect size of 0.23. This result is further confirmed through the visual exploration of Figure 3, which shows that while students' data at that level are skewed towards 0 (i.e., not knowing the word), teachers' data present the opposite pattern, being skewed towards 1 (i.e., knowing the word).

Table 1: Independent-Samples Mann-Whitney U Tests of responses by Course Level.

	SPA 1	SPA 2	SPA 3
Mann-Whitney U	6047.000	7407.500	6558.500
Wilcoxon W	11933.000	13293.000	12444.500
Standard Error	458.658	458.914	459.040
Asymptotic significance (2-sided test)	0.639	0.001*	0.114
Effect size (r)	0.11	0.23	0.03

Since teachers in SPA 2 are the ones who present the distribution of responses that differs the most from that of the students enrolled at that same course level, it would be interesting to verify if there are words at specific frequency ranks that are driving those differences. Concretely, are teachers in SPA 2 less accurate in assessing students' knowledge of words at lower frequency ranks?

3.3 RQ3: In course levels where teachers tend to have less accurate judgments of their students' lexical knowledge, are teachers' intuitions more, or less, accurate for words in different frequency ranks?

Three Mann Whitney U tests were run, one per word frequency rank (i.e., rank 1=1–1,000 most frequent words, rank 2 = 1,001–2,000 most frequent words, rank 3 = 2,001–3,000 most frequent words), comparing teachers' and students' percentages of *yes* responses in SPA 2. As evidenced in Table 2, significant differences arose at all frequency ranks with medium (or close to medium) effect sizes, showing

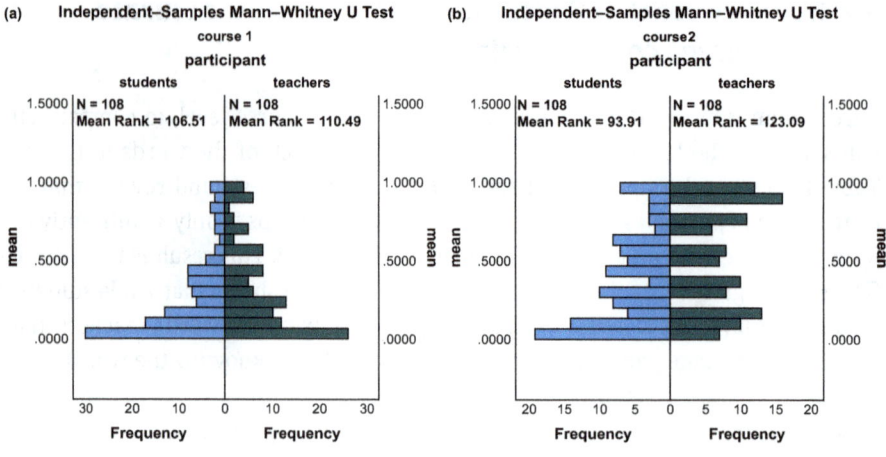
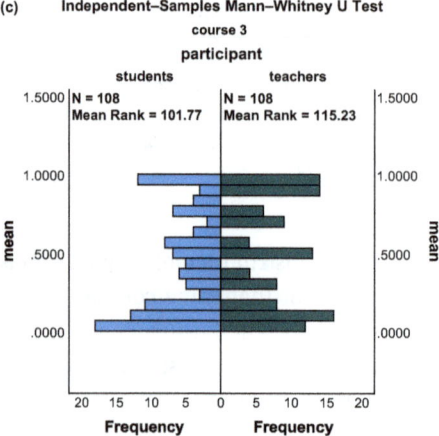

Figure 3: Histograms of the Distribution of Responses by Teachers and Students in SPA 1 (course 1), SPA 2 (course 2) and SPA 3 (course 3).

Table 2: Independent-Samples Mann-Whitney U Tests by Frequency Ranks in SPA 2.

	Rank 1	Rank 2	Rank 3
Mann-Whitney U	892.000	895.500	834.000
Wilcoxon W	1558.000	1561.500	1500.000
Standard Error	88.402	88.681	88.633
Asymptotic significance (2-sided test)	0.006*	0.005*	0.036*
Effect size (r)	0.32	0.32	0.24

that teachers tended to overestimate their students' knowledge at all frequency ranks, and not only for lower frequency words.

3.4 RQ4: Does the amount of teaching experience at a particular course level impact the accuracy of teachers' judgment accuracy in that level?

This study also aims to research the effect of an instructor's teaching experience at a particular course level on their accuracy levels when predicting students' knowledge (as reported by the students themselves) of the words in the test. In order to obtain a parameter that could approximate an instructor's closeness to the real knowledge of students enrolled in the course level they teach, we subtracted the mean result of the students at that level from each teacher's average response. For example, in SPA 1, the average knowledge of the students was of 0.26 (i.e. 26%). If an instructor's average was 0.56 (i.e., 56%), the difference would be of 0.3 (i.e., 30%). Upon making this calculation for each instructor, a Spearman correlation was run between this difference and the number of times that the instructor had taught that particular course level. Results from this analysis did not show any significant correlation ($r= -.185$; $p= .267$), indicating that the teachers' distance to students' declared knowledge were not correlated with their amount of experience teaching that particular course level. This analysis, however, is a first approximation to this question and would need to be re-run with a larger sample of teachers in future studies.

4 Discussion

The goal of this study was to research Spanish teachers' intuitions about their students' lexical knowledge by addressing the following questions:

RQ1: How accurate are teachers' intuitions about L2 students' reported lexical knowledge?

RQ2: Are teachers' intuitions more, or less, accurate at different course levels?

RQ3: In course levels where teachers tend to have less accurate judgments of their students' reported lexical knowledge, are teachers' intuitions more, or less, accurate for words in different frequency ranks?

RQ4: Does the amount of teaching experience at a particular course level impact the accuracy of teachers' judgment accuracy in that level?

With respect to RQ1, the quick response is: *Yes!* Instructors in this study tended to be overall accurate in their intuitions about the lexical knowledge of students enrolled in the course level they were teaching at the time, as revealed in the strong correlation between students' and teachers' responses. However, when comparing the distribution of *yes* responses in both groups of participants at each course level, teachers' responses tended to present very similar distributions to those of students in SPA 1 and SPA 3, while SPA 2 teachers tended to believe that many words were known by the students when students had declared not knowing them. Therefore, in response to RQ2, the accuracy of teachers' intuition does seem to depend on the course level, with overall lower accuracy in SPA 2. Given the teaching context (i.e., three consecutive courses taught by TAs who generally start teaching SPA 1 and move on to SPA 2 and 3), these results may be due to the fact that instructors in SPA 3 had generally taught SPA 1 and 2 in the past, which provided them an advantageous longitudinal overview of all the levels. Indeed, not only did they have experience with each of the chapters of the book used in all three courses, which may have provided useful information about the vocabulary that students are exposed to (Cubillos 2014), but they also had personally interacted with students at all levels by teaching all courses in the language program. Teachers in SPA 1, on the other extreme, only had experience working with SPA 1 students and (accurately) assumed that these knew very few words. Instructors in SPA 2 found themselves in an uncomfortable in-between position, where they probably realized that their current students knew more words than those in SPA 1 but they had not yet been exposed to SPA 3 students. This incomplete set of information may have favored a tendency towards overestimation. Moreover, their misguided intuition may also have been driven by the very real fact that the percentage of additional words learned from SPA 1 to SPA 2 is much higher, according to this study's data, (i.e., 12%) than that observed between students in SPA 2 and those in SPA 3 (i.e., 4%).

In response to RQ3, when digging deeper into the specific words for which SPA 2 teachers tended to overestimate students' knowledge, no differences arose between frequency ranks. Concretely, teachers overestimated their students' knowledge for words that were among the first most frequent in Spanish, but also for lower frequency words. It may be that teachers do not rely as much on a frequency criterion when determining whether a word is expected to be known or not known by students at a particular course level, or that, in line with what was found in previous research, they may not have a fine-tuned awareness of frequency differences between words (McCrostie 2007). What we do know from previous research is that teachers give a lot of importance to a words' usefulness (Dang, Webb and Coxhead 2020; Garnier and Schmitt 2015; He and Godfroid 2019; Laufer and Nation 2012; Stein 2017), which can provide a potential explanation for some of the words for which teachers tended to overestimate students declared knowledge. For instance, in SPA 1, 54% of instructors thought that their students knew the verb *borrar* 'to erase', which is in frequency rank 3, whereas only 16% of students declared knowing it. This word, although not highly frequent in native speakers' Spanish corpora, is used repeatedly in the classroom when erasing information from the blackboard. Similar trends are observed with other words that are used often in the classroom but are not very frequent in a native corpus, such as *adivinar* 'to guess' or *desafío* 'challenge', which teachers may generally think are known because they are regularly utilized when giving instructions about typical exercises and activities.

Another source of information about what students may or may not know is the presence or absence of words in textbook activities and glossaries. As is discussed in Marcos Miguel and Cubas in this volume, teachers greatly rely on textbook contents and activities when teaching vocabulary in their classes. In this context, it would not be surprising if they (sometimes wrongly) assumed that words that are included in the textbook are known by the students. An interesting example of one such word is *alimento* 'food item', which 90% of the teachers in SPA 2 thought was mastered by their students when only 27% of them reported knowing it. The word is in frequency rank 2 but generally serves as a title for lists of food items in textbook glossaries and it would be easy to imagine that teachers use it when talking about food in general. However, it does not point to any specific food item that students can use when going grocery shopping or ordering a dish in a restaurant. This could be an example of how teachers' intuitions may be partially biased by what they know their students are exposed to in the textbooks, rather than on the observation of actual students' use, or recognition, of the words. However, research shows that simple exposure to a word does not ensure incidental learning unless occurrences of a word are frequent enough (i.e., 10 to 20 repetitions) and that words that are taught explicitly in class have a better chance of being learned (Dóczi and Kormos 2016; Folse 2010). Thus, even though students may have seen the word *alimento* in the textbook, if no particular attention was given to it since it was not necessary to complete any of the activities, there would be little chances of them learning the word.

This last idea calls the attention to the fact that, when we talk about lexical frequency, we are referring to calculations that are based on native speaker corpora. If we want to better understand the impact of lexical frequency on students' word recognition and lexical knowledge, frequency counts need to be extracted from corpora of classroom recordings. Even if textbooks can serve as "proxies" of what happens in the classroom, they may not be good indicators of how much emphasis is given to specific words. For example, knowing that the word *alimento* appears in the textbook is not enough to assume that it is repeated enough times during class to facilitate incidental learning, or that it is taught explicitly. Having the information about what ultimately happens in the classroom would allow us to use frequency counts that correspond to the actual input students are exposed to and to better understand the relation between what appears in the textbooks and what teachers do with it. This information, in turn, would make it possible to assess whether students' and teachers' responses in studies similar to ours may be driven by classroom frequency and explicit treatment of certain words, instead of relying on native speakers' frequency counts which are disconnected from the realities of L2 classrooms. Unfortunately, no such corpus has been created and shared so far, to the best of our knowledge.

The hypotheses proposed above about the driving forces behind teachers' intuitions of student learning currently remain at the hypothetical level, but they would certainly deserve further inquiry in future studies on L2 teachers' intuitions about students' lexical knowledge. Importantly, in response to RQ4, no matter the criteria that may have driven teachers' responses, the accuracy of said responses does not seem to be influenced by the level of experience that the teacher has at that specific course level. However, again, this needs to be studied further, with more course levels and course types, as well as additional instructors with a broader range of teaching experiences.

Going back to the issue of vocabulary selection in L2 classes, the literature proposes three distinct criteria that could prove useful in fulfilling this arduous task: (1) corpus-based word frequency data (Schmitt and Schmitt 2014), (2) teachers' perception of usefulness (Dang, Webb, and Coxhead 2020; Garnier and Schmitt 2015; He and Godfroid 2019; Laufer and Nation 2012), and (3) students' actual vocabulary knowledge (Brysbaert, Keuleers and Mandera 2020). Based on previous research, teachers do not rely on the first source of data (Dang and Webb 2020; Sánchez-Gutiérrez, Robles-García and Pérez Serrano 2022), and very few currently available wordlists incorporate teachers' subjective ratings of usefulness (Dang, Webb and Coxhead 2020). In the case of Spanish, there is simply none of the sort. To date, there are no wordlists in Spanish that adopt the bottom-up approach proposed by Brysbaert, Keuleers and Mandera (2020), which entails organizing words based on the number of students who know them. Because no such database exists in Spanish, teachers have to rely on their own intuitions about which words their students may know and which they may not in order to make daily decisions about vocabulary teaching. As evidenced in this study, teachers have relatively accurate perceptions of their students' reported word knowledge, especially when those are beginners or when they are taking the last course in a first-year language program. Nevertheless, there are still mismatches between students' reported knowledge and the knowledge that is assumed from them by their teachers. This is particularly true for certain specific words that teachers may want their students to know and thus assume most of their students acquired. While more research is needed in this respect, those inconsistencies in teachers' and students' data demonstrate that vocabulary selection decisions should not rely solely on teacher's intuitions but rather on observed student knowledge, assessed by consistent vocabulary tests. Therefore, we propose that teachers increase the number and frequency of vocabulary assessments in their courses in order to gather reliable data about their students' lexicon, which will in turn allow them to make better decisions about which words to teach.

5 Conclusion

This study aimed to explore the extent to which L2 Spanish teachers are good judges of their students' reported lexical knowledge. Upon analyzing the results of a self-reported vocabulary test that was completed by students enrolled in three consecutive beginner language courses and comparing them to the assessment of their word knowledge provided by teachers in those same courses, teachers seem to have a relatively accurate perception of students' reported knowledge. However, this is far from being true with all words in the test, and more research is needed that analyzes the criteria that underlie teachers' intuitions about their students' (self-reported) knowledge of certain vocabulary. While the creation of a wordlist that determines the words that should be taught at different proficiency levels based on a large-scale inquiry of student data would be much welcome in the longer term, teachers can, in the meantime, systematically assess their students' lexical knowledge through continuous testing.

While this study offers an initial exploration into teachers' awareness about students' vocabulary knowledge, it presents several limitations. First, *yes/no* tests, such as the one used in this study, are known to overestimate learners' knowledge, since they do not require to provide any evidence of actually knowing the meaning of the word and thus depend on learners' reported knowledge rather than proof of actual knowledge (Schmitt et al. 2020; Stoeckel et al. 2021). However, at the moment, no meaning recall vocabulary test has been designed in Spanish that is validated and published for public use, which limits researchers' ability to investigate students' actual lexical knowledge. Another limitation of the test is that it focuses only on one type of vocabulary knowledge: the form-meaning link. As is pointed out in Zyzik and Marqués Pascual (this volume), the overfocus on this aspect of lexical knowledge does not reveal the whole picture of what knowing a word means. For instance, it may be that students would not be able to translate a word directly but would know that it is related to other words in its lexical family, thus revealing knowledge of word parts. In future studies, as more validated vocabulary tests become available in Spanish, it would be advisable to use a meaning-recall test, but it would be even better to test different aspects of word knowledge as well.

Additionally, teachers in this study were asked to respond to the test items thinking about the probability that a general group of students (e.g., those in SPA 3) would know a word. Given that students in a class may vary greatly in the amount of vocabulary they know, teachers may provide responses that either focus on the students they think know the most or the ones that know the least. Depending on what subgroup of students they were considering when completing the test, they may have over-or under-estimated their knowledge, adding a lot of variability to the teachers' results. In future studies, it would be better to match teachers with students from the specific class they are teaching at the time of testing. An alternative (or perhaps complementary) way of addressing this issue would be to provide teachers with a scale instead of a *yes/no* response, which would allow them to indicate how sure they are that students at that proficiency level would know each word or not or what percentage of their students they think would know it. Finally, this study was merely exploratory and only looked at beginner courses and at a limited number of instructors. Future studies would benefit from adding more proficiency levels and including a larger number of instructors.

Appendix 1

item	SPA 1		SPA 2		SPA 3	
	students	teachers	students	teachers	students	teachers
encontrar	0.58	0.85	0.85	0.90	0.81	1.00
pequeño	0.83	0.92	0.95	1.00	0.96	1.00
esperar	0.40	0.54	0.72	0.90	0.96	1.00
tiempo	0.88	1.00	0.99	1.00	0.99	1.00
trabajo	0.98	1.00	1.00	1.00	0.98	1.00
solo	0.76	0.69	0.91	0.90	0.95	1.00
cuerpo	0.28	0.77	0.56	1.00	0.89	1.00
creer	0.68	0.46	0.87	0.90	0.96	1.00
mano	0.80	0.92	0.90	1.00	0.99	1.00
todo	0.86	1.00	0.94	1.00	0.95	1.00
meter	0.35	0.00	0.52	0.20	0.44	0.07
cara	0.39	0.69	0.65	1.00	0.80	0.93
mostrar	0.14	0.23	0.28	0.80	0.49	0.87
empresa	0.41	0.54	0.55	0.80	0.56	0.73

(continued)

item	SPA 1		SPA 2		SPA 3	
	students	teachers	students	teachers	students	teachers
fuerza	0.11	0.31	0.44	0.80	0.36	0.67
dinero	0.82	0.92	0.97	1.00	1.00	1.00
descubrir	0.68	0.54	0.58	0.80	0.70	0.80
antiguo	0.23	0.23	0.50	0.80	0.62	0.80
lanzar	0.04	0.00	0.06	0.10	0.09	0.13
suerte	0.50	0.69	0.68	0.70	0.82	0.87
asunto	0.03	0.08	0.05	0.10	0.03	0.20
dolor	0.35	0.38	0.60	0.80	0.76	0.73
crecer	0.32	0.54	0.42	0.50	0.56	0.47
cerrar	0.40	0.69	0.60	0.90	0.74	1.00
enviar	0.24	0.46	0.62	0.90	0.58	0.80
rey	0.21	0.46	0.33	1.00	0.47	0.53
abierto	0.23	0.77	0.58	0.90	0.65	0.93
vivo	0.99	0.69	1.00	1.00	0.98	0.93
rato	0.35	0.23	0.65	0.40	0.59	0.27
lluvia	0.36	0.92	0.61	0.90	0.66	1.00
cuento	0.53	0.46	0.81	0.90	0.75	0.87
colocar	0.02	0.15	0.05	0.30	0.03	0.13
recuerdo	0.41	0.31	0.75	0.80	0.88	0.80
caballo	0.43	0.46	0.74	1.00	0.74	0.87
recoger	0.42	0.23	0.66	0.60	0.74	0.27
piedra	0.18	0.08	0.25	0.40	0.28	0.53
seco	0.11	0.08	0.24	0.60	0.33	0.47
esconder	0.10	0.15	0.26	0.80	0.18	0.47
vuelta	0.10	0.00	0.40	0.40	0.46	0.27
grito	0.20	0.00	0.44	0.60	0.46	0.53
encargar	0.08	0.00	0.19	0.30	0.14	0.00
ruido	0.19	0.38	0.25	0.90	0.61	0.60
labio	0.25	0.23	0.21	0.70	0.35	0.80
saltar	0.41	0.62	0.42	0.60	0.38	0.53
alimento	0.13	0.54	0.27	0.90	0.42	0.47
desnudo	0.06	0.00	0.12	0.40	0.06	0.33
temor	0.04	0.15	0.06	0.40	0.14	0.40
pérdida	0.12	0.00	0.32	0.20	0.26	0.40
confianza	0.18	0.31	0.32	0.60	0.36	0.60
cadena	0.05	0.00	0.08	0.10	0.08	0.20
bailar	0.96	1.00	1.00	1.00	0.99	1.00
cuello	0.30	0.38	0.24	0.90	0.74	0.87
robar	0.13	0.15	0.41	0.90	0.51	0.53
muestra	0.27	0.15	0.53	0.20	0.54	0.27
callar	0.12	0.31	0.14	0.40	0.07	0.40
esquina	0.11	0.23	0.41	0.40	0.36	0.20

(continued)

item	SPA 1		SPA 2		SPA 3	
	students	teachers	students	teachers	students	teachers
lejano	0.01	0.23	0.02	0.40	0.01	0.27
fiel	0.06	0.15	0.09	0.10	0.18	0.13
carretera	0.10	0.31	0.30	0.60	0.21	0.47
traje	0.29	0.23	0.83	0.80	0.87	0.87
mentira	0.13	0.38	0.37	0.90	0.46	0.93
pasear	0.63	0.54	0.52	0.80	0.68	0.87
rama	0.06	0.08	0.11	0.20	0.05	0.00
humo	0.07	0.00	0.13	0.20	0.09	0.47
asomar	0.02	0.00	0.01	0.00	0.00	0.00
sucio	0.25	0.62	0.37	0.60	0.58	0.87
escalera	0.41	0.23	0.58	0.40	0.76	0.67
obrero	0.00	0.00	0.04	0.10	0.01	0.20
rueda	0.12	0.08	0.15	0.30	0.20	0.13
bolsillo	0.03	0.08	0.11	0.10	0.14	0.40
dulce	0.50	0.54	0.79	0.90	0.95	0.80
perdido	0.31	0.46	0.54	0.70	0.50	0.67
borrar	0.16	0.54	0.32	0.50	0.51	0.73
adivinar	0.03	0.38	0.06	0.70	0.27	0.67
cárcel	0.05	0.15	0.11	0.70	0.07	0.53
alcalde	0.00	0.15	0.03	0.50	0.02	0.20
rezar	0.04	0.23	0.04	0.10	0.01	0.13
ancho	0.05	0.00	0.14	0.40	0.05	0.07
orilla	0.15	0.08	0.09	0.10	0.17	0.00
pecado	0.12	0.00	0.29	0.10	0.20	0.00
alegre	0.57	0.92	0.65	0.80	0.85	0.87
sudor	0.05	0.00	0.05	0.30	0.02	0.27
huella	0.04	0.08	0.03	0.20	0.01	0.20
pisar	0.35	0.00	0.30	0.20	0.27	0.00
vientre	0.18	0.00	0.09	0.00	0.07	0.07
pálido	0.03	0.00	0.05	0.30	0.04	0.20
socio	0.37	0.08	0.45	0.60	0.50	0.60
gota	0.16	0.00	0.14	0.20	0.18	0.13
castigar	0.06	0.23	0.12	0.30	0.10	0.07
tonto	0.45	0.46	0.55	0.50	0.55	0.67
picar	0.13	0.00	0.32	0.30	0.10	0.13
orgulloso	0.10	0.23	0.23	0.50	0.30	0.47
suelto	0.09	0.00	0.20	0.00	0.13	0.00
eje	0.03	0.00	0.04	0.00	0.03	0.00
apellido	0.88	0.92	0.47	0.90	0.59	0.93
docente	0.03	0.15	0.06	0.20	0.04	0.13
colega	0.05	0.23	0.06	0.70	0.05	0.73
cerro	0.33	0.08	0.41	0.20	0.27	0.07

(continued)

item	SPA 1		SPA 2		SPA 3	
	students	teachers	students	teachers	students	teachers
uña	0.49	0.31	0.50	0.50	0.53	0.13
chiste	0.14	0.15	0.38	0.50	0.34	0.60
desafío	0.02	0.46	0.05	0.30	0.07	0.27
penumbra	0.04	0.00	0.07	0.00	0.10	0.00
resaltar	0.09	0.00	0.17	0.20	0.16	0.07
ahogar	0.05	0.00	0.11	0.00	0.15	0.20
hueco	0.04	0.08	0.08	0.10	0.08	0.07
sabiduría	0.01	0.08	0.00	0.20	0.01	0.00
tibio	0.09	0.00	0.07	0.20	0.09	0.00
cumbre	0.03	0.00	0.06	0.00	0.02	0.00

References

Aizawa, Kazumi, Masamichi Mochizuki & Paul Meara. 2001. Intuition about word frequency: What does it tell us about vocabulary knowledge. *Research Reports of the Faculty of Engineering* 20. 75–82. Tokyo Denki University.

Alcaraz Mármol, Gema. 2009. Vocabulary in EFL textbooks: Frequency levels. In Pascual Cantos Gómez & Aquilino Sánchez Pérez (eds.), *A survey on corpus-based studies*, 862–875. Murcia, Spain: AELINCO (Asociación Española de Lingüística de Corpus). http://www.um.es/lacell/aelinco/contenido/index.html (accessed 12 March 2021).

Alderson, Charles. 2007. Judging the frequency of English words. *Applied Linguistics* 28(3). 383–409. https://doi.org/10.1093/applin/amm024

Brezina, Vaclav & Dana Gablasova. 2015. Is there a core general vocabulary? Introducing the new general service list. *Applied Linguistics* 36. 1–22. https://doi.org/10.1093/applin/amt018

Brysbaert, Marc & Boris New. 2009. Moving beyond Kučera and Francis: A critical evaluation of current word frequency norms and the introduction of a new and improved word frequency measure for American English. *Behavior Research Methods* 41. 977–990. https://doi.org/10.3758/BRM.41.4.977

Brysbaert, Marc, Emmanuel Keuleers & Paweł Mandera. 2020. Which words do English non-native speakers know? New supernational levels based on yes/no decision. *Second Language Research* 37(2). 207–231. https://doi.org/10.1177/0267658320934526

Creighton, Theodore B. 2007. *School and data: The educator's guide for using data to improve decision making*. London: Sage.

Criado, Raquel & Aquilino Sánchez. 2009. Vocabulary in EFL textbooks: A contrastive analysis against three corpus-based word ranges. In Pascual Cantos Gómez & Aquilino Sánchez Pérez (eds.), *A survey on corpus-based studies*, 862–875 AELINCO: Murcia. http://www.um.es/lacell/aelinco/contenido/index.html (accessed 12 March 2021).

Cubillos, Jorge H. 2014. Spanish textbooks in the US: Enduring traditions and emerging trends. *Journal of Spanish Language Teaching* 1(2). 205–225. https://doi.org/10.1080/23247797.2014.970363

Daller, Michael, John Turlik & Ian Weir. 2013. Modelling vocabulary growth in a foreign language: Defining and measuring lexical diversity. In Scott Jarvis & Michael Daller (eds.), *Vocabulary knowledge: Human ratings and automated measures*, 185–218. Amsterdam: John Benjamins.

Dang, Thi Ngoc Yen & Stuart Webb. 2020. Vocabulary and good language teachers. In Carol Griffiths & Zia Tajeddin (eds.), *Lessons from good language teachers*, 203–218. Cambridge University Press.

Dang, Thi Ngoc Yen, Stuart Webb & Averil Coxhead. 2020. Evaluating lists of high-frequency words: Teachers' and learners' perspectives. *Language Teaching Research*, Online First. 1–25. https://doi.org/10.1177/1362168820911189

Davies, Mark. 2005. Vocabulary range and text coverage: Insights from the forthcoming Routledge frequency dictionary of Spanish. In David Eddington (ed.), *Selected proceedings of the 7th Hispanic Linguistics Symposium*, 106–115. Somerville, MA: Cascadilla Proceedings Project.

Davies, Mark, & Kathy Hayward Davies. 2017. *A frequency dictionary of Spanish: Core vocabulary for learners*, Second Edition. New York: Routledge.

Davies, Mark &Timothy L. Face. 2006. Vocabulary coverage in Spanish textbooks: How representative is it? In Nuria Sagarra & Almeida Jacqueline Toribio (eds.), *Selected Proceedings of the 9th Hispanic Linguistics Symposium*, 132–143. Somerville, MA: Cascadilla.

Donzelli, Giovanna. 2007. Foreign language learners: Words they hear and words they learn: A case study. *Estudios de Lingüística Inglesa Aplicada* 7. 103–125. https://revistas.uned.es/index.php/ELIA/article/view/18092

Dóczi, Brigitta & Judit Kormos. 2016. *Longitudinal developments in vocabulary knowledge and lexical organization*. Oxford: Oxford University Press.

Earl, Lorna & Steven Katz. 2006. *Leading in a data rich world*. Thousand Oaks, California: Corwin press.

Epstein, Seymour. 2008. *Intuition from the perspective of cognitive experiential self-theory*. New York: Erlbaum.

Folse, Keith. 2010. Is explicit vocabulary focus the reading teacher's job? *Reading in a Foreign Language* 22(1). 139–160. http://nflrc.hawaii.edu/rfl

Garnier, Mélodie & Norbert Schmitt. 2015. The PHaVE List: A pedagogical list of phrasal verbs and their most frequent meaning senses. *Language Teaching Research* 19(6). 645–666. https://doi.org/10.1177/1362168814559798

He, Xuehong & Aline Godfroid. 2019. Choosing words to teach: A novel method for vocabulary selection and its practical application. *TESOL Quarterly* 53(2). 348–371. https://doi.org/10.1002/tesq.483

Horst, Marlise. 2013. Mainstreaming second language vocabulary acquisition. *The Canadian Journal of Applied Linguistics* 16(1). 171–188. https://journals.lib.unb.ca/index.php/CJAL/article/view/21299

Laufer, Batia. 1989. What percentage of text-lexis is essential for comprehension? In Christer Lauren & Marianne Nordman (eds.), *Special language: From humans thinking to thinking machines*, 316–323. Clevedon: Multilingual Matters.

Laufer, Batia &Paul Nation. 1999. Vocabulary size and use: Lexical richness in L2 written production. *Applied Linguistics* 16(3). 307–322. https://doi.org/10.1093/applin/16.3.307

Laufer, Batia & Geke C. Ravenhorst-Kalovski. 2010. Lexical threshold revisited: Lexical coverage, learners' vocabulary size and reading comprehension. *Reading in a Foreign Language* 22(1). 15–30. http://nflrc.hawaii.edu/rfl

Laufer, Batia & Paul Nation. 2012. Vocabulary. In Susan M. Gass & Alison Mackey (eds.), *The Routledge Handbook of Second Language Acquisition*, 163–176. London, England: Routledge.

Lipinski, Silke. 2010. A frequency analysis of vocabulary in three first-year textbooks of German. *Die Unterrichtspraxis/Teaching German* 43(2). 167–174. https://doi.org/10.1111/j.1756-1221.2010.00078.x

López Bastidas, Lani & Claudia Sánchez-Gutiérrez. 2020. Vocabulary selection and word repetitions in beginner L2 Spanish textbooks. *Revista Electrónica de Lingüística Aplicada* 19(2). 48–63. https://www.aesla.org.es/ojs/index.php/RAEL/article/view/432

Martini Oliveira Pisani, Juliane. 2012. *High frequency vocabulary in a secondary Quebec ESL textbook corpus*. Montreal, Canada: Concordia University MA thesis. https://spectrum.library.concordia.ca/id/eprint/974698/

McCrostie, James. 2005. A further investigation of word frequency intuitions. *The East Asian Learner* 2(1). 26–36. https://doi.org/10.1177/0033688206076158

McCrostie, James. 2007. Investigating the Accuracy of Teachers' Word Frequency Intuitions. *RELC Journal* 38(1). 53–66. https://doi.org/10.1177/0033688206076158

Meara, Paul. 1980. Vocabulary acquisition: A neglected aspect of language learning. *Language Teaching and Linguistics Abstracts* 13(3–4). 221–246. https://doi.org/10.1017/S0261444800008879

Milton, James. 2009. *Measuring second language vocabulary acquisition*. Bristol, UK: Multilingual Matters.

Nation, Paul. 2006. How large a vocabulary is needed for reading and listening? *Canadian Modern Language Review* 63(1). 59–82. https://7doi.org/10.3138/cmlr.63.1.59

Nation, Paul. 2012. *The BNC/COCA word family lists*. http://www.victoria.ac.nz/lals/about/staff/paul-nation (accessed 20 March 2021).

Nation, Paul. 2013. *Learning vocabulary in another language*, 2nd edn. Cambridge: Cambridge University Press.

Ringeling, Tobi. 1984. Subjective Estimations as a Useful Alternative to Word Frequency Counts. *Interlanguage Studies Bulletin* 8. 59–69. https://www.jstor.org/stable/43135301

Robles-García, Pablo. 2020a. 3K-LEx. Desarrollo y validación de una prueba de amplitud léxica en español. *Journal of Spanish Language Teaching* 7(1). 1–13.

Robles-García, Pablo. 2020b. *¿Cuántas palabras conocen los aprendientes de español como lengua extranjera? Competencia léxica y oportunidades de aprendizaje léxico en el aula de ELE*. Davis, CA: University of California Davis dissertation.

Sánchez-Gutiérrez, Claudia H., Pablo Robles-García & Mercedes Pérez Serrano. 2022. L2 Spanish vocabulary teaching in US universities: Instructors' beliefs and reported practices. *Language Teaching Research*. Online First. 1–23.

Sánchez-Gutiérrez, Claudia, Nausica Marcos Miguel & Michael K. Olsen. 2018. Vocabulary coverage and lexical characteristics in L2 Spanish textbooks. In Peter Ecke & Susanne Rott (eds.), *Understanding vocabulary learning and teaching: Implications for language program development*, 78–98. Boston, MA: Cengage. http://hdl.handle.net/10125/69783

Schmitt, Norbert & Bruce Dunham. 1999. Exploring native and non-native intuitions of word Frequency. *Second Language Research* 15(4). 389–411. https://doi.org/10.1191/026765899669633186

Schmitt, Norbert & Diane Schmitt. 2014. A reassessment of frequency and vocabulary size in L2 vocabulary teaching. *Language Teaching* 47(4). 484–503. https://doi.org/10.1017/S0261444812000018

Schmitt, Norbert, Karen Dunn, Barry O'Sullivan, Laurence Anthony & Benjamin Kremmel. 2020. Introducing knowledge-based vocabulary lists (KVL). *TESOL Journal* 12(4). 1–10. https://doi.org/10.1002/tesj.622

Stæhr, Lars Stenius. 2008. Vocabulary size and the skills of listening, reading and writing. *Language Learning Journal* 36. 139–152. https://doi.org/10.1080/09571730802389975

Stein, Gabriele. 2017. Some thoughts on the issue of core vocabularies: A response to Vaclav Brezina and Dana Gablasova: 'Is there a core general vocabulary? Introducing the new general service list. *Applied Linguistics* 38(5). 759–763. https://doi.org/10.1093/applin/amw027

Stoeckel, Tim, Stuart McLean & Paul Nation. 2021. Limitations of size and levels tests of written receptive vocabulary knowledge. *Studies in Second Language Acquisition* 43(1). 181–203. https://doi.org/10.1017/S027226312000025X

Sun, Ye & Thi Ngoc Yen Dang. 2020. Vocabulary in high-school EFL textbooks: Texts and learner knowledge. *System* 93. 1–13. https://doi.org/10.1016/j.system.2020.102279

Vanlommel, Kristin, Ross Van Gasse, Jan Vanhoof & Peter Van Petegem. 2017. Teachers' decision-making: Data based or intuition driven? *International Journal of Educational Research* 83. 75–83. https://doi.org/10.1016/j.ijer.2017.02.013

Van Zeeland, Hilde & Norbert Schmitt. 2013. Lexical coverage in L1 and L2 listening comprehension: The same or different from reading comprehension? *Applied Linguistics* 34(4). 457–479. https://doi.org/10.1093/applin/ams074

Yang, Lu & Averil Coxhead. 2020. A corpus-based study of vocabulary in the New Concept English textbook series. *RELC Journal*. Online First. 1–15. https://doi.org/10.1177/0033688220964162

Nausica Marcos Miguel, Mari Félix Cubas Mora
Chapter 11
Interpreting the designated curriculum: Teachers' understanding of vocabulary instruction and adherence to the textbook

1 Introduction

In the last thirty years, SLA research has extensively focused on L2 vocabulary acquisition, primarily on learners' cognitive development in L2 English (see Milton 2009; Nation 2001; Schmitt 2008). Within the classroom, there has been research on how instructed learners acquire vocabulary (e.g., Dobinson 2001; Zimmerman 1997), what activities are more effective for vocabulary learning (e.g., Laufer and Hulstijn 2001; Keating 2008), how teachers teach vocabulary (e.g., Sanaoui 1996; Swain and Carroll 1987), and what motivates teachers' classroom practices (e.g., Niu and Andrews 2012; Zhang 2008). This research has shown three main findings. First, some explicit teaching is necessary for successful learning (see Nation and Webb 2011). Second, the cognitive load of an activity can make a difference in vocabulary learning (e.g., Keating 2008). Third, both vocabulary size and vocabulary depth, i.e., the set of features that constitute word knowledge, are important (see Schmitt 2014). However, instructors' beliefs and practices have scarcely been considered in English L2 teaching (see Bergström, Norberg and Nordlund 2021; Niu and Andrews 2012; Rossiter, Abbott and Kushnir 2016), much less in Spanish L2 teaching (e.g., Marcos Miguel 2015, 2017; Miguel García 2005; Sánchez-Gutiérrez, Robles-García and Pérez Serrano 2022).

Despite the prevalent use of textbooks in the L2 classroom, there is still much we do not know about their influence in vocabulary learning and instruction. Although not all classroom environments include a textbook, textbook use is ubiquitous in higher education institutions in the U.S., particularly in those offering multi-section language courses taught by Teaching Assistants (TAs), lecturers, and adjuncts. The textbook is generally seen as 'a reference point orienting classroom instruction and learning' (Allen 2008: 11). Moreover, TAs have identified vocabulary instruction 'as the aspect of FL learning facilitated most by textbook materials' (14). Because of the importance of textbooks in this educational context, they

---
Nausica Marcos Miguel, Ghent University
Mari Félix Cubas Mora, University of Pittsburgh

https://doi.org/10.1515/9783110730418-011

play a part in orienting teachers' understanding of how to develop effective vocabulary instruction (see Hutchinson and Torres 1994). Yet previous research on the role of textbooks in L2 vocabulary instruction has focused almost exclusively on lexical content and types of vocabulary practice available in textbooks (see Brown 2011 for English L2; Neary-Sundquist 2015 for German L2; López Jiménez 2014, and Robles García and Sánchez-Gutiérrez 2016, for Spanish L2). Little research has explored the way that classroom vocabulary acquisition is influenced by the interaction of textbook and teacher.

Moreover, while attention to textbooks in Spanish L2 research has been on the increase, this has not been the case for another ubiquitous element in language classrooms, i.e., the syllabus. As a norm, this document contains a description of the course, course goals, major assignments, methods of grading, and a schedule (e.g., Slattery and Carlson 2005). Given the role of the syllabus in summarizing the content of the course, vocabulary goals should be addressed in an L2 syllabus (see Fink 2012; Graves 2000). Nevertheless, to our knowledge, no study has analyzed syllabus content regarding vocabulary instruction.

In brief, this study will enhance the literature on classroom L2 vocabulary instruction by exploring it from two curricular perspectives (see Remillard and Heck 2014): (1) the extent to which textbooks and syllabi (i.e., the designated curriculum) exhibit the characteristics of effective L2 vocabulary instruction, and (2) the extent to which teachers' reported practices (i.e., the intended curriculum) aligned with characteristics of effective L2 vocabulary instruction. Understanding how teachers interact with the designated curriculum – the syllabus and the textbook – can shed light on how vocabulary instruction takes shape in the teacher-intended curriculum, that is, how teachers conceptualize and plan vocabulary instruction for their classroom practice based on the 'blueprint' given in the designated curriculum. Studying the designated and the intended curriculum puts the focus on the stages that precede classroom instruction. While previous studies have focused on the individual features of vocabulary activities, in the present study, vocabulary activities are viewed as parts of a learning sequence.

In the following sections, we will first discuss the notions of the designated and the intended curriculum within the curricular framework put forth by Remillard and Heck (2014). Next, we will explain how the teacher-intended curriculum can be analyzed through the lens of teacher cognition research (Borg 2006). We will then summarize the role of vocabulary in the Communicative Language Teaching (CLT) approach, which is typically preferred in Spanish L2 textbooks in the U.S. (Cubillos 2014) as well as in the training of TAs (see Savignon 2007; Shrum and Glisan 2009). Finally, we will discuss the tools used to analyze the effectiveness of vocabulary instruction in both the designated curriculum (textbooks and syllabi) and the intended curriculum (instructors' plans for implementing vocabulary instruction). These tools are a simplified version of Nation and Webb's (2011) Technique Feature Analysis Checklist (TFAC) and a modified version of the Word Knowledge List (WKL) based on Nation (2001) and Brown (2011). The TFAC and WKL as well as Remillard and Heck's curricular framework connect current research recommendations for vocabulary teaching and learning with instructors' reported practices.

1.1 The designated and the intended curriculum

Drawing from Remillard and Heck's (2014) framework, four curricular levels can be identified in U.S. college-level Spanish L2 classrooms:
1. the official curriculum (the course as approved by the university),
2. the designated curriculum (the textbook and the syllabus),
3. the teacher-intended curriculum (how the teacher plans to enact the official and designated curricula), and
4. the enacted curriculum (what happens in the classroom).

For college-level practitioners, the layout of the textbook serves as the basis from which to organize a course. Moreover, the course syllabus establishes curricular adaptations of the textbook within a language program and situates the course goals and assessments within the departmental context (see Graves 2000). The teacher interacts with the designated curriculum and, in the process, produces an interpretation of that designated curriculum (the intended curriculum), which corresponds to their understanding not only of the designated curriculum but also of how to put it into action (see Stein, Remillard and Smith 2007). The role of the teacher as agent, in the process of making the designated curriculum materialize in the classroom, introduces one level of specificity and variation in the intended curriculum and, finally, in the enactment of the curriculum. The importance of the intended curriculum is especially significant when most aspects of word knowledge are left to the learner's own discovery and to the teacher's discretion. Despite the activities' focus, the instructor's choices will influence vocabulary instruction (e.g., Folse 2010; Marcos Miguel 2017). The next section will delve into the theoretical and methodological frameworks used in the current study to analyze participants' teacher-intended curriculum.

1.2 Teacher cognition on vocabulary learning and instruction as a means to analyze the teacher-intended curriculum

According to Borg's (2006) model, teacher cognitions are shaped by the teacher's own schooling experiences and professional coursework. These previous experiences will be influenced and modified by the contextual factors associated with the school or institution where they teach. Interest in teacher cognition of vocabulary teaching has increased in the last few years. Studies in English L2 in Sweden and Spanish L2 in the U.S. have found that instructors do not have clear vocabulary goals in their classes (Bergström, Norberg and Nordlund 2021; Sánchez-Gutiérrez, Robles-García and Pérez Serrano 2022). Despite teachers being aware of the importance of vocabulary for communication, vocabulary learning is mostly an incidental endeavor as little time is devoted to explicit instruction (Bergström, Norberg and Nordlund 2021). These findings pointing to incidental vocabulary instruction are also consistent with observational studies which indicate that word formation, a fundamental part of word knowledge, is taught in an unplanned, incidental manner (Marcos Miguel 2017).

Furthermore, studies focusing on teacher cognition have also yielded insights with regard to the fundamental role of textbooks and course syllabi for Spanish L2 instructors in U.S. colleges and universities, especially for TAs, when choosing which vocabulary to teach (Allen 2008; Sánchez-Gutiérrez, Robles-García and Pérez Serrano 2022) as well as what activities to select (Marcos Miguel 2015). These studies indicate that teacher cognition provides a path to exploring how the teacher understands what needs to be taught and how. Therefore, Borg's framework for analyzing teacher cognition is applicable to this study of the teacher-intended curriculum, i.e. what the teacher intends to do with the designated curriculum in the classroom.

Previous research on teacher cognition of vocabulary instruction and learning has relied on interviews (e.g., Bergström, Norberg and Nordlund 2021; Sánchez-Gutiérrez, Robles-García and Pérez Serrano 2022) or the pairing of interviews with classroom observations to compare teachers' reported practices and their actual practices in the classroom (e.g., Marcos Miguel 2015, 2017; Zhang 2008). This study provides a novel approach: the interview is complemented with a task in which the participating TAs analyzed the vocabulary activities in a textbook chapter. This task gauged participants' degree of familiarity with both the TFAC, a tool for identifying activities that are most likely to facilitate vocabulary acquisition, and the WKL, a tool for identifying those aspects of word knowledge that are most likely to be learned in an activity. These tools will be further discussed in section 1.4.

1.3 Vocabulary instruction in Communicative Language Teaching (CLT) textbooks

CLT is the main approach to language teaching in Spanish L2 college-level courses in the U.S. This instructional framework is emphasized in L2 teaching methods courses (see Savignon 2007; Shrum and Glisan 2009). Although vocabulary instruction is not the primary focus of CLT (Zimmerman 1997), most textbooks used in methods courses discuss strategies for vocabulary presentation, practice, and retention (see Arnold 2013 for a compilation of textbooks used in these courses).

In CLT, textbooks are 'a way of influencing the quality of classroom interaction and language use' (Richards and Rodgers 2001: 153). However, according to these authors, CLT is open to interpretation concerning textbook design. Beginner and intermediate textbooks published in the U.S. generally organize their lessons around themes – such as the house, food, or leisure activities – and functional categories, such as expressing desires and preferences, extending invitations, or describing daily routines. Thus, context is established through themes and functional categories.

Activities in a textbook based or inspired by CLT range from *mechanical* – e.g., substitution drills – to *meaningful* – i.e., activities in which students 'are required to make meaningful choices when carrying out practice' (Richards 2006: 16) with controlled language – to *communicative* – i.e., activities in which students 'us(e) the language within a real communicative context' (16). These *meaningful* and *communicative* classroom activities are meant to be carried out in pairs or in groups. Following this progression of activities, Spanish L2 textbooks generally scaffold students' ability to engage with open-ended activities, such as role-play, by first presenting a series of relevant closed activities, such as matching activities, fill-in-the-blank, multiple choice, and true/false formats (e.g., López-Jiménez 2014; Marcos Miguel and Cubas Mora 2017).

The selection of lexical items included in these textbooks is usually based on 'subjective assessments of the usefulness of words' (Zimmerman 1997: 14) rather than lexical frequencies (see Godev 2009; Lipinski 2010; Sánchez-Gutiérrez, Marcos Miguel and Olsen 2018). Analyses of the aspects of word knowledge required by textbook vocabulary activities suggest that the main goal of textbook vocabulary instruction is to facilitate students' recognition of the link between form and meaning (Brown 2011 in English L2; Neary-Sundquist 2015, and Retelj 2014 in German L2; Zyzik and Marqués-Pascual, this volume, and Sánchez-Gutiérrez, Robles García and Alins Breda 2021 in Spanish L2).

1.4 The Technique Feature Analysis Checklist (TFAC) and the Word Knowledge List (WKL)

The Technique Feature Analysis Checklist (TFAC), based on Nation and Webb (2011), identifies those components of an activity that facilitate vocabulary acquisition. The TFAC is formulated as a series of yes/no questions that assess the extent to which an activity or technique exhibits the following five criteria, which have been deemed effective in promoting vocabulary learning: (a) motivation, (b) noticing, (c) retrieval, (d) generation, and (e) retention (Nation and Webb 2011). Each "yes" answer on the TFAC is worth 1 point, for a maximum score of 18 points. The authors maintain that tasks with a higher score are more effective at promoting vocabulary learning. Studies that have evaluated activities with the TFAC support this assertion (see Hu and Nassaji 2016).

The TFAC has primarily been used in research to analyze isolated activities that learners completed on their own, such as "[creating] flashcards [and] word lists, [completing] fill-in-the-blanks, and writing words in sentences and compositions" (Webb, Yanagisawa and Uchihara 2020: 716). This checklist has also been used to assess activities within Spanish L2 graded readers (Alins Breda 2021). Clearly, TFAC can also be used as a pedagogical tool to help instructors choose textbook activities that are most likely to be effective in promoting vocabulary acquisition; therefore, we chose to include the TFAC in the present study. Table 1 presents a simplified version of the TFAC that is better suited to use with textbook activities since some of the original TFAC questions do not apply when activities are organized and sequenced within a textbook chapter (see Marcos Miguel and Cubas Mora 2017). As it is still not clear what criteria can be more decisive for vocabulary learning, our recommendation is for instructors to include a variety of activities with different scores and distribution of scores when sequencing a vocabulary lesson.

Table 1: Simplified TFAC list (based on Nation and Webb 2011) (Marcos Miguel and Cubas Mora 2017: 37–38).

Criteria	Scores
Motivation	
Does the activity motivate learning?	(0/1)
Do the learners select the words?	(0/1)
Noticing	
Does the activity focus attention on the target words?	(0/1)
Does the activity raise awareness of new vocabulary learning?	(0/1)
Does the activity involve negotiation?	(0/1)

Table 1 (continued)

Criteria	Scores
Retrieval	
Does the activity involve retrieval of the word? *(Either meaning in L1 or form in L2 is provided; students must supply the other element.)*	(0/1)
Is it productive retrieval? *(Meaning in L1 is provided; students must supply the form in L2.)*	(0/1)
Is it recall? *(Students must supply L2 form directly; there are no options from which to choose.)*	(0/1)
Generation	
Is it productive? *(Students must use the word in a new linguistic context.)*	(0/1)
Retention	
Does the activity ensure successful linking of form and meaning?	(0/1)
Final Total Score	0–10/10

The adjustments in Table 1 were made to align the content of TFAC with the vocabulary component within the structure of Spanish L2 textbooks, which typically contain sequenced activities for explicit vocabulary practice within a chapter (see Marcos Miguel and Cubas Mora 2017). For instance, in *motivation*, the question "is there a clear vocabulary learning goal?" was removed from the simplified list because most vocabulary activities in Spanish textbooks are found in a section that explicitly targets vocabulary learning. In *retrieval*, the questions "are there multiple retrievals of each word?" and "is there spacing between retrievals?" were eliminated, as these questions can be difficult to assess without a digitized version of the textbook and the necessary software expertise to search for each token. In *generation*, the questions "does the activity involve generative use?" and "is there a marked change that involves the use of other words?" were also deleted. The former was deleted because most activities in textbooks include generative use, i.e., "meeting a word used in a new way" (Nation and Webb 2011: 9), and the latter because it implies a level of detailed analysis that may not be necessary for instructors. For *retention*, the two questions about "instantiation" and "imaging" were deleted because both may depend on the student rather than the activity. Furthermore, given that Spanish textbooks typically organize chapters around a common theme, the question "does the activity involve interference?" was also eliminated. That is, these three *retention* questions provide little information when analyzing Spanish L2 textbooks.

In addition to the TFAC, the Word Knowledge List (WKL), based on Nation (2001) and Brown (2011), can be used to analyze the aspects of word knowledge addressed in a vocabulary learning activity. These aspects of word knowledge correspond to the notion of *vocabulary depth*, which is based on the understanding that knowing a word is more than the ability to link form and meaning. The concept of word knowledge recognizes the different aspects of a word's form, meaning, and use (see Nation 2001). Brown (2011) reformulated Nation's WKL to facilitate the evaluation of textbook activities. Whereas Nation's (2001) list focuses on individual words, Brown (2011) proposes a way to evaluate an entire vocabulary activity. For this reason, we have adopted Brown's version with minor modifications for its application to the evaluation of an activity within a sequence (see Table 2).

Table 2: WKL (adapted from Brown 2011).

spoken form	Activities that draw attention to the spoken form of the word and its connection with the written form.
written form	Activities that draw attention to the spelling of the word.
word parts	Activities focused on the different forms of a word.
form-meaning	Activities focused on recalling form from meaning or vice versa.
polysemy (concept-referents)	Activities focused on comparing meanings of the same word form.
word associations	Activities focused on the different meaning relationships between items.
grammatical functions	Activities focused on the grammatical specifications of a word.
collocations	Activities that draw attention to the combinatorial possibilities of a word.
stylistics/dialectal registers/frequency	Activities focused on contextual features of words.

2 Research questions

This chapter explores two questions:
1. How does the approach to vocabulary instruction promoted in the designated curriculum of beginning (1st and 2nd semester) and intermediate (3rd and 4th semester) Spanish courses correspond to the criteria identified in the TFAC and WKL?

2. How does the approach to vocabulary instruction promoted in the teacher-intended curriculum of beginning (1st and 2nd semester) and intermediate (3rd and 4th semester) Spanish courses correspond to the criteria identified in the TFAC and WKL?

These analyses complement a previous quantitative study of the same participants using the TFAC and the WKL to score a set of vocabulary activities (see Marcos Miguel and Cubas Mora 2017).

3 Methodology

This case study follows a mixed-methods design by combining a quantitative analysis of textbooks and syllabus (see section 3.2) and a qualitative analysis of seven TA interviews (see section 3.3).

3.1 Context

This study focuses on the first- and second-year language sequence at a U.S. university. The courses in this sequence include first through fourth semester Spanish (two elementary level and two intermediate level courses) and one accelerated elementary course combining first and second semester geared to false beginners. To fulfill language requirements for the university, students must test out of the second semester of Spanish or successfully complete either the second semester course or the accelerated course. Students who take the intermediate-level courses are those who plan to continue with their language studies, completing a major, minor or an area studies certificate.

The textbooks for these elementary- and intermediate-level courses were chosen by the language program coordinators (LPCs) (see Table 3). One common syllabus for each course was prepared by the LPCs and distributed to the instructors. Most of the instructors in this program were TAs completing their doctoral studies in literature or linguistics.

3.2 The designated curriculum: Textbooks and syllabi

3.2.1 Textbook sampling and activities analysis

A chapter was selected from each of the three textbooks used in the program. In addition, a chapter was selected for analysis from a textbook that the researchers considered to be well-known among experienced instructors. The selected chapters in the elementary textbooks (*Mosaicos, Puentes,* and *Vistas*) introduced vocabulary related to housing, and the selected chapter in the intermediate textbook (*Enfoques*) introduced vocabulary related to employment. In each chapter analysis, only activities with an explicit vocabulary-learning goal were included. Activities were not included if vocabulary learning was not the explicit goal of the activity and/or if knowledge of thematic vocabulary was not needed to complete the activity.

The activities in the chapters were examined using the simplified version of the TFAC (see Table 1). To analyze aspects of word knowledge, both researchers used Brown's (2011) adapted WKL (see Table 2). The researchers first scored the activities independently and subsequently cross-checked their scores to reach full agreement. The goal of these discussions was to ensure that the researchers as coders understood the meaning of each category in the same way. This scoring process is similar to the one described by Zyzik and Marqués-Pascual (this volume). Table 3 includes the textbooks analyzed and the semesters in which they are used.

Table 3: Textbooks by course.

Course	Textbook
1st and 2nd semester (beginning courses, 1st year)	*Mosaicos*
Accelerated course (1st and 2nd semester together in a semester) (beginning course)	*Puentes*
3rd and 4th (intermediate courses, 2nd year)	*Enfoques*
Additional textbook (designed for beginning courses)	*Vistas* (see 4.1.1)

3.2.2 Syllabi sampling and analysis

The five syllabi used in the basic language sequence courses were analyzed (see Table 3). All passages in the syllabi that explicitly referred to vocabulary instruction and assessment were copied into an Excel spreadsheet and classified according to the questions in the TFAC that they address (see Table 1). Next, the same process was done for those passages of the syllabus that made explicit reference to the practice and/or assessment of word knowledge (Nation 2001), as measured by the elements listed in Table 2.

3.3 The intended curriculum: TAs' perspectives

3.3.1 TA sampling

The target group was TAs who were teaching or had recently taught basic language courses in the program. Having received IRB approval, the researchers reached out to potential participants directly. An email message was sent out explaining that the researchers were conducting a study on approaches to vocabulary instruction. Seven TAs were interviewed. Pseudonyms are given in Table 4.

Table 4: Participants' profiles.

Participant	1st language	Time teaching	Graduate studies
George	English	1 year	Literature
Marta	Spanish	1 year	Literature
Elena	Portuguese	1 year	Literature
Paco	Spanish	3 years	Literature
Lola	Spanish	3 years	Literature
Anthony	English	5 years	Linguistics
Mary	English	5 years	Linguistics

3.3.2 TA Interviews

An interview was carried out in Spanish, English, or both depending on the TA's choice. The interview started with a set of questions focused on the participant's perspectives and experiences with vocabulary teaching and learning as well as their understanding of the role of textbooks in classroom instruction (see Appendix). Information was gathered about the participant's education, professional training, experiences in connection to teaching, and beliefs and practices about vocabulary instruction and the textbook.

The interview also included a task in which the TAs analyzed nine explicit vocabulary activities from a chapter of an elementary Spanish textbook (Blanco and Donley 2012) using TFAC and WKL. The use of this task as part of the interview ensured explicit discussion on what guides TAs' decisions of vocabulary activities and aspects of word knowledge to teach. Moreover, the inclusion of standardized tools (the TFAC and the WKL) enabled us to compare responses not only across participants but also with our analyses of both the textbooks and the syllabi. By introducing the task in the second part of the interview, we ensured that the TAs had the opportunity to refer to the topics they valued more without being primed by the TFAC or the WKL. Figure 1 outlines the interview process.

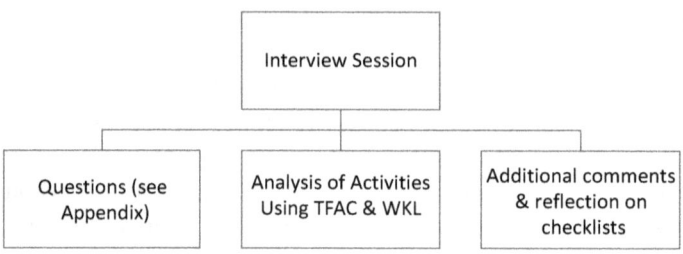

Figure 1: Data gathering process during TAs' interviews.

During the interview process, TAs analyzed vocabulary activities from the chapter dealing with houses in *Vistas*. The vocabulary section occupies the first three pages of the chapter, starting with an image of a house with furniture and other decorative elements. This section includes word labels, a glossary of new words, and a text box drawing attention to lexical variation. While vocabulary activities in this chapter incorporate activities with a variety of scores in TFAC (see Figure 2), most activities focus explicitly on only one aspect of word knowledge: linking form and meaning (Figure 3). During the interview, the activities were discussed in the order in which they appear in the book. Even though the chapter did not cover all aspects of the TFAC and WKL, the process of analyzing textbook activities served the purpose of engaging participants in conversation about the qualities of effective vocabulary activities and the aspects of word knowledge that should be taught.

3.3.3 Analysis of TAs' interviews

The interviews were transcribed verbatim. As a first step, the researchers read the transcripts and identified excerpts related to the following aspects of the interview: (a) participants' experience as L2 vocabulary learners, (b) participants' experience learning about vocabulary teaching in their training, (c) their beliefs about vocabulary learning and teaching, (d) their practices with regard to vocabulary teaching, (e) difficulties arising from the use of TFAC and WKL, and (f) general comments about the checklists. Categories (a) to (d) were based on Borg's framework (2006) of teacher cognition, assuming beliefs and practices to be influenced by both professional development and learning experiences.

Then, each researcher independently took notes identifying the main themes in these excerpts (see Ryan and Bernard 2003). After this initial analysis, the authors exchanged their transcript selections and notes and identified recurrent themes. Through this process, the following themes were identified as the areas of vocabulary instruction and learning most relevant to the TAs' intended curriculum: 1) linking form and meaning, 2) interaction, 3) context, 4) emotional factors, 5) adaptation of textbook activities, and 6) scaffolding. In brief, their process of exploration and discussion through several meetings followed the usual steps in analyzing and interpreting interviews as qualitative data (see Cresswell 2012). Consistent with this process, the authors reached an agreement after discussion of their preliminary analysis. This process ensured consistency of meaning between the coders (see Madill, Jordan and Shirley 2000).

4 Results

4.1 Results: The designated curriculum

4.1.1 Textbook activities' scoring results

Figure 2 shows the total number of activities included in each analyzed chapter (one chapter per textbook). Each textbook chapter is represented by a different color. Each dot represents an activity and its score according to the TFAC. For example, the first dot in purple represents an activity in *Enfoques* with the prompt "Listen to the ad about *creditinstant* and decide if the sentences are true or false. Correct the false ones." This activity scored only four points. The eighth dot in purple represents an activity in the same chapter with the prompt "What do you think? In pairs, answer the questions and share your opinion with the class," which received nine points.

To complement Figure 2, Table 5 summarizes activity scores, presented as averages for each textbook.

Each chapter includes a different number of vocabulary activities. Activities in all textbooks exhibit a wide range of scores, from 3 to 9. *Mosaicos* has more activities than the rest, and these activities include a variety of scores. In contrast, the intermediate textbook chapter, *Enfoques*, has the smallest number of activities, and the relatively low scores of the activities in *Enfoques* can likely be explained by the smaller number of open-ended activities in the chapter. Meanwhile, the vocabulary activities

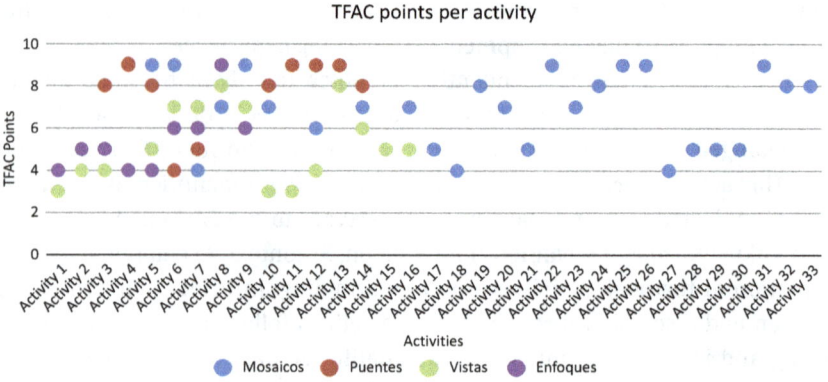

Figure 2: TFAC scores per activity.

Table 5: TFAC scores: Descriptive statistics of analyzed activities.

	Level of textbook	Number of activities analyzed	Average activity score	SD	range
Mosaicos	Beginner (1st and 2nd semester)	33	7	1.9	(4–9)
Puentes	Beginner (Accelerated 2nd semester)	14	7.1	2	(4–9)
Vistas	Beginner (1st and 2nd semester)	16	5.2	1.8	(3–8)
Enfoques	Intermediate (3rd and 4th semester)	9	5.4	1.6	(4–9)

in the accelerated elementary textbook, *Puentes*, has a similar average score to *Mosaicos* (Table 5), although with a smaller variety of scores overall (Figure 2).

Table 6 provides the raw number of possible points for each chapter. As the number of possible points varies according to the criteria (e.g., *retention*=1 possible point; *noticing*=3 possible points) and each chapter had a different number of activities (see Figure 2), the denominator in the ratio varies according to the number of points of the criteria and the number of activities in the chapter. Half of the activities across textbooks included at least four criteria. The fifth criterion – *retention* – was present in only five activities.

Figure 3 shows the percentage of activities that practice each aspect of word knowledge. Although an activity can target more than one aspect, most activities across textbook chapters focus on the same aspects. Activities that link form and meaning are the most prevalent, while other aspects of word knowledge, such as word parts or collocations, are barely addressed.

Table 6: Points by criteria in TFAC.

	Motivation (2 points)	Noticing (3 points)	Retrieval (3 points)	Generation (1 point)	Retention (1 point)
Mosaicos (33 activities)	55/66	79/99	73/99	17/33	5/33
Puentes (14 activities)	24/28	36/42	31/42	9/16	0/16
Vistas (16 activities)	15/32	22/48	39/48	7/16	0/16
Enfoques (9 activities)	9/18	20/27	12/27	4/9	0/9

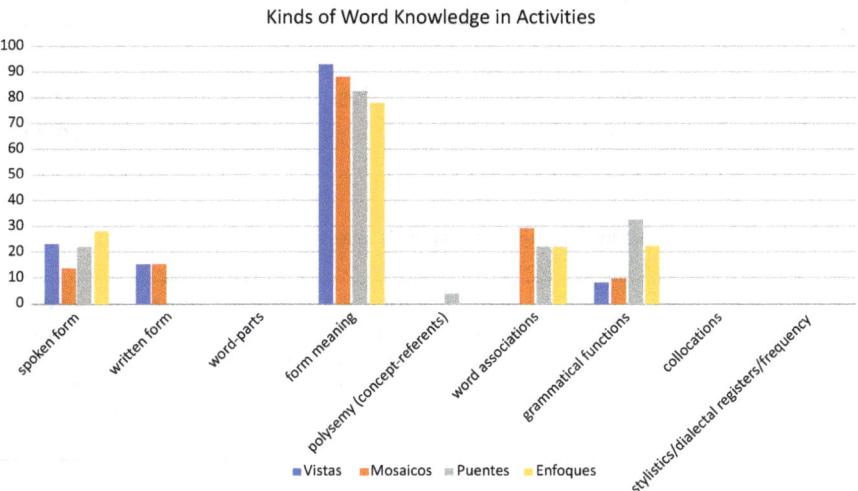

Figure 3: Percentage of word knowledge practice in activities.

4.1.2 Syllabi scores

The syllabi analyzed for this study included information about vocabulary in two main sections: the description of the assessments, and the rubrics. Additionally, the syllabus of the first-semester course included a brief mention of vocabulary in the learning outcomes section.

Exams and compositions were the only assessments in the syllabus that included vocabulary learning in their description. Table 7 shows the TFAC scores for these forms of assessment. The characteristics of these assessments did not differ across levels.

Table 7: TFAC Scores for Assessments in the Syllabi.

Assessments	Syllabus section	TFAC Score (Maximum score 10)
Speaking test: Interview	speaking test, interview (description of interview)	9.5
	speaking test, interview (assessment, instructions)	9.5
Composition	compositions (description)	8.5
Exams	midterm (description)	8
	final exam (description)	8

Table 7 shows that these assessments had a high score on the TFAC. When considering TFAC criteria separately, all criteria appeared relatively well-represented in these assessments, as shown in Table 8.

Table 8: Descriptive statistics by criteria in TFAC (syllabi's assessments).

	Motivation 2 points (M, SD)	Noticing 3 points (M, SD)	Retrieval 3 points (M, SD)	Generation 1 point (M, SD)	Retention 1 point (M, SD)
All three assessments (speaking test, compositions, exams)	1.3 (.27)	2.6 (.55)	3 (0)	1 (0)	.8 (.45)

Table 9 shows the specific aspects of word knowledge that were emphasized in the designated curriculum; namely, in the rubrics included in the syllabus. At least five aspects were present in each rubric, and most aspects were included in two rubrics, except for collocations and frequency. These two aspects of word knowledge were not mentioned in any of the rubrics.

Three aspects were consistently mentioned in the rubrics: vocabulary size (present in the syllabus in terms such as "range", "varied", and "rich"), accuracy, and appropriateness of register/style. These aspects overlap with the concept of

Table 9: Number of WKL aspects included in the rubrics.

Aspect	Speaking test (Interview rubric)	Speaking test (Debate rubric)	Composition (Rubric)	Composition (Symbols to correct)	Number of rubrics with a WKL aspect
Pronunciation	1	1	0	0	2
Spelling	0	0	1	1	2
Word form	1	1	1	1	4
Meaning	1	1	1	1	4
Polysemy (concept and referents)	0	0	0	1	1
Word associations	0	0	0	1	1
Grammatical functions	1	0	1	1	3
Collocations	0	0	0	0	0
Stylistics/dialectal registers	1	1	1	0	3
Frequency	0	0	0	0	0
Total number of criteria (10)	5	4	5	6	NA
Average number of aspects in all rubrics (10)			5		2

vocabulary size, but not necessarily with the concept of depth (see introduction chapter in this volume for further discussion on these terms).

4.2 Results: Teacher-intended curriculum

As noted in 3.3.3, the researchers identified six main themes related to vocabulary instruction and learning that seemed to be most relevant in revealing the TAs' intended curriculum. These themes are as follows: 1) linking form and meaning, 2) interaction, 3) context, 4) emotional factors, 5) adaptation of textbook activities, and 6) scaffolding.

4.2.1 Linking form and meaning

All participants were aware of the importance of linking form and meaning in vocabulary instruction and learning. They conceptualized this linking process as *visualization* or as a combination of *visualization* and *memorization*. The final product of linking form and meaning was always seen as positive, i.e., *knowing the word*. However, the process involved in achieving that goal could be considered both positive and negative. Whereas most of the teachers viewed rote memorization in a negative light, Mary had a positive reaction to the first vocabulary activity analyzed during her interview, noting that "your mind wasn't thinking that you were memorizing". Figure 4 displays teachers' understanding of the process of linking form and meaning.

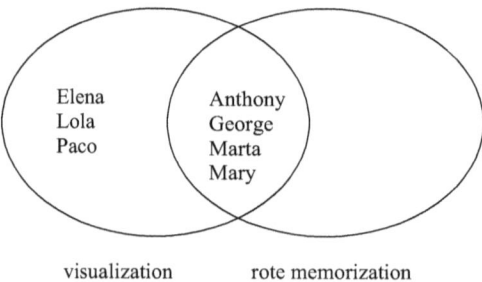

Figure 4: Linking form and meaning in vocabulary teaching and learning.

The TAs recognized the role of the textbook in this process as providing the corpus of target words for each textbook theme; that is, the words that needed to be memorized and visualized. *Visualization* was understood as an aid in the learning process achieved by presenting realia as well as illustrations and photographs in PowerPoint slides or textbook activities. For all participants, the use of pictures had been emphasized in their CLT training.

4.2.2 Interaction

The conceptualization of this theme follows from the *Interaction Hypothesis*, i.e., negotiation through interaction facilitates language acquisition by 'potentially drawing attention to linguistic problems and leading them to notice the gaps between their production and the target language' (Gass and Mackey 2006: 4). Although only Mary explicitly used the term *interaction*, a number of comments in the interviews were linked to this idea, i.e., interacting with peers, teachers, and materials to learn. Nevertheless, some of the participants also asked for clarification about the meaning of *negotiation*, which was brought up in the question *'does the activity involve negotiation?'* (see Table 1). TAs' views are displayed in Figure 5.

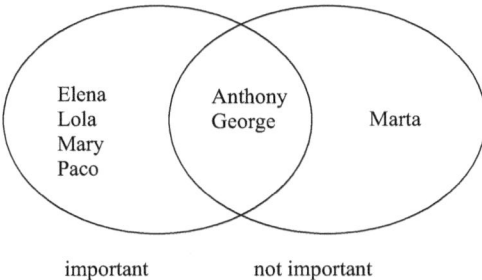

Figure 5: Interaction in vocabulary teaching and learning.

Most participants pointed out the importance of partner activities – such as creating a skit or a dialogue, or discussing a topic with another student – as a way to foster vocabulary acquisition. In the same vein, they also found interaction with the teacher and the whole class to be very positive. The TAs represented in the middle of Figure 5, Anthony and George, did not make any explicit comment that could be clearly connected with their perspective on the importance of the theme. None of the TAs explicitly mentioned the textbook as an instrument for facilitating this interaction process.

4.2.3 Context

Context was one of the most complex terms that repeatedly appeared in the interviews. Two main definitions emerged: 1) context as the theme of the textbook chapter and/or a subsection, and 2) context as the situation of a reading or speaking task (see Figure 6). Context as a theme implies that words related, for example, to the beach, the house, or the school are taught together. Context as a reading/speaking situation refers to the whole dialogue or text, i.e., to a situation with its pragmatic rules. Supplying words in context was considered to be a way of ensuring that students would notice new words.

All participants agreed that words should not be taught in isolation. As George explained, "When you have the actual ability to discuss it with some kind of context instead of it just being 'this vocabulary word, this vocabulary word' I think it is better." Elena also brought an example of her own learning of a heritage language, "Entonces yo más o menos memorizaba las frases y no los vocabularios sueltos. [. . .]

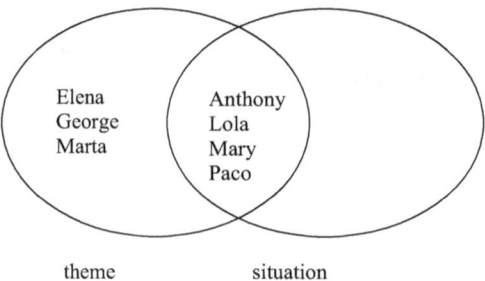

Figure 6: Context in vocabulary teaching and learning.

Entonces creo que era un poquito mejor porque al menos estaba en un contexto [. . .] estudiábamos creo que un texto por semana [. . .] los vocabularios estaban más o menos contextualizados." [Then, I kind of memorized the sentences and not isolated words. [. . .] I believe it was a little bit better because it was at least in context [. . .] we studied, I think, a text per week [. . .] the words were more or less contextualized [in that text].]

Overall, the TAs recognized that contextualized vocabulary teaching had been emphasized in their CLT training. No participant pointed out any need or inclination to address themes or clusters of words different from or in addition to those included in the textbook. On occasion, the term *context* appeared to be a buzzword picked up from their training courses, something that these TAs knew was appropriate to mention in a discussion on vocabulary instruction. The concept also came up while discussing the simplified TFAC (see Table 1): the phrase "linguistic context" appears within the *generation* criteria with the indication that productive generation implies "*Using the word in a new linguistic context.*" Still, the TAs did not explain why their notion of context, either theme or situation, could facilitate vocabulary learning. In brief, context was used as equivalent to theme, i.e., as the theme of the chapter, or to situation, i.e., talking about learning a word in a dialogue, in a song, and/or from a text (aural or written) where the learners had background knowledge. Both notions were associated with effective vocabulary learning and, as such, considered to be important for classroom practice.

4.2.4 Emotional factors

Participants' decisions of what textbook activities to include in their lesson plans were dependent on their own preferences as well as on other emotional factors, i.e., entertainment level of the activity or the activity's relevance to learners' interests or daily lives. Figure 7 shows the elements encompassed by the term *emotional factors*.

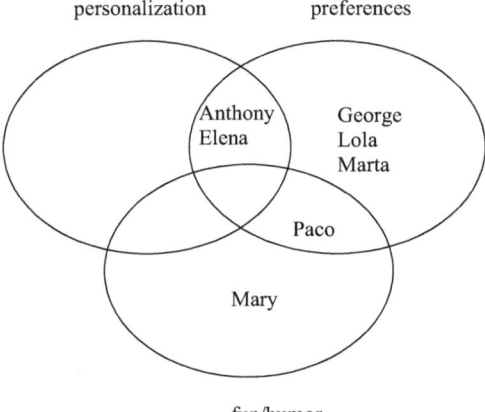

Figure 7: Emotional factors in vocabulary teaching and learning.

Teacher preferences rested mostly on the participants' previous experiences with similar activities, both as teachers and as learners. The term *personalization* related to the students, such as whether the textbook activity was relevant to the students' personal lives. For example, Elena pointed out that activities about chores at home are not conducive to successful learning because such activities are disconnected from the daily experience of university students living in dorms.

Several teachers also discussed the importance of including *humor* and *fun* activities to increase learners' motivation. Such activities were incorporated into the class primarily through the use of external materials. Criticism of the textbook stemmed from the perception that textbooks contain few personalized and entertaining activities. This lack was considered to be a shortcoming intrinsic to the use of any textbook in teaching vocabulary.

4.2.5 Adaptation of textbook activities

Participants described three different behaviors in regard to the adaptation of textbook activities: 1) they used textbook activities with some modifications, 2) they used textbook activities without any modifications, and 3) they used their own activities. Figure 8 reflects the information participants provided regarding adaptations.

As the intersecting circles in Figure 8 show, these behaviors were not mutually exclusive. Teachers believed that modifying activities and using their own activities were positive practices. Examples of commonly used modifications included pre-

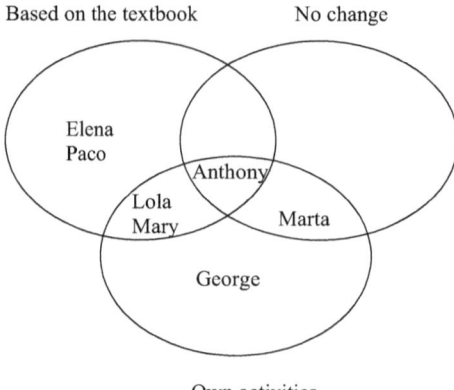

Figure 8: Adaptation of textbook activities for vocabulary instruction.

senting the vocabulary in a PowerPoint or creating a new activity based on an existing textbook activity.

For example, Mary pointed out that her activities are "Not directly from the book but we'll do something similar. I use that to give me ideas [. . .]". The lack of modifications was either due to lack of time for preparation or because they considered the activities suitable, as Anthony acknowledged.

Participants concurred that the textbook determined the vocabulary that had to be taught and the time needed for teaching it explicitly. They reported that they adhered to the textbook in this respect. Consequently, in this regard, the intended curriculum aimed at following the designated curriculum.

4.2.6 Scaffolding

The sequencing of activities in the classroom was one of the most revealing issues to emerge from the interviews. Except for Marta, all participants discussed this topic, which we labeled *scaffolding*, since this was the term some of them explicitly used.

According to these TAs, learners must start with guided activities involving *motivation* and *noticing* before moving onto open-ended activities with a focus on *retrieval*. A vocabulary practice session should not start with an open-ended activity that requires knowledge of many new words. The idea of scaffolding is grounded in the fact that an extremely demanding task will be counterproductive and hinder vocabulary learning. The concept of scaffolding was also applied to the sequence of activities within a chapter and to the whole textbook sequence. Figure 9 shows the participants' understanding of how scaffolding should work. It encompasses: 1) the order of activities presented in the classroom, 2) the activities that are chosen as

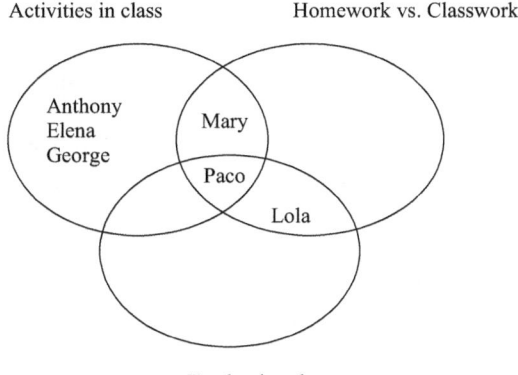

Figure 9: Scaffolding in vocabulary teaching and learning.

homework versus those for classroom use, and 3) textbook sequencing of vocabulary throughout the chapters.

While not all participants provided detail about how to scaffold activities, they recognized the need to do so when dealing with vocabulary instruction. Mary offered the most methodological definition. She explained the steps for scaffolding vocabulary instruction up to the last step, production: "Starting out with that where it's just *recognition*, going to like *a yes-no question, going to a choice* and then finally getting *the repetitions*, so they are hearing it multiple times."

Mary also pointed out that these steps came from her teacher training and her own language learning. Most of the participants commented on scaffolding after having used the TFAC and WKL to assess textbook vocabulary activities and rank those activities from least to most effective. That is, participants did not consider scaffolding to be a main issue until they had to decide which activities were more conducive to successful learning as part of the interview.

5 Discussion

Content analysis of the textbook chapters and course syllabi was used to answer the first research question: *How does the approach to vocabulary instruction promoted in the designated curriculum of beginning (1st and 2nd semester) and intermediate (3rd and 4th semester) Spanish courses correspond to the criteria identified in the TFAC and WKL?* All four textbooks had a similar structure and promoted similar practices. These results are consistent with Cubillos' (2014) analysis of U.S.-published textbooks. Similar to Zyzik and Marqués-Pascual (this volume), the elementary-level textbooks placed greater emphasis on explicit vocabulary instruction, as reflected in the higher number of activities, than the intermediate textbook.

In terms of the qualities measured by the TFAC, the activities in the four textbooks covered a range of scores, with four points being the most common score (see Figure 2). *Puentes*, probably because of its focus on high-beginners, offered more open-ended activities, which is reflected in the high TFAC scores of most activities. It is interesting to note that *Mosaicos*, while having a similar average score in Table 5, was the best at sequencing, since it included activities that scaffolded vocabulary instruction and clearly integrated vocabulary instruction with other non-vocabulary focused activities. Thus, similar scores in TFAC in a chapter can point to different sequencing configurations.

TFAC points were relatively evenly divided among *motivation, noticing, retrieval,* and *generation* (see Table 6), which suggests that the textbooks connect with the TFAC criteria. However, despite the focus on form and meaning, few activities ensure successful linking of form and meaning (i.e., *retention*), as many activities could be completed without necessarily having linked the form and meaning of the target words. One difficulty when interpreting these scores is that TFAC does not suggest an order of points. That is, most research has compared activities with different scores in isolation, but no consideration has been made in the research as to how these activities can be best arranged in sequential order within the lesson.

In terms of word knowledge (see Figure 3), activities fostered recognition and production, emphasizing the link between form and meaning. Similar to the findings of Neary-Sundquist (2015) and Brown (2011), our content analysis indicated that the practice of grammatical functions was the second most commonly emphasized aspect of word knowledge. Because of the chapters' thematic nature, some practice with word associations was also included: activities requiring students to organize words into categories appeared occasionally in the vocabulary practice sections. The limited focus on aspects of word knowledge in these four textbooks is consistent with other analysis of Spanish L2 textbooks (e.g., Zyzik and Marqués-Pascual this volume; Sánchez-Gutiérrez, Robles García and Alins Breda 2021).

The syllabi, like the textbooks, emphasized instruction of form and meaning but also included reflection on vocabulary use by focusing on different registers. There was no change in the assessments across the four semesters, i.e., learners were expected to demonstrate mastery of the same aspects of word knowledge in all four semesters of the course sequence. Most aspects of the WKL were present in two of the four rubrics (see Table 9) included in the syllabi. Whereas all assessments focused on word form and meaning, no mention was made of collocational knowledge or frequency in any assessment. Interestingly, the syllabi, specifically the assessment and rubrics sections, included more information on word knowledge than the textbook activities. Moreover, the TFAC score of the assessments was high (see Table 7). In brief, the designated curriculum (when considering both elements, i.e., the textbooks and syllabi) scored well on both the TFAC and the WKL. While some aspects of vocabulary instruction deemed relevant in vocabulary research were omitted, the vocabulary activities and assessments of the designated curriculum were found to be largely effective in promoting vocabulary acquisition at both the elementary and intermediate levels.

Interviews with participating TAs were used to answer the second research question: *How does the approach to vocabulary instruction promoted in the teacher-intended curriculum of beginning (1st and 2nd semester) and intermediate (3rd and 4th semester) Spanish courses correspond to the criteria identified in the TFAC and WKL?* The interviews revealed five primary themes: 1) linking form and meaning, 2) interaction, 3) context, 4) emotional factors, 5) adaptation of textbook activities, and 6) scaffolding. The TAs' intended curriculum was unfolded through these themes, especially with regard to their plans for adapting and scaffolding the textbook activities in their lessons. Although participants occasionally held different perspectives than those embedded in the textbook and course syllabi, they generally described an intended curriculum that was consistent with the designated curriculum.

While some of the themes (*interaction, context,* and *scaffolding*) came from participants' training experiences, others (*emotional factors* and *adaptation*) came from their own experiences as learners and practitioners. In particular, *linking form and meaning* seems to be a basic tenet that the TAs extracted from their own experiences as L2 learners. This finding is consistent with the research on teachers' cognition about vocabulary teaching/learning (e.g., Bergström, Norberg and Nordlund 2021; Niu and Andrews 2012).

The TAs showed some degree of recognition/familiarity of the criteria from the TFAC and the WKL that were reflected in the textbooks and syllabi. The interview themes revealed all five TFAC criteria: *motivation, noticing, retrieval, generation,* and *retention. Retention,* i.e., *linking form and meaning,* appears as the main goal of vocabulary instruction. The interview theme of *interaction* indicated that TAs valued the goals of *noticing* and *retention.* TAs' reflections on *context* suggest several constructs taken into consideration in TFAC, namely *noticing, retrieval, generation,* and *motivation.* All instances of *emotional factors* elucidated how important the criterion of *motivation* was for these TAs. Although the idea of *scaffolding* is not part of the TFAC, since each activity is analyzed separately, the way these TAs approached *scaffolding* illustrates the concepts of *motivation, noticing,* and *retention.*

In terms of the WKL, the interview themes only revealed that the concept of *linking form and meaning* was the main area raised in TAs' interviews. No other aspects of word knowledge were mentioned. A reason for this could be that since beginner- and intermediate-level textbooks, as a general rule, devote limited to no attention to aspects of word knowledge other than linking form and meaning, these aspects do not figure in the teachers' cognition. This absence of practice of vocabulary depth in the textbooks (e.g., Brown 2011) may also contribute to the teachers' apparent lack of awareness of these areas of word knowledge.

Contextual factors in the classroom and teachers' previous experiences as both learners and teachers shape their opinions and help them understand their intended curriculum (Borg 2006). For example, the *emotional factors* theme that emerged from the interviews revealed that TAs critically examined the textbook from their own experiences, noting that vocabulary activities were not consistently relevant for learners. However, the TAs accepted the textbook "as is" regarding vocabulary selection, and the aspects of word knowledge presented. With the exception of more experienced TAs such as Mary, participants did not discuss their training on vocabulary instruction in detail.

Within the designated and intended curriculum model, students' voices are heard through teachers' interpretations of what they like and dislike; as a result, students' opinions influence the TAs' intended curriculum. For example, under the theme *adaptation of activities*, the TAs consistently indicated that they modified textbook activities or created new textbook-based activities in response to students' preferences and patterns of classroom engagement. Nevertheless, these interview findings suggest that TAs typically align their intended curriculum with the designated curriculum, i.e., they rely on the textbook, while recognizing the need to create an intended curriculum that appeals to their students.

In summary, the participants considered vocabulary selection to be the prerogative of the textbook. As textbooks focus on explicit instruction, most of the instructors accordingly planned for explicit instruction rather than considering the role of implicit learning. Finally, in alignment with the textbook's content, these instructors limited vocabulary instruction to the goal of linking form and meaning. Nevertheless, all instructors agreed that they carried out textbook adaptations (see McGrath 2013), e.g., adding visual support to the practice or skipping activities from the textbook. Still, the adaptations were made within the boundaries of the designated curriculum.

Some scholars have claimed that novice teachers are not helped by the dismissive stance towards textbooks that is sometimes found in teacher education, as beginning teachers are still unprepared when they enter the classroom or lack the necessary experience to develop their own curriculum and materials (Ball and Feiman-Nemser 1988; Hutchinson and Torres 1994; Richards 2001). This lack of critical discussion, combined with novice teachers' limited knowledge about research on vocabulary instruction, makes it difficult for TAs to improve on the instruction offered by the textbook. Therefore, given the close alignment of the designated and the intended curriculum revealed in this study, it could be unrealistic to expect more novelty in vocabulary instruction by novice instructors. Further research should explore whether this is also the case with experienced instructors.

Moreover, future research can analyze L2 vocabulary teaching in a more ecologically-based environment, so that relevant recommendations can be made to L2 practitioners about how to use their textbooks more effectively. Further research on vocabulary instruction requires analysis of in-class use of vocabulary activities, assessment materials, i.e., teachers' enactment of the curriculum. Additionally, further studies should consider the role of an instructor's individual characteristics. For example, Mary seemed to be more informed than the rest of the participants, which we attributed to the fact that she had more teaching experience than the other participants. Additionally, she was a linguistics graduate student and a non-native speaker. Further studies should explore the effects of a TA's L1 (Spanish or another language) as well as the effects of the PhD program (literature vs. linguistics) in which the TA is enrolled.

With regard to the designated curriculum, an analysis of textbooks from other publishers using the TFAC and the WKL could provide further insights into vocabulary instruction. It is also important to keep in mind that we adapted the TFAC and the WKL to analyze activities in a chapter and, thus, to recognize their usefulness for vocabulary learning within that context. One reviewer pointed out that our operationalization of concept-referents to tally whether an activity included reflection/practice of polysemic words may differ from other analyses (e.g., Zyzik and Marqués-Pascual, this volume). Other possible interpretations of the WKL could also be operationalized with the goal of helping instructors see what combination of activities contributes most effectively to vocabulary learning. Furthermore, additional research can explore textbooks from the perspective of the publisher to understand the motivations behind the designated curriculum, as there is a need "to critically examine production norms of the publishing industry" (Harwood 2021: 182). Extending research to include the perspective of textbook publishers offers a complete picture of materials research. Case studies of language programs can likewise inform vocabulary research in ecologically valid ways.

6 Conclusions

This analysis uses a simplified version of the TFAC (Nation and Web 2011) and an adapted version of WKL (Brown 2011; Nation 2001) to explore the designated and intended curriculum model (Remillard and Heck 2014) in a Spanish L2 language program. That is, this study helps identify the aspects of word knowledge and the methods of vocabulary instruction that are considered in post-secondary Spanish L2 curricula in the U.S.

This case study shows close alignment between the designated curriculum and the TAs' intended curriculum. Apart from some adaptations because of insufficient visual support and students' preferences of topics, most TAs adhered to the corpus and aspects of vocabulary instruction presented in the textbooks. Even though the syllabi included elements of word knowledge going beyond the prevalent focus on the link between meaning and form, the TAs did not seem to be aware of this fact and, therefore, did not indicate that they integrated these aspects of word knowledge into their lessons. To increase TAs' effectiveness in teaching vocabulary, teacher training programs should offer explicit training on vocabulary instruction and strive to support TAs in developing a more complex understanding of vocabulary teaching and learning. Moreover, the curricular model suggests that teaching materials can be used to support TAs in implementing effective vocabulary instruction. The use of materials that integrate the components of effective vocabulary learning featured in TFAC and that encourage students to learn several aspects of word knowledge could help instructors include more research-based practices in their teaching.

Appendix

Semi-structured Interview Questions
Adapted from Borg (1998) and Zhang (2008).

Section 1: Education

1. Did you learn other foreign languages at school?
    a) What do you recall about these lessons?
    b) What kinds of methods were used?
    c) Do you recall whether you enjoyed such lessons or not?
    d) How was vocabulary taught?
    e) How did you learn vocabulary?
2. What about at the college level? Did the study of language play a role there?
3. Do you feel that your own education as a student has had any influence on the way you teach today?
4. Have you ever been to other countries? If yes, how did this experience impact your teaching?

Section 2: Entry into the Profession and Development as a Teacher

1. 1. Why did you become a Spanish teacher?
    a) What recollections do you have about your earliest teaching experiences?
    b) Were these particularly positive or negative?
    c) What kinds of teaching methods and materials did you use?
2. Tell me about your formal teacher training experiences.
    a) Do they promote a particular way of teaching?
    b) Do they encourage teachers to approach vocabulary in a particular way?
    c) Which aspect(s) of the course(s) did you find most memorable?
3. What has been the greatest influence on your development as a teacher?
4. What qualities do you think a qualified Spanish teacher should have?

Section 3: Reactions on Teaching

1. What is the most satisfying aspect of teaching Spanish, and what is the hardest part of the job?
2. What are your strengths as a Spanish teacher, and your weaknesses?
3. Can you describe one particularly good experience you have had as a Spanish teacher, and one particularly bad one?
4. What is your idea of a "successful" lesson?

Section 4: The School

1. Does the school you work for promote any particular style of teaching?
2. Are there any restrictions on the kinds of materials you use or on the content and organization of your lessons?

Section 5: Vocabulary instruction

1. Which do you think is the most important in Spanish teaching: reading, vocabulary, grammar, listening, speaking, or writing? Why?
    a. What role do you think vocabulary plays in learning Spanish?
2. In general, what do you think vocabulary learning involves?
3. How do you evaluate that your students have commanded the vocabulary you require them to learn?

4. What do you think vocabulary teaching involves?
5. If your students asked you how to enlarge their vocabulary, what suggestions would you give them?
6. What type of vocabulary do you think you need to teach? What type of vocabulary don't you think you need to teach?
7. What are the hardest and the easiest things about teaching vocabulary?

Section 6: The textbook

1. Do you use the textbook to teach vocabulary in your classroom?
2. Do you use the textbook as the main element in the classroom? Or do you include other materials in the class?
3. What kind of foreign language textbooks do you like?
4. How do textbooks teach vocabulary?
5. What are the weaknesses and the strengths of the textbook that you are currently using?
6. How do you make up for the gaps in the textbook in terms of vocabulary instruction?
   a) For example, do you modify vocabulary activities in the textbook?
   b) If so, how?

References

Alins Breda, Diego. 2021. Do activities in graded readers promote vocabulary learning? A Technique Feature Analysis study. *Revista Nebrija de Lingüística Aplicada a la Enseñanza de Lenguas* 15(30). 103–117.

Allen, Heather Willis. 2008. Textbooks materials and foreign language teaching: Perspectives from the classroom. *NECTFL Review* 62. 5–28.

Arnold, Nike. 2013. The role of method textbooks in providing early training for teaching with technology in the language classroom. *Foreign Language Annals* 46(2). 230–245. doi:10.1111/flan.12020

Ball, Deborah L. & Sharon Feiman-Nemser. 1988. Using textbooks and teachers' guides: A dilemma for beginning teachers and teacher educators. *Curriculum Inquiry* 18(4). 401–423. doi:10.1080/03626784.1988.11076050

Bergström, Denise, Cathrine Norberg & Marie Nordlund. 2021. "Words are picked up along the way"–Swedish EFL teachers' conceptualizations of vocabulary knowledge and learning. *Language Awareness*. 1–17. doi:10.1080/09658416.2021.1893326

Borg, Simon. 1998. Teachers' pedagogical systems and grammar teaching: A qualitative study. *TESOL Quarterly* 32(1). 9–38. https://www.jstor.org/stable/3587900

Borg, Simon. 2006. *Teacher cognition and language education. Research and practice*. Norfolk: Continuum.
Brown, Dale. 2011. What aspects of vocabulary knowledge do textbooks give attention to? *Language Teaching Research* 15(83). 83–97. doi:10.1177/1362168810383345
Creswell, John W. 2012. *Educational research: Planning, conducting, and evaluating quantitative and qualitative research*. Boston: Pearson.
Cubillos, Jorge. 2014. Spanish textbooks in the US: enduring traditions and emerging trends. *Journal of Spanish Language Teaching* 1(2). 205–225. doi:10.1080/23247797.2014.970363
Dobinson, Toni. 2001. Do learners learn from classroom interaction and does the teacher have a role to play? *Language Teaching Research* 5(3). 189–211. doi:10.1177/136216880100500302
Fink, Susan B. 2012. The many purposes of course syllabi: Which are essential and useful? *Syllabus Journal* 1(1). 1–12.
Folse, Keith. 2010. Is explicit vocabulary focus the reading teacher's job? *Reading in a Foreign Language* 22(1). 139–160.
Gass, Susan & Alison Mackey. 2006. Input, interaction, and output. *AILA Review* 19. 3–17. doi:10.1075/aila.19.03gas
Godev, Concepción B. 2009. Word-frequency and vocabulary acquisition: an analysis of elementary Spanish college textbooks in the USA. *Revista de Lingüística Teórica y Aplicada* 47(2). 51–68.
Graves, Kathleen. 2000. *Designing language courses: A guide for teachers*. Boston: Heinle & Heinle.
Harwood, Nigel. 2021. Coda: An expanding research agenda for the use of instructional materials. *The Modern Language Journal* 105(S1). 175–184. doi:10.1111/modl.12683
Hu, Hsueh-Chao Marcella & Hossein Nassaji. 2016. Effective vocabulary learning tasks: Involvement Load Hypothesis versus Technique Feature Analysis. *System* 56. 28–39. doi:10.1016/j.system.2015.11.001
Hutchinson, Tom & Eunice Torres. 1994. The textbook as agent of change. *ELT Journal* 48(4). 315–328. doi:10.1093/elt/48.4.315
Keating, Gregory D. 2008. Task effectiveness and word learning in a second language: The involvement load hypothesis on trial. *Language Teaching Research* 12(3). 365–386. doi:10.1177/1362168808089922
Laufer, Batia & Jan Hulstijn. 2001. Incidental vocabulary acquisition in a second language: The construct of Task-Induced Involvement. *Applied Linguistics* 22(1). 1–26. doi:10.1093/applin/22.1.1
Lipinski, Silke. 2010. A frequency analysis of vocabulary in three first-year textbooks of German. *Die Unterrichtspraxis/Teaching German* 43(2). 167–174. doi:10.1111/j.1756-1221.2010.00078.x
López-Jiménez, Mª Dolores. 2014. A critical analysis of the vocabulary in L2 Spanish Textbooks. *Porta Linguarum* 21. 163–181. doi:10.30827/Digibug.30489
Madill, A., Jordan, A. and Shirley, C., 2000. Objectivity and reliability in qualitative analysis: Realist, contextualist and radical constructionist epistemologies. British journal of psychology, 91(1), pp.1–20.
McGrath, Ian. 2013. *Teaching materials and the roles of EFL/ESL teachers*. London: Bloomsbury.
Marcos Miguel, Nausica. 2015. Textbook consumption in the classroom: Analyzing classroom corpora. *Procedia-Social and Behavioral Sciences* 198. 309–319. doi:10.1016/j.sbspro.2015.07.449
Marcos Miguel, Nausica. 2017. Instruction in derivational morphology in the Spanish L2 classroom: What do teachers believe and do? *Konin Language Studies* 5(1). 37–60. doi:10.30438/ksj.2017.5.1.2
Marcos Miguel, Nausica, & Mari Félix Cubas Mora. 2017. Proposing a framework to analyze and evaluate textbook vocabulary activities in the foreign language classroom. In Laura Torres Zúñiga & Thomas H. Schmidt (eds.), *New methodological approaches to foreign language teaching*, 31–51. Newcastle upon Tyne: Cambridge Scholars Publishing.

Miguel García, Mª Lourdes de. 2005. La enseñanza del léxico del español como lengua extranjera. Resultados de una encuesta sobre la metodología aplicada en el aula. *marcoELE. Revista de Didáctica Español Lengua Extranjera* (1). 1–21.

Milton, James. 2009. *Measuring second language vocabulary acquisition*. Bristol: Multilingual Matters.

Nation, I. S. Paul. 2001. *Learning vocabulary in another language*. Cambridge: Cambridge University Press.

Nation, I. S. Paul & Stuart Webb. 2011. *Researching and analyzing vocabulary*. Boston: Heinle Cengage Learning.

Neary-Sundquist, Colleen A. 2015. Aspects of vocabulary knowledge in German textbooks. *Foreign Language Annals* 48(1). 68–80. doi:10.1111/flan.12126

Niu, Ruiying & Stephen Andrews. 2012. Commonalities and discrepancies in L2 teachers' beliefs and practices about vocabulary pedagogy: A small culture perspective. *TESOL Journal* 6. 134–154.

Retelj, Andreja. 2014. Evaluation of textbooks for German as a foreign language in the basis of the Common European Framework of Reference for Languages: learning, teaching, assessment. *Linguistica* 54(1). 61–75. doi:10.4312/linguistica.54.1.61-75

Remillard, Janine T. & Daniel J. Heck. 2014. Conceptualizing the curriculum enactment process in mathematics education. *ZDM-International Journal of Mathematics Education* 46(5). 705–718. doi:10.1007/s11858-014-0600-4

Richards, Jack C. 2001. *Curriculum development in language teaching*. Cambridge: Cambridge University Press.

Richards, Jack C. 2006. *Communicative Language Teaching today*. Cambridge: Cambridge University Press.

Richards, Jack C. & Theodore S. Rodgers. 2001. *Approaches and methods in language teaching. A description and analysis*. Cambridge: Cambridge University Press.

Robles García, Pablo & Claudia H. Sánchez-Gutiérrez. 2016. La morfología derivativa en los manuales de español elemental estadounidenses: Un estudio exploratorio. *RAEL: Revista Electrónica de Lingüística Aplicada* 15(1). 70–86.

Rossiter, Marian, Marilyn Abbott & Andrea Kushnir. 2016. L2 vocabulary research and instructional practices: Where are the gaps? *TESL-EJ* 20(1). 1–25.

Ryan, Gery W. & H. Russell Bernard. 2003. Techniques to identify themes. *Field Methods* 15(1). 85–109. doi:10.1177/1525822X02239569

Sanaoui, Razika. 1996. Processes of vocabulary instruction in 10 French as a second language classrooms. *The Canadian Modern Language Review* 52(2). 179–199. doi:10.3138/cmlr.52.2.179

Sánchez-Gutiérrez, Claudia H., Nausica Marcos Miguel & Michael K. Olsen. 2018. An analysis of vocabulary coverage and lexical characteristics in L2 Spanish textbooks. In Peter Ecke & Susanne Rott (eds.), *Understanding vocabulary learning and teaching: Implications for language program development. American Association of University Supervisors, Coordinators, and Directors of Language Programs (AAUSC) Volume 2018*, 78–98. Boston: Cengage.

Sánchez-Gutiérrez, Claudia H., Pablo Robles García & Diego Alins Breda. 2021. Unidades temáticas y aspectos del conocimiento léxico en los manuales de ELE. *Revista Nebrija de Lingüística aplicada a la enseñanza de Lenguas* 15(31). 179–193.

Sánchez-Gutiérrez, Claudia H., Pablo Robles-García & Mercedes Pérez Serrano. 2022. L2 Spanish vocabulary teaching in US universities: Instructors' beliefs and reported practices. *Language Teaching Research* (online first). 1–23. doi:10.1177/13621688221074443

Savignon, Sandra J. 2007. Beyond communicative language teaching: What's ahead? *Journal of Pragmatics* 39(1). 207–220. doi:10.1016/j.pragma.2006.09.004

Schmitt, Norbert. 2008. Review article: Instructed second language vocabulary learning. *Language Teaching Research* 12(2). 329–363.
Schmitt, Norbert. 2014. Size and depth of vocabulary knowledge: What the research shows. *Language Learning* 64(4). 913–951. doi:10.1177/1362168808089921
Shrum, Judith & Eileen Glisan. 2009. *Teacher's handbook*. Boston: Cengage Learning.
Slattery, Jeanne M. & Janet F. Carlson. 2005. Preparing an effective syllabus: Current best practices. *College Teaching* 53(4). 159–164. doi:10.3200/CTCH.53.4.159-164
Stein, Mary Kay, Janine Remillard & Margaret S. Smith. 2007. How curriculum influences student learning. In Frank K. Lester (ed.), *Second handbook of research on mathematics teaching and learning*, 319–369. Charlotte: Information Age Publishing.
Swain, Merrill & Susanne Carroll. 1987. The immersion observation study. In Birgit Harley, Patrick Allen, Jim Cummins & Merrill Swain (eds.), *The development of bilingual proficiency. Final report*, 192–222. Ontario: Ontario Institute for Studies in Education, Modern Language Centre.
Webb, Stuart, Akifumi, Yanagisawa & Takumi Uchihara. 2020. How effective are intentional vocabulary-learning activities? A meta-analysis. *The Modern Language Journal* 104(4). 715–738. doi:10.1111/modl.12671
Yanagisawa, Akifumi & Stuart Webb. 2021. To what extent does the Involvement Load Hypothesis predict incidental L2 vocabulary learning? A meta-analysis. *Language Learning* 71. 487–536. doi:10.1111/lang.12444
Zhang, Weimin. 2008. *In search of English as a Foreign Language (EFL) teachers' knowledge of vocabulary instruction*. Atlanta, GA: GSU Dissertation.
Zimmerman, Cheryl Boyd. 1997. Historical trends in second language vocabulary instruction. In James Coady & Thomas Huckin (eds.), *Second Language vocabulary acquisition*, 5–19. Cambridge: Cambridge University Press.

Textbooks examined

Blanco, José A. & Philip Donley. 2012. *Vistas. Introducción a la lengua española*. 4th edn. Boston: Vista Higher Learning.
Blanco, José A. & Maria Colbert. 2012. *Enfoques. Curso intermedio de lengua española*. 3rd edn. Boston: Vista Higher Learning.
Castells, Matilde Olivella de, Elizabeth Guzman, Paloma Lapuerta & Judith E. Liskin-Gasparro. 2008. *Mosaicos: Spanish as a world language*. 5th edn. Upper Saddle River: Prentice Hall.
Marinelli, Patti & Lizette Mujica Laughlin. 2014. *Puentes. Spanish for intensive and high-beginner courses*. Boston: Heinle Cengage Learning.

Eve C. Zyzik, Laura Marqués-Pascual

Chapter 12
Do you really know this word? Dimensions of vocabulary knowledge in Spanish textbooks

1 Introduction

Traditional vocabulary teaching and learning techniques usually follow a form-meaning approach that prioritizes learning the meaning of new words and phrases. Studies on classroom teaching practices support this view of vocabulary instruction (Marcos-Miguel and Cubas-Mora this volume, Sanaoui 1996). The same is true for textbooks, as previous research has shown that vocabulary activities tend to focus on consolidating the form-meaning link, with some attention to other aspects of vocabulary knowledge (Brown 2011; Neary-Sundquist 2015; Vu and Michel 2021). A point of departure for our study is to conceptualize vocabulary knowledge as consisting of various components (see section 2) that include, but are not limited to, the form-meaning link. Afterwards, we discuss previous analyses of English and German textbooks that serve as an impetus for the current study in which we examine how Spanish textbooks at three different proficiency levels incorporate the various dimensions of vocabulary knowledge.

2 Components of vocabulary knowledge

Although meaning is a central part of vocabulary, research has shown that vocabulary learning involves many additional layers of knowledge (see Fernández Pérez and González Pereira, this volume).[1] Nation (2001, 2013) identified nine dimensions of vocabulary knowledge that must be considered when discussing what it means to know a word. These nine dimensions are generally understood

---

[1] Fernández-Pérez & González-Pereira (this volume) show the multiple ways in which vocabulary learning enhances grammatical knowledge and vice versa, showing how the lexicon is much more that simple meaning-form pairings.

Eve C. Zyzik, University of California, Santa Cruz
Laura Marqués-Pascual, University of California, Santa Barbara

to constitute vocabulary depth, which refers to how well a word is known (see Schmitt 2014, for more details about the concept of vocabulary depth and its relationship to vocabulary size). Nation's conceptualization of vocabulary knowledge, shown in Figure 1, involves both receptive and productive knowledge within each component. For example, a learner may be able to recognize the meaning of a particular word (displaying receptive knowledge of the form-meaning link) but not be able to recall the word when presented with a stimulus or a communicative need.

Table 1: Aspects of vocabulary knowledge (adapted from Nation 2001: 27).

Major category		Specific aspect	Description
FORM	F1	Spoken form	What does the word sound like? How is the word pronounced?
	F2	Written form	What does the word look like? How is the word spelled?
	F2	Word parts	What parts are recognizable in this word? What word parts are needed to express this meaning?
MEANING	M1	Form and meaning	What meaning does this word signal? What word can I use to express this meaning?
	M2	Concepts and referents	What is included in the concept? What items can the concept refer to?
	M3	Associations	What other words does this word make us think of? What other words could we use instead?
USE	U1	Grammatical functions	In what patterns does the word occur?
	U2	Collocations	What words occur with this one?
	U3	Constraints on use	When, where, and how would we expect to use this word?

Although Table 1 might lead to the assumption that these nine components are separate entities, it is more likely that they are interrelated. Indeed, this is a question that researchers have investigated empirically. González-Fernández and Schmitt (2020) approached this question from two angles: first, they set out to determine the degree of relatedness between the components, and second, they asked whether some components are acquired before others (cf. Laufer and Goldstein 2004). They investigated four types of vocabulary knowledge from Nation's model: form-meaning links, collocations, derivatives (i.e., word parts), and multiple meanings. Each component was tested in both recognition and recall formats. Their results showed strong positive correlations between the various components (between .70 and .94), which confirms that the various types of vocabulary knowledge are highly interrelated. With respect to a potential implicational scale or an acquisition order, González-Fernández and Schmitt concluded that recognition knowledge is mastered before any type of recall knowledge. Within recognition, the form-meaning link is acquired first, followed by collocations, then multiple-meanings, and finally derivatives. This implicational scale was based on participants' responses, with 80% being considered the level at which a given aspect is mastered.

Another question stemming from Nation's model of vocabulary knowledge is whether each component benefits from or requires intentional learning. Specifically, it seems that some types of knowledge develop incidentally as a result of exposure to input. Collocations are a case in point, and for some researchers, this means that knowledge of collocations is largely implicit in nature (Ellis 2004). Furthermore, González Fernández and Schmitt (2015: 98) maintain that the acquisition of collocational knowledge depends on "the kind of high-quality engagement with language that presumably occurs in a socially-integrated environment." Although collocations can be taught in the classroom via different kinds of direct instruction (cf. Boers et al. 2014, Laufer and Girsai 2008, Peters 2016), there may be limits to how well collocations can be learned in a classroom environment and/or with pedagogical exercises. Nevertheless, Brown (2011: 85) maintains that textbooks should address all aspects of vocabulary knowledge because all aspects "can benefit from intentional learning, even if some may primarily be learnt by other means." We concur with Brown's position in that not all aspects should necessarily receive equal attention, but that textbook activities should address all aspects to some degree. In the next section, we review studies that have analyzed the various kinds of vocabulary activities in textbooks.

3 Vocabulary in textbooks

Textbooks for L2 learners have been analyzed from multiple vantage points because, as noted by Cubillos (2014: 205), "published materials tend to define the content, pace, and pedagogical orientation of language courses at all levels." Given the goals of the present study, we review the existing analyses of textbooks with respect to vocabulary. One major goal of research in this area has been to determine the degree of overlap between high-frequency words and the vocabulary items included in textbooks (i.e., vocabulary selection). For Spanish, this question has been examined by Davies and Face (2006), Godev (2009), and most recently by Sánchez-Gutiérrez, Marcos Miguel and Olsen (2018). Sánchez-Gutiérrez et al. carried out an analysis of sixteen Spanish textbooks at the elementary and intermediate levels, focusing on the glossaries of each book in order to conduct a frequency analysis. Their results revealed that generally less than half of the 3000 most frequent words were included in the textbooks. These results are in line with previous studies on vocabulary selection in Spanish textbooks (cf. Davies and Face 2006, Godev 2009), indicating that criteria other than frequency are used in determining which vocabulary words are included in textbooks. Consequently, Sánchez-Gutiérrez et al. suggest complementing classroom vocabulary exercises with homework that targets the 3000 most frequently-used words.

The presentation of new vocabulary and corresponding activities in Spanish textbooks have also been studied. For example, López-Jiménez (2014) analyzed the various ways in which new vocabulary is introduced in Spanish textbooks (visual lists, translations, texts, etc.), and the types of activities that followed. Activities were classified into five categories: mechanical exercises, closed exercises, open activities, communicative activities, and ambiguous activities (see López-Jiménez for how each activity type is defined). The analysis shows that most vocabulary activities are closed exercises (57%) with only one correct answer and approximately one-third are open activities in which more than one answer is valid. Although the distinction between closed exercises and open activities may be useful, it could be argued that both types of activities are needed and that neither is inherently superior to the other. The same could be argued for input-based versus output-based vocabulary activities, which were analyzed by Yoon (2019). Input-based activities do not require students to produce any specific vocabulary words, but instead require comprehension in order to complete the activity successfully (e.g., matching a picture with a description). The textbooks surveyed by Yoon showed a tendency towards output-based instruction, with an emphasis on production of new words learned.

Nation's (2001) framework has been used to explore the lexical focus of textbook activities. Brown (2011) provided an analysis of the vocabulary activities found in nine general English textbooks for the beginner and intermediate levels. Crucially, the notion of 'vocabulary activity' here is broad: "any activity that focuses on the form, meaning or use of an item or items" (p. 87). This includes activities that might be found in the 'grammar' or 'reading' sections of the textbook. Brown adopted Nation's component view of vocabulary knowledge (see Table 1) and explained that some activities involved more than one component. The results indicate a clear preference for activities focusing on the form-meaning link (nearly 52%), followed by grammatical functions (29%), and then spoken form (nearly 15%). The remaining activities focused on collocations (8%), associations (7%), and concepts and referents (6%). The other components, such as word parts, written form, and constraints on use, were rarely targeted in the textbooks examined. For example, Brown found only four activities targeting constraints on use, which may be due to the fact that the basic vocabulary items included in the textbooks are not constrained by register.

Neary-Sundquist (2015) replicated Brown's (2011) study by analyzing five German textbooks at the beginner level. Her results showed that vocabulary activities involving *form* were the least common overall, representing only 11.5% of the total number of activities. Activities that focused on *meaning* were more frequent (39.9%), and within this category, the vast majority of activities were designed to strengthen form-meaning connections. Finally, the *use* category was most common, accounting for nearly half of all vocabulary activities (48.5%). The distribution within this category was skewed towards activities that focused on grammatical functions. Neary-Sundquist also noted that certain types of vocabulary activities were almost completely absent from the German textbooks. Specifically, activities focusing on *word parts* accounted for less than 1% of the sample even though affixation and compound words are prevalent in German. Likewise, within the global category of *meaning*, activities focused on *concepts and referents* were conspicuously absent (less than 1%). In the *use* category, *collocation* activities were very infrequent (less than 1%) and *constraints on use* were also rarely included (1.5%). Neary-Sundquist concludes that the German textbooks followed the same general trends described by Brown (2011) for the ESL/EFL textbooks. Nevertheless, the ESL/EFL textbooks devoted more attention to spoken word form and to collocations than the German textbooks.

Most recently, Vu and Michel (2021) applied Nation's framework to the analysis of English textbooks at the upper-intermediate (B2) and advanced (C1) levels. They hypothesized that English for Academic Purposes (EAP) textbooks would differ from the general English textbooks analyzed by Brown (2011). Indeed, their results reveal that EAP textbooks focus more on the *use* dimension of vocabulary, with nearly half of all activities (48.4%) belonging to this category. Within *use*, Vu and Michel note the preponderance of activities that focus on grammatical functions, with fewer activities targeting collocations and constraints on use. Activities that focused on *meaning* accounted for one-third of all vocabulary activities whereas the *form* dimension was less emphasized (18.6%) in these EAP books. However, within the category of *form*, activities focusing on word parts were common given that academic language requires knowledge of prefixes, suffixes, and nominalizations. In their interpretation of these data, Vu and Michel argue that higher proficiency learners should be expected to go beyond form-meaning connections. Thus, the fact that meaning (and especially form-meaning) is not as visible in the vocabulary activities of EAP textbooks is justifiable. Methodologically, they noted that it was not always easy to determine which aspect of word knowledge was being targeted.

The present study is a conceptual replication of the studies by Brown (2011), Neary-Sundquist (2015), and Vu and Michel (2021). We extend the analysis to Spanish textbooks, adopting the same theoretical framework (Nation 2001, 2013) and the same broad definition of what constitutes a vocabulary activity. We adopt Nation's framework because we are particularly interested in the dimensions of lexical knowledge rather than the pedagogical features that a particular activity might have (e.g., whether it is a closed or open activity as in López-Jiménez 2014). Because the point of departure for our study was Nation's framework, we followed the same methodology used in the studies we replicate. Since Spanish textbooks tend to devote considerable attention to inflectional morphology (e.g., gender agreement, verb inflections), we wanted to determine if the original components of vocabulary knowledge, as described in Nation (2001), can be applied without modification to the analysis of Spanish textbooks. Finally, we also wanted to gain a clearer understanding of the activities classified by previous research as involving more than one component of vocabulary knowledge. None of the previous studies have provided details regarding the typical pairing components. In other words, when an activity involves more than one component of vocabulary knowledge, which are typically included in the pairing? For this reason, in our study we have also included an analysis of activities with a dual focus on two aspects of vocabulary knowledge.

4 Methodology

4.1 The textbooks

Eight Spanish textbooks were analyzed in this study, ranging from beginner to advanced levels. All textbooks analyzed are designed for L1 English learners of Spanish in the United States and were currently available and widely used across higher education institutions. We selected textbooks from three major publishers in order to examine the overall trend in vocabulary instruction across different editorial teams. We selected three beginner Spanish textbooks and three intermediate Spanish textbooks from three different publishers (one each from Wiley, Vista Higher Learning and McGraw-Hill). Most advanced Spanish textbooks currently available focus on grammar and composition, and not all of them include vocabulary activities and/or a focus on vocabulary instruction. In addition, since the market for advanced Spanish is more limited, we could only find two textbooks at this level from two of the three publishers that could be included in the analysis. Table 2 lists the textbooks used for the analysis.

Table 2: Textbooks used in the study.

Title	Authors	Publisher	Year	Level
Panorama (6th ed)	José A. Blanco Philip R. Donley	Vista Higher Learning	2020	Beginner
¡Pura vida! (2nd ed)	Norma López-Burton Laura Marqués-Pascual Cristina Pardo-Ballester	Wiley	2019	Beginner
Tu mundo (2nd ed)	Magdalena Andrade Jeanne Egasse Elías Miguel Muñoz María Cabrera-Puche	McGraw-Hill	2019	Beginner
Imagina (3rd ed)	José A. Blanco C. Cecilia Tocaimaza-Hatch	Vista Higher Learning	2015	Intermediate
Punto y aparte (6th ed)	Sharon Foerster Anne Lambright	McGraw-Hill	2020	Intermediate
En tu medio	Leah Fonder-Solano Casilde A. Isabelli María Isabel Martínez Mira	Wiley	2018	Intermediate
Repase y escriba (7th ed)	Maria Canteli Dominicis John J. Reynolds	Wiley	2014	Advanced
Taller de escritores (3rd ed)	Paula Cañón	Vista Higher Learning	2020	Advanced

4.2 Coding procedures

The textbooks varied in length and number of chapters. All the beginner level textbooks included at least 12 chapters; the intermediate level textbooks ranged from 5 to 10 chapters and the advanced-level textbooks had 6 and 14 chapters. Following Brown (2011) and Neary-Sundquist (2015) odd-numbered chapters from each textbook were analyzed in order to include a representative sample of the contents of each book. Since all elementary textbooks had at least 10 chapters we decided to analyze chapters 3, 5, 7 and 9. In the intermediate and advanced textbooks we analyzed chapters 1, 3, 5 and chapter 7 if applicable.

The first step was to identify all the vocabulary activities in the given chapters. We understand "activity" to be largely synonymous with "exercise" in the sense that there is a focus on discrete, pre-selected language items (Boers et al. 2014). Following Brown (2011), we adopt a broad definition of what constitutes a vocabulary activity. In practice, this means that many activities in textbook sections targeting "grammar," "pronunciation" or "reading" were indeed vocabulary-related. Finally, an activity must require the students to do something rather than simply present vocabulary words. For example, we noted that many Spanish textbooks present regional vocabulary as part of a "culture" section, but students are not required to do anything with these words. Thus, the mere presentation of vocabulary is not included in our analysis.

In the initial screening of each book for vocabulary activities, we quickly realized that a decision needed to be made regarding activities that target inflectional forms exclusively (i.e., without any focus on lexical meaning). Since Spanish is a highly inflected language, textbooks include many activities that ask students to manipulate word form in some way, such as conjugating verbs or inflecting adjectives for gender and number. Technically, these types of activities would fall into the category of Form and specifically "Word parts". Nation (2001: 100) gives the example of having to "change the stem to the appropriate *inflected or derived form* to complete the sentence" (emphasis added). In our analysis, we opted to restrict the category of "Word parts" to activities focusing on derivation and word families (e.g., *happy, happiness*). Activities that focus only on inflectional forms are not included as vocabulary activities. An example of such an activity is shown in (1). Note that the activity below does not require students to know the meaning of the verb 'correr' or to choose a verb that makes sense in the context. It is a mechanical drill (VanPatten 2002) and, as such, excluded from our analysis.

(1) *Panorama*, p. 89

Provide the appropriate present tense forms of these verbs.
correr
Graciela _____
Tú _____
Yo _____
Sara y Ana _____

Once all the vocabulary activities in each chapter had been identified, each one was assigned a code based on its primary focus and, if applicable, the secondary focus. In order to guarantee that we were applying the classification scheme consistently, we began by coding two chapters from one of the intermediate texts (*En tu medio*) in order to establish inter-rater reliability. Each author coded thirty activities independently; we compared our coding for these thirty activities, which resulted in 90% agreement (27 out of 30 activities were coded identically). Next, we proceeded with the analysis by coding four textbooks together (two at the beginner level and two at the intermediate level). One of the researchers coded half of the chapters in each text and the other coded the other half. We then discussed all problematic cases or activities that were difficult to categorize. By identifying problematic activity types, we were able to further refine the criteria for each subcategory. Subsequently, each author coded the remaining four textbooks independently. Afterwards, we reviewed any remaining problematic cases and resolved all disagreements.

As noted by Brown (2011) and Neary-Sundquist (2015), many vocabulary activities have a dual focus. For example, an activity can target *spoken form* by having students check a box next to each word they hear in an audio segment and also target *form-meaning* connections by having them match those words to a definition. This dual focus is shown in sample activity (2):

(2) *Panorama*, p. 301

Ahora escucha la conversación entre Josefina y Rosa. Cuando oigas una de las palabras de la columna A, usa el contexto para identificar el sinónimo o la definición en la columna B.

"Now listen to the conversation between Josefina and Rosa. When you hear one of the words in column A, use the context to find the synonym or the definition in column B."

The presence of dual-focus activities complicates the quantitative analysis in some ways. For example, Brown (2011) presents data in a table in which the totals exceed 100% in certain categories due to the presence of such dual-focus activities. To resolve this issue and simplify the presentation of the data, we opted to double count such activities. For example, if a textbook has 100 vocabulary activities and 20 of them are dual-focus, we present the percentage of activities in each category (form, meaning, and use) out of 120. In this way, we avoid percentages exceeding 100.

5 Results

A total of 541 vocabulary activities were identified and analyzed in this study. These activities are unevenly distributed across the instructional levels, as shown in Table 3. The second row of Table 3 presents the number of dual-focus activities, which are a subset of the total number of activities.

Let us first consider the results of the beginner-level textbooks. One of the textbooks (*Panorama*) had more activities than the other two. This means that when comparing raw numbers, *Panorama* is likely to have more activities across categories. The data for the beginner books are presented in Table 4.

Table 3: Number of vocabulary activities per instructional level.

	Beginner texts	Intermediate texts	Advanced texts
Total number of vocabulary activities	326	140	75
Number of dual-focus vocabulary activities	49	28	25

Table 4: Token counts and frequencies for beginner textbooks.

	Panorama	*Pura Vida*	*Tu Mundo*	Category total
Totals for Form	25	10	2	37 (10%)
spoken form	22	3	2	27
written form	2	4	0	6
word parts	1	3	0	4
Totals for Meaning	114	89	90	293 (78%)
form and meaning	86	67	62	215
concepts and referents	13	19	25	57
associations	15	3	4	22
Totals for Use	26	6	13	45 (12%)
grammatical functions	24	3	11	38
collocations	2	3	0	5
constraints on use	0	0	0	0
Activity total	165	105	105	375 (100%)

A clear trend emerges from the three first-year textbooks: activities focused on meaning are prevalent, accounting for 78% of all vocabulary activities. Within this broader category, activities designed to consolidate the form-meaning link are most numerous, followed by concepts and referents, and then associations. The activities dedicated to the form dimension are not evenly distributed among the three textbooks. Here we note that *Panorama* has many more activities that focus on spoken word form, which skews the distribution of the activities within this category. Activities that focus on written form and word parts are practically absent from all three textbooks. Considering all three textbooks together, 10% of the vocabulary activities are focused on word form, with the caveat that not all textbooks devote the same amount of attention to this dimension. Similar results are observed for the use dimension, which accounts for 12% of all vocabulary activities. Here we see an unequal distribution across textbooks (numerically in favor of *Panorama*) and within the category (skewed towards activities that target grammatical functions). Activities focusing on collocation were almost completely absent from all three books. Finally, we did not document any vocabulary activities that were designed to teach constraints on use in our sample of first-year books.

The results for the intermediate textbooks show very similar trends, although there were fewer vocabulary activities overall. These data are summarized in Table 5.

Table 5: Token counts and frequencies for intermediate textbooks.

	Imagina	*Punto y aparte*	*En tu medio*	Category total
Totals for Form	1	7	10	18 (10.7%)
spoken form	0	6	7	13
written form	0	0	3	3
word parts	1	1	0	2
Totals for Meaning	53	36	36	125 (74.4%)
form and meaning	43	21	25	89
concepts and referents	4	10	0	14
associations	6	5	11	22
Totals for Use	2	19	4	25 (14.9%)
grammatical functions	1	18	1	20
collocations	1	1	2	4
constraints on use	0	0	1	1
Activity total	56	62	50	168 (100%)

Note: Totals reflect double-counting of dual-focus activities.

The three intermediate textbooks were similar in terms of the total number of activities. In terms of their distribution among the three dimensions, vocabulary activities that focus on meaning predominate (74.4%). Within this category, most activities focus on strengthening the form-meaning connection. Activities that focused on the use dimension (14.9%) were primarily targeting grammatical functions, although it must be noted this is due to only one textbook (*Punto y Aparte*). Activities targeting collocations and constraints on use were negligible. Finally, in terms of word form (10.7%), these were primarily activities that targeted spoken word form in two of the textbooks: *Punto y Aparte* and *En tu Medio*.

The results for the advanced-level textbooks, albeit fewer in number, also focused primarily on the meaning dimension (66%). These results are shown in Table 6.

Despite the overall focus on meaning, we see more attention to collocations in these advanced level books. In fact, within the use dimension (17.5%), we see the largest number of activities dedicated to collocations. Similarly, within the

Table 6: Token counts and frequencies for advanced textbooks.

	Taller de escritores	*Repase y escriba*	Category total
Totals for Form	14	2	16 (16.5%)
spoken form	2	0	2
written form	5	0	5
word parts	7	2	9
Totals for Meaning	27	37	64 (66%)
form and meaning	25	29	54
concepts and referents	0	3	3
associations	2	5	7
Totals for Use	7	10	17 (17.5%)
grammatical functions	2	2	4
collocations	5	8	13
constraints on use	0	0	0
Activity total	48	49	97 (100%)

Note: Activity totals reflect double-counting of dual-focus activities

form dimension (16.5%) there are more activities that target word parts, at least in one of the textbooks (*Taller de Escritores*).

To summarize the data thus far, it is useful to compare the distribution of each dimension (form, meaning, and use) in each of the three instructional levels. This is shown in Figure 1, with the bars representing the tokens of activities in each dimension.

The picture that emerges from this analysis is that beginner, intermediate, and advanced Spanish textbooks are relatively homogeneous in terms of the variety of vocabulary activities offered. The meaning dimension is clearly favored: activities with a focus on meaning account for 66%-78.6% of the total. In order to determine if there was an association between textbook level and the number of activities in each category (form, meaning, and use), we created a frequency table (i.e., crosstab) with the three textbook levels, the three categories, and the number of observations in each cell. A Chi-square test of independence reveals no association between textbook level and category ($\chi^2(4)= 7.25$, $p= .123$).

We turn now to the dual-focus activities that were identified in our analysis. As shown in Table 3, there were a total of 102 activities that focused on more than one aspect of vocabulary knowledge. In our analysis, we found that the large majority (93%) included attention to some aspect of meaning. In other words, meaning was central to these activities even if they also emphasized an additional aspect of

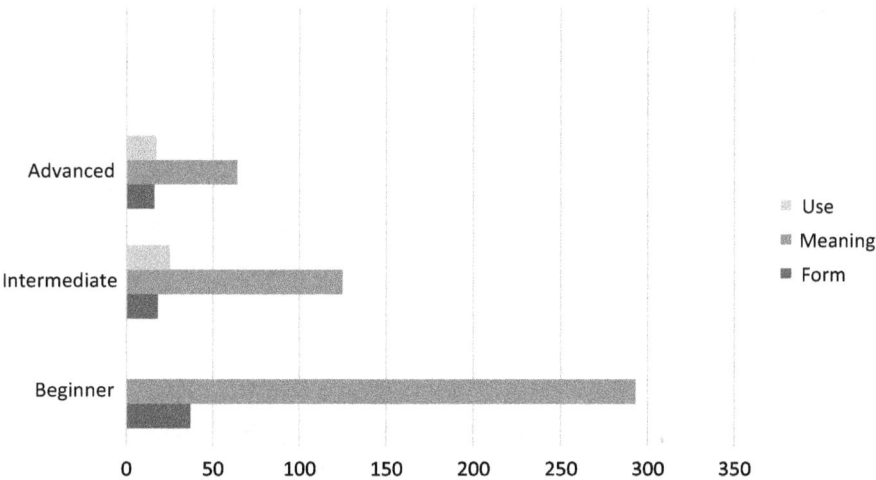

Figure 1: Distribution of each dimension of vocabulary knowledge across textbooks in three proficiency levels.

form or use. In fact, 27% of the dual-focus activities attended to dual aspects of meaning (e.g., form-meaning link and associations). Activities that combined form-meaning links and grammatical functions accounted for 43% of dual-focus activities. However, none of these activities focused on collocations and constrains on use (which is not surprising due to the fact that those two aspects in the Use category are hardly present in the activities analyzed in these textbooks). Finally, there were activities that combined a focus on meaning and some aspect of form (either spoken form, written form, or word parts). This latter combination represented 23% of the dual-focus activities. Results for dual-focus activities are shown in Table 7.

Table 7: Token counts and frequencies for dual-focus activities.

Book	Dual focus activities	Activities with focus on meaning	M1+U1	M1+ F1/F2/F3	M1+ M2/M3
Panorama	20	20	9	5	6
Pura Vida	15	15	6	3	6
Tu mundo	14	14	6	2	6
Punto y Aparte	11	11	7	4	0
Imagina	8	8	2	1	5
En tu medio	9	6	2	2	2

Table 7 (continued)

Book	Dual focus activities	Activities with focus on meaning	M1+U1	M1+ F1/F2/F3	M1+ M2/M3
Taller de escritores	13	10	5	5	0
Repase y Escriba	12	11	7	1	3
TOTAL	102 (100%)	95 (93%)	44 (43%)	23 (23%)	28 (27%)

6 Discussion

We begin the discussion by summarizing the main trends in the Spanish textbooks and comparing our results to those of Brown (2011), Neary-Sundquist (2015), and Vu and Michel (2021). Next, we provide more detail about the types of activities that were most commonly found as well as what could be considered shortcomings in the three main dimensions: form, meaning, and use.

6.1 Main trends: Application of Nation's framework to Spanish textbooks

For ESL/EFL, Brown (2011) found that textbook activities focus primarily on linking form and meaning, and to a lesser degree, on the words' grammatical functions. Neary-Sundquist (2015) found similar trends in German textbooks, although these books devoted more attention to grammatical functions. Neary-Sundquist reported that 46.4% of all activities were classified as having a focus on grammatical functions, which is very similar to the results found in EAP textbooks by Vu and Michel (2021). In contrast, our study found a much smaller proportion of activities with a focus on grammatical functions: 11.5% for all textbook levels combined. What might explain these differences between EAP and German and Spanish textbooks? One possibility is that our coding of these activities differed from that of Neary-Sundquist, although this is unlikely because we adhered to the original description provided by Brown (2011: 88), who defined this category in the following way: "an activity that requires students to manipulate a word in some way with respect to a sentence, for example, by adding it to the sentence in the correct position." Neary-Sundquist provided examples from the German textbooks in which students are asked to formulate questions with specific lexical items (e.g., semi-structured interviews, autograph games or surveys). The Spanish textbooks we analyzed also contained interviews and surveys, but the target words were generally included in the interview questions so that no manipulation was necessary. A typical interview format from one of the Spanish texts is shown in (3), taken from the chapter on parts of the house and domestic chores.

(3)   *Tu mundo*, p. 235

   ¿Tienes lavadora en tu casa o vas a una lavandería automática para lavar tu ropa?

   "Do you have a washing machine at home or do you go to a laundromat to wash your clothes?"

Note that this type of interview activity requires knowledge of the meaning of the vocabulary items (*lavadora, lavar la ropa*) in order to answer the question, but it does not require the student to manipulate the word(s) with respect to a sentence. It is likely that the German textbooks required an additional element of manipulating word order in such activities, which would result in a higher percentage of activities in the "grammatical functions" category.

With respect to dual-focus activities, we found that almost all included attention to some aspect of meaning. In other words, meaning was targeted alongside another component of vocabulary knowledge such as grammatical functions or spoken form. One way to interpret this finding is that meaning is so central to the notion of what constitutes "vocabulary" that it is practically impossible to ignore. Consider, for example, an activity in which a table setting (e.g., plate, fork, knife, etc.) is depicted with a picture and students have to make sentences with the target vocabulary using phrases to describe their location (e.g., *a la derecha de* "to the right of"). In this case, the learner has to manipulate the words with respect to a sentence, employing their knowledge of grammatical functions. At the same time, however, it is impossible to complete this activity without knowing the meaning of the words *tenedor* ("fork") and *cuchillo* ("knife"). Other dual-focus activities combined two components belonging to the larger "meaning" category. For example, consider an interview activity in which students have to ask each other about what one does in certain rooms of the house (e.g., What do we do in the kitchen?). This type of activity requires meaning recognition of the word *cocina* ("kitchen"), but also involves considering what is included in a word's meaning (concepts and referents). In this sense, the word "cocina" might evoke different activities such as talking with family members, washing the dishes, or even watching television. In fact, examining vocabulary in this way (concepts and referents) may provide a platform for discussing culturally-specific meanings of words and phrases.

With respect to potential differences between beginner, intermediate, and advanced textbooks, the results do not reveal any statistically significant association between levels and activity types. However, the sheer number of vocabulary activities decreases drastically at the intermediate level and again at the advanced level. Consider, for example, that the total number of vocabulary activities in the two advanced-level books (97) is only 26% of the total number found in the first-year books (375). In fact, any given chapter in the two advanced textbooks included on average of 11 activities focused on vocabulary, whereas the beginner textbook chapters included an average of 27 activities that focused on some aspect of vocabulary knowledge. Why is it that advanced-level Spanish books have fewer vocabulary activities? There are at least two possible reasons. First, it may be that textbook authors assume that advanced learners are exposed to various types of authentic materials (e.g., written texts such as novels or short stories) and that vocabulary will be acquired incidentally through exposure. Another possibility is that at the advanced level it becomes more difficult to find a common denominator of what vocabulary to teach (see Sánchez-Gutiérrez et al., this volume, for insights about the difficult task of vocabulary selection). At the beginner level, vocabulary selection is determined in large part by semantic or thematic sets (e.g., food, kinship terms, parts of the house). In contrast, at the advanced level, these semantic sets are no longer the driving force in vocabulary selection and thus, textbook authors approach vocabulary differently, generally by creating vocabulary lists from the texts that students will read or listen to. The result is that there are far fewer vocabulary activities per chapter at the advanced level. We note, however, that the upper-intermediate and advanced EAP books analyzed by Vu and Michel (2021) contained a plethora of vocabulary activities. Thus, the lack of attention to vocabulary in advanced-level Spanish books is not a necessary condition; it is a deliberate decision on the part of the materials developers.

Finally, as noted in the methodology section, we opted to limit the category of "word parts" to activities that focused only on derivation. In our understanding of Nation (2001), this category is conceptualized broadly to include both inflection and derivation, and Brown (2011) includes both inflection and derivation activities as examples. For example, inflection could target the three degrees of adjectives (e.g., *short, shorter, shortest*) and derivation might target different members of a given word family (e.g., *happy* versus *happiness*). Given the highly inflected nature of the Spanish language, activities that focus on inflection are abundant in all the textbooks we surveyed. A perusal of any Spanish language textbook will show that inflection is targeted from the very beginning of instruction, especially with respect to adjectives (gender/number agreement) and verb conjugations. Inflection continues to be a major focus across instructional levels as stem-changing verbs are introduced and additional tenses are presented. In our coding scheme, we excluded activities that targeted inflection in the format of mechanical drills because it is difficult to justify them as vocabulary activities in the first place. To be clear, the problem with mechanical drills is not that there is only one correct answer, but that the activity can be completed without any consideration of the meaning of the target words (cf. Wong and VanPatten 2003). It is worth asking how our results might be different had we included mechanical drills that target inflection. First, such a decision would have drastically increased the total number of "vocabulary" activities in our data; second, it would have increased the number of activities within the "word parts" category. In sum, we believe that the decision to exclude inflection from the category of "word parts" is justified for Spanish and that future studies should consider distinguishing between inflection and derivation so that this category is clearly delimited. In what follows, we address each major component of vocabulary (form, meaning, and use) in more detail.

6.2 Activity types and shortcomings

In this part of the discussion, we address each major component of vocabulary in more detail in order to critically examine how textbooks address (or fail to address) each component. Whenever possible, we include suggestions that could be incorporated in order to diversify and strengthen the vocabulary activities in textbooks.

6.2.1 Form

There were relatively few activities that targeted spoken word form (42 activities or 7.8% of the total). Furthermore, these were unevenly distributed among the textbooks, with one first-year textbook (*Panorama*) accounting for more than half of the activities of spoken form. Although *Panorama* is an outlier, let us consider the kinds of activities that were included to target spoken form. In *Panorama*, each chapter has a brief section dedicated to pronunciation, which give tips for pronouncing specific sounds (e.g., diphthongs) or provide short explanations about the correspondence between letters and sounds. The activities require students to read a series of words and sentences containing the target sound(s). Similar activities are found in *En tu Medio*, one of the intermediate books. For example, students listen to a set of words with the letters "c" and "z" in order to decide if the pronunciation is typical of Peninsular Spanish or Latin American Spanish. In sum, activities focusing on spoken word form are typically included in the "pronunciation" section of a given chapter.

Orthography is generally overlooked as a component of vocabulary knowledge by these textbooks, as evidenced by the paucity of activities focusing on written form. As such, learning the conventions of orthography is assumed to happen implicitly. Spanish is described as having a shallow orthography given the general one-to-one correspondence between phonemes and graphemes in most cases (Defior, Martos and Cary 2002). For example, contrary to English, the phoneme /f/ is always spelled as "f," and the letter "f" is always read as /f/. However, Spanish orthography contains a few complex sound-letter correspondences that lead to frequent spelling errors among heritage language learners (cf. Llombart-Huesca 2018). Despite these complexities in the orthographic code (e.g., /b/ can be written with "b" or "v"), L2 learners of Spanish make relatively few mistakes in spelling. In an analysis of written compositions, Elola and Mikulski (2016) reported that spelling errors accounted for less than 10% of errors for the L2 group, compared to 27% of all errors for the heritage speakers. Thus, for L2 learners, an explicit emphasis on spelling is probably not warranted because they typically learn new vocabulary items with simultaneous exposure to the written form.

Within the larger category of form, there were only 15 activities (2.7%) that targeted word parts. As noted earlier, we limited this category to derivation and compounding, excluding activities that were exclusively focused on inflection. Derivation is a very important word-formation process in Spanish, with more than one hundred suffixes (Cantos Gómez and Almela Pérez 2009). Recognition of these suffixes is also a major cue to word class; learners who are sensitive to the most frequent suffixes in Spanish will be able to categorize a newly learned word as a noun, verb, adjective, or adverb. Previous research (Zyzik and Azevedo 2009) has demonstrated that L2 learners of Spanish often know the general meaning of a word but not its lexical category. For example, learners may confuse pairs of words such as *fuerte/fuerza* 'strong/strength' and *cariñoso/cariño* 'affectionate/ affection'. Zyzik (2009: 161) concludes that word class information is not automatically available from the L1 and that "words can exist in the L2 lexicon for some time without specification of their category membership." The implication for pedagogy is that some explicit attention to word class may be beneficial and perhaps even necessary. Although many of the textbooks we examined group vocabulary items into nouns, verbs, and adjectives at the end of each chapter, this is clearly insufficient for drawing attention to the derivational suffixes that indicate word class (e.g., noticing that all words ending in *-dad* are nouns).

Vocabulary researchers have advocated for the explicit instruction of derivative forms as a way of expanding learners' vocabulary (cf. Morin 2003, 2006). Robles García and Sánchez Gutiérrez (2016) examined the presentation of eight different suffixes in Spanish textbooks and found that suffixes such as *-ción* and *-dad* are generally taught in order to show patterns of grammatical gender rather than as a word formation strategy. Given the productive nature of derivation in Spanish, the absence of vocabulary activities that address suffixes and prefixes (word parts) is a major oversight of these commercial textbooks. We are not suggesting that textbooks present lengthy lists of Spanish suffixes (see Sánchez Gutiérrez, Marcos Miguel and Robles García 2020 for a proposal of which suffixes should be targeted). Crucially, vocabulary activities could be developed in a way that highlights relationships between words belonging to the same family; for example, if the adjective *viejo* "old" appears in the active vocabulary of a given chapter, a vocabulary activity could ask students to create the related noun (*vejez*) and verb (*envejecer*).

6.2.2 Meaning

As shown in the results section, meaning-focused activities were abundant in all of the textbooks analyzed. Thus, the issue with meaning-focused activities is not their lack of representation in textbooks but rather the lack of variety within this category. The majority of activities were focused on consolidating the form-meaning link (66%). In terms of format, these activities involved matching definitions with words from a list or asking students to come up with a definition for a set of words. Fill-in-the-blank activities (e.g., cloze sentences) were also common across textbooks. In discussing options for vocabulary activities, Folse (2004: 146) notes that "Too often we tend to limit ourselves to two or three kinds of exercises, but there are numerous permutations of vocabulary exercises." This is certainly true of the textbooks analyzed here. Within the category of concepts and referents, the predominant activity type was "preguntas personales" (i.e., interview questions seeking preferences or opinions about a topic). Associations, a subcategory of meaning, were targeted with activities that Folse (2004) calls "odd-man out", which asks students to identify the word that does not belong in a set.

Notably, the textbooks seem to ignore polysemy as a characteristic of word meaning. Recall that González-Fernández and Schmitt (2020) included multiple meanings in their assessment of participants' vocabulary knowledge. The fact that many vocabulary words have more than one meaning is occasionally noted in the definition of the word (and in the word list at the end of the chapter), but we found no activities that address multiple meanings. For example, the verb *llevar* is highly polysemous, but let us focus on two common meanings: to wear (an item of clothing) and to take (someone or something somewhere). This verb is often presented in textbooks in the chapter on clothing, but the other meaning of *llevar* (to take) is also introduced implicitly in other chapters or activities. However, an important addition would be activities in which students have to disambiguate the meanings of *llevar* and other common verbs. For example, the activity could present sentences such as (5a) and (5b).

(5a) Omar debe llevar el auto al mecánico. "Omar should take his car to the mechanic."
(5b) Omar siempre lleva una corbata cuando va a la oficina. "Omar always wears a tie when he goes to the office."

Given a list of sentences such as (5a) and (5b), students must decide which ones express the meaning "to wear". There are many other high frequency verbs with multiple meanings (e.g., *dejar, quedar, probar*) that could be targeted in vocabulary activities. Of course, nouns and adjectives can also be polysemous, but the presentation of vocabulary in semantic and thematic sets leads to only one of many meanings being targeted.

6.2.3 Use

As mentioned earlier, "grammatical functions" accounted for a large percentage of activities within the *use* category. These activities required students to manipulate the word(s) and/or place them in the correct place within a sentence or the appropriate syntactic frame. Specifically, activities that consisted of dehydrated sentences in which students have to add functional elements were the most common type of activity in this category. Also common were activities that required students to use the word(s) in a sentence given a prompt or other kind of stimulus, as in the example below:

(6) *Taller de escritores*, p. 18

Comparativos y superlativos
Expresa tus ideas sobre los siguientes grupos de palabras. Para cada grupo escribe dos oraciones: una con comparativos y otra con superlativos. Incluye algunos ejemplos de superlativo absoluto en tus oraciones.
Modelo:
burros/perros/gatos (inteligente)
→ *Los gatos son más inteligentes que los burros, creo. Pero, para mí, los perros son los más inteligentes de todos. De hecho, son inteligentísimos.*

"Comparatives and superlatives. Express your ideas about the following groups of words. Write two sentences for each group: one using a compara-

tive sentence and one using a superlative structure. Include some examples of absolute superlatives as well in your sentences.
Model:
donkeys/dogs/cats (intelligent)
→ *Cats are more intelligent than donkeys, I think. But for me, dogs are the most intelligent of all. In fact, they are really intelligent".*

In our analysis, we identified a total of 25 activities that targeted collocations (4.6% of all vocabulary activities). The majority of these activities can be found in the advanced-level textbooks. In contrast, the beginner and intermediate books have very few activities of this type, despite the fact that multi-word vocabulary is included in the active vocabulary in each textbook. For example, here is a brief selection of verbal collocations found across chapters of *En tu Medio* (intermediate level): *dar por sentado, echar de menos, desmentir un rumor, quedarse en casa,* and *hacer diligencias.* Although vocabulary selection was not the focus of our analysis, a perusal of the active vocabulary in each textbook reveals the presence of many multi-word items. However, the activities that target this multi-word vocabulary are few and far between. The first-year books present collocations in the thematic unit that includes emotions, which inevitably includes common expressions with the verb 'tener' such as *tener miedo, tener hambre, tener frío,* etc. These expressions are typically presented as intact collocations and the corresponding activities ask students to match the expressions with a picture or a written situation, as shown in example (7).

(7) *Pura vida*, p. 115

La fiesta del abuelo
Match the following situations with tener expressions in the second column to describe this birthday party.

6. Mi padrastro abre la ventana porque. . . . .   e. tiene frío

The variety of collocation activities in the Spanish textbooks seems to be quite limited. Boers et al. (2014) describe six common formats of collocation activities, including connecting the parts of a collocation (i.e., matching format), inserting the word in a meaningful context, underlining the word in context, inserting the intact collocation in context, correcting the collocation, and eliminating the word from a series of options that does not make a collocation. Boers et al. argue for the superiority of exercises that present intact collocations since this format should diminish the risk of erroneous collocations being created by the learner (see also Boers, Dang, and Strong 2017). Our analysis of the Spanish textbooks reveals two types of collocation exercises: inserting the word in a meaningful context and inserting intact collocations. An example of inserting intact collocations is presented below from one of the advanced-level texts.

(8) *Repase y escriba*, p. 192

   Maneras de hacer las cosas
   Haga comentarios basándose en las siguientes oraciones y usando las expresiones adverbiales con la preposición **a**.

   Modelo:
   Rosa tiene que escribir una carta y su impresora no funciona.
   → *Rosa tiene que escribir una carta a mano*.

   "Ways of doing things. Make comments based on the following sentences using adverbial expressions with **a**".

It is widely acknowledged that L2 learners often struggle with knowing which words pattern together despite having relatively advanced language proficiency (cf. Foster 2009, Nesselhauf 2003, Siyanova and Schmitt 2008, among others). The Spanish textbooks seem to acknowledge the importance of collocations at the advanced level, with an increasing number of collocation activities in the two advanced books that were examined. From our perspective, greater emphasis on collocations could also be included at the beginner and intermediate levels. In addition to the common expressions with 'tener' mentioned earlier, other collocations could be emphasized as well. Adjectives could be presented with either 'estar' or 'ser' depending on the most common combination. For example, instead of presenting the adjectives *dispuesto/a, estresado/a,* and *agotado/a* in isolation (*Imagina*), these adjectives could be presented and practiced as multi-word units with the verb 'estar'. Similarly, states or emotional reactions could be presented as collocations with the verb 'ponerse' (e.g., *ponerse nervioso/a*).

7 Limitations and directions for future research

The findings reported here should be interpreted in light of the limited nature of the analysis (eight Spanish textbooks) and the methodological choices in analyzing these materials. First, we did not analyze the vocabulary activities with respect to the distinction between word recognition and word recall. González-Fernández and Schmitt (2020: 501) concluded that recognition knowledge is mastered before any type of recall knowledge, leading to the following pedagogical suggestion: "perhaps the focus of pedagogy should be shifted towards pushing learners' knowledge from receptive towards productive mastery." This kind of approach implies a commitment to vocabulary recycling, which would involve presenting new vocabulary items for recognition purposes first (e.g, matching the word to its definition) and later building on this knowledge with subsequent activities that require word recall, ideally with attention to collocations, derivations, and multiple meanings.

Second, it must be noted that we did not evaluate the efficacy of any particular type of activity. There is a lengthy tradition in applied linguistics that compares different activity types and their impact on vocabulary learning and retention (cf. Folse 2006 and Keating 2008, among others). For example, San Mateo and Chacón-García (2019) compared three types of activities: choosing the right definition, gap-fill, and writing sentences. They found that sentence writing was the most effective activity, followed by gap-fill. Matching the word to its definition was the least effective for retention. They explain these results in terms of task-induced involvement load (Hulstijn and Laufer 2001). In our analysis of the Spanish textbooks, however, we found that matching words to definitions and gap-fill exercises were extremely common. From the perspective of textbook authors, these activities are relatively easy to create and also easy to grade. Although sentence-writing activities are not difficult to design, they require instructor feedback, making them a less popular choice overall.

A final limitation of the current study is that we did not analyze the digital or supplementary online materials that usually accompany these textbooks. All but one of the books examined in this study are accompanied by a digital platform that includes many additional activities. Although we could assume that those activities are created by the same authors and that the coverage of vocabulary would follow the same trend as the print textbooks, this is not always the case. Many activities included in the online platforms are often created by third party providers hired by the editorial team and are included in all the textbook programs published by the same company. It could be informative to analyze such ancillaries and examine these additional materials about the types of lexical knowledge targeted there.

8 Conclusions

The current analysis of Spanish textbooks confirms that meaning continues to be the primary driver of vocabulary activities in commercial teaching materials. More specifically, the proportion of meaning-focused activities ranges from 66% in advanced-level books to 78% in beginner-level books. Our analysis also highlights several issues that are worth exploring in greater detail. First, the systematic reduction in the number of vocabulary activities as learners progress through their classroom experience (from beginner to intermediate to advanced levels), suggests that materials designers assume that vocabulary will be learned incidentally from exposure to texts, both oral and written. Second, we have highlighted that Nation's original category of "word parts" as a dimension of vocabulary knowledge may not be adequate for highly inflected languages such as Spanish. Since Spanish textbooks continue to emphasize inflection at the expense of derivation, it is important to distinguish between these two facets of "word parts" in analyzing textbook materials. Finally, given that textbooks influence teaching practices and teachers' and students' beliefs (Willis Allen 2008), we maintain that it is crucial to diversify the kinds of vocabulary activities that are included in textbooks. A more comprehensive approach to vocabulary that incorporates collocations, derivations, and polysemy would benefit learners and teachers alike.

References

Boers, Frank, Tu Cam Thi Dang & Brian Strong. 2017. Comparing the effectiveness of phrase-focused exercises: A partial replication of Boers, Demecheleer, Coxhead and Webb (2014). *Language Teaching Research* 21(3). 362–380. https://doi.org/10.1177/1362168816651464

Boers, Frank, Murielle Demecheleer, Averil Coxhead & Stuart Webb. 2014. Gauging the effects of exercises on verb–noun collocations. *Language Teaching Research* 18(1). 54–74. https://doi.org/10.1177/1362168813505389

Brown, Dale. 2011. What aspects of vocabulary knowledge do textbooks give attention to? *Language Teaching Research* 15(83). 83–97.

Cantos Gómez, Pascual & Ramón Almela Pérez. 2009. Estudio cuantitativo de los afijos en español. Bulletin of Hispanic Studies 86(4). 453–468.

Cubillos, Jorge. 2014. Spanish textbooks in the US: enduring traditions and emerging trends. *Journal of Spanish Language Teaching* 1(2). 205–225. https://doi.org/10.1080/23247797.2014.970363

Davies, Mark & Timothy L. Face. 2006. Vocabulary coverage in Spanish textbooks: How representative is it. In Nuria Sagarra & Almeida Jacqueline Toribio (eds.), *Selected proceedings of the 9th Hispanic Linguistics Symposium*, 132–143. Cascadilla Proceedings Project.

Defior, Sylvia, Francisco Martos & Luz Cary. 2002. Differences in reading acquisition development in two shallow orthographies: Portuguese and Spanish. *Applied Psycholinguistics* 23(1). 135–148.

Ellis, Rod. 2004. The definition and measurement of L2 explicit knowledge. *Language Learning* 54. 227–275.

Elola, Idoia & Ariana. M. Mikulski. 2016. Similar and/or different writing processes? A study of Spanish foreign language and heritage language learners. *Hispania* 99(1). 87–102.

Folse, Keith S. 2004. *Vocabulary myths: Applying second language research to classroom teaching*. Ann Arbor: University of Michigan Press.

Folse, Keith S. 2006. The effect of type of written exercise on L2 vocabulary retention. *TESOL quarterly* 40(2). 273–293.

Foster, Pauline. 2009. Lexical diversity and native-like selection: The bonus of studying abroad. In Brian Richards, Michael Daller, David Malvern, Paul Meara, James Milton & Jeanine Treffers-Daller (eds.), *Vocabulary studies in first and second language acquisition*, 91–106. Hampshire, United Kingdom: Palgrave Macmillan.

Godev, Concepción B. 2009. Word-frequency and vocabulary acquisition: an analysis of elementary Spanish college textbooks in the USA. *Revista de Lingüística Teórica y Aplicada* 47(2). 51–68.

Gómez, Pascual C., & Ramón A. Pérez. 2009. Estudio cuantitativo de los afijos en español. *Bulletin of Hispanic Studies* 86(4). 453–469.

González Fernández, Beatriz & Norbert Schmitt. 2015. How much collocation knowledge do L2 learners have? *ITL-International Journal of Applied Linguistics* 166(1). 94–126.

González-Fernández, Beatriz & Norbert Schmitt. 2020. Word knowledge: Exploring the relationships and order of acquisition of vocabulary knowledge components. *Applied Linguistics* 41(4). 481–505.

Hulstijn, Jan & Batia Laufer. 2001. Some empirical evidence for the involvement load hypothesis in vocabulary acquisition. *Language Learning* 51(3). 539–558.

Keating, Gregory D. 2008. Task effectiveness and word learning in a second language: The involvement load hypothesis on trial. *Language Teaching Research* 12(3). 365–386.

Laufer, Batia & Zahava Goldstein. 2004. Testing vocabulary knowledge: Size, strength, and computer adaptiveness. *Language learning* 54(3). 399–436.

Laufer, Batia & Nany Girsai. 2008. Form-focused instruction in second language vocabulary learning: A case for contrastive analysis and translation. *Applied Linguistics* 29(4). 694–716.

Llombart-Huesca, Amàlia. 2018. Understanding the spelling errors of Spanish heritage language learners. *Hispania* 101(2). 211–223.

López-Jiménez, Mª Dolores. 2014. A Critical Analysis of the Vocabulary in L2 Spanish Textbooks. *Porta Linguarum* 21. 163–181.

Morin, Regina. 2003. Derivational morphological analysis as a strategy for vocabulary acquisition in Spanish. *The Modern Language Journal* 87(2). 200–221.

Morin, Regina. 2006. Building depth of Spanish L2 vocabulary by building and using word families. *Hispania* 89(1). 170–182.

Nesselhauf, Nadja. 2003. The use of collocations by advanced learners of English and some implications for teaching. *Applied Linguistics* 24(2). 223–242.

Nation, Paul. 2001. *Learning vocabulary in another language*. Cambridge: Cambridge University Press.

Nation, Paul. 2013. *Learning vocabulary in another language*. 2nd edn. Cambridge: Cambridge University Press.

Neary-Sundquist, Colleen A. 2015. Aspects of Vocabulary Knowledge in German Textbooks. *Foreign Language Annals* 48(1). 68–80. https://doi.org/10.1111/flan.12126

Peters, Elke. 2016. The learning burden of collocations: The role of interlexical and intralexical factors. *Language Teaching Research* 20(1). 113–138. https://doi.org/10.1177/1362168814568131

Robles García, Pablo & Claudia H. Sánchez-Gutiérrez. 2016. La morfología derivativa en los manuales de español elemental estadounidenses: Un estudio exploratorio. *RAEL: revista electrónica de lingüística aplicada* 15(1). 70–86.

Sanaoui, Razika. 1996. Processes of Vocabulary Instruction in 10 French as a second language classrooms. *The Canadian Modern Language Review* 52(2). 179–199.

San Mateo Valdehíta, Alicia & Carmen Chacón-García. 2019. Learning word class in a second language through vocabulary learning activities: definition-choosing, gap-filling, and sentence writing. *Journal of Spanish Language Teaching* 6(1). 49–63. https://doi.org/10.1080/23247797.2019.1590001

Sánchez-Gutiérrez, Claudia H., Nausica Marcos Miguel & M. Olsen. 2019. An analysis of vocabulary coverage and lexical characteristics in L2 Spanish textbooks. In P. Ecke & S. Rott (eds.) *Understanding Vocabulary Learning and Teaching: Implications for Language Program Development*. American Association of University Supervisors, Coordinators, and Directors of Language Programs (AAUSC) Volume 2018. Boston, MA: Cengage.

Sánchez-Gutiérrez, Claudia H., Nausica Marcos Miguel & Pablo Robles García. 2020. What derivational suffixes should we teach in Spanish as a Second Language courses? *Hispanic Linguistics: Current issues and new directions* 26. 75.

Sánchez-Gutiérrez, Claudia H. & Pablo Robles-García. This volume. Vocabulary in the Spanish classroom: What students know and what their instructors believe they know. In Irene Checa-García & Laura Marqués-Pascual (eds.), *Current Perspectives in Spanish Lexical Development*. Berlin, Boston: De Gruyter Mouton.

Schmitt, Norbert. 2014. Size and Depth of Vocabulary Knowledge: What the Research Shows. *Language Learning* 64(4). 913–951.

Siyanova, Anna & Norbert Schmitt. 2008. L2 learner production and processing of collocation: A multi-study perspective. *Canadian Modern Language Review* 64(3). 429–458.

VanPatten, Bill. 2002. *From input to output: A teacher's guide to second language acquisition*. McGraw-Hill.

Vu, Duy Van & Marije Michel. 2021. An exploratory study on the aspects of vocabulary knowledge addressed in EAP textbooks. *Dutch Journal of Applied Linguistics* 10. 1–15.

Willis Allen, Heather. 2008. Textbooks Materials and Foreign Language Teaching: Perspectives from the classroom. *NECTFL Review* 62. 5–28.

Wong, Wynne & Bill VanPatten. 2003. The evidence is IN: Drills are OUT. *Foreign Language Annals* 36(3). 403–423.

Yoon, Jiyoung. 2019. Teaching and learning vocabulary as L2: Approaches in Spanish textbooks. *Language Teaching and Educational Research* (LATER) 2(2). 114–131. DOI: https://doi.org/10.35207/later.647156

Zyzik, Eve. 2009. Noun, verb, or adjective? L2 learners' sensitivity to cues to word class. *Language Awareness* 18. 147–164.

Zyzik, Eve & Clara Azevedo. 2009. Word class distinctions in second language acquisition: An experimental study of L2 Spanish. *Studies in Second Language Acquisition* 31(1). 1–29.

Index

3K-LEx 12, 251–2

Available lexicon 76–77, 79, 87, 91, 100, 103
Availability list 11–12, 17
Accuracy 4, 13–15, 17, 49, 51–54, 58, 60–69
Approach
– Observational approach 26, 35–37
– Lexical approach 6, 8–9, 33–35, 40

CAF (complexity, accuracy, fluency) 4, 8
Case study 277, 296
Centros de interés 12, 104
CHAT 13, 123, 149
CLAN (Computerized Language Analysis) 13, 123, 148–9
Cognitive process(es) 30, 39, 42, 78–79
Cognitive prototype(s) 80, 82
COILA 91–97, 102, 104
COILD 91–100, 103–4
Collocation(s) 5, 9–10, 12, 34–36, 39–40, 110, 216–217, 276, 283–285, 304–307, 312–315, 323–326
Common European Framework of Reference for Languages 12, 28
Concordances 5, 9, 10, 36, 39
Construction grammar 6, 32
Content words 110, 112, 123, 128–9
Corpora 5, 8–11, 13, 17, 35–42, 45, 166, 182, 246–248, 259
CREA 10, 39
Curriculum 4, 19, 76, 130, 269–272, 276–279, 281, 284–285, 290–291, 293–296

Data-driven learning 9, 38
DispoCen 87
Dispolex 12

Explicit instruction 9, 33–34, 40–42, 269, 272, 275, 292, 294, 320

Frequency
– Band (based) frequency 16, 148, 150, 182
– Count (based) frequency 16, 113, 123, 182, 259

– Frequency list(s) 11, 16, 77, 113, 123–124, 131, 149, 162–163, 174–176, 178, 180–182, 193
– Word frequency 6, 11, 77, 82, 182, 247, 247, 249, 255, 260
Fuzzy sets 69, 80–83, 85–86, 92, 102, 104

Giraud's Index 15, 112–113, 148, 153

Incidental learning 8–9, 32–33, 40–41, 130, 259–260, 272
Interference 115–116, 215, 275
Interlanguage 17, 40, 115, 117, 221

Lemma(s) 10, 15, 110–112, 114, 123–124, 143, 149–150, 175, 182, 251
Lexerr/W 148, 150–151, 156
Lexerr/T 148, 150–151, 156
Lexical
– Accuracy 4, 13–15, 17, 75–76, 109–110, 119, 141–143, 145, 148, 150–152, 154–156
– Amplitude 76, 84, 87–88, 91, 102, 104
– Lexical vailability 4, 7, 9, 12, 16, 17, 77, 79, 81, 82, 84, 87, 90, 110, 162
– Breadth 3–4, 13, 17, 75–76, 79, 81–85, 87, 90–91, 94, 100–101, 103–104, 109, 130
– Competence 11, 18–19, 33, 35, 39, 44–45, 119
– Complexity 14–15, 129, 141
– Decentralization 76, 84–92, 94–96, 103–104
– Density 15–17, 69, 75–76, 109–111, 113, 119–121, 123–126, 128–130, 142–144, 155
– Deployment 14–15, 17, 144, 148, 150–151, 155–156
– Depth 3–4, 13, 17, 50, 109, 113, 269, 276, 285, 294, 304
– Diversity 4, 7–8, 10–11, 13–15, 17, 39, 41, 75–76, 109–114, 117, 119, 121–126, 128–131, 141–143, 145, 148, 150–155, 161–163, 165, 167–169, 180, 183
– Fluency 4, 14–15, 17, 29–30, 33–34, 40, 43–44, 120, 140–143, 153, 155
– Innovation(s) 189–191, 197
– Measure(s) 8, 49, 52, 92, 110–111, 124, 126–129, 140–144, 148, 150–153, 155–156, 162–166, 168, 174–179

– Richness 4, 8, 11, 13–15, 17, 75–76, 80–81, 84, 101, 104, 109–114, 117–121, 125–127, 129, 142, 148, 155, 161–163, 166, 168–169, 173, 183
– Sophistication 8, 15–17, 75–76, 109–111, 113–114, 119–121, 122–131, 142–144, 145, 148–151, 153–156, 161–167, 169–170, 174–178, 180–183
– Transfer 7, 17, 109–111, 141–121, 128–13, 148–149
– Variation 78, 100, 219, 280
Lexical Frequency Profile 4, 164
Lexical input processing (lex-IP) 42

MATTR (Moving-Average of Type-Token Ratio) Index 14, 112
Mechanical drills/exercises 29, 41, 273, 306, 310, 319
Mental lexicon 3, 35, 49, 77, 161, 180, 189, 191, 211
MTLD (Measure of Textual Lexical Diversity) Index 14, 112
MOR 123, 149
Multiword items 5–6, 9–10, 12–13

Nation's framework of vocabulary knowledge 3–4, 36–38, 276, 304–308, 316

Orthographic form(s) 49, 51–52

Passive vocabulary knowledge 161, 163–167, 169–170, 172, 174–178, 180–182
Phonological form(s) 49, 51–53, 67, 69
Polysemy 109, 182, 276, 283–284, 32, 326

SILD 88–89, 103
Sound-spelling correspondence 51, 53, 57, 65, 68–69
Study Abroad 7–8, 111, 137, 145, 154, 166, 181, 217, 237
Syllabus 6, 40, 146, 170, 270–271, 277, 279, 284

Tasks
– Decision-making task 162–163, 167–169, 172–174, 176
– Forced choice task 53–56, 58–64, 66–68
– Lexical decision task 8, 12, 50, 53, 59, 193, 251
Task complexity 168, 172–173, 181
Text length 110, 112, 123, 129, 147, 163
TFAC (Technique Feature Analysis Checklist) 271–272, 274–285, 295–296
T-unit 14, 148
TTR (Type to Token Ratio) index 14–15, 112

Vocabulary
– Vocabulary activity 276, 286, 306, 308–309, 321
– Vocabulary depth. See Lexical depth
– Vocabulary knowledge rating(s) 59–64, 67
– Vocabulary size 3–4, 8, 11–12, 17, 31, 49, 52, 56, 59, 103, 119, 130, 269, 284–285, 304
– Vocabulary specificity 76, 84–85, 90, 92, 103–104
Vocabulary Levels Test 4, 12, 49, 52
Vocabulary Size Test 4, 12, 49

Word formation (rules) 44, 189–191, 194–195, 199–200, 204, 206–211, 272, 320–321

www.ingramcontent.com/pod-product-compliance
Lightning Source LLC
Chambersburg PA
CBHW050514170426
43201CB00013B/1949